EVERYDAY LIFE IN VIKING-AGE TOWNS
SOCIAL APPROACHES TO TOWNS IN
ENGLAND AND IRELAND, C. 800–1100

edited by

D. M. Hadley and Letty ten Harkel

OXBOW | books
Oxford & Philadelphia

First published in 2013. Reprinted in paperback in 2021 and 2023 in the United Kingdom by
OXBOW BOOKS
The Old Music Hall, 106–108 Cowley Road, Oxford OX4 1JE

and in the United States by
OXBOW BOOKS
1950 Lawrence Road, Havertown, PA 19083

Paperback Edition: ISBN 978-1-78925-546-1
Digital Edition: ISBN 978-1-78297-009-5 (epub)

A CIP record for this book is available from the British Library

Library of Congress Cataloging-in-Publication Data

Everyday life in Viking-age towns : social approaches to towns in England and Ireland, c.
800-1100 / [edited by] D. M. Hadley and Letty ten Harkel.
       pages cm
  Includes bibliographical references.
  ISBN 978-1-84217-532-3
  1. City and town life--England--History--To 1500. 2. City and town life--Ireland--History-
-To 1500. 3. Sociology, Urban--England--History--To 1500. 4. Sociology, Urban--Ireland-
-History--To 1500. 5. Great Britain--History--To 1066. 6. Ireland--History--To 1172. 7.
Urban economics--History--To 1500. I. Hadley, D. M. (Dawn M.), 1967- II. Ten Harkel,
Letty.
  DA152.2.E94 2013
  307.760942--dc23
                              2013025374

Printed in the United Kingdom by CMP (UK) Ltd

For a complete list of Oxbow titles, please contact:

UNITED KINGDOM   UNITED STATES OF AMERICA
Oxbow Books   Oxbow Books
Telephone (0)1226 734350   Telephone (610) 853-9131, Fax (610) 853-9146
Email: oxbow@oxbowbooks.com   Email: queries@casemateacademic.com
www.oxbowbooks.com   www.casemateacademic.com/oxbow

Oxbow Books is part of the Casemate Group

Front cover: An artist's impression of Viking-Age Lincoln at dawn (by Marcus Abbott)

CONTENTS

Dublin

Limerick

Waterford

Wexford

Cork

Woodstown

Locations of places referred to in the volume (drawn by Letty ten Harkel).

PREFACE

D. M. Hadley and Letty ten Harkel

The study of early medieval towns has frequently manifested itself as an investigation of urban beginnings and the search for broadly applicable definitions of urban characteristics. While the catalyst for urbanisation remains contested (*e.g.* Scull 1997; Valante 2008), the chronological development of towns has become more clearly understood over the course of the last quarter of the 20th century following large-scale urban excavations in advance of development (see Griffiths, this volume). Far less attention, in contrast, has been paid to the experience of living in towns, and, accordingly, this volume focusses on urban identities, as expressed through material culture, and on what characterised urban dwellers as different from their contemporaries in the countryside during the Viking Age (*c.* 800–1100).

Towns: origins and definitions

The most influential definition of 'the town' for early medieval archaeology in the British Isles is undoubtedly that provided in a study of Anglo-Saxon towns by Martin Biddle (1976, 99–100) a generation ago. He suggested that the identification of Anglo-Saxon towns demanded the presence of at least three or four of the following characteristics: defences; a planned street-system; a market; a mint; legal autonomy; a role as a central place; a relatively large and dense population; a diversified economic base; plots and houses of 'urban' type; a complex religious organisation; and a judicial centre. Over the years, Biddle's definition of a town has been both adapted (*e.g.* Wickham 2006, 591–6) and criticised, since some of his characteristics rely on historical evidence that is often not forthcoming in an early medieval context, while others (such as markets and judicial activities) can be found in undoubtedly non-urban contexts (Scull 1997, 271). In addition, scholars have commented on the difficulty of distinguishing between small 'towns' and large 'villages', as both may share the same characteristics (Gardiner 2006, 24). Meanwhile, others have doubted the value of identifying defining characteristics for towns on the grounds that 'towns carry different meanings to different people at different times' (Perring 2002, 9).

In the context of Scandinavian settlement, debates about towns have tended to focus on whether the settlers were the catalyst to the emergence of towns, or whether they merely added a new dimension to existing processes of urbanisation in England and Ireland (Hinton 1990, 92–6). It is widely acknowledged that when Scandinavian raiding and settlement commenced, English and Irish societies were essentially non-urban, even if in England the ruins of the – largely deserted – Roman towns still served as tangible reminders of a period when they were an integral part of everyday life. Nonetheless, in the centuries following the decline of these Roman towns, various settlement forms developed that have been identified as important stages in the re-emergence of urbanism. The middle Anglo-Saxon trading centres known as *wics* – such as Ipswich

(Suffolk), *Hamwic* (Southampton, Hampshire) and *Eoforwic* (York) – undoubtedly provide the best examples (Scull 1997), although more recently Blair (2005, 248–9) has argued in favour of middle Anglo-Saxon minsters as the forerunners to the late Anglo-Saxon town, on the grounds that they were focal points for manufacture and trade. Even more importantly in his opinion, the minsters corresponded more closely than *wics* to the idea of the *civitas* that was envisioned in Biblical texts and explored in early medieval writing, such as St Augustine's *De Civitate Dei* ('The City of God'). As Blair (2005, 249) has observed, 'it was within the stone walls of Romano-British ruins, so enthusiastically adopted by monastic founders, that lay perceptions of special places in the landscape coalesced with literary ones of the heavenly and earthly Jerusalems'. Ireland, in contrast, was not incorporated into the Roman Empire and therefore had no urban legacy comparable to that of England (Edwards 1990, 1–5). As a result, discussions about the origins of urban settlement forms have been less extensive, and largely restricted to considerations of the emergence of towns in the wake of Scandinavian influence in the 10th and 11th centuries (Valante 2008, 57–80). It has certainly been argued in some studies that the Irish monastic settlements of the 7th and 8th centuries were every bit as complex as the *wics* and minsters from the Anglo-Saxon realm (Doherty 1985; Clarke 1990), but the extent to which they were really the direct fore-runners to the towns of later centuries has been doubted (Valante 2008, 26–30).

Despite the fact that traces of urban activity can be identified in the 7th and 8th centuries, many of the sites concerned were abandoned or relocated in the 9th century (*e.g.* Hall 2004, 488–97), and the period from the later 9th to 11th centuries is now widely regarded as having witnessed the (re-)emergence and growth of the towns that were largely to provide the urban framework of the Middle Ages (Astill 2009, 262–5). These developments coincided with the conquests of the Scandinavian raiders-turned-settlers in England and Ireland, and the degree to which the Scandinavian settlers were responsible for urban origins and development has been subject to much debate. For example, in Wessex and Anglo-Saxon Mercia, the construction of defensive *burhs* as a response to the Viking raiders in the late 9th and early 10th centuries has long been seen as a first stage in the re-urbanisation process in those regions. These *burhs* subsequently acquired a range of urban characteristics, including a market, a mint, a diversified economic base and a large population (Hill and Rumble 1996; Astill 2006, 236, 243, 254; 2009, 262–5). Without the benefit of hindsight, King Alfred's biographer Asser already attributed the construction of 'cities and towns … where previously there were none' to his king (Asser, *Life of King Alfred* ch. 91; Stevenson 1904), inspiring – at least in part – the school of thought that viewed urbanisation as an intentional and ideological act on the part of the West Saxons and Mercians (*e.g.* Carver 1993; 2000; 2010; 2011). In contrast, in northern and eastern England, as in Ireland, the Vikings have often been held more directly responsible for the development of towns, which were seen as trading and manufacturing sites having developed out of the base camps of various segments of the armies that were now in the process of settling down and colonising the regions they had previously plundered (Hall 1981, 95–9). However, the paucity of diagnostically Scandinavian material culture from some towns has often appeared puzzling (Biddle 1976, 122–3; Hall 1980, 152–3, 205), and many studies have accordingly looked to the influence of other factors in urban development in those regions, such as trading links within Britain and with the continent, as much as to the impact of Scandinavian settlement (*e.g.* Hall 2000; see also Blinkhorn, this volume).

In northern and eastern England, whatever level of influence has been ascribed to Scandinavian settlers in the development of urbanism, towns of the 9th and 10th centuries have always been recognised as being integral to existing economic networks, even if their relationship with surrounding rural regions remains under-explored and consequently poorly understood (Roskams

1996, 280). In Ireland, however, the absence of diagnostically Scandinavian material culture in the countryside has posed considerable challenges in understanding how the urban places of the 9th and 10th centuries functioned, and the nature, if any, of interactions between towns and their rural hinterland has been a particular focus for debate. The notion emerged that towns in Ireland were merely 'colonial way-stations' on the sea routes linking the Baltic and the areas of Scandinavian colonisation with the Mediterranean and North Africa (De Paor 1976, 33), while Richard Hodges (1982, 195) deduced that Viking towns in Ireland were:

> Evidently dependent on their Scandinavian contacts in England and the Baltic Sea countries ... [with] virtually no evidence of interaction between the Viking colonies isolated on the coastlines and the great heartland of Ireland with its dense population.

However, in countering these interpretations, John Bradley (1988) drew attention to resources excavated in Dublin – such as cattle, copper, lead, iron, fruits, berries, timber and wattles – that must have been acquired from the rural hinterland, suggesting that towns were, indeed, integrated, in some way, into their localities.

Opinions about the reasons why towns developed in England and Ireland in the late 9th to 11th centuries will undoubtedly continue to differ, as scholars focus in varying degrees on economic, political or ideological factors. Opinions on *how* they developed are, on the other hand, increasingly unanimous, largely as a result of the rescue and developer-funded investigations that took place during the period of urban regeneration of the later 20th century. Although more work remains to be done, the development of many individual towns, from their early medieval emergence to their present day existence, is understood in much greater detail than twenty years ago, when Helen Clarke and Björn Ambrosiani published their 1991 book on *Towns in the Viking Age*. This proliferation of urban excavations has given rise to many excellent town-specific archaeological publications, making available the results of the excavations in, for example, Dublin (Bradley 1988; Simpson 2005; 2010), York (Hall 2004) and Lincoln (Stocker 2003), to name a few towns that feature prominently in the current volume. However, the nature of commercial archaeology has undergone many changes as well, as a result of ongoing negotiations between planners, developers and archaeologists. The outcome of this – at the current time – is a situation whereby extensive open-area excavations are now largely a thing of the past, being substituted increasingly by 'preservation *in situ*' and occasional keyhole investigations, whereas current economic pressures in England and, to a much more serious extent, Ireland, have severely diminished the quantity of large-scale urban regeneration projects being carried out (Aitchison 2010; Eogan 2010). This means that the rapid increase in archaeological data from urban development areas, retrieved during the later 20th century, has slowed down significantly. Consequently, excavation in the wake of urban development will continue to add further detail to the basic chronological timelines that have been established during the rescue era, but may not significantly change our understanding of the chronology of urban development for the foreseeable future.

Life in towns

Changes in the organisation and priorities of developer-funded archaeology may herald the end of one era, but that is not to say that the study of early medieval urbanism is at an end. As stated at the start of this preface, for a long time research on towns was concerned with urban beginnings and chronology ('urbanisation'), driven by a desire to understand the roots of our own society. Paradoxically, however, few scholars have asked 'what was it like to live in those early towns?' or 'who were the people who inhabited the emerging towns of Viking-Age England and Ireland?'. Instead, the emphasis has rested largely on issues of stratigraphy and dating, which, however useful and important in their own right, has meant that the human element of these early towns, so important for their growth and development, has often been entirely removed. This has sometimes resulted in discussions of towns full of artefacts and structures but devoid of people, resulting in the kind of empty townscape depicted in the impression of Viking-Age Lincoln on the front cover of this book (created by Marcus Abbott). It is hoped that the contents of this volume, bringing together a selection of articles from established and early career researchers from Ireland and England, will to an extent repopulate these early medieval towns.

The study of everyday life in Viking-Age towns in England and Ireland is a huge subject. The thirteen chapters in this book, therefore, do not claim to be exhaustive, neither in terms of subject matter nor geographical coverage, but rather they present a selection of new research of established and early career researchers that falls within the remit of this theme. Although historical sources are addressed, the emphasis of the volume is overwhelmingly archaeological, paying homage to the wealth of new material that has become available since the advent of urban archaeology in the 1960s. It is hoped that this collection of case-studies will provide a starting point for future research on early medieval urbanism. The first chapter by David Griffiths sets the scene for the volume by charting the development of developer-funded and rescue archaeology in England and Ireland in the context of the themes explored in the following chapters. The next two chapters – written by Gareth Williams, and Emer Purcell and John Sheehan respectively – provide a broad discussion of urbanisation in both countries, placed firmly within a socio-political framework, drawing on both historical and archaeological material.

The remainder of the volume is divided into two parts. The first – 'constructing and experiencing urban landscapes' – is thematically arranged around the experiences of different groups of individuals who inhabited Viking-Age towns. Focusing on the recently excavated *longphort* of Woodstown (Co. Waterford), Stephen H. Harrison paints a picture of life in this earliest phase of Irish towns. The domestic sphere is investigated by Rebecca Boyd and Deirdre McAlister, who analyse Viking-Age housing and childhood respectively. The chapters by D. M. Hadley and David Stocker, on the other hand, look more closely at more public aspects of urban life through analysis, in turn, of male identities and the dynamics behind parish formation.

The final part of the book – 'urban trades and activities' – is almost entirely object-based, including analyses of animal bone assemblages (Kristopher Poole) and pottery (Paul Blinkhorn), as well as metalwork (Letty ten Harkel) and combs (Steven P. Ashby). The final chapter, written by Maurice F. Hurley, takes a more conceptual approach to urban trades and activities, by focusing on the distinction between craft and handiwork through analysis of wood, antler and bone objects from Ireland's western towns. The emphasis on artefactual evidence to recreate urban identities is a departure from much traditional work on early medieval towns, which has tended to use objects primarily as dating evidence, or at best to discuss economic relations between towns, or towns and rural areas.

Although extended discussions of definitions of urbanism are not a feature of this volume, there is one such definition that deserves special attention, as it was an important source of inspiration during the conceptual stages of the present volume. In the context of a study of the towns of *Domesday Book*, Susan Reynolds (1987, 295) suggested that the emergence of an urban *identity* is a necessary prerequisite for the existence of a town:

> Because of the distinctive functions of towns their inhabitants normally regard themselves, and are regarded by outsiders, as a different sort of people. However deeply they are divided among

themselves they tend to be united at least in regarding themselves as united in their urbanity against the country bumpkins around.

Whether the inhabitants of the Viking-Age towns of England and Ireland already felt united in their urbanity remains open to discussion, depending on whether one prefers to regard urbanisation as an agency-driven development, or as a more organic process that led to increasing settlement complexity, eventually resulting in a situation where towns were undeniably part of the landscape. In the context of this volume, rather than continuing to pursue these extensively discussed issues, it was decided to focus on shedding more light on the people who inhabited these settlements. Thus, the chapters in this volume focus not on urban development but on urbanism, or – to refer to a definition by the American urban sociologist Gottdiener (1994, 102) – life *in* towns: on the people who were born, lived, worked and died in the emerging 'Viking' towns of England and Ireland.

Acknowledgements

We would like to thank the contributors for their hard work in making this volume possible, and Claire Litt from Oxbow for her assistance with bringing the volume to publication. We are also grateful to Marcus Abbott for producing the reconstruction image for the cover. Finally, we would like to thank our respective families for their support during the production of this volume: Oliver and Isabelle Jessop, and Thom and Marri ten Harkel.

Bibliography

Aitchison, K. (2010) United Kingdom archaeology in economic crisis. In N. Schlanger and K. Aitchison (eds) *Archaeology and the Global Economic Crisis: multiple impacts, possible solutions*, 25–30. Tervuren, Culture Lab Éditions.

Astill, G. (2006) Community, identity and the later Anglo-Saxon town: the case of southern England. In W. Davies, G. Halsall and A. Reynolds (eds) *People and Space in the Middle Ages 300–1300*, 233–54. Turnhout, Brepols.

Astill, G. (2009) Medieval towns and urbanization. In R. Gilchrist and A. Reynolds (eds) *Reflections: 50 Years of Medieval Archaeology, 1957–2007*, 255–70. Society for Medieval Archaeology Monograph 30. Leeds, Maney.

Biddle, M. (1976) Towns. In D. M. Wilson (ed.) *The Archaeology of Anglo-Saxon England*, 99–150. London, Thames and Hudson.

Blair, J. (2005) *The Church in Anglo-Saxon Society*. Oxford, Oxford University Press.

Bradley, J. (1988) The interpretation of Scandinavian settlement in Ireland. In J. Bradley (ed.) *Settlement and Society in Medieval Ireland*, 49–78. Kilkenny, Boethius Press.

Carver, M. O. H. (1993) *Arguments in Stone: archaeological research and the European town in the first millennium*. Oxford, Oxbow.

Carver, M. O. H. (2000) Town and anti-town in the first millennium in Europe. In A. Buko and P. Urbańczyk (eds) *Archeologia w Teorii i w Praktyce*, 373–96. Warsaw, DiG.

Carver, M. O. H. (2010) *The Birth of a Borough: an archaeological study of Anglo-Saxon Stafford*. Woodbridge, Boydell.

Carver, M. O. H. (2011) What were they thinking? Intellectual territories in Anglo-Saxon England. In H. Hamerow, D. A. Hinton and S. Crawford (eds) *The Oxford Handbook of Anglo-Saxon Archaeology*, 914–47. Oxford, Oxford University Press.

Clarke, H. B. (1990) The topographical development of early medieval Dublin. In H. B. Clarke (ed.) *Medieval Dublin: the making of a metropolis*, 52–69. Blackrock, Irish Academic Press.

Clarke, H. and Ambrosiani, B. (1991) *Towns in the Viking Age*. Leicester, Leicester University Press.

De Paor, L. (1976) The Viking towns of Ireland. In B. Almqvist and D. Greene (eds) *Proceedings of the Seventh Viking Congress*, 29–38. Dublin, Viking Society for Northern Research.

Doherty, C. (1985) The monastic town in early medieval Ireland. In H. B. Clarke and A. Simms (ed.) *The Comparative History of Urban Origins in Non-Roman Europe*, 45–75. British Archaeological Reports International Series 255(i). Oxford, British Archaeological Reports.

Edwards, N. (1990) *The Archaeology of Early Medieval Ireland*. London, Batsford.

Eogan, G. (2010) The impact of the recession on archaeology in the Republic of Ireland. In N. Schlanger and K. Aitchison (eds) *Archaeology and the Global Economic Crisis: multiple impacts, possible solutions*, 19–24. Tervuren, Culture Lab Éditions.

Gardiner, M. (2006) Review of medieval settlement research, 1996–2006. *Medieval Settlement Research Group Annual Report* 21, 22–8.

Gottdiener, M. (1994) *The New Urban Sociology*. New York, McGraw-Hill Inc.

Hall, R. A. (1980) The Five Boroughs of the Danelaw: a review of present knowledge. *Anglo-Saxon England* 18, 149–206.

Hall, R. A. (1981) The markets of the Danelaw. In E. Roesdahl, J. Graham-Campbell, P. Connor and K. Pearson (eds) *The Vikings in England and their Danish Homeland*, 95–140. London, The Anglo-Danish Viking Project.

Hall, R. A. (2000) Anglo-Scandinavian attitudes: archaeological ambiguities in late ninth- to mid-eleventh-century York. In D. M. Hadley and J. D. Richards (eds) *Cultures in Contact: Scandinavian settlement in England in the ninth and tenth centuries*, 311–24. Turnhout, Brepols.

Hall, R. A. (ed.) (2004) *Aspects of Anglo-Scandinavian York*. The Archaeology of York 8 (4). York, Council for British Archaeology.

Hill, D. and Rumble, A. (eds) (1996) *The Defence of Wessex: the Burghal Hidage and Anglo-Saxon fortifications*. Manchester, Manchester University Press.

Hinton, D. A. (1990) *Archaeology, Economy and Society. England from the fifth to the fifteenth centuries*. London, Routledge.

Hodges, R. (1982) *Dark Age Economics. Origins of towns and trade, AD600–1000*. London, Duckworth.

Perring, D. (2002) *Town and Country in England: frameworks for archaeological research*. Council for British Archaeology Research Report 134. York, Council for British Archaeology.

Reynolds, S. (1987) Towns in Domesday Book. In J. C. Holt (ed.) *Domesday Studies*, 295–310. Woodbridge, Boydell.

Roskams, S. (1996) Urban transition in early medieval Britain: the case of York. In N. Christie and S. T. Loseby (eds) *Towns in Transition: urban evolution in late Antiquity and the early Middle Ages*, 213–34. Aldershot, Scolar Press.

Simpson, L. (2005) Viking warrior burials in Dublin: is this the *longphort*? In S. Duffy (ed.) *Medieval Dublin VI*, 11–62. Dublin, Four Courts Press.

Simpson, L. (2010) The first phase of Viking activity in Ireland: archaeological evidence from Dublin. In J. Sheehan and D. Ó Corráin (eds) *The Viking Age. Ireland and the West*, 418–29. Dublin, Four Courts Press.

Scull, C. (1997) Urban centres in pre-Viking England. In J. Hines (ed.) *The Anglo-Saxons from the Migration Period to the Eighth Century*, 269–98. Woodbridge, Boydell.

Stevenson, W. H. (ed.) (1904) *Asser's Life of King Alfred, together with the Annals of St Neots erroneously ascribed to Asser*. Oxford, Clarendon Press.

Stocker, D. (ed.) (2003) *The City by the Pool: assessing the archaeology of the City of Lincoln*. Lincoln Archaeological Studies 10. Oxford, Oxbow.

Valante, M. (2008) *The Vikings in Ireland: settlement, trade and urbanisation*. Dublin, Four Courts Press.

Wickham, C. (2006) *Framing the Early Middle Ages: Europe and the Mediterranean 400–800*. Oxford, Oxford University Press.

1

LIVING IN VIKING-AGE TOWNS

David Griffiths

As outlined in the preface to this volume, early medieval urban studies are now progressing well beyond the traditional empirical themes that have dominated them until recently: a search for definition, and an emphasis on physical topography and stratigraphy. These represent essential preoccupations in the progression of research into early towns, but their predominance in the debate on urban origins can now be seen, in retrospect, as expressions of the academic and practical concerns of their own time, and particularly of the 1960s, 1970s and 1980s. Objectifying 'The Town' was accompanied by an objectification of the archaeological process, and reporting style stuck closely and cautiously to identification and description of separate categories of site data. Delving further into the lives of individuals and communities, and the challenges and opportunities they faced whilst inhabiting early towns, were seen until recently as belonging to an unseen and untapped realm of hyper-interpretation, somewhat beyond the responsibility of those writing up excavations on stretched post-excavation resources. By the 1990s, academic discourse in early medieval urban studies could justifiably have been accused of presenting a dehumanised picture. Process, development and physical structure had all but eclipsed the potential for approaching individual human experience in early towns. Yet for the general public, excavation-based reconstructions and re-enactments such as the 'Jorvik Viking Centre' and 'Dublinia' have prompted a popular appetite for engagement with past lives, which demands a broader academic response. In academic circles, the rise of post-processual thinking in the 1990s and 2000s has emphasised the role of human agency and ideology as a counter to broad-brush notions of environmental determinism and social and economic evolution. Research bridging the formerly restrictive urban-rural divide has proliferated (*e.g.* the various papers in Giles and Dyer 2007). A renewed interest has arisen in ethnicity and acculturation in the Viking Age (*e.g.* Hadley 2011), in domestic cultures and the social construction of space (Davies *et al.* 2006; Astill 2006; 2009), in gender and childhood (*e.g.* Stoodley 2011; Hadley and Hemer 2011; Lucy 2011) and in the body and the life-course (Crawford 2011).

A re-interrogation of the vast and rich archives of raw and semi-raw data from urban excavations has until recently been overdue. A new generation of university-based doctoral and post-doctoral researchers has begun to produce creative syntheses, with greater theoretical and anthropological content, which is reflected in the work of contributors to this volume. The human dimension has returned to centre stage, giving new force to some basic questions. What was it like to live in a Viking-Age town? What was it like to be a child, elderly, sick, unfree or excluded? How did warmth, privacy, play, work and leisure function in these crowded environments? How did people deal with the effects of crime, security, fires, epidemics, refuse, dirt, noise, smells and social nuisances? How distinct was the feeling of difference between town-dwellers and country-dwellers? Some of these questions may yet be some time in the answering, but it is worth asking them nevertheless as a prompt to yet more creative ways forward. As demonstrated in this volume, the long-awaited synthesis of primary site data into a stimulating series of interpretive and humane themes is now substantially under way.

Definitions

The widespread rise of 'rescue' urban excavation from the 1960s onwards coincided with an increased willingness on the part of historians, historical and human geographers, and archaeologists, to question the traditional basis of urban definitions. Defences, street plans, churches, bridges, harbours, place-names and street-names are the physical representations of urbanism, but hitherto a town was only acceptably defined as such in historical terms if it met certain institutional or legal criteria, such as having a borough or market charter. This created a potential nonsense whereby a town or city could only be said to have existed by dint of its legal or ecclesiastical definition, even if it was a failed enterprise with few or no residents, whereas a place with many or all the physical attributes of urbanism may not qualify as such if it lacked confirmation of institutional status. By the 1970s, as the influential definitions of Martin Biddle (1976a) and Susan Reynolds (1977) demonstrate (see also Hadley and Ten Harkel, this volume), there was a widespread move away from rigid classificatory historicism towards a more nuanced and multi-dimensional picture, based largely on social and economic process rather than political status, for which Biddle's 'menu' of urban characteristics was devised. These definitions were in many ways expressions of the evolutionary and processual thinking, which defined 'New Archaeology' at that time (for a retrospective study of this era, see Gerrard 2003, 172–80).

One important aspect of urban discovery from the 1960s to 1980s, which gave rise to new debates about trade, coinage and early political systems, was the discovery of the pre-Viking 'wics' or *emporia* at *Hamwic* (Southampton, Hampshire), *Gipeswic* (Ipswich, Suffolk) and *Eoforwic* (York), later joined by Aldwych/*Lundenwic* (London) in the 1990s (Hill and Cowie 2001). These open or poorly-defended trading sites, located away from the former Roman cities, with regularly laid-out building forms and extensive evidence of ceramic production and imports, closely paralleled a group of riverine or estuarial sites on the near Continent such as Dorestad in the Netherlands and Quentovic in Normandy. Richard Hodges's influential book *Dark Age Economics* (1982) revitalised interest in urban origins, and sought to create a taxonomy of 'gateway communities' as places of secular/royal patronage which may have given rise to incipient urbanism. Among archaeologists, trade, and trading networks, rose in importance and perception, eclipsing the institutional status of early towns as a factor in their rise. Yet, Hodges's argument was criticised as overly normative and prescriptive, and it took perceptive critiques such as those by Grenville Astill (1991; 2000) to balance Hodges's predilection for core/periphery models of state formation and systems theory, with themes of locality, agricultural context, and diversity of political and religious impetus. Accompanying this diversification of approach was an increased interest in 'proto-urbanism', where informal beach markets, monasteries and minsters were variously argued to be responsible for generating urban momentum (*e.g.* Blair 2001; Griffiths 2003). The search for common urban origins produced a wealth of comparative studies, including an important collection of papers edited by Howard Clarke and Anngret Simms (1985). This sought to bring together the early histories of towns in non-Roman Europe, implying a commonality of urban experience outside the legacy of the Roman Empire. *Dark Age Economics* came as a revitalising contribution to a debate on European trade and the legacy of the Roman Empire, which dated back to Henri Pirenne's *Medieval Cities* (1927) and *Mohammed and Charlemagne* (published posthumously in French in 1937 and in English in 1939). The critical debate that these seminal contributions provoked had considerable influence on academic thinking about the Viking Age. Excavations in Ribe (Denmark), Hedeby/Haithabu (Germany), Kaupang (Norway) and Birka (Sweden) extended the focus on North Sea trading networks to cover the rise of Scandinavian kingdoms in the late Iron Age and Viking periods. The 1991 book by Helen Clarke and Björn Ambrosiani, *Towns in the Viking Age*, sought to draw together common threads across Europe, but came a little too early to capture the full richness of the evidence from former communist countries in Eastern Europe.

A significant problem with evolutionary notions of proto-urbanism is that few of the trading sites that showed significant signs of urbanism in the 8th or 9th centuries went on to become fully-fledged towns in the 10th or 11th centuries. The North Sea *emporia,* with one or two exceptions, failed in the mid-9th century, becoming derelict and abandoned, and later urban activity took place on different (if in some cases nearby) sites. In England, the sites of *Hamwic, Eoforwic* and *Lundenwic* all lapsed into disuse, and only *Gipeswic* survived *in situ,* by the narrowest thread of continuity through the 9th century. This decline was, ironically, blamed by historical commentators such as Peter Sawyer (1982) on the effects of North Sea Viking raids, although Hodges and others preferred to point to systems collapse due to changing emphases in early state formation, and the decline of the Carolingian Empire. The *longphort* settlements of Ireland (see Harrison, this volume) are another case largely of discontinuity. Until recently the location of the settlement of 9th-century Dublin was a mystery, indicated only indirectly by the rich pagan cemeteries of Kilmainham/Islandbridge and smaller clusters of furnished graves elsewhere along the lower River Liffey. The townscape of Dublin was commonly accepted to have begun to develop after the interruption of Scandinavian rule between 902 and 917, as demonstrated most extensively by Wallace's excavations at Wood Quay/Fishamble Street (Wallace 1992; 2001; 2008). Excavations at Temple Bar West in the 1990s revealed 9th-century domestic occupation for the first time (Simpson 2000), and even some relatively limited evidence for continuity of use into the 10th century, suggesting that some inhabitants stayed on after their rulers were expelled by native Irish forces in 902. The early Scandinavian presence around the former *Dubh Linn* ('black pool') on the River Poddle near its entrance to the Liffey is confirmed by a series of warrior burials on its south side (Simpson 2005). But attributes of the other *longphort* sites such as defences, hoards, trade objects such as merchant weights, and early metalworking, are still lacking from Dublin's 9th-century phase. Elsewhere in Ireland, considerable doubt remains about the relationships between *longphort* sites and later towns, such as that between Woodstown and Waterford, and historically-recorded 9th-century Viking camps at Cork and Limerick with the 11th- and 12th-century towns that arose there. Outwardly very similar 9th-century sites in Britain, such as the riverside camps at Repton (Derbyshire) and Torksey (Lincolnshire), have only very distant and qualified developmental relationships with the 'Five Boroughs' of the North and East midlands (see Williams, this volume).

It is clear that discontinuity, change and localism are as powerful factors in the story of early towns as a broad-brush notion of urban evolution. What might be termed the 'processual phase' of urban studies was long-lasting and pervasive, but itself is now subject to critique and revision. An emphasis on urban origins has given way to a stronger interest in the nature of urban life itself. A 'town' is no longer seen as a site-type and therefore an interpretive end in itself, but as a shorthand term for a concentration of spatial, social and economic complexity which is perhaps more interesting in its variations than its conformity. Indeed the question 'what is a town?', for example, is seen as looking jaded or 'hackneyed and old fashioned' (Giles and Dyer 2007, 2). The emphasis on urban definitions has also produced something of a false dichotomy between town and countryside. Perceptive historians and archaeologists had always recognised the interconnections and interdependencies between cities, suburbs, and their rural hinterlands (Dyer and Lilley 2012). Yet the divergences of approach between urban and rural archaeology conspired against breaking down the town-country divide. This led to long-running debates on urban origins, and on the formation of early medieval villages and field systems in the rural landscape, taking place virtually in isolation from each other. This was a major opportunity missed, as the chronological and regional similarities between intensified urbanism and the growth of urban markets in the 10th and 11th centuries, and the move towards village nucleation in large swaths of England, are too close and interesting to be overlooked any longer (Griffiths 2011). The shiring of later Anglo-Saxon England, based on hides and hundreds, local assemblies, and comparable developments in the Danelaw (Hadley 2000) are evidence that local governance and institutions were developing around a pattern of social and economic urban-rural dependencies. Civil defence in later Anglo-Saxon England depended on co-organisation of town defences and roads, settlements, beacons and look-outs across the rural landscape (Baker *et al.* in press).

It is clear by the later 11th century that some aspects of town life were beginning to develop a sense of separateness from the countryside (Reynolds 1977), but that rural connections and interdependencies were still extremely strong. Major Viking-Age towns such as Dublin, Chester, Lincoln and York had hinterlands consisting of rural estates, rivers, coastlines and uplands, which supplied them with timber, wool, fish, livestock and cereal production. Dublin's shire, the *Dyflinarskíri*, was extensive (although by no means dominated by Scandinavian settlers), and the later Hiberno-Norse towns at Waterford, Wexford, Cork and Limerick, all had 'home territories' which can be traced in medieval sources (Bradley 1988). Many elite citizens had both rural and urban residences, and these personal connections and power structures gave dynamism to the redistribution of rural productive surpluses via urban markets. It is probable that many lower-ranking individuals and families, and itinerant smiths, metalworkers and boneworkers (see Ashby, this volume), passed between town and country on a regular, perhaps seasonal basis. Hunting and animal husbandry in the countryside and in forests, the gathering and picking of herbs and wild nuts and fruit, the exploitation of shorelines and marshlands, wildfowling and fishing, and the geography of droving, carting, exchange and supply, are all vital to understanding the patterns of consumption and diet revealed by botanical and animal bone assemblages from urban excavations (see Poole, this volume). When medieval documentary sources begin to show more detail of urban-rural social dependencies and links in later centuries, the extent of their complexity and quirkiness becomes clear. An extreme example of these comes in the form of the rights of certain powerful merchants in Bristol and Chester to grain production in Ireland following the Anglo-Norman Conquest of 1171 (Thacker 2003, 29–30), which led to primary foodstuffs being imported over great distances of sea. Simple core-periphery models, and neatly exclusive catchment analyses borrowed from human geography, generally are misleading.

Contacts between town and country depended on familial connections, institutional rights and traditions, which operated sometimes over great distances. Despite less documentary evidence, there is good reason to assume that in the Viking Age, particular and sometimes surprising urban-rural dependencies and geographical imbalances probably also occurred. This may help to explain regionally biased distributions of pottery and metalwork types (see Blinkhorn, this volume; Ten Harkel, this volume).

The legacy of urban excavation

Prior to the mid-1960s, medieval urban studies were almost exclusively a historical domain. Medieval deposits in towns were only subject to archaeological attention by happenstance, as had occurred on a partial basis, for instance, during the construction of the New Bodleian underground bookstore in Oxford in the later 1930s (Bruce-Mitford 1939). In the Victorian era and the early 20th century, the emphasis in excavation technique was on exposing masonry structures. In some English towns such as Chester, where the Roman-enthusiast Robert Newstead held sway over city excavations in the period 1910–1940, post-Roman layers were considered to be of little academic interest, and were liable to be removed by workmen or by machine before 'archaeological excavation' started, although some of the more eye-catching medieval finds of this excavation era were kept. Attitudes improved after the Second World War. Excavation during post-war reconstruction in London, such as the exposure and re-siting of the Wallbrook Mithraeum in the mid-1950s (Grimes 1968), raised public awareness of the buried past in historic cities and prompted a growing demand for research and excavation. This era coincided with the growth of contributions by individual pioneers of urban archaeology outside London, such as W. A. Pantin in Oxford, L. P. Wenham in York, and F. H. Thompson in Chester. Wenham and Thompson, in particular, used teams of local volunteers to investigate sites opened up by clearance and development, prefiguring the spread during the 1960s of paid teams of excavators in increasing numbers of towns (Gerrard 2003, 133–8). A longstanding tradition taken from urban historical geography underlies the rise of urban archaeology, and influential early exercises in the mapping of townscapes, such as those of Torksey and York in the 1960s by M. W. Barley (1964) and Rosemary Cramp (1967), generated much archaeological impetus.

The first modern urban excavation in Ireland took place in Dublin Castle in 1961 (Simpson 2000) and larger-scale campaigns followed, run by the National Museum of Ireland at High Street, Winetavern Street and Christchurch Place in the period 1962–76, and Wood Quay from 1976–81 (Murray 1983; Wallace 1992). In Britain, some city and local museums were active in excavating their own townscapes, in London and Chester, for instance. However the UK's national museums remained almost entirely detached from urban excavation. The most influential operational model arose in Winchester, where a series of major excavations took place from 1961 to 1971. An Excavations Committee consisting of influential citizens was formed to raise funds, and a Director (Martin Biddle) appointed, giving rise to the creation of a professional 'research unit' which occupied its own premises, acquired its own equipment, and employed excavators and specialists alongside students and volunteers (Gerrard 2003, 98–9). Attempting to create a national response to the destruction of archaeological layers in historic towns by development, the Council for British Archaeology created an Urban Research Committee in 1970, which led to the influential 1972 report *The Erosion of History* (Heighway 1972). The 'city unit' model, often constituted as a charitable trust, was replicated (with some variation in

David Griffiths

Fig. 1.1 Excavations at Flaxengate, Lincoln (England) in the mid-1970s (photograph by Lincoln Archaeological Trust; supplied by John Herridge, and reproduced courtesy of City of Lincoln Council).

size and operational remit) in Canterbury, York, Southampton, Exeter, Lincoln (fig. 1.1), Bath, Bristol, Oxford, Gloucester, Hereford, Stafford, Shrewsbury, Carlisle and Perth. Comparable city excavation offices emerged in Waterford (fig. 1.2) and Cork. In other areas, such as Wales, East Anglia, the North-East and East Midlands, urban excavation was carried out by county, regional or university-based units. Assisted by government schemes for the unemployed such as the Youth Opportunities Programme and the Manpower Service Commission, urban excavation ahead of redevelopment was widespread in the 1970s and early 1980s (Gerrard 2003, 171).

The urban archaeological boom saw a transformation in the quality and intensity of excavation techniques. Frequently working in rushed and sometimes dangerous circumstances, the archaeologists of that era produced an astonishingly rich and multi-dimensional cull of evidence, the implications of which are still being explored. Major innovations included the adoption of single-context recording (accompanied by the 'Harris Matrix', an innovative graphical model originating at Winchester, for systemizing and depicting stratigraphic relationships), which opened the way to making sense of the intensely complex depositional histories that were encountered, environmental sampling, and the conservation of organic materials. In a largely pre-computer age, all notation and drawing was by hand, using analogue materials, producing bulky and unwieldy site archives. The excavation boom was succeeded by a post-excavation funding crisis, which produced protracted delays in analysis and publication. Even in the most capable hands, the intensely complex and expensive job of writing up major urban excavations was a mountainous and sometimes near-impossible task. Many of the urban excavations in Britain and Ireland which pre-dated the onset of direct developer-funding in the early 1990s lacked adequate financial provision for this vital, but expensive and time-consuming phase (Carver 1993; 2010). Once the 'dig' was over, site teams having dispersed, and public interest having waned, it proved difficult enough to sustain anything more than the creation of basic structural reports, referring to major stratigraphic events and phases, with building plans and quantifications and basic identifications and descriptions of finds. Broader analyses, often presented as concluding

Fig. 1.2 Excavations at Peter Street, Waterford (Ireland) in the later 1980s (reproduced with kind permission of Maurice Hurley).

discussions, were predominantly historical in theme, and included some insightful studies of urban functions, such as those of Winchester (Biddle 1976b, 449–88).

Many published excavation reports took decades to produce, and in some cases, this primary level of publication has yet to be achieved. There were many reasons for the delay. Site archives often had to be moved on from their original premises to often unsatisfactory temporary storage, as many of the original urban units closed or were amalgamated with other institutions as competitive tendering took over the 1990s and 2000s. Plans, site records and photographs created in difficult conditions up to twenty years previously, were often found to be in a deleterious state, and some excavation archives have lost crucial elements due to the exigencies of several decades' worth of oversight or benign neglect. We are fortunate today in that a reasonable number of the people who undertook the original work are still with us (although some, sadly, are not), and state or publicly-funded organisations such as the Office of Public Works and the Discovery Programme in Ireland, and English Heritage, Historic Scotland and the Archaeology Data Service in Britain, have been willing to support publication programmes for excavation archives which have long-since parted company with their original sponsors.[1] For excavations conducted since the early 1990s, however, progress towards publication has somewhat improved. This has been helped by three factors: principally that of more adequate resourcing based on developer-funding, a better standard of project management following innovations such as MAP2 (English Heritage, 1991), and also a reduced scale of activity, with more new developments being designed to obviate the need for deep excavation.

A broader interrogation and synthesis of the results of major urban excavations since the 1960s is in many cases only now getting under way. In published monographs, fascicules, or 'grey literature' site reports, structures and deposits were largely written up in the terms in which they had been recorded. Text of this genre generally emphasises numbers and systematic description. Plans (usually black and white hachured replications of pencil originals drawn at scale onto permatrace) are sometimes accompanied in reports by similarly colourless isometric reconstructions of buildings, which give a spurious impression of completeness and very rarely depict human beings (an exception being the fine series of colour reconstructions of Dublin's urban environment produced by Michael Heffernan, which are used to illustrate Wallace 2001). Finds groups were largely reported upon by specialists according to type, date and material, with little reference to their placing within domestic space, their relationships to gender, age, social groupings, status or, indeed, each other. Contextual sequences, redeposition, residuality, along with boundaries, walls, floors, paths, postholes and pits dominated the interpretive language of reports and monographs, revealing a concern towards documenting and classifying 'things' and an innate aversion towards explicitly registering 'people'. Excavations of burials came slightly closer to approaching the human dimension, even though in almost all cases the personal identities of the bodies were unknown. Records and statistics on height, age and pathologies were gathered, but confronted by large numbers of inhumations, many truncated or otherwise disrupted, few archaeologists felt it necessary to enquire further into individual biographies.

The record of site data deriving from fifty years' worth of urban excavation is patchy. Techniques of description, interpretation and retrieval varied considerably over time and geography, although a semi-itinerant workforce – the 'Circuit' as it was known – helped to spread and consolidate common excavation methods across Britain and Ireland (but which, nonetheless, continued to differ in important respects from European and Scandinavian styles of excavation). Archaeological science made a slow, incremental impact. Soil chemistry analysis such as phosphate mapping of house floors, soil micromorphology, and integrated radiocarbon and luminescence-based dating techniques are all relatively recent in their impact, which has hitherto been largely felt on rural settlement sites of the Viking Age, such as Bornais in the Outer Hebrides (Sharples 2005). Most dating and phasing in the 1970s and 1980s was by relative sequence, based on datable finds such as coins, with only limited use of radiocarbon dating and dendrochronology. In Dublin, radiocarbon dating was barely used in constructing the chronological sequences for the excavations of the 1960s to 1980s, but was applied more extensively to sites excavated in the 1990s and 2000s. Of these, excavations at Temple Bar West were the first to reveal unambiguous evidence of 9th-century occupation, and the seven 'warrior' burials south of the 'Pool' at South Great George Street and Great Ship Street returned remarkably early radiocarbon determinations, suggesting they could have been placed there as early as the end of the 8th century or the beginning of the 9th century (Simpson 2000; 2005; O'Donovan 2008; Griffiths 2010 for critique). Scientific dating and other analyses from more recently excavated sites suggest that reappraisals of the outcomes of earlier excavations are needed, with new determinations and analyses on surviving archived organic material wherever possible.

Most urban excavation teams routinely gathered larger pieces of animal, bird and fish-bone by hand as 'bulk finds', but fewer attempted to collect it using wet-sieving to retrieve smaller or microscopic remains. Archaeobotanical remains were only collected from certain sites, or from certain contexts such as refuse pits. The York Archaeological Trust (founded in 1972) became arguably the leading organisation in applying environmental archaeological techniques to urban excavation. Its close relationship with the Environmental Archaeology Unit at the University of York ensured that scientific inquisitiveness and expertise, together with academic research facilities, were brought to bear on the richly preserved, deep waterlogged organic deposits encountered on sites in central York, most notably at 16–22 Coppergate which was excavated under the direction of Richard Hall between 1977 and 1982 (Hall 1984), giving rise subsequently to the creation of the Jorvik Viking Centre on the site. This long-running and highly publicised campaign cast unprecedented light on the conditions of daily life for the Viking-Age residents of narrow, congested urban tenements. The wood, wattle and other constructional materials from the houses were subjected to experimental conservation techniques. The presence of bees and other small ephemeral fauna was detected in the urban environment. Diet, health, and rudimentary sanitation emerged as research themes and provoked unprecedented public interest. Descriptions, and in some cases the actual display, of the remains of intestinal parasites, insects, faeces and body lice prompted curiosity and the imaginative and empathetic feelings of modern observers towards their urban forbears of a millennium ago. A glimpse of the human and corporeal dimension of urban archaeology continues to strike a particularly resonant note with adult visitors and children. The instinctive reaction of the general public towards the archaeology of human life and death in Viking-Age York demonstrates an innate emotional curiosity about past individual experience, with which, through over-familiarity and scientific distance, the academic discourses of archaeologists and urban historians have been in some danger of losing touch.

Material environments and urban identities

Any search for Scandinavian influence on towns outside Denmark, Norway or Sweden is hampered by the lack of an original or convincing archetype of 'Viking' urbanisation. Townscapes in Scandinavia were generally smaller and more specialised than those elsewhere in Europe. Excavations of early trading settlements at Ribe, Kaupang, Hedeby and Birka have shown some potential inspirations for developments elsewhere. Dagfinn Skre's excavations at Kaupang between 1999 and 2003 (Skre 2007; 2008; 2011) showed a 9th-century trading environment rich in silver, amber and continental pottery, and houses which may partly have inspired the Hiberno-Norse Type 1 buildings (see Boyd, this volume) although their sill-beam construction technique differs somewhat from the internal roof-supports of the Irish examples. The effects of Scandinavian influence are far more complex than originally foreseen when 'Viking Dublin' and 'Viking York' were in the hey-day of excavation, in the later 1970s and early 1980s. Then, there was a widespread media perception that they were almost twin Viking cities, two-of-a-kind, and irrefutable evidence of the profound impact which the Vikings had had on both Ireland and northern England. Both cities had been ruled by dynasties with Scandinavian ancestral backgrounds, sometimes the same one, between 841 and 1052 in the case of Dublin, and 876 and 954 in the case of York (although their continuing symbolic significance to Scandinavians may explain the failed Norwegian attempts to re-take them in 1066 in the case of York, and 1102–3 in the case of Dublin). In modern times, therefore, the permissible adjective 'Viking' for these two cities was used as a convenient shorthand for excitement, colour, internationalism, and a hint of violence. In the Irish Republic, the term 'Viking' carried a certain 'otherness' which distinguished the archaeology of the capital from the officially-approved notion of Celtic national origins, and provoked controversy during the 1979 sit-ins at Wood Quay as demonstrators sought to prevent the city corporation from destroying the site in order to build concrete office blocks (the outcome was a compromise on the time made available for excavation). Archaeologists therefore straddled the line between terminological probity and marketing language somewhat uneasily, but most were prepared to go along with the 'Viking' concept for their cities, perhaps reassured by the subtle use of 'Viking Age' wherever possible to water down overly simplistic direct ethnic associations with Scandinavia. The aftermath of major urban excavations in Dublin and York has shown that direct Scandinavian influences were much more muted and partial than hitherto admitted. Building types, artefacts, diet and technologies owed at least as much to the traditions of the host country than to Scandinavia, despite a reasonable representation in both cases of Scandinavian imports amongst the excavated finds, and local re-interpretations of Scandinavian art styles and language on the urban fabric. There has been a dawning realisation amongst archaeologists and historians over the past twenty years that drawing upon external 'influences' alone is wholly inadequate to help us understand the growth of complex urban cultures. What came to exist in 10th- and 11th-century Dublin, York, Lincoln, Chester and many other towns, could not simply be characterised in terms of intersecting national or ancestral traditions deriving from Ireland, Anglo-Saxon England or Scandinavia. Each town had its own specific combinations of agency unique to their particular circumstances. In particular, it is now recognisable that the experience of living in an early town produced its own momentum towards transmuted ethnic identity. Townspeople sought to distinguish themselves in some ways from country-dwellers, yet in most cases did not entirely sever that connection, as familial rural links remained important. The rise of commerce meant that urban identities were construed through living amongst a dense and cacophonous multitude of locals, visitors and strangers. For reasons of wealth, rank, occupation, external origin, reputation, religious belief, or social exclusion on the grounds of physical or mental impairment, people living in towns had some things in common with each other and some things not. Even in apparently planned and conforming urban housing plots, subtle contra-distinctions existed between immediate neighbours, as potently as on any larger scale and perhaps more so. The selection by townspeople of attributes to support individual identities, from dress display to the use of domestic space, traditions of children's play, and attitudes to privacy, warmth and cleanliness, was particular down to the level of the individual household and belies any attempt to characterise a whole town's identity in too-simplistic a light (see the chapters by Ten Harkel, Boyd and McAlister, this volume). Choice of materials, construction techniques, decorative and craft specialisations, and the use, display and discard of personal possessions are all indicative of the 'performance' of identity in the practices of everyday life.

A renewed theorisation of the particular and the domestic in urban archaeologies must be accompanied by an increased emphasis on the experience of living in townscapes. Phenomenology, the study of how people experience the world, is perhaps more commonly debated by archaeologists and anthropologists in relation to prehistoric landscapes and monumentality (*e.g.* Tilley 1994; Bradley 1998; Ingold 2000) but there is no doubt that it has its potential applications to studying life in early towns. Urban environments conditioned the lives of early medieval citizens in both practical and cognitive ways. Dominating (if derelict) Roman architecture surrounded those living in 10th- and 11th-century York, Chester, Leicester and Lincoln, setting their experience at variance with those inhabiting Dublin, Oxford or Nottingham. The legacy of Roman buildings, in terms of stone, tile and mortar rubble, infused the Viking-Age environments of former Roman cities with a particular materiality that was absent elsewhere. Occupation of former Roman structures and plots seems in many cases to have been reserved for certain groups in early medieval urban society, and densely-packed tenements and market places often grew up on the margins of these. Coppergate in York lies outside the Roman walls, and the most complete evidence for occupation of 10th-century Chester was found at 26–42 Lower Bridge Street, on sloping land between the southern wall of the Roman fortress and the River Dee (Mason 1985). Numerous churches, their dedications, graveyards and interlocking city parishes (see Stocker, this volume), gave texture to complex intra-urban religious and social allegiances. Earthen and stone defences, quaysides, towers, place-names, bridges, open spaces, streets, and public monuments such as the 'Thingmote' assembly mound of Viking Dublin and its near neighbour, the curious standing stone on the harbour's edge known as the 'Steine' (Ó Floinn 1998), represented an urban landscape of phenomenological power and complexity to those living in it, and those visiting or transiting through it.

Reconstructing the experience of living in Viking Age towns is an extremely tall order for present-day researchers and may well ultimately be impossible. It is however legitimate to recognise that the rich freight of information already available from histories and excavations of towns has barely begun to yield its full interpretive potential. Breaking out from the 'tyranny' of the individual empirical site report to a fuller, more integrated interrogation of past urban environments is essential. Synthesis and reappraisal of materials, spatial constructs and chronologies will generate new research questions, and it is to be hoped that these will have their effect in guiding future excavation strategies. Above all, we must concentrate on putting the human-scale experience with all its conflicting attitudes, rational or irrational beliefs and emotions back into our perceptions of early medieval towns. The following chapters provide a stimulating step along that road.

Note

1   For a case-study, see http://www.ahds.ac.uk/creating/case-studies/newham/index.htm

Bibliography

Astill, G. (1991) Towns and town hierarchies in Anglo-Saxon England. *Oxford Journal of Archaeology* 10, 95–117.

Astill, G. (2000) General survey 600–1300. In D. M. Palliser (ed.) *The Cambridge Urban History of Britain, Volume 1, AD 600–1400*, 27–49. Cambridge, Cambridge University Press.

Astill, G. (2006) Community, identity and the later Anglo-Saxon town: the case of Southern England. In W. Davies, G. Halsall and A. Reynolds (eds) *People and Space in the Middle Ages, 300-1300*, 233–54. Studies in the Early Middle Ages 28. Turnhout, Brepols.

Astill, G. (2009) Medieval towns and urbanization. In R. Gilchrist and A. Reynolds (eds) *Reflections: 50 Years of Medieval Archaeology, 1957–2007*, 255–70. Society for Medieval Archaeology Monograph 30. Maney, Leeds.

Barley, M. W. (1964) The medieval borough of Torksey, excavations 1960–62. *Antiquaries Journal* 44, 165–8.

Baker, J., Brookes, S. and Reynolds, A. (eds) (in press) *Landscapes of Defence in the Viking Age*. Studies in the Early Middle Ages series. Turnhout, Brepols.

Biddle, M. (1976a) Towns. In D. M. Wilson (ed.) *The Archaeology of Anglo-Saxon England*, 99–150. London, Methuen.

Biddle, M. (1976b) *Winchester in the Early Middle Ages. An edition and discussion of the Winton Domesday*. Winchester Studies 1. Oxford, Clarendon Press.

Blair, J. (2001) Small towns, 600–1270. In D. M. Palliser (ed.) *The Cambridge Urban History of Britain, Volume 1, AD 600–1400*, 245–72. Cambridge, Cambridge University Press.

Bradley, J. (1988) The interpretation of Scandinavian settlement in Ireland. In J. Bradley (ed.) *Settlement and Society in Medieval Ireland: Studies Presented to F. X. Martin*, 49–78. Kilkenny, Boethius Press.

Bradley, R. (1998) *The Significance of Monuments: on the shaping of human experience in Neolithic and Bronze Age Europe*. London, Routledge.

Bruce-Mitford, R. L. S. (1939) The archaeology of the site of the Bodleian Extension in Broad Street, Oxford. *Oxoniensia* IV, 89–146.

Carver, M. O. H. (1993) *Arguments in Stone: archaeological research and the European town in the first millennium*. Oxford, Oxbow.

Carver, M. O. H. (2010) *The Birth of a Borough: an archaeological study of Anglo-Saxon Stafford*. Woodbridge, Boydell.

Clarke, H. and Ambrosiani, B. (1991) *Towns in the Viking Age*. London, Leicester University Press.

Clarke, H. B. and Simms, A. (eds) (1985) *The Comparative History of Urban Origins in Non-Roman Europe*. British Archaeological Reports International Series 255i. Oxford, British Archaeological Reports.

Cramp, R. J. (1967) *Anglian and Viking York*. Borthwick Papers 33. York, St Anthony's Press.

Crawford, S. (2011) Overview: the body and life course. In H. Hamerow, D. A. Hinton and S. Crawford (eds) *The Oxford Handbook of Anglo-Saxon Archaeology*, 623–40. Oxford, Oxford University Press.

Davies, W., Halsall, G. and Reynolds, A. (eds) (2006) *People and Space in the Middle Ages, 300–1300*. Studies in the Early Middle Ages 28. Turnhout, Brepols.

Dyer, C. and Lilley, K. (2012) Town and countryside, relationships and resemblances. In N. Christie and P. Stamper (eds) *Medieval Rural Settlement: Britain and Ireland AD 800–1600*, 81–98. Oxford, Windgather Press.

English Heritage (1991) *Management of Archaeological Projects* 2 (MAP 2). London, English Heritage.

Gerrard, C. (2003) *Medieval Archaeology: understanding traditions and contemporary approaches*. Abingdon, Routledge.

Giles, K. and Dyer, C. (eds) (2007) *Town and Country in the Middle Ages: contrasts, contacts and interconnections, AD 1100–1500*. Society for Medieval Archaeology Monograph 22. Leeds, Maney.

Griffiths, D. (2003) Exchange, trade and urbanisation. In W. Davies (ed.) *From the Vikings to the Normans*, 73–104. Short Oxford History of the British Isles. Oxford, Oxford University Press.

Griffiths, D. (2010) *Vikings of the Irish Sea: conflict and assimilation AD 790–1050*. Stroud, The History Press.

Griffiths, D. (2011) Towns and their hinterlands. In J. Crick and L. Van Houts (eds) *A Social History of England 900–1200*, 152–78. Cambridge, Cambridge University Press.

Grimes, W. F. (1968) *Excavation of Roman and Mediaeval London*. London, Routledge and Kegan Paul.

Hadley, D. M. (2000) *The Northern Danelaw: its social structure* c. *800–1100*. London, Leicester University Press.

Hadley, D. M. (2011) Ethnicity and acculturation. In J. Crick and L. Van Houts (eds) *A Social History of England 900–1200*, 235–46. Cambridge, Cambridge University Press.

Hadley, D. M. and Hemer, K. A. (2011) Microcosms of migration: children and early medieval population movement. *Childhood in the Past* 4, 63–78.

Hall, R. A. (1984) *The Viking Dig*. London, The Bodley Head.

Hill, D. and Cowie, R. (2001) *Wics: the early medieval trading centres of northern Europe*. Sheffield, Sheffield University Press.

Heighway, C. M. (1972) *The Erosion of History: archaeology and planning in towns*. London, Council for British Archaeology.

Hodges, R. A. (1982) *Dark Age Economics*. London, Duckworth.

Ingold, T. (2000) *The Perception of the Environment. Essays in livelihood, dwelling and skill*. Abingdon, Routledge.

Mason, D. J. P. (1985) *Excavations at Chester, 26–42 Lower Bridge Street: the Dark Age and Saxon periods*. Grosvenor Museum Archaeological Excavation and Survey Reports 3. Chester, Chester City Council.

Lucy, S. (2011) Gender and gender roles. In H. Hamerow, D. A. Hinton and S. Crawford (eds) *The Oxford Handbook of Anglo-Saxon Archaeology*, 688–703. Oxford, Oxford University Press.

Murray, H. (1983) *Viking and Early Medieval Buildings in Dublin*. British Archaeological Reports British Series 119. Oxford, British Archaeological Reports.

O'Donovan, E. (2008) The Irish, the Vikings and the English: new archaeological evidence from excavations at Golden Lane, Dublin. In S. Duffy (ed.) *Medieval Dublin VIII*, 36–130. Dublin, Four Courts Press.

Ó Floinn, R. (1998) The archaeology of the early Viking Age in Ireland. In H. B. Clarke, M. Ní Mhaonaigh and R. Ó Floinn (eds) *Ireland and Scandinavia in the Early Viking Age*, 131–65. Dublin, Four Courts Press.

Pirenne, H. (1927) *Medieval Cities*. Princeton, Princeton University Press.

Pirenne, H. (1939) *Mohammed and Charlemagne*. London, Unwin.

Reynolds, S. (1977) *An Introduction to the History of English Medieval Towns*. Oxford, Clarendon Press.

Sawyer, P. H. (1982) *Kings and Vikings*. London, Methuen.

Simpson, L. (2000) Forty years a-digging: a preliminary synthesis of archaeological investigations in medieval Dublin. In S. Duffy (ed.) *Medieval Dublin I*, 11–68. Dublin, Four Courts Press.

Simpson, L. (2005) Viking warrior burials in Dublin: is this the longphort? In S. Duffy (ed.) *Medieval Dublin VI*, 11–62. Dublin, Four Courts Press.

Sharples, N. (2005) *A Norse Farmstead in the Outer Hebrides: excavations at Mound 3, Bornais, South Uist*. Oxford, Oxbow.

Skre, D. (ed.) (2007) *Kaupang in Skiringssal*. Kaupang Excavation Project Publication Series Volume 1, Norske Oldfunn XXII. Aarhus, Aarhus University Press.

Skre, D. (2008) The development of urbanism in Scandinavia. In S. Brink and N. Price (eds) *The Viking World*, 83–93. Abingdon, Routledge.

Skre, D. (2011) *Things from the Town: artefacts and inhabitants in Viking-Age Kaupang*. Kaupang Excavation Project Publication Series Volume 3, Norske Oldfunn XXIV. Aarhus, Aarhus University Press.

Stoodley, N. (2011) Childhood to old age. In H. Hamerow, D. A. Hinton and S. Crawford (eds) *The Oxford Handbook of Anglo-Saxon Archaeology*, 641–66. Oxford, Oxford University Press.

Thacker, A. T. (2003) Early medieval Chester. In C. P. Lewis and A. T. Thacker (eds) *Victoria History of the County of Chester, Volume 5*, 16–33. Woodbridge, Boydell, for Institute of Historical Research.

Tilley, C. (1994) *A Phenomenology of Landscape*. Oxford, Berg.

Wallace, P. F. (1992) *The Viking Age Buildings of Dublin*. Medieval Dublin Excavations 1962–81, Series A, Volume 1 (2 vols). Dublin, Royal Irish Academy.

Wallace, P. F. (2001) Ireland's Viking Towns. In A.-C. Larsen (ed.) *The Vikings in Ireland*, 37–50. Roskilde, Viking Ship Museum.

Wallace, P. F. (2008) Archaeological Evidence for the different expressions of Scandinavian settlement in Ireland. In S. Brink and N. Price (eds) *The Viking World*, 434–8. London, Routledge.

2

TOWNS AND IDENTITIES IN VIKING ENGLAND

Gareth Williams

Historical narratives of the Viking settlement in England tend to focus on towns (or at least on settlements which became towns), in common with Ireland and with Russia, but in contrast to other areas of Viking settlement. Of the four main terms used for regions of Viking settlement in England, two – 'The Kingdom of York' and 'The Five Boroughs' – take their names from specific towns, while two – 'The Danelaw' and 'East Anglia' – do not. Of these four terms, only the last can be shown to be a contemporary term, and this causes some problems for our understanding of the relationship between towns and political identities. Nevertheless, there is no doubt that the emerging towns played some part in the shaping of political and cultural identities in areas of Scandinavian settlement, while the expansion of West Saxon authority in the early 10th century into areas of Viking settlement is expressed in terms of the capture by one side or the other of a succession of towns of varying sizes, and of the submission of military forces associated in some way with individual named towns. This chapter will address the role of the emerging towns for the emerging political and cultural identities of Viking-Age England.

The development of Viking towns in England

The importance of towns in the West Saxon conquest of Viking England prompts the question of what was meant in terms of political authority when a 'town' submitted or was captured. It also prompts the question of why towns formed such an important element in Viking England and Ireland, but not in other areas of settlement, as towns were by no means universal across the Viking diaspora. In part, the emergence of towns in the already relatively densely settled territories of England and Ireland and their absence elsewhere may relate to whether the Viking settlements were superimposed onto pre-existing settlements, or represented the colonisation of more or less virgin territory. The narrative of the 'land-taking' in Iceland, by contrast with England and Ireland, is one of the establishment of farms, rather than towns, of land-taking by wealthy individuals with their extended households, rather than by armies or other large groups, and of wider regions defined in relation to the landscape as much as by the farms themselves, and the whole island functioning to some extent as a single extended community (Byock 2001, 9–11, 84–8; Sigurðsson 2008, 571–2). However, although relatively few Viking-Age rural settlements have yet been excavated in England (Richards 2001, 269; 2008, 371–2), the overall distribution of Scandinavian place-names together with widespread use of individual place-names referring to farms of one sort or another suggest that the bulk of the Scandinavian settlement there was also based around rural estates (Hadley 2000, 99–104), while towns (considered in this context purely as settlements, rather than as territorial centres) are not representative of the bulk of the Scandinavian or Anglo-Scandinavian settlement.

If the towns were not entirely representative of Viking-Age settlement in England, they were not evenly distributed either: there was a sprinkling in the former kingdom of Mercia, a sparser sprinkling in East Anglia, with York alone north of the Humber, while there were no identifiable Viking towns west of the Pennines. The nature of pre-Viking settlement alone does not explain this distribution. North-west England was previously settled, as were most if not all of the areas of Scotland colonised by the Vikings, together with the few areas of Viking settlement in Wales, but none of these regions witnessed the development of towns, although some beach-markets and other sites showing evidence of trade developed in these areas, fulfilling some of the economic functions of towns (Griffiths 1992; 2010, 109–18; Redknap 2004; 2009; Griffiths *et al.* 2007). It is also difficult to relate the pattern of urbanisation directly to the places of origin of different Viking groups who settled in different areas of Britain and Ireland. Although much of the secondary literature refers to areas of 'Danish' or 'Norwegian' settlement, and one can point to the existence of towns (or at least settlements with some urban characteristics) in Denmark but not in Norway (assuming that Kaupang and the Vestfold region are seen as under Danish rule, which is not firmly established (Wamers 2002; Skre 2007, 463–8)), recent thinking has questioned the applicability of such ethnic labels either in Britain or in Scandinavia in this period (Downham 2009), and settlements such as Hedeby (Germany, formerly in Denmark), Ribe (Denmark) and Kaupang (Norway) were, in any case, no more typical of 9th-century Denmark than York was of the north of England (Hall and Williams in prep.). Furthermore, towns were to form a major element in the Viking settlement of Ireland, much of which apparently came from Norway. It is true that there were many other settlements in southern Scandinavia and the Baltic that showed some urban characteristics (Tummuscheit 2003; Bogucki 2007; 2010; Sindbæk 2010; Hall and Williams in prep.), but these were not sufficiently developed to provide a model for Anglo-Scandinavian urbanisation.

A stronger factor in the development of towns in Viking-Age England may have been the existence there of earlier towns as a model. This is not to say that there were existing Anglo-Saxon precursors to all of the Anglo-Viking towns which developed in the late 9th and 10th centuries. Pre-Viking towns were very limited in number, and those few were divided between areas settled by Vikings and those which remained under Anglo-Saxon control with Ipswich (Suffolk) and York falling under Viking control, while London, Canterbury (Kent) and Southampton (Hampshire) remained Anglo-Saxon (Hall 2011, 602–4). Worcester also shows some urban characteristics (see below) by the late 9th century (Brooks 1996, 143–4; Hall 2011, 607), while Tamworth (Staffordshire), Hereford and Winchcombe (Gloucestershire) all have defences that have been identified as evidence of pre-Viking urbanism in south-western Mercia, and even across Mercia as a whole (Haslam 1987; Bassett 2007; 2008). This latter view, however, seems to go beyond the currently available evidence, and pre-Viking towns in Mercia seem not to have been a major influence in the development of Viking towns in that area. A variety of other types of pre-Viking settlement showed some urban characteristics, especially those relating to specialised production and exchange, including both ecclesiastical centres (minsters), and secular emporia and production centres (*wics*) (Hodges 1982; Pestell and Ulmschneider 2003;

Blair 2005, 246–90; Pestell 2011). However, these pre-urban sites lacked the range of social, administrative and defensive functions typical of the 10th- and 11th-century town, and while they could provide a starting point for further development, they did not provide a full model for urbanisation. Moreover, many of them did not develop into towns at all, while others saw significant shifts in the exact location of urban activity in relation to continued settlement in the same town, *e.g.* the apparent relocation of settlement at London in the course of the 9th century from Aldwych/the Strand to within the Roman city walls (Hobley 1988).

In addition to any models for urbanism that may have existed by the time of the settlements of the mid- to late 870s, a further model may have been provided by the development of *burhs* in Alfredian Wessex from the late 9th century. The network of *burhs* developed under Alfred, and in the early years of the reign of Edward the Elder, is listed in the so-called Burghal Hidage, which was probably compiled early in the reign of Edward the Elder (899–924), and indicates the number of hides of land relating to military service in each of the named *burhs,* together with a mechanism for relating the hidage to the length of the defensive enclosure (Hill and Rumble 1996). This list provides interesting parallels to some of the Viking towns further north. Firstly, many (although not all) developed into towns, with a wide range of functions (see further below). However, in most cases the *burhs* were not fully developed until the 10th century, and several of the *burhs* listed in the Burghal Hidage seem to have disappeared very quickly, reflecting the fact that *burhs* had a primarily military role in the Alfredian phase, and many of them quickly became obsolete in the changing strategic landscape of the 10th century (Hall 2011; Williams 2013).

Secondly, the assignment of men for the defence of the Burghal Hidage *burhs* raises an important point for our understanding of how an emerging town might function as a focus for a wider regional identity. The manpower required to man the entire network was on a massive scale, and must have been drawn from much wider areas than from the emerging *burhs* themselves. Although interpretations of exactly which land was assigned to each *burh* differ, comparisons with the hidage assessment of *Domesday Book* suggest that most, if not all, of the hidated land in Wessex was assigned to individual *burhs* (Brooks 1996; Hinton 1996). This meant that the rural population was tied by specific obligations to individual towns, and it would be strange if this did not lead to a degree of identification with those towns. Prior to Alfred's burghal programme, the *Anglo-Saxon Chronicle* (*ASC*) refers to the military levies raised from individual shires (*e.g.* the mustering of the men of Somerset, Wiltshire and part of Hampshire in 878; *ASC* A & E, *sub* 878). From the latter part of the reign, burghal garrisons were capable of functioning as field armies when required, as well as defending their own individual *burhs* (*e.g. ASC* A, *sub* 894 [893]; Abels 1997). This sense of a regional army directly relating to a town seems very much to prefigure the description of the Viking 'armies' of the early 10th century, as these are also routinely described by the *Anglo-Saxon Chronicle* as relating to individual towns. The Alfredian system was extended northwards by his successors in the course of the 10th century (Higham 1988; Hill and Rumble 1996; Abels 1997; Griffiths 2001; Ward 2001; Williams 2013), and it is not always clear how much of the urban development in areas of Scandinavian settlement took place under the impetus of local Anglo-Scandinavian rulers and how much as a consequence of the West Saxon expansion. At the same time, however, there is a danger that Anglo-Saxon sources may imply misleading degrees of similarity between Anglo-Saxon and Anglo-Scandinavian towns through the assumption that Anglo-Scandinavian towns shared the characteristics of the towns with which the Anglo-Saxon authors themselves were familiar.

Alfred's burghal strategy was in part a response to the strategy of the *micel here* ('great raiding army') in the 860s and 870s. This strategy was based on establishing 'camps' each winter, which could provide both security and command of local sources of supply over the winter, and which could provide a base for the next season's campaigning before the army moved on to the next camp. The use of these bases was combined with unusual strategic mobility through the use of both ships and horses, and it is this, more than prowess on the battlefield or military technology, that distinguishes the Vikings from their contemporaries (Williams 2008b). Alfred's *burhs* denied strategic mobility to the enemy, and at the same time protected the sort of sites that might otherwise be taken over as winter camps. It has been noted that Alfred's *burhs* were varied in nature, including former Roman towns, hillforts and new foundations in strategic locations, although some of these made use of estate centres, such as Reading (Berkshire) and Wantage (Berkshire). In the same way, the *micel here* made use of towns (including London and York), royal estates (such as Reading and Chippenham (Wiltshire)) and ecclesiastical centres (*e.g.* Repton (Derbyshire)) as well as strategically placed sites which cannot, as yet, be demonstrated as being sites of any great significance in the immediate pre-Viking period (*e.g.* Torksey (Lincolnshire)). In some cases, the absence of evidence for prior occupation may simply reflect poor documentation and lack of archaeological investigation, and the prior status of places like Thetford (Norfolk), which went on to become an important Anglo-Scandinavian town, is currently unclear. These winter camps have some similarity with the phenomenon of the *longphort* (pl. *longphuirt*) in Ireland; *longphuirt* were also camps developed at least in part for the temporary domination of the surrounding area and as bases for raiding further afield (Ó Floinn 1998; Sheehan 2008; Williams forthcoming; for further discussion of *longphuirt*, see Harrison, this volume).

These winter camps may themselves have played an important part in establishing a pattern of pre-urban settlement. It is important to note here the scale of such encampments. For a long time, the paradigm for such camps has been the enclosure at Repton excavated by Martin Biddle and Birthe Kjølbye-Biddle (2001). With a total enclosed area of 1.46 hectares/3.65 acres, this could perhaps accommodate an army based on the minimalist interpretation of the size of Viking forces proposed by Peter Sawyer (1962, 117–28), but not the larger forces accepted by most scholars following the refutation of Sawyer's argument by Nicholas Brooks (1979). However, more recent investigations of sites in both England and Ireland suggest that even if the Repton enclosure has been correctly reconstructed, it is likely to have been only part of a much larger encampment. Irish *longphuirt* seem to have been rather larger, despite the fact that the force that occupied Repton is repeatedly described as *micel* ('great' or 'large') (Simpson 2005, 21–5). The Viking winter camp at Torksey, occupied the year before Repton, can be shown to have occupied a total area of around *c.* 26 hectares/65 acres (Blackburn 2011a, 221), while another comparable site from North Yorkshire, also showing an apparent peak of occupation in the 870s, is even larger at *c.* 31 hectares/76 acres, although this site is not mentioned in the historical record (Hall and Williams in prep.). These sites certainly compare in size to the emerging towns of the late 9th and 10th centuries, and many of the settlers must have become accustomed to over-wintering in such large camps for a period of several years before settlement.

While interpretation of the Viking presence at Repton has focused on the defensive structures and the graves, with relatively few stray finds (Biddle and Kjølbye-Biddle 2001), the bulk of our understanding of the Torksey and North Yorkshire camps, as well as the Woodstown *longphort*, is primarily derived from finds recovered with metal detectors, with only limited excavation, and the large number of finds from all three sites indicates a range of activities which reflect at least some of the core characteristics of an early medieval town, as defined by Martin Biddle (1976, 99–100; see also the preface to this volume): defences; a planned street-system; a market(s); a mint; legal autonomy; a role as a central place; a relatively large and dense population; a diversified economic base; plots and houses of 'urban' type; social differentiation; complex religious organisation; and a judicial centre. Biddle indicated that at least three or four of these characteristics needed to be present for a settlement to qualify as a town, and to these one might add a prolonged period of occupation/activity in the same settlement, even if the focus of settlement might move short distances, as seems to have occurred at London (see above) and whole towns might occasionally relocate, as in the replacement of Hedeby by nearby Schleswig in southern Denmark (Roesdahl 1982, 52).

Not all of Biddle's urban characteristics are visible archaeologically, and the historical references to Viking camps provide little detailed information to enable us to assess how they conformed to these characteristics. However, there is some evidence to suggest that the occupants of the winter-camps sometimes involved themselves in activities with an urban flavour. For example, several accounts of the Vikings over-wintering refer to them 'making peace' with neighbouring/ surrounding kingdoms. Such peace-making is likely to have included arrangements for trade/ markets for the duration of the truce. A surviving treaty between Alfred of Wessex and the Viking leader Guthrum makes specific allowance for trade between their two peoples (Keynes and Lapidge 1983, 171–2), and although this treaty appears to date from after Guthrum and his men had settled in East Anglia, there are parallels in accounts of the Vikings over-wintering on the Continent (Valante 2008, 41–2). Furthermore, recent interpretations of the *longphort* phenomenon also point to trading activity as a significant function rather than them fulfilling a purely military role (Sheehan 2008; Valante 2008, 41–5; Harrison, this volume; Williams forthcoming). This is significant, because both Torksey and the North Yorkshire site have yielded evidence of widespread exchange, in the form of coins, bullion and weights (similar weights have also been associated with the historically documented Viking camp at Wareham (Archibald 1998)), together with evidence of metalworking as well as other more domestic activities, such as textile manufacture. The same is true of the *longphort* at Woodstown (O'Brien *et al.* 2005). Woodstown and the North Yorkshire site also had defensive earthworks, and although no comparable earthworks have yet been discovered at Torksey, archaeological investigation of the site has so far been extremely limited. The evidence for both production and exchange is, then, consistent with Biddle's requirement for a town to have a 'market' and 'diversified economic base', and the scale certainly indicates 'a relatively large and dense population', while 'defences' are known from two of the three sites and suspected at the third (Hall and Williams in prep.).

We can see, then, that even with limited historical and archaeological evidence for the winter camps, there are a number of features that enable them to fit Biddle's minimum of three to four urban characteristics, and while some of the other Biddle characteristics definitely seem to have been absent (planned street-system, mint, plots and houses of 'urban' type), the remainder are harder to determine. Nevertheless, these sites do not feel like 'towns', perhaps because the immediately recognisable core physical characteristics of street-systems and houses/plots are missing (albeit archaeological investigation at all three sites has been limited).

Although the Viking winter camps did not have the regular and organised lay-outs that we tend to associate with towns, living in such camps for several months each year must have accustomed the members of the *micel here* to living within the constraints of something not unlike an urban environment. This must have led to a degree of socialisation to living in pre-urban conditions, and temporary arrangements for assigning accommodation, resolving disputes, and so on, must have been in place, prefiguring the more permanent urban planning and the role of justice associated with the later towns. It also seems likely that the camps provided an element of shared identity for what was otherwise a heterogeneous group, composed of many smaller elements, probably with diverse origins. Furthermore, this shared identity may have extended beyond the physical site itself. The *Annals of St Bertin* (*ASB*) (*sub* 861) describe a Viking force comparable to the *micel here* dividing into individual *sodalidates* while overwintering along the whole length of the Seine between Paris and the sea (*ASB, sub* 861). It seems likely that the *micel here* was also obliged to fragment, with the camps providing a focus for the more-extended temporary settlement of a particular region, and a place of refuge in addition to a centre for production and trade. Some of this is admittedly speculative, but there is no question that these camps were effective in temporarily controlling the territories and resources of the surrounding regions. From this it was a short step to a more permanent relationship between town and hinterland.

The fundamental difference between towns and winter camps in this respect was in the nature of that relationship to the hinterland. In the case of the winter camps, there was a necessity for reaching some kind of accommodation (however enforced) with the surrounding population in terms of the use of space and resources, since a population equivalent to that of a town was abruptly imposed onto the landscape. They needed to eat and drink, to repair or replace worn clothing and shoes, to maintain and repair ships and military equipment, and to construct winter accommodation, however temporary. This meant access to a wide variety of commodities and raw materials, much of which would have been drawn from the surrounding areas, although some may have required raiding or trading further afield. However, while it will have been a concern for those of the local population who remained, there was no need for the Viking leaders to consider directly the long-term consequences on the land of their temporary exploitation. Would the Vikings have respected the need to set part of the harvest aside as seed for the following year, knowing that they would move on? We have no way to tell, but it seems unlikely. By contrast, once the Vikings themselves turned to permanent settlement, the long-term sustainability of both urban and rural settlements became a concern. The towns could not develop and survive without a permanent relationship with the hinterland, while the towns provided a focus for defence of an Anglo-Scandinavian population dispersed across rural areas, which still contained a significant native population, as well as defence against potential external enemies.

Towns and territories

It is in the context of a relationship between towns and extended territories that the emphasis on towns in the West Saxon conquest and unification of England should be seen. With the capture or submission of each 'town' came the defeat or submission of a local *here* ('raiding army') and the surrounding area. In this respect, the Anglo-Scandinavian towns were probably similar to the West Saxon *burhs,* with the bulk of the garrison dispersed over an area of land attached to each *burh.*

Control of the town gave control of the associated territory and vice versa. Control of the surrounding territory meant control of the food supply, as seen in the pre-urban phase when a

Viking force had to abandon Chester in 893–4 because the Anglo-Saxons took all the cattle outside, burnt the crops, and ate the surrounding countryside bare with their horses, so that the Vikings were forced to move on to Wales because of lack of supplies (*ASC* A, *sub* 894–5 [893–4]). Equally, without a defensive centre to house a garrison, it was impossible to dominate the surrounding area in the event that claims to authority were contested. Thus, after the raiding army at Bedford had submitted to Edward the Elder in 918, the raiding army of Huntingdon, together with a force from East Anglia, established a fortification at nearby Tempsford (Bedfordshire) in 920, reverting to a pre-urban military encampment to contest Bedford's control of its hinterland, although they were defeated and driven out later the same year (*ASC* A, *sub* 919 [918], 921 [920]). This site probably only had a short-lived importance, as once the Tempsford raiding army was defeated there was no military, economic or administrative need for a second *burh* so close to Bedford, while the two would have continued to compete for the resources of the surrounding countryside. The diversity of the Viking urban or semi-urban settlements reflects a wider similarity with the West Saxon *burhs* in that some Viking towns were based around established or revitalised urban centres (including former Roman towns) such as York and Lincoln, others apparently used Roman forts (Derby, Towcester (Northamptonshire)), others were related to established estate centres, whether secular or monastic (Northampton), while the remainder have less certain origins, possibly representing new creations. It is problematic that, with the exception of York and Lincoln, few historically documented Viking towns have so far produced much archaeological evidence, so that the exact relationship between Viking settlement and previous settlements is not always clear (Hall 1989; 2001; 2011; Vince 2001). Like the *burhs*, some were of lasting significance as regional centres, while others, like Tempsford, were little more than temporary forts, and many more were probably somewhere in between. It seems likely that the more substantial urban centres, like the *burhs*, exercised a range of social and administrative functions beyond their military and economic roles, but the paucity of historical records from the period of Viking rule makes this hard to determine with any accuracy.

The roles of the emerging towns are likely to have included that of power centre for the surrounding area, consequently drawing the focus of regional identity towards these towns. The interdependency between town and hinterland has already been discussed, but in the context of identity, the issue is not so much the geographical or economic hinterland as the sense of an associated territory. Both Torksey and Stamford (Lincolnshire) were important centres of ceramic production (Hinton 1990, 82–4) and must have interacted economically with the surrounding countryside in addition to their wider economic role as centres of production and exchange. By the mid-late 10th century both were certainly *burhs*, and they should probably also be considered as towns before the West Saxon conquests, and there is no reason to doubt that the urban population identified with these towns. It is less clear that the population of the surrounding countryside identified with these towns, rather than with the larger but more distant Lincoln, or with broader regions, such as Lindsey and Kesteven, instead of with towns. It is notable that while several known Viking towns later became the focus of shires, others, including both Torksey and Stamford, did not. Both towns formed part of the emerging shire of Lincolnshire, which was much larger than any of the southern shires and on economic and geographical criteria alone could presumably have been divided into much smaller shires. The same is true of Yorkshire and Norfolk.

When considering the relationship between towns and wider territories, comparison with Viking towns in Ireland may be at the same time both informative and misleading. In Ireland, the major Viking towns of Dublin, Limerick, Cork, Waterford and Wexford emerged as distinct political units, each with its surrounding territory. In an influential article, John Bradley (1988) argued for the importance of seeing the towns not purely as urban settlements, but as territorial units comprising both town and hinterland. This is demonstrably the case with Dublin, and its associated territory of *Dyflinaskiri*, and Bradley makes a strong case for the other towns having similar territories. He has recently (Bradley 2009) argued further for pushing these territories back to the 9th century, although Howard Clarke (1998, 353–68) has questioned whether any of the towns on the list above can really be considered to be towns before the late 10th century, and particularly whether there was permanent occupation there. It is true that there is now more evidence than when Clarke wrote for continued occupation in Dublin between the *longphort* phase in the late 9th century and the more 'urban' phases of the 10th century (Simpson 2005; 2010), but elsewhere Clarke's arguments still appear to hold; even at Dublin in the *longphort* phase, it is not clear that the settlement required the sort of hinterland to support it at this stage that it later required. The scale of the settlement remains uncertain, and unless it had a more substantial permanent population than has so far been demonstrated, Dublin could have supported itself through a combination of what could be raised in the immediate locality, trade with surrounding areas not under Viking control, and plunder/tribute. References in Irish sources to cattle raiding and specifically to 'cattle-tribute' are likely to relate to the need for cattle for food as much as, or more than, their economic value (Valante 2008, 84–5).

As stated previously, the *longphort* phase in this respect, as in others, resembles the phase of the winter-camps in England rather than a phase of permanently settled towns. Thus, while Bradley's model of extended territories with urban foci remains persuasive for Ireland in the late Viking Age, there is currently little evidence (with the possible exception of Dublin) that this dates back as far as the main period of urban development in England in the late 9th and 10th centuries. This is to some extent conjectural, since the argument is largely derived from absence of evidence. However, there is a more fundamental difference between the development of Viking towns in England and Ireland in that the Irish towns, and their associated territories, were carved out of neighbouring kingdoms (often placed on the border between two kingdoms), with the remainder of those kingdoms surviving as distinct political entities, so that the Viking towns, however large their territories, were distinct units which were effectively islands surrounded by unconquered native kingdoms. By contrast, the Viking settlement of England involved the conquest, settlement and partition of entire kingdoms, or large parts of kingdoms, and effectively divided England into large blocks of territory under Anglo-Saxon or Viking control, rather than isolated territories as in Ireland, where that very isolation forced distinct identities on the towns and their territories.

This pattern of wider territorial conquest meant that there was scope for pre-Viking identities to survive in England on a much larger scale, although the exact nature of this survival is not always clear. The pre-Viking kingdoms of Northumbria and East Anglia survived in some sense (see further below), but their boundaries were not necessarily the same, nor were they perhaps even stable. Regional identities, perhaps preserving older political units, also seem in some cases to have survived. The prime example here is Lindsey, formerly an independent kingdom, then a sub-kingdom contested by Northumbria and Mercia, and subsequently a Mercian province for nearly two centuries before the Viking conquest (Foot 1993). The term Lindsey has survived as a regional name up to the present day, and was certainly in use in the late Anglo-Saxon period (see below). The fact that Lincolnshire did not fit the pattern of southern shires has already been mentioned. Is this because existing regional identities were too strong to be worth overcoming when the concept of the shire was introduced?

The date of the emergence of the shire itself is a problem. The former Anglo-Scandinavian territories were certainly divided into shires by the 11th century, and it is likely that the shiring took place in the course of the late 10th century, as West Saxon authority became more firmly established. The shire formed an important tier of royal administration, above the hundred/wapentake and the *burh* (Williams 2013). However, it is not clear that units reflecting the later shire boundaries necessarily existed before the West Saxon conquest. Most of the towns recorded in the narrative of the conquest were those that gave their names to the shires even if some, like Buckingham, never developed into major centres. However, some of them, like Towcester and the Lincolnshire examples already mentioned, never developed shires of their own. Other towns and their inhabitants seem to have had links which crossed shire boundaries, such as the men 'of Bedford and Northampton' in 917 (*ASC* A, *sub* 918 [917]), and the men 'of Northampton as far north as the Welland' (and therefore incorporating part of what later became Leicestershire) in 920 (*ASC* A, *sub* 921 [920]), although it is not clear to what extent these represent shared identities, or temporary alliances between groups with distinct identities. Perhaps shires existed on a less formal basis before the late Anglo-Saxon shiring. The OE term *scir* and its ON cognate *skiri* imply a district associated with a particular focus, as in *Dyflinaskiri*, but this does not mean that the term always carried the significance accorded to shires in late Anglo-Saxon legal and administrative documents. Hadley (2000, 107–8) points to the existence of a number of 'shires' attached to relatively minor settlements, which later got swallowed up into the larger Yorkshire. Such small shires may reflect a network of territories that took their identities from settlements with some urban characteristics, even if not all of them could be defined as 'towns' in the Anglo-Scandinavian period according to the criteria identified above. Once again, however, the number of such settlements and shires, and exactly how, when and why they developed into the larger shires that followed remains a matter of conjecture.

Regional identities

Moving to still larger units, there are also problems with a group of political identities that appear in the secondary literature, none of which can reliably be dated back to the late 9th or even the 10th century. These include the Danelaw, the Kingdom of York and the Five Boroughs. Of these, the issues surrounding the concept of the Danelaw have been discussed in detail by others (Hart 1992, 3–24; Abrams 2001; Holman 2001), and only a summary is necessary here. As the name implies, the name refers to legal status, and when the term is first recorded in the early 11th century, it appears as a strictly legal distinction between customary legal practice in different parts of the newly unified kingdom of England, referring to the 'Danish' law which had applied in some areas before the expansion of authority under the West Saxon dynasty, and which they permitted to continue for a while as part of the process of cementing their new-found authority. As such, it is a term which only became meaningful within that unified kingdom, and one may reasonably doubt whether it had any currency before the reign of Edgar. While it implies a shared cultural identity, it says nothing about political identity, and the fact that the two early (12th-century) lists of the shires that constituted the Danelaw conflict with each other (Abrams 2001, 130–1) diminishes the value of the term still further.

In addition to legal practice, the term Danelaw has been used by modern scholars as an indicator variously of cultural, linguistic, religious and political identity, although again the area which it is taken to cover varies considerably, depending on whether it is used to indicate merely a distinction between Anglo-Saxon and Viking rule, or to indicate an additional distinction between supposed areas of 'Danish' and 'Norwegian' settlement. There are further discrepancies between use of the term to indicate the full extent of Scandinavian settlement in the late 9th century, or to indicate more flexibly the areas under Anglo-Scandinavian political authority at any given moment in the process of West Saxon expansion and Anglo-Scandinavian reaction in the 10th century. All of these usages suggest a sense of unity that goes far beyond anything which can be observed in contemporary sources. The creation of further artificial sub-divisions, such as the 'Northern Danelaw', 'Southern Danelaw' and 'Outer Danelaw', as suggested by Cyril Hart (1992, 8–19), has even less firm foundation in contemporary sources, and again represent modern constructed identities imposed onto the 10th-century landscape.

To a great extent the same problem concerning use of terminology exists with the 'Kingdom of York'. This term is never used in contemporary English sources, which tend to continue to refer to Northumbria (Rollason 2003), one of the pre-Viking kingdoms settled in the late 9th century. Matters are complicated by the fragmentary nature of the historical record both before and after the Viking conquest. The existence throughout the 10th century of a local Anglian dynasty based at Bamburgh (Northumberland), coupled with limited evidence of Scandinavian place-names or sculpture north of the Tees, suggests that to some extent Northumbria fragmented into areas broadly corresponding to the 7th-century kingdoms of Bernicia and Deira, although there may have been times that the Anglian rulers of Bamburgh acknowledged the rule of their 'Northumbrian' neighbours to the south. David Rollason (2003, 244–8) has also emphasised the need to accommodate in the political landscape the Community of St Cuthbert, a major landholder north of the Tees, which probably exercised a considerable degree of autonomy in return for acknowledging and perhaps even supporting the rule of the Viking kings of Northumbria. A further issue exists over the status of the area between the Pennines and the Irish Sea. A distinction is often made between the 'Danish' 'Kingdom of York', and the 'Norwegian' north-west, which is again absent in the historical record, although the area between Chester and the kingdom of Cumbria receives little mention in this period, and its history is hard to determine (Higham 2004). No major centre of political power can be identified in this area with any certainty, although it has been suggested that there may have been such a centre in the vicinity of the Ribble valley (Higham 1988), while the concentration of both silver hoards and sculpture in the Penrith area (figs 2.1 and 2.2) may indicate that this was also a significant centre of power, a possibility perhaps reinforced by Athelstan's meeting with various northern rulers at Eamont Bridge (or Dacre) just outside modern Penrith (Cumbria) in 927, when he had secured control of Northumbria (Williams 2011a). The north-west could therefore represent a distinct but historically invisible identity (or more than one), but it could equally well have been seen as part of the kingdom of Northumbria, together with the area around York. Certainly, recent analysis of the hoards suggests that the north-west formed part of the same economic area as Yorkshire, despite the fact that York was probably the location of the only mint in Northumbria (Williams 2009).

All of the above may seem a digression from the question of towns and identity, but York is one of the prime examples of a town that might be expected to generate an identity of its own. It undoubtedly was a mint town; Viking rulers of Northumbria can be placed there on several

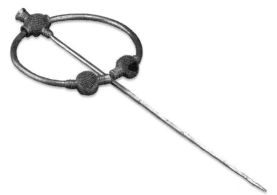

Fig. 2.1 Hiberno-Scandinavian brooch (BM 1909, 0624.2) found at Flusco Pike, near Penrith (Cumbria), probably in the same field as two other Viking hoards.

Fig. 2.2 Penrith (Cumbria) 4–9, taken from the south-east (CASSS 2/494) (copyright Corpus of Anglo-Saxon Stone Sculpture. Reproduced courtesy of Derek Craig; photographer T. Middlemass).

occasions; and it has plausibly been suggested that the archbishops of York were active supporters of the Viking kings as means of maintaining their own status and a degree of Northumbrian independence in the face of the expanding authority of the West Saxon dynasty (and with it that of the archbishops of Canterbury) (*e.g.* Smyth 1975–9, II, 91–4). Extensive archaeological evidence leaves no doubt that York was a major Viking/Anglo-Scandinavian settlement from the late 9th century onwards (Hall 2008, 380–2), and unfortunately the importance of York as an urban settlement is easily confused with the importance of York as a distinct political entity. Here matters are not helped either by the fact that the excavation of Viking Dublin was also extensive, and took place at much the same time, causing the two to be seen very much as a pair (*e.g.* Smyth 1975–79). Comparison between the two has been extremely important for developing an understanding of many aspects of urban life, but what is misleading for our understanding of the political identity of York is that Dublin, as discussed above, was a political entity in its own right, with a hinterland permanently linked to the town, and with the name *Dyflinaskiri* implying something along the lines of an Anglo-Saxon shire as a unit of administrative, judicial and military significance, with its identity derived from a major settlement. The fact that for a period in the 10th century Dublin and York fell under the rule of a single dynasty (with dynastic ties perhaps beginning as early as the late 9th century; Smyth 1975–79; Dumville 2005; Downham 2007) adds to the expectation that the two towns might show similarities as kingdoms as well as urban settlements.

The tendency to view York and Dublin together ignores the fact that much of our understanding of Dublin derives from the later 10th and even 11th centuries, by which time the political axis between Dublin and York had been firmly broken. It also ignores a fundamental difference in the way that the two towns developed. The 10th-century town of Dublin grew out of the 9th-century *longphort* and, like other *longphuirt*, Dublin was established on the borders of two existing kingdoms, rather than in an existing political centre (even if it took over the estates, and perhaps even some of the economic functions of one or more existing monasteries) (Bradley 1988; Valante 2008, 51–2). As Dublin became more established (and there is nothing more than hindsight to suggest that it was initially intended to be any more permanent than many other temporary camps elsewhere in Ireland, England and Francia), *Dyflinaskiri* emerged as a new geographical unit as well as a political entity. By contrast, York was not only an existing settlement, defined by surviving Roman walls, but a town of some importance at the heart of a major kingdom. Lack of surviving documentation means that pre-Viking York is no better understood than in the early Viking period with regard to its character as a centre of royal authority, and its role in royal administration, justice, taxation and military organisation is unclear, although it was at York that the Vikings defeated the last Anglian kings of Northumbria (*ASC* A &E, *sub* 867 [866]). Although the focus of urban occupation within York apparently shifted following the Viking settlement, it retained its role as an ecclesiastical centre, and it recovered its pre-Viking role as the only known mint in Northumbria. It may well have developed a role as a political capital in other respects in the Anglo-Scandinavian period, but as the centre of what remained of the Northumbrian political identity rather than defining a new identity as Dublin did. The concept of a 'Kingdom of York' reflects the importance of York as a major Viking town, and York, like other towns, is likely to have defined the identity of the surrounding area. However, to suggest that the whole of the territory normally associated politically and culturally with York in this period defined its identity in terms of York rather than Northumbria flies in the face of the evidence, and risks fundamentally misleading us on the nature of both York and Anglo-Scandinavian society in northern England.

The southern boundary of Northumbria is also problematic. Northumbrian influence had extended periodically into Lindsey at various points in the pre-Viking period, in competition with Mercia, and although there tends to be an assumption that Mercian authority in this area was permanent after the so-called Mercian supremacy of the 8th and early 9th centuries, the eclipse of Mercian power in the 820s calls this into question. Furthermore, the fact that Northumbrian stycas of the 9th century are found in Lindsey may point to economic if not political links in the immediate pre-Viking period. However, recent discoveries in both Lincolnshire and Yorkshire may indicate that there was greater use of stycas for some years following the Viking conquest and settlement than has previously been recognised, so the styca evidence points less definitely to pre-Viking economic ties across the Humber than was formerly the case, although this is a subject which would repay more detailed study (Blackburn 2011a; Williams 2011b). Historical records from both areas for the 9th century add nothing to our understanding. David Stocker (2000) has argued for sculptural links between Northumbria and Lindsey in the 10th and 11th centuries (*e.g.* fig 2.3), and there are arguments for linking various aspects of material culture between the two areas in the early Viking Age. However, the extent of such links has recently been called into question by Letty ten Harkel (2010; in press), largely on the basis of analysis of the Lincoln coinages. Lindsey apart, the boundary between Northumbria and Mercia had been contested in earlier periods, and again there is no reason to assume that this was completely stable in the 9th century, either in the pre-Viking or Viking periods. The only (somewhat inconclusive) evidence here for the settlement period is the suggestion by Mark Blackburn (2001, 128) on stylistic grounds that a solitary coin in the name of the Viking ruler Guthfrith of Northumbria (d. 895) (fig. 2.4a), was minted south of the Humber, perhaps

Fig. 2.3 Crowle (Lincolnshire) 1A (CASSS 5/145) is made of Yorkshire Millstone Grit and displays clear decorative parallels with the Yorkshire sculpture tradition (Everson and Stocker 1999, 151) (copyright Corpus of Anglo-Saxon Stone Sculpture. Reproduced courtesy of Derek Craig; photographer J. O'Neill).

indicating Northumbrian control in this area. However, there is also evidence for distinct (if rare) issues minted in Lincoln (figs 2.4b and c) and Leicester by the 890s, with no relationship to the more extensive coinage minted in York from *c.* 895 (Blackburn 2001, 128–30; 2006) (fig. 2.4d), which indicates that Lincoln and Leicester were not always under Northumbrian control. A similar problem exists with East Anglia. Here, again, an existing kingdom retained its political identity, but boundaries may have shifted. The phrasing of the oft-cited treaty between Alfred and Guthrum suggests that the area controlled by Guthrum extended well to the west of the established East Anglian kingdom (Keynes and Lapidge 1983, 171–2), and it has also been suggested that some of the coinage of Viking 'East Anglia' may also have been minted in what had historically been eastern Mercia (Blackburn 2001; 2005).

The area between Northumbria and East Anglia was part of the former kingdom of Mercia. Western Mercia remained under Anglo-Saxon rule, initially under the Mercian king Ceolwulf II and subsequently under West Saxon overlordship, although the exact status of the West Saxon-Mercian relationship under Ealdorman Æthelred and his (West Saxon) wife Æthelflæd, Lady of the Mercians, remains a matter of debate (*e.g.* Davidson 2001; Keynes 2001). In contrast, there is no record of any coherent authority across the whole of 'Danish' Mercia. Parts may have fallen under the domination of the Viking rulers of East Anglia and Northumbria, but for the most part the area seems to have fragmented into smaller territories, based around individual towns ruled by different *jarls*. The assumption that these *jarls* were necessarily subject to a king is based on anachronistic assumptions of social hierarchy based on the evidence of the 11th century and later. Relatively few of these *jarls* can be identified by name, nor can the exact territories pertaining to each *burh* be determined.

References in the *Anglo-Saxon Chronicle* suggest some affinities between specific towns, although the exact nature of these affinities is generally unclear. Only one grouping has traditionally been seen as a single unified territory. This is the so-called 'Five Boroughs' of Lincoln, Stamford, Nottingham, Derby and Leicester. However, I would argue that this is also a modern construction, based simply on the fact that the figure of five *burhs* is mentioned on separate occasions, rather than on any concrete references to these particular five *burhs* functioning as a single group. There are three key references here, spanning a period of around seventy years. Only one of these references mentions the towns by name, and the reading of each of these references has been influenced to some extent by the others, and by the assumption that there

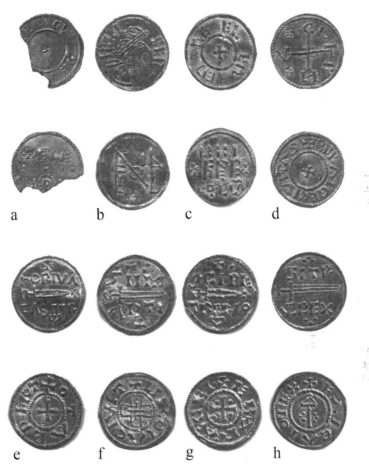

a   b   c   d

e   f   g   h

Fig. 2.4 a) Silver penny of Guthfrith of Northumbria, c. AD 895 (BM 1984, 0414.3); b) silver penny, Lincoln monogram type, c. AD 880–95 (BM 1867.0716, 13); c) silver penny with LINCOLLA mint signature, c. AD 880–95 (BM 1838, 0710.30); d) silver penny of Cnut with York ('Ebraice') mint signature (BM 1838, 0738.1354); e) silver penny with RORIVACASTR mint signature, c. AD 921–7 (BM); f) silver penny of St Martin of Lincoln, c. AD 921–7 (BM); g) silver penny of St Peter of York, c. AD 921–7 (BM); h) Silver penny of Sihtric of Northumbria, probably minted in the Midlands, c. AD 921–7 (copyright all images: Trustees of the British Museum).

was a single stable group of five *burhs*, which retained its identity through the West Saxon conquest and the subsequent unification of England.

The earliest reference is a poem preserved in several recensions of the *Anglo-Saxon Chronicle*, celebrating the success of Edmund in re-establishing West-Saxon authority in 942, after a brief period of independence following the death of Athelstan. This mentions five boroughs by name (text and translation following Downham 2009, 146–8):

Her Eadmund cyning Engla þeoden	In this year King Edmund, lord of the *Engle*,
maga mundbora Myrce geode	protector of men, conquered Mercians,

dyre dædfruma swa Dor scadeþ	noble doer of deeds, as the Dore divides,
Hwitanwylles geat and Humbra ea	Whitwell gate and Humber's river,
brada brimstream burga fife	broad sea stream, five boroughs,
Ligoraceaster and Lincylene	Leicester and Lincoln,
and Snotingaham swylce Stanford eac	and Nottingham and Stamford also,
and Deoraby Dane waeran æror	and Derby – they were previously *Dene* –,
under Nordmannum nyde gebegde	oppressed in need under Northmen,
on hæþenra hæfteclommum	in the fetter-chains of heathens
lange þrage oþ hie alysde eft	for a long time, until he freed them again
for his weorþscipe wiggendra hleo	for his glory, shield of warriors,
afera Eadweardes Eadmund cyning.	offspring of Edward: King Edmund.

The key lines here are
... burga fife
Ligoraceaster and Lincylene
and Snotingaham swylce Stanford eac
and Deoraby
(five boroughs, Leicester and Lincoln, and Nottingham and Stamford also, and Derby)

The surrounding lines show the pattern of the poem with each line divided into half-lines, with the beginning of the two halves of each line alliterating. The description of the five boroughs is carefully balanced: Leicester with Lincoln, 'Snotingaham' with Stamford, and Derby with the Danes. Simply reading the poem as if it were a prose account ignores the extent to which not only the syntax but also the choice of boroughs may reflect the needs of the poet. If Edmund subdued the territory to the south of the Dore, Whitwell Gap and the Humber, he presumably also subdued Edward the Elder's *burh* at Bakewell (Derbyshire), as well as Torksey, and perhaps also the putative late 10th-century *burhs* of Caistor and Horncastle (both Lincolnshire), to name only a few. Were these omitted because 'the Five Boroughs' was really a recognised political entity, or because they were the five most important towns in the region, or simply because they did what the poet wanted and alliterated? It may also be noted that there is no definite article linked with *burga fife*. This is not in itself conclusive, since definite articles are not always included in Old English where the meaning is understood, but, taken alone, the passage can be translated as 'five boroughs' with more immediate justification than 'the Five Boroughs of', and there is nothing in the poem to indicate any links between the five, other than that the five had all been captured as part of the process of Edmund establishing his authority over north-east Mercia.

The second reference to five *burhs* comes from the so-called Wantage Code, a law code prepared fairly early in the reign of Æthelræd II, and which certainly relates to an area of former Viking settlement, since it refers to the organisation of land in wapentakes rather than hundreds. This code refers to breach of the peace in *Fif burga* (Liebermann 1916, I, 228–9, *Æthelred* III.1, 1), and since the terms of the law are similar to terms specified for breach of the peace in Nottinghamshire and Derbyshire, this can be interpreted as a reference to the same Five Boroughs as the 942 poem (if one accepts that as a grouping, *contra* my argument above) (Hart 1992, 20–3). Once again, however, there is no definite article to indicate a set group of five boroughs, and no mention of any individual borough by name. Furthermore, seen in context together with the preceding and following sections (*Æthelred* III.1–1, 2), this reference forms part of a sliding scale of the breaches of the peace beginning with the king's own peace, for which no atonement is possible, through breaches of the peace of royal officials over five boroughs, down to one borough and eventually down to a single alehouse. Seen in this context, the reference to five *burhs* reads more naturally as a simple indication of the sliding scale of the offence (a recurrent pattern within Anglo-Saxon law-codes) than as a reference to a specific political unit.

The final piece of evidence for the Five Boroughs dates from the early 11th century. The *Anglo-Saxon Chronicle* tells us that the men of the Five Boroughs submitted to Svein Forkbeard (*ASC* E, *sub* 1013). This does seem to be a reference to a distinct and recognised group of towns, although none of them are named, and the reference immediately follows a report of the submission of the men of Lindsey. This raises doubts as to whether Lincoln can therefore have been one of the Five Boroughs concerned, and even if it was, it would suggest that Lincoln was on the fringe of the Five Boroughs, and that the area of Lindsey did not form part of the territory of the Five Boroughs despite the fact that Lincoln north of the Witham is normally interpreted as being in Lindsey (Jones and Stocker 2003, 13). The term appears again in the *Anglo-Saxon Chronicle* two years later, together with a reference to the Seven Boroughs (*ASC* E, *sub* 1015). Again, individual *burhs* are not named in either case, but the context suggests that the two groups overlap, or at least were in the same region. Stenton (1971, 283) suggested that the Seven Boroughs may have been the Five Boroughs together with Torksey and York, but this is only conjecture, and if it is correct, suggests that the Five Boroughs was a less dominant entity than is generally supposed, if the same towns formed parts of both a five-town and a seven-town grouping. There is absolutely nothing in these 11th-century references to indicate that these were the same towns mentioned in the 942 poem, or the Wantage code, other than the repetition of the number five.

Pushing back to the period before the West Saxon conquest, we may also note that while there is no mention of any combination of the five acting together in any political circumstances in the early 10th century, and each of the five seems to have submitted separately to Æthelflæd or Edward, there is a reference to the *here* ('raiding army') of Northampton and Leicester attacking Towcester in 920 (*ASC* A, *sub* 921[920]). Rather than suggesting a grouping of the Five Boroughs, this implies that one of those boroughs (Leicester) was actually linked strongly with another (Northampton) outside this notional grouping.

The western frontier of the area of the Midlands under Viking control also probably fluctuated. Accounts of Anglo-Saxon conquests in the early years of the reign of Edward the Elder suggest that he and his sister Æthelflæd were forced to re-establish control over areas previously controlled by Alfred under the terms of his treaty with Guthrum, while Staffordshire and northern Warwickshire show little evidence of extensive Scandinavian settlement despite the fact that we only hear of *burhs* being established by Edward and Æthelflæd at Warwick, Tamworth and Stafford as late as the second decade of the 10th century. However, a pocket of Scandinavian place-names straddles the Staffordshire/Derbyshire border near Ashbourne (Derbyshire), and a group of sculptures showing Anglo-Scandinavian influences also extends across the shire boundaries (Sidebottom 2000). In the same area, Anglo-Scandinavian minting may also have taken place at the former Roman fort of Rocester (Staffordshire), which controlled an important route from western Mercia (and the Irish Sea) towards the better-documented towns of Derby and Nottingham. This interpretation depends on the reading of a unique coin of the 920s (fig. 2.4e) as RORIVACASTR, and the identification of RORIVACASTR as an early (but otherwise unrecorded) form of the place-name Rocester (Williams 2008a). Neither the reading nor the attribution are beyond question (Blackburn 2011b, 377), although no convincing alternative attribution has yet been suggested.

What does seem clear is that Anglo-Scandinavian minting took place in the Midlands in the

920s, although the established chronology based on the *Anglo-Saxon Chronicle* leaves this area firmly under West Saxon control from 920. Lincoln, unlike the other main Midland towns, is not specifically recorded as submitting before this date, and certainly coins were minted afterwards that displayed some affinity with Scandinavian York (Blackburn 2006; Ten Harkel in prep.). Whether or not RORIVACASTR can be identified with Rocester, it appears to represent minting at a town (in some sense) that had its origins in a Roman fort, in common with major Viking towns such as York, Lincoln, Leicester and perhaps Derby, and lesser towns such as Towcester. The same is probably true of CASTRA EORT, an unidentified mint that appears on Anglo-Viking coins of the 920s (Blackburn 2006, 215). The name perhaps represents OE *Eorþ burh* ('earthern fortification'), which gives rise to place names such as Arbury and Yarborough, but which could relate to a large number of potential places, inside or outside the territory of the 'Five Boroughs'. The Anglo-Viking 'Sword' types of the 920s seem likely on the grounds of distribution to have been minted predominantly in the East Midlands (Blackburn 2006), with minting certainly taking place at Lincoln (fig. 2.4f), as well as at York (fig. 2.4g), despite the fact that (with the exception of the Lincoln and York coins) most of the coins appear to have been issued under the authority of Sihtric of Northumbria (*c.* 921–7). However, most of the Sword types in the name of Sihtric (fig. 2.4h), or with blundered inscriptions, cannot be attributed to specific mints, and do not in themselves support any specific grouping of towns. Thus, not only is there nothing in contemporary sources that specifically identifies the supposed Five Boroughs as a political entity, but there is evidence to suggest a more complicated and perhaps more fluid grouping of Anglo-Scandinavian towns within the Midlands, with some association with Northumbria (Williams 2011a).

Conclusion

It is clear that towns played an important part in Anglo-Scandinavian society, and it is likely that individual towns provided a sense of identity for a dispersed rural population as well as for the inhabitants of the towns themselves. How far this stretched on an individual basis, and what the relationship was between neighbouring towns, is generally much less clear. The understanding of individual towns, and their interrelationship, may be improved through further excavation, by mapping similarities in material culture, and through exploring in detail the relationships and identities in contemporary sources. However, beyond the level of individual towns, the continued use in scholarly literature of terms such as the Danelaw, the Kingdom of York and the Five Boroughs may be actively misleading both in terms of the specific identities within each area, and for the understanding of the role and significance of towns more broadly in a society with a predominantly rural population.

Bibliography

Abels, R. P. (1997) English logistics and military organisation, 871–1066: the impact of the Viking wars. In A. Nørgård Jørgensen and B. L. Clausen (eds) *Military Aspects of Scandinavian Society in a European Perspective, AD 1–1300*, 257–65. Copenhagen, National Museum of Denmark.

Abrams, L. (2001) Edward the Elder's Danelaw. In N. J. Higham and D. H. Hill (eds) *Edward the Elder, 899–924*, 128–43. London, Routledge.

Archibald, M. M. (1998) Two ninth-century Viking weights found near Kingston, Dorset. *British Numismatic Journal* 68, 11–20.

Bassett, S. (2007) Divide and rule? The military infrastructure of eighth- and ninth-century Mercia. *Early Medieval Europe* 15, 53–85.

Bassett, S. (2008) The middle and late Anglo-Saxon defences of western Mercian towns. *Anglo-Saxon Studies in Archaeology and History* 15, 180–239.

Bately, J. M. (ed.) (1986) *The Anglo-Saxon Chronicle 3 MS A*. Woodbridge, Boydell.

Biddle, M. (1976) Towns. In D. M. Wilson (ed.) *The Archaeology of Anglo-Saxon England*, 99–150. Cambridge, Cambridge University Press.

Biddle, M. and Kjølbye-Biddle, B. (2001) Repton and the 'great heathen army', 873–4. In J. Graham-Campbell, R. A. Hall, J. Jesch and D. N. Parsons (eds) *Vikings and the Danelaw: select papers from the proceedings of the thirteenth Viking Congress, 21–30 August 1997*, 45–96. Oxford, Oxbow.

Blackburn, M. A. S. (2001) Expansion and control: aspects of Anglo-Scandinavian minting south of the Humber. In J. Graham-Campbell, R. A. Hall, J. Jesch and D. N. Parsons (eds) *Vikings and the Danelaw: select papers from the proceedings of the thirteenth Viking Congress, 21–30 August 1997*, 125–55. Oxford, Oxbow.

Blackburn, M. A. S. (2005) Presidential address 2004. Currency under the Vikings. Part 1: Guthrum and the earliest Danelaw coinages. *British Numismatic Journal* 75, 18–43.

Blackburn, M. A. S. (2006) Presidential address 2005. Currency under the Vikings. Part 2: the two Scandinavian kingdoms of the Danelaw, c. 895–954. *British Numismatic Journal* 76, 204–26.

Blackburn, M. A. S. (2011a) The Viking winter camp at Torksey, 872–3. In M. A. S. Blackburn, *Viking Coinage and Currency in the British Isles*, 221–64. British Numismatic Society Special Publications 7. London, Spink/British Numismatic Society.

Blackburn, M. A. S. (2011b) Supplements to the Articles 2011. In M. A. S. Blackburn, *Viking Coinage and Currency in the British Isles*, 371–90. British Numismatic Society Special Publications 7. London, Spink/British Numismatic Society.

Blair, J. (2005) *The Church in Anglo-Saxon Society*. Oxford, Oxford University Press.

Bogucki, M. (2007) Coin finds in the Viking Age emporium at Janów Pomorski (Truso) and the *Prussian phenomenon*. In S. Sucholdoslki and M. Bogucki (eds) *Monetary Circulation in Antiquity, the Middle Ages and Modern Times. Time, range, intensity*, 79–106. Warsaw, Avalon.

Bogucki, M. (2010) Viking Age emporia around the Baltic Sea – a cul-de-sac of the European urbanization? In A. Buko and M. McCarthy (eds) *Making a Medieval Town: patterns of early medieval urbanization*, 150–65. Warsaw, Polish Academy of Sciences/University of Warsaw.

Bradley, J. (1988) The interpretation of Scandinavian settlement in Ireland. In J. Bradley (ed.) *Settlement and Society in Medieval Ireland. Studies presented to F. X. Martin OSA*, 49–78. Kilkenny, Boethius.

Bradley, J. (2009) Some reflections on the problem of Scandinavian settlement in the hinterland of Dublin in the ninth century. In J. Bradley, A. J. Fletcher and A. Simms (eds) *Dublin in the Medieval World. Studies in honour of Howard B. Clarke*, 39–62. Dublin, Four Courts Press.

Brooks, N. P. (1979) England in the crucible of defeat, *Transactions of the Royal Historical Society* (5) 29, 1–20.

Brooks, N. P. (1996) The administrative background to the Burghal Hidage. In D. Hill and A. R. Rumble (eds) *The Defence of Wessex: the Burghal Hidage and Anglo-Saxon fortifications*, 128–50. Manchester, Manchester University Press.

Byock, J. (2001) *Viking Age Iceland*. Harmondsworth, Penguin.

Clarke, H. B. (1998) Proto-towns and towns in Ireland and Britain. In H. B. Clarke, M. Ní Mhaonaigh and R. Ó Floinn (eds) *Ireland and Scandinavia in the Early Viking Age*, 331–80. Dublin, Four Courts Press.

Cubbin, G. P. (ed.) (1996) *The Anglo-Saxon Chronicle 6 MS D*. Woodbridge, Boydell.

Davidson, M. (2001) The (non)submission of the northern kings in 920. In N. J. Higham and D. H. Hill (eds) *Edward the Elder, 899–924*, 200–11. London, Routledge.

Downham, C. E. (2007) *Viking Kings of Britain and Ireland: the dynasty of Ívarr to AD 1014*. Edinburgh, Dunedin Academic Press.

Downham, C. E. (2009) 'Hiberno-Norwegians' and 'Anglo-Danes': anachronistic ethnicities and Viking-Age England. *Mediaeval Scandinavia* 19, 139–69.

Dumville, D. N. (2005) Dubliners and New Dubliners in Ireland and Britain: a Viking-Age story. In S. Duffy (ed.) *Medieval Dublin* 6, 78–93. Dublin, Four Courts Press.

Everson, P. and Stocker, D. (1999) *Corpus of Anglo-Saxon Stone Sculpture Volume 5: Lincolnshire*. Oxford, Oxford University Press.

Foot, S. (1993) The kingdom of Lindsey. In A. Vince (ed.) *Pre-Viking Lindsey*, 128–40. Lincoln Archaeological Studies 1. Lincoln, City of Lincoln Archaeological Unit.

Griffiths, D. (1992) The coastal trading ports of the Irish Sea. In J. Graham-Campbell (ed.) *Viking Treasure from the North West: the Cuerdale hoard in its context*, 63–72. Liverpool, Liverpool Museum.

Griffiths, D. (2001) The North-West frontier. In N. J. Higham and D. H. Hill (eds) *Edward the Elder, 899–924*, 167–87. London, Routledge.

Griffiths, D. (2010) *Vikings of the Irish Sea*. Stroud, The History Press.

Griffiths, D., Philpott, R. A. and Egan, G. (2007) *Meols: the archaeology of the North Wirral Coast. Discoveries and observations in the 19th and 20th centuries, with a catalogue of collections*. Oxford University School of Archaeology Monograph 68. Oxford, Oxford University School of Archaeology.

Hadley, D. M. (2000) *The Northern Danelaw: its social structure, c. 800–1100*. London and New York, Leicester University Press.

Hall, R. A. (1989) The Five Boroughs of the Danelaw: a review of present knowledge. *Anglo-Saxon England* 18, 149–208.

Hall, R. A. (2001) Anglo-Scandinavian urban development in the East Midlands. In J. Graham-Campbell, R. A. Hall, J. Jesch and D. N. Parsons (eds) *Vikings and the Danelaw: select papers from the proceedings of the thirteenth Viking Congress, 21–30 August 1997*, 143–56. Oxford, Oxbow.

Hall, R. A. (2008) York. In S. Brink and N. Price (eds) *The Viking World*, 379–84. London and New York, Routledge.

Hall, R. A. (2011) Burhs and boroughs: defended places, trade and towns. Plans, defences, civic features. In H. Hamerow, D. A. Hinton and S. Crawford (eds) *The Oxford Handbook of Anglo-Saxon Archaeology*, 600–21. Oxford, Oxford University Press.

Hall, R. A. and Williams, G. (with B. Ager and N. S. H. Rogers) (in prep.) A riverine site near York.

Haslam, J. (1987) Market and fortress in England in the time of Offa. *World Archaeology* 19.3, 76–93.

Hart, C. (1992) *The Danelaw*. London, Hambledon Continuum.

Higham, N. J. (1988) The Cheshire burhs and the Mercian frontier to AD 924. *Transactions of the Antiquarian Society of Lancashire and Cheshire* 98, 193–222.

Higham, N. J. (2004) Viking-Age settlement in the north-western countryside: lifting the veil? In J. Hines, A. Lane and M. Redknap (eds) *Land, Sea and Home: settlement in the Viking period. Proceedings of a conference on Viking-period settlement, at Cardiff, July 2001*, 297–312. Society for Medieval Archaeology Monograph 20. Leeds, Maney.

Hill, D. H and Rumble, A. R. (eds) (1996) *The Defence of Wessex: the Burghal Hidage and Anglo-Saxon fortifications*. Manchester, Manchester University Press.

Hinton, D. A. (1990) *Archaeology, Economy and Society: England from the fifth to the fifteenth century*. London, Routledge.

Hinton, D. A. (1996) The fortifications and their shires. In D. Hill and A. R. Rumble (eds) *The Defence of Wessex: the Burghal Hidage and Anglo-Saxon fortifications*, 151–9. Manchester, Manchester University Press.

Hobley, B. (1988) Saxon London: *Lundenwic* and *Lundenburh*: two cities rediscovered. In R. Hodges and B. Hobley (eds) *The Rebirth of Towns in the West, AD 700–1050*, 69–82. Council for British Archaeology Research Report 68. London, Council for British Archaeology.

Hodges, R. (1982) *Dark Age Economics: the origins of towns and trade in the West AD 600–1000*. London, Duckworth.

Holman, K. (2001) Defining the Danelaw. In J. Graham-Campbell, R. A. Hall, J. Jesch and D. N. Parsons (eds) *Vikings and the Danelaw: select papers from the proceedings of the thirteenth Viking Congress, 21–30 August 1997*, 1–11. Oxford, Oxbow.

Irvine, S. (ed.) (2004) *The Anglo-Saxon Chronicle 7 MS E*. Woodbridge, Boydell.

Jones, M. J. and Stocker, D. (2003) Geological and topographical background. In D. Stocker (ed.) *The City by the Pool: assessing the archaeology of the City of Lincoln*, 13–18. Oxford, Oxbow.

Keynes, S. D. (2001) Edward, king of the Anglo-Saxons. In N. J. Higham and D. H. Hill (eds) *Edward the Elder, 899–924*, 40–66. London, Routledge.

Keynes, S. D. and Lapidge, M. (ed. and trans.) (1983) *Alfred the Great. Asser's Life of King Alfred and other contemporary sources*. Harmondsworth, Penguin.

Liebermann, F. (1916) *Die Gesetze der Angelsachsen* (3 vols). Halle, Max Niemeyer.

Nelson, J. L. (trans.) (1991) *The Annals of St Bertin*. Manchester, Manchester University Press.

O'Brien, R., Quinney, P., and Russell, I. (2005) Preliminary report on the archaeological excavation and finds retrieval strategy of the Hiberno-Scandinavian site of Woodstown 6, County Waterford. *Decies: Journal of the Waterford Archaeological and Historical Society* 61, 13–122.

O'Brien O'Keefe, K. (ed.) (2001) *The Anglo-Saxon Chronicle 5 MS C*. Woodbridge, Boydell.

Ó Floinn, R. (1998) The archaeology of the early Viking Age in Ireland. In H. B. Clarke, M. Ní Mhaonaigh and R. Ó Floinn (eds) *Ireland and Scandinavia in the Early Viking Age*, 131–65. Dublin, Four Courts Press.

Pestell, T. (2011) Markets, *emporia, wics*, and 'productive' sites: pre-Viking trade centres in Anglo-Saxon England. In H. Hamerow, D. A. Hinton and S. Crawford (eds) *The Oxford Handbook of Anglo-Saxon Archaeology*, 556–79. Oxford, Oxford University Press.

Pestell, T. and Ulmschneider, K. (eds) (2003) *Markets in Early Medieval Europe: trading and 'productive' sites, 650–850*. Bollington, Windgather Press.

Redknap, M. (2004) Viking-Age settlement in Wales and the evidence from Llanbedrgoch. In J. Hines, A. Lane and M. Redknap (eds) *Land, Sea and Home: settlement in the Viking period. Proceedings of a conference on Viking-period settlement, at Cardiff, July 2001*, 139–76. Society for Medieval Archaeology Monograph 20. Leeds, Maney.

Redknap, M. (2009) Silver and commerce in Viking-Age North Wales. In J. Graham-Campbell and R. Philpott (eds) *The Huxley Viking Hoard: Scandinavian settlement in the North West*, 29–41. Liverpool, National Museums Liverpool.

Richards, J. D. (2001) Finding the Vikings: the search for Anglo-Scandinavian rural settlements in the northern Danelaw. In J. Graham-Campbell, R. A. Hall, J. Jesch and D. N. Parsons (eds) *Vikings and the Danelaw: select papers from the proceedings of the thirteenth Viking Congress, 21–30 August 1997*, 269–78. Oxford, Oxbow.

Richards, J. D. (2008) Viking settlement in England. In S. Brink and N. Price (eds) *The Viking World*, 368–74. London and New York, Routledge.

Roesdahl, E. (1982) *Viking Age Denmark*. London, British Museum Publications Ltd.

Rollason, D. (2003) *Northumbria, 500–1100: creation and destruction of a kingdom*. Cambridge, Cambridge University Press.

Sawyer, P. H. (1962) *The Age of the Vikings*. London, Edward Arnold.

Sheehan, J. (2008) The *longphort* in Viking Age Ireland. *Acta Archaeologica* 79, 282–95.

Sidebottom, P. (2000) Viking Age stone monuments and social identity in Derbyshire. In D. M. Hadley and J. D. Richards (eds) *Cultures in Contact: Scandinavian settlement in England in the ninth and tenth centuries*, 213–36. Turnhout, Brepols.

Sigurðsson, J. V. (2008) Iceland. In S. Brink and N. Price (eds) *The Viking World*, 571–8. London and New York, Routledge.

Simpson, L. (2005) Viking warrior burials in Dublin: is this the *longphort*? In S. Duffy (ed.) *Medieval Dublin VI*, 11–62. Dublin, Four Courts Press.

Simpson, L. (2010) The first phase of Viking activity in Ireland: archaeological evidence from Dublin. In J. Sheehan and D. Ó Corráin (eds) *The Viking Age. Ireland and the West*, 418–29. Dublin, Four Courts Press.

Sindbæk, S. M. (2010) Close ties and long-range relations: the emporia network in early Viking-Age exchange. In J. Sheehan and D. Ó Corráin (eds) *The Viking Age. Ireland and the West*, 430–40. Dublin, Four Courts Press.

Skre, D. (2007) *Kaupang in Skiringssal.* Kaupang Excavation Project Publication Series 1: Norske Oldfunn XXII. Oslo, University of Oslo/Aarhus University Press.

Smyth, A. P. (1975–79) *Scandinavian York and Dublin* (2 vols). New Jersey/Dublin, Templekieran.

Stenton, F. M. (1971) *Anglo-Saxon England* (3rd edn). Oxford, Oxford University Press.

Stocker, D. (2000) Monuments and merchants: irregularities in the distribution of stone sculpture in Lincolnshire and Yorkshire in the tenth century. In D. M. Hadley and J. D. Richards (eds) *Cultures in Contact: Scandinavian settlement in England in the ninth and tenth centuries,* 179–212. Turnhout, Brepols.

Taylor, S. (ed.) (1983) *The Anglo-Saxon Chronicle 4 MS B.* Woodbridge, Boydell.

Ten Harkel, A. T. (2010) *Lincoln in the Viking Age: A 'town' in context.* Unpublished PhD thesis, University of Sheffield.

Ten Harkel, L. (in press) The urbanisation of Viking-Age Lincoln: a numismatic perspective.

Tummuscheit, A. (2003) Gross Strömkendorf: a market site of the eighth century on the Baltic Sea coast. In T. Pestell and K. Ulmschneider (eds) *Markets in Early Medieval Europe: trading and 'productive' sites, 650–850,* 208–20. Bollington, Windgather Press.

Valante, M. (2008) *The Vikings in Ireland. Settlement, trade and urbanisation.* Dublin, Four Courts Press.

Vince, A. (2001) Lincoln in the Viking Age. In J. Graham-Campbell, R. A. Hall, J. Jesch and D. N. Parsons (eds) *Vikings and the Danelaw: select papers from the proceedings of the thirteenth Viking Congress, 21–30 August 1997,* 157–80. Oxford, Oxbow.

Wamers, E. (2002) The 9th century Danish Norwegian conflict: maritime warfare and state formation. In A. Nørgård Jørgensen, J. Pind, L. Jørgensen and B. L. Clausen (eds) *Maritime Warfare in Northern Europe: technology, organisation, logistics and administration 500BC–1500AD,* 237–48. Copenhagen, National Museum of Denmark.

Ward, S. (2001) Edward the Elder and the re-establishment of Chester. In N. J. Higham and D. H. Hill (eds) *Edward the Elder, 899–924,* 160–66. London, Routledge.

Williams, G. (2008a) RORIVA CASTR: a new Danelaw mint of the 920s. *Scripta varia numismatico Tuukka Talvio sexagenario dedicate. Suomen Numismaattisen Yhdistyksen julkaisuja* 6, 41–7. Helsinki, Finnish Numismatic Society.

Williams, G. (2008b) Raiding and warfare. In S. Brink and N. Price (eds) *The Viking World,* 93–103. London and New York, Routledge.

Williams, G. (2009) Hoards from the northern Danelaw from Cuerdale to the Vale of York. In J. Graham-Campbell and R. Philpott (eds) *The Huxley Viking Hoard: Scandinavian settlement in the North West,* 73–83. Liverpool, National Museums Liverpool.

Williams, G. (2011a) Coinage and monetary circulation in the northern Danelaw in the 920s in the light of the Vale of York hoard. In T. Abramson (ed.) *Studies in Early Medieval Coinage 2,* 146–55. Woodbridge, Boydell.

Williams, G. (2011b) Silver economies, monetisation and society: an overview. In J. Graham-Campbell, S. Sindbæk and G. Williams (eds) *Silver Economies, Monetisation and Society in Scandinavia AD 800–1100,* 337–72. Aarhus, Aarhus University Press.

Williams, G. (2013) Military and non-military functions of the Anglo-Saxon *burh, c.* 878–978. In J. Baker, S. Brookes and A. Reynolds (eds) *Landscapes of Defence in the Viking Age: Anglo-Saxon England and comparative perspectives,* 78–98. Turnhout, Brepols.

Williams, G. (forthcoming) Viking camps and the means of exchange in Britain and Ireland in the ninth century. In R. Johnson and H. B. Clarke (eds) *Viking Ireland and Beyond.* Dublin, Royal Society of Ireland/Four Courts Press.

3

VIKING DUBLIN: ENMITIES, ALLIANCES AND THE COLD GLEAM OF SILVER

Emer Purcell and John Sheehan

Dublin was Ireland's most important Viking town and was second only to York in the Viking world of north-western Europe. This chapter is not directly concerned with the economic growth and development of the town, but rather examines the history of the Viking kingdom of Dublin and, through the lens of the silver-hoard evidence, attempts to understand more fully the nature and extent of its relations and interactions with the most important Irish kings and kingdoms of the 9th and 10th centuries. The study is confined to the northern half of Ireland – Leth Cuinn – which was dominated by the Northern and Southern Uí Néill dynasties (fig. 3.1). The main Southern Uí Néill dynasties were Clann Cholmáin, who ruled the kingdom of Mide, and Síl nÁedo Sláine, who ruled Brega, while their northern cousins were Cenél nEógain and Cenél Conaill. Tara was the symbolic seat of the premier kingship in Ireland, and from the early 8th century the right to hold that position alternated between Clann Cholmáin of Southern Uí Néill and Cenél nEógain of Northern Uí Néill. Entries in the Irish annals detail Viking raids and battles, but more often than not reveal Vikings in alliance with various Irish kings, as they fought one another, and in particular with those who vied for the position of king of Tara. Within these power struggles, both national and local, alliances tended to shift and fluctuate considerably and rapidly. Some trends emerge from the present analysis. For example, Brega (comprising modern county Meath, north Dublin and south Louth) was divided between the kings of Northern Brega, based at Knowth (Co. Meath), and Southern Brega, based at Lagore (Co. Meath). Northern Brega dynasts had a more hostile relationship with their Dublin neighbours, though there is a notable period in the mid- to late 10th century when alliances were formed. Dublin's relationship with the dominant Clann Cholmáin dynasty of Mide (mainly comprising modern county Westmeath and parts of Longford and Offaly) is almost always one of enmity, though even this dynasty was prepared to employ Viking assistance when it suited its purpose. Cenél nEógain (with territory in Inishowen, Co. Donegal, and counties Tyrone and Derry) and Cenél Conaill (located in Co. Donegal) were overlords of Airgialla and other territories in the northern part of Ireland, stretching to modern county Louth. Relations between Northern Uí Néill and Dublin are a little harder to characterise.

Silver and hoards

Many years ago the art-historian Françoise Henry (1967, 112) commented on how desirable

Fig. 3.1 Map of Ireland showing the kingdoms and principal locations mentioned in the text.

the 'cold gleam of silver' became in Viking-Age Ireland. Silver was the principal medium of economic exchange throughout the Viking world, though recent thinking has suggested that various forms of commodity monies, such as *vádmál* (cloth), *kýrlag* (cattle) and iron, were also of some importance as means of exchange (Gullbekk 2011; Skre 2011). Though coin usage and minting did develop in 10th-century Dublin, silver was generally used in non-numismatic form in Viking-Age Ireland in a type of bullion or metal-weight economy, while imported coins were generally valued by weight. Therefore, ornaments of various types, as well as ingots, sometimes cut up into what is termed 'hack-silver', served as a form of bullion currency. Ornaments, such as arm- and neck-rings as well as brooches, served a dual purpose in that they could also be used as display and status items in the social economy. Given the nature and duration of Scandinavian settlement and interaction in Ireland it is not surprising that large amounts of Viking-Age silver have been found there. In fact, 125 silver hoards of 9th- and 10th-century date are on record, representing a concentration of deposits that is not equalled elsewhere outside of Scandinavia during this period.[1] Just over half of these are 'coinless hoards', finds composed exclusively of non-numismatic silver, while the remainder comprises either 'mixed hoards', in which coins occur with non-numismatic silver, or coin hoards.

Given that almost half of Ireland's hoards contain coins, it may initially seem that there are good prospects for dating hoards and relating them to trends or events evident in the historical record. Unfortunately, however, the matter is not so clear-cut. It is complicated, for instance, by the fact that all of the mixed hoards were deposited during the 10th century, while the coinless hoards have a wider date-range, potentially dating from the second half of the 9th century onwards. Only four of the coin hoards date from the 9th century, while for the most part they date from 940 onwards. In addition, the issue of the varying bullion values of the hoards contributes towards the complexity of the matter, for many of the coin hoards appear to have been rather small finds while the coinless and mixed hoards tend to be significantly heavier. Consequently, it is the latter types of hoards which generally account for the great bulk of the considerable amount of silver wealth in Ireland during the 9th and 10th centuries, and many of these cannot be closely dated. As a result of these and other issues it is difficult to relate the hoards to particular historically-attested events, but this is always a problematical type of exercise. What are more realisable and worthwhile exercises, however, are identifying and comparing the general hoarding horizons and geographical distributions of silver in the important Irish kingdoms of the 9th and 10th centuries. This may be achieved purely on the basis of the number of hoard find-spots in each kingdom, but is also possible to estimate the overall amount of silver, in bullion terms, that is on record from these areas. It must be noted that this latter exercise is sometimes inevitably based on a process of assumption and supposition in relation to the quality of antiquarian's accounts of some hoards, but nonetheless its results seem at least broadly valid (Sheehan forthcoming a). Comparing and contrasting the totality of the silver hoard material with the historical evidence may contribute to an understanding of the nature and extent of Dublin's relationships with the kingdoms considered in this chapter.

No less than forty-nine Viking-Age silver hoards of 9th- or 10th-century date are on record from the Southern Uí Néill kingship, within Mide, Northern Brega and Southern Brega (fig. 3.2), the greatest numbers of which are coinless hoards. This impressive quantity of silver is even more remarkable when it is compared with the appreciably lesser amounts known from Ireland's other five kingdoms. Therefore, Southern Uí Néill, as an immediate political context for Dublin, is of interest in that it was a kingdom of some considerable silver wealth in the 9th and 10th centuries. It is clear, from both general distributional considerations and from the tendency for many of the finds to derive from Irish sites, such as royal centers, ringforts and crannógs, that the Southern Uí Néill hoards represent Irish, rather than Scandinavian, wealth, even if it was the existence of Viking Dublin which made the silver available to them (Kenny 1987, 512). Reflection on how this silver wealth was acquired often mainly focuses on the economic relationships that must have existed between the Irish and the Scandinavians. Graham-Campbell (1998, 106), for instance, suggests Dublin exchanged silver 'not only for

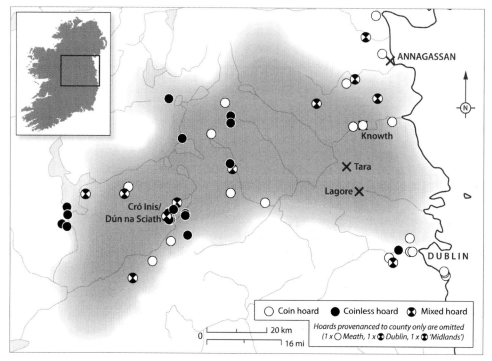

Fig. 3.2 The distribution of 9th- and 10th-century Viking-Age silver hoards in Southern Uí Néill.

the commodities required to sustain daily life – to build houses and boats, to eat, drink and dress – but also for trade goods, including slaves'. While this is undoubtedly true, it does not take account of the importance of other potential mechanisms for silver exchange, such as political alliances, gift-exchange, ransoming and, perhaps most importantly, tribute. Some of the finds appear to be socially-motivated, such as ornament hoards, others may have been more economically inspired and represent the use of silver as currency, such as hack-silver hoards, while others appear more likely to signify tribute, such as large bullion hoards, and each of these distinctive types of hoards are represented in Southern Uí Néill. In general terms, however, given the dating limitations noted above, few, if any, of the Southern Uí Néill finds may be expressly related to the 9th-century *longphort* at Dublin, even though this likelihood seems more than probable, and the possibility should be borne in mind that many of the hoards may well relate to other temporal, social and economic contexts in the region, including 10th-century Dublin, and its hinterland, as well as the Irish centers of power.

There are thirty-one Viking-Age silver hoards of 9th- or 10th-century date recorded from Mide, forming two-thirds of the total from the Southern Uí Néill kingship as well as the greatest number, by far, from a single kingdom in Viking-Age Ireland. The estimated bullion weight of these hoards amounts to a remarkable 56 kg, a quantity which overshadows the combined total from the remainder of Ireland, with most of it deriving from a number of finds from Lough Ennell (Ryan *et al.* 1984), the location of the kingdom's royal centre at Cró Inis/Dún na Sciath. The finds from Mide comprise seventeen coinless, six mixed and eight coin hoards. The numerical dominance of non-numismatic hoards is noteworthy and indicates that this kingdom had a different relationship with Viking Dublin than did neighbouring Northern Brega, which is distinguished by its almost complete lack of such finds. Unlike the hoards from the latter area, which are dominated by coin and mixed hoards, in most cases containing only ingots in addition to the coins, the hoards from Mide feature examples of most varieties of Viking-Age silver artefact known from Ireland's hoards, as well as the ubiquitous ingot. Other types of archaeological evidence from Mide also contribute towards a picture of a kingdom which had deep connections with Viking Dublin, whether through trade, tribute, ransom or loot. The crannóg at Coolore Demesne (Co. Westmeath), for instance, which has produced two silver hoards as well as some decorated lead weights and pans from a balance scales, has also yielded a range of other relevant artefacts (Kelly 2007, 93–103). Likewise, Ballinderry crannóg (Co. Offaly) yielded a number of high-status artefacts that can only have been acquired through contact with Viking Dublin, including a decorated game board, for *hnefatafl* (Purcell 1995, 109–10), a rare Irish example of an Ulfberht sword (Walsh 1998, 230–2) and a unique longbow of Scandinavian background (Halpin 2008, 37–8, fig. 8), while the crannóg at Newtownlow (Co. Westmeath), in addition to a coin hoard, produced a bronze plaque decorated in Ringerike style (Kelly 1991, 86, pl. 3).

There are eight Viking-Age silver hoards on record from Northern Brega. While this may seem like a moderate number compared to Mide, a sense of how considerable it is may be arrived at by taking into account that it represents almost the same number of find-spots as is evident from the area under control of Viking Dublin. Each of the Northern Brega finds is either a 'mixed' or a coin hoard, and the absence of non-numismatic finds, which are a strong feature of neighbouring Mide, is notable. It is reckoned that the overall bullion weight of these hoards is around 9 kg. Whatever about the usefulness of the estimation, which may well be skewed by the antiquarian accounts of the lost coin hoard from Drogheda (see Dolley 1966, 26–7), it is certainly the case that what appears to be Northern Brega's rather impressive bullion estimate is greatly overshadowed by the amount of silver from Clann Cholmáin, its Southern Uí Néill overlords.

There are ten hoards on record from Southern Brega and the border area of Laigin, immediately to its south. Each of these, however, is from within the bounds of the modern county of Dublin. This geographical focus is significant as Bradley (2009, 47–51) has concluded that 9th- and 10th-century Dyflinarskíri, the region under control of the Vikings, was always confined to the area of this county, apart from a short time in the 10th century. Consequently, it is reasonable to suppose that these ten hoards represent the wealth of Dublin, rather than that of the Southern Brega kingship. The finds comprise one coinless and two 'mixed' hoards, as well as seven coin hoards, a hoarding profile that is comparable to that of Northern Brega but rather dissimilar from that of Mide. The coinless find is the only hoard of this type on record from the entire eastern half of the Southern Uí Néill kingdom and is the only recorded hoard that could conceivably have been deposited here during the second half of the 9th century, Dublin's *longphort* phase. The estimated bullion weight value of the Dublin finds is only a quarter of that from Northern Brega.

There are seventeen Viking-Age silver hoards recorded from Northern Uí Néill (fig. 3.3), ten of which are composed entirely of non-numismatic material. Five of the finds are from on or close to the Inishowen peninsula and together these represent one of the more noteworthy distributions of Viking-Age hoards within a geographically restricted area on record from Ireland.

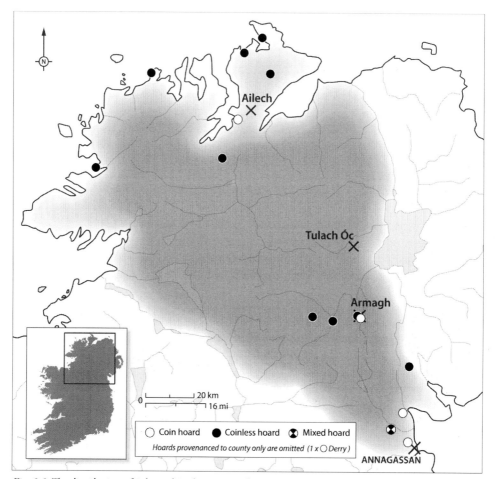

Fig. 3.3 The distribution of 9th- and 10th-century Viking-Age silver hoards in the over-kingdom of Northern Uí Néill.

These hoards are distributed fairly close to Ailech, the royal centre of the Northern Uí Néill kingship prior to its move to Tullach Óc (Tullaghogue, Co. Tyrone) during the late 10th/11th century (MacCotter 2008, 224). This tendency for silver hoards to cluster around royal centres is also paralleled in the kingdoms of Northern Brega and, most exceptionally, Clann Cholmáin. The Northern Uí Néill hoards, however, are distinct in one important respect from the finds from the other kingdoms considered here, in that they generally tend to contain complete ornaments. This may indicate that their relationship with the Scandinavians was more socially than economically motivated, and was perhaps based on tribute or gift-exchange. It is estimated that the amount of silver from the kingdom, in bullion terms, amounts to around 4.5 kg, most of which is accounted for by these hoards from Cenél nEógain. This is greater than the estimated value for the hoards from Dublin, though it should be noted that non-numismatic finds, such as characterise Northern Uí Néill, are generally significantly heavier than the coin hoards that are more distinctive of Dublin. In fact, the only cluster of coin hoards from Northern Uí Néill, and the only example of a mixed hoard, is from the southern limits of the over-kingdom, all in modern Co. Louth. These hoards are distinctive in nature from the remaining finds from this kingdom and, unsurprisingly, given their geographical location on the east coast, they share more in common with the hoards from Northern Brega and Dublin than with their fellows in Northern Uí Néill.

Enmities and alliances: the 9th century

The Vikings were active on the east coast of Ireland long before the establishment of the *longphort* at Dublin in 841. One of the most notable events occurred in 837 when two large fleets arrived. The annals relate:

> A fleet of three score ships of the Norsemen upon the Boyne. Another fleet of three score ships on the River Liffey. These two fleets afterwards plundered Mag-Life and Mag-mBrega between churches, and forts, and houses. A victory of the men of Brega, over the foreigners, at Deoninne in Mugdorna-Brega, when six score of them were slain. A battle [was gained] by foreigners, at Inber-na-mbarc, over the Uí Néill from the Shannon to the sea, where a slaughter was made that has not been reckoned; but the chief kings escaped (*Annals of the Kingdom of Ireland by the Four Masters* (hereafter AFM), *s.a.* 836).[2]

In the pre-Viking period, the River Liffey formed the boundary between Brega and Laigin, and the strategic importance of Dublin in political terms is exemplified here. The annal reference is a precursor of the expansion of Scandinavian territory, and territory under Scandinavian influence, in the later 10th century, from their Dublin base north into Brega, south into Laigin and west into Mide. These territories form the focus of the initial raids after the establishment of the *longphoirt* in 841:

> There was a naval camp (*longphort*) at Linn Duachaill from which the peoples and churches of Tethba were plundered. There was a naval camp at Dublinn from which the Laigin and the Uí Néill were plundered, both states and churches, as far as Sliab Bladma (*Annals of Ulster* (hereafter AU)).

AU records the establishment of another *longphort* on the Boyne at Linn Ross (Rossnaree) in 842. Downham (2003–4, 238) suggests that the settlement at Rossnaree, only a short distance from Knowth, the royal centre of Northern Brega, may have been founded with the consent of the kingship, and it may be significant that this is also the year of the earliest recorded alliance between the Irish and the Vikings, when Commán, abbot of Linn Duachaill, was killed by them (AU).

The Vikings were to prove useful allies in Brega's struggle against their traditional overlords, Clann Cholmáin of Mide. The year 848 was a devastating one for the Vikings, in which four defeats involving significant losses of men are recorded in battles against the kings of Mumu, Laigin, Southern Brega and Clann Cholmáin (AU). Even though the figures noted in the annals may have been exaggerated, the Vikings must have been considerably weakened by significant losses of troops in these battles. This may explain why in 849 *Chronicum Scotorum* (hereafter CS) records: 'Duiblinn was attacked by Máel Sechnaill and by Tigernach, king of Lagore'. Máel Sechnaill son of Máele Ruanaid, king of Mide and overlord of Brega, accompanied by Tigernach, king of Southern Brega, appear to have taken advantage of the depletion of Viking forces to attack the settlement at Dublin. As a result of this joint attack, the following year, the Vikings were only too happy to ally with Cináed son of Conaing, king of Northern Brega, when he rebelled against Máel Seachnaill. Cináed also took the opportunity to subjugate his rival Tigernach, king of Lagore, plundering his royal site (AU 850). Máel Sechnaill and Tigernach took their revenge the following year, and drowned Cináed (AU 851). The *Fragmentary Annals of Ireland* (hereafter FA), complied in the 11th century, preserves a tradition that Auisle, one of three kings of Viking Dublin in the mid-9th century, was married to one of Cináed's daughters (FA §234), though it has been suggested that this might have been Cináed mac Alpín (Downham 2007, 140). While there may be some doubt about the existence of this marriage alliance, it is clear that within a decade of the establishment of *longphoirt* in Southern Uí Néill the Vikings had become embroiled in local power plays between Mide, Northern Brega and Southern Brega. The arrival in 853 of Amlaíb (ON Óláfr), son of the king of Lochlainn, must have considerably altered the state of play for the annals record that the foreigners who had been in Ireland prior to his arrival submitted to him, and that he exacted tribute from the Irish (AU).

The detailed integration of the Dublin Vikings in local power plays and internal dynastic disputes in Southern Uí Néill, and beyond, belies the impression of them as mere outsiders. Máel Sechnaill, king of Mide, fought hard during this period to retain his hold on the kingship of Tara, and although he was opposed to the Dublin Vikings, he was happy to employ the support of the Gallgoídil – most likely a mixed band of Gaelicised Scandinavians who originated in the Western Isles (AU 856). In the mid-9th century, the kingdom of Osraige attempted to assert itself under the leadership of Cerball son of Dúnlange. He quickly recognised the military benefits of the Vikings and formed alliance with the kings of Dublin. In 859, along with Amlaíb and Ímar (ON Ívarr), he launched a raid into Mide (AU), but eventually submitted to Máel Sechnaill. The following year the Dublin Vikings had found a new ally in Áed Findliath, king of Cenél nEógain. In common cause against Máel Sechnaill, who was now joined by Cerball, they battled at Armagh and, subsequently, Áed and Amlaíb invaded Mide (FA §279; AU 861). In 861, Máel Sechnaill successfully defeated the Dublin Vikings (CS). In 862, in yet another raid into Mide, Áed and the kings of the foreigners were joined by Flann son of Conaing, king of Northern Brega. Flann's motivations were to resist the over-lordship of Máel Sechnaill but, in the following year, Amlaíb, Ímar and Auisle plundered his kingdom, in what appears to have been a massive attack on the royal and sacred sites of Brega:

> The caves of Achad Aldai, and of Cnodba, and of Boadán's Mound above Dubad, and of Óengoba's wife, were searched by the Foreigners – something which had never been done before. This was the occasion when three kings of the Foreigners, i.e. Amlaíb and Ímar and Auisle, plundered the land of Flann son of Conaing; and Lorcán son of Cathal, king of Mide, was with them in this (AU 863).

They plundered Newgrange, Knowth and Dowth, and throughout Flann's kingdom, and the last part of the annalistic entry relates that they were accompanied on this expedition by Lorcán, king of Mide. Áed Finnliath exacted his revenge the following year when he blinded Lorcán (AU 864) and, as Downham (2007, 20) points out, Amlaíb drowned Conchobar son of Domnall, Lorcán's rival, at Clonard.

The kingship of Tara passed to Áed Finnliath after Máel Sechnaill's death (AU 862). The Vikings served their purpose for him while he was king-in-waiting, but by 866 he had no further need of them. He turned on those settled in his own backyard:

> Áed son of Niall plundered all the strongholds of the foreigners i.e. in the territory of the North, both in Cenél Eógain and Dál Araidi, and took away their heads, their flocks, and their herds from camp by battle (?). A victory was gained over them at Loch Febail and twelve score heads taken thereby (AU).

Fig. 3.4 Silver hoard from 'near Raphoe' (Co. Donegal) (photograph: Sotheby's, London).

The reference implies that there were a number of *longphoirt*, with associated hinterlands, along this northern coastline, and Ó Corráin (1997, 90) proposes that Áed Finnliath was taking the littoral back from Viking control. FA preserve a tradition that Áed was married to Amlaíb's daughter (§292). It is difficult to date this marriage alliance though the most appropriate context is the early 860s, when the two kingdoms were in military alliance against Máel Sechnaill. If the genealogy of Clann Eruilb – another branch of Cenél nEógain, descended from Áed Allán – is reliable, it may also have formed marriage alliances with the Vikings at this time (Thornton 1996). It is tempting to associate some of the hoards from the Inishowen area, all from around Ailech, the royal centre of the Northern Uí Néill, with these later 9th-century Scandinavian/ Cenél nEógain marriage alliances. The finds, from north-west Inishowen, Roosky, Carrowmore/ Glentogher and 'near Raphoe' (all Co. Donegal), exhibit features in common, suggesting that they may represent a shared hoarding horizon (fig. 3.4). It is possible, given they each contain complete ornaments, little or no hack-silver and no coins, that these finds are hoards that should be interpreted in social terms (Sheehan 2004, 181–4), though other interpretations are also possible (see below).

A major attack by Irish kings on Viking Dublin occurred in 867:

> Amlaíb's fort at Cluain Dolcáin was burned by Gaíthíne's son and Máel Ciaráin son of Rónán, and the aforesaid commanders caused a slaughter of a hundred of the leaders of the foreigners in the vicinity of Cluain Dolcáin on the same day (AU).

Cennétig son of Gaíthíne, was king of Loígis and Máel Ciaráin son of Rónán, was a member of the family who were hereditary abbots of Clondalkin, a monastic settlement in west Dublin. Doherty (2000, 185) argues that this attack may represent a concerted strike on what was the border of the 9th-century Viking kingdom. Events of the 860s culminated in 868 at the battle of Killineer when Flann, king of Northern Brega, and the Vikings of Dublin were heavily defeated by Áed Finnliath (AU). So, although, Flann had suffered at the hands of the Dublin Vikings in 863, it seems he was prepared to ally himself with them a few years later if it meant keeping Áed Finnliath at bay.

In 873 Ímar, described in AU as 'king of all the Norsemen in Britain and Ireland', died (AU), and Amlaíb disappears from the Irish sources. The loss of these two powerful kings, who had controlled Dublin for over twenty years, signalled a decline in the power of the kingdom. Internal strife amongst the leaders of Dublin ultimately led to their downfall. For a period in 882, Flann Sinna, of Southern Uí Néill, and king of Tara, allied with Dublin and they attacked Armagh, in what is an obvious assault on Northern Uí Néill (AU). CS 883 records the death of Auisle's son at the hands of Ottir son of Eirgne, and of Muirgel, daughter of Máel Sechnaill. This Ottir (ON Óttarr) may be the son of Iernce (ON Iárnkné) who, along with Stain (ON Stein), was defeated during the battle at Carlingford Lough between the Dubgennti and the Finngenti in 852 (AU). It appears from FA that Iargna formed an alliance with Matudán son of Muiredaig, king of Ulaid (FA §235). The Dál Fiatach kings of Ulaid were not averse to forming alliances with the Vikings, and may have found common cause with them against the power of the Cenél nEógain. In the late 9th century, Ottir's brother, Eoloir, was responsible for the death of Éremón son of Áed, one of two kings of Ulaid; incidentally a rival branch of the family to that of Matudán son of Muiredaig, so this may support FA's record of an alliance, demonstrating once again how involved the Vikings were in Irish dynastic disputes. The Irish equivalent translation of Iárnkné or 'Ironknee', Glún Iairn, later emerged as a personal name associated particularly with the Dublin Vikings. Such names demonstrate a level of social interaction lying beneath the political alliances recorded in the annals.

At some point, a marriage alliance was formed between Mide and these northern Vikings, presumably in common cause against Northern Uí Néill, perhaps during the reign of Muirgel's father, Máel Sechnaill, or more likely in that of her brother, Flann Sinna, which would suggest a date in the early 880s. By 888, the Dublin Vikings and Flann Sinna were in opposition, and Flann suffered a massive defeat (AU). The following year, the Vikings joined forces with Domnall son of Áed, king of Northern Uí Néill, against Flann (AU 889). Dissension amongst the Dublin Vikings reached a new level in the 890s when Sigfirth the Earl took power from the son of Ímar. It is possible that different factions within the Dublin dynasty formed alliances with Flann Sinna and Domnall son of Áed, though this is not specifically recorded (as in most cases the annals only note the involvement of the Vikings of Dublin without specifying the names of the leaders). However, in 895, the Dublin Vikings were in alliance with Mide once more when Máel Ruanaid son of Flann Sinna, and the son of Ímar raided Osraige (AFM *s.a.* 890). In 896, the Dublin dynasty lost three of its key players: Sicfrith (ON Sigfrøðr) was 'treacherously' killed by his own kinsmen, while his brother, Amlaíb, and his nephew, Glún Tradna son of Glún Iairn, were killed by the king of Ulaid in Conaille (AU/CS). In the same year, Flannacán son of Cellach, king of Northern Brega, was killed by the Vikings.

It is difficult to relate particular silver hoards to the historically-attested interactions that took place between Viking Dublin and the kingdoms of the Northern and Southern Uí Néill dynasties during the 9th century, partly due to the fact that the deposition of so few hoards may be firmly assigned to this period. There are, however, significant numbers of coinless hoards that could potentially date to the second half of the 9th century on the basis of the date-ranges of the ornaments they contain. Broad-band arm-rings, for instance, were already familiar in Ireland during the closing decades of the 9th century, and it is also evident that hack-silver, which on the basis of the evidence of mixed hoards alone appears to be a 10th-century phenomenon, was also current in Ireland during the second half of the 9th century. Thus, any number of the coinless hack-silver hoards from Northern or Southern Uí Néill could potentially date to this period. The dominance of hack-silver at the recently-discovered *longphort* at Woodstown (Co. Waterford), as well as the occurrence there of a large number of lead scale weights, clearly indicates that these types of sites had important economic functions and were more than just fortified military settlements (see Harrison, this volume). It is evident that the economic outcomes of the activities traditionally associated with *longphoirt* – such as raiding, ransoming and slaving – were sufficient to set up trading undertakings. It is noteworthy that significant finds of Viking-Age silver and gold are on record from the immediate vicinity of the potential *longphort* site at Ballaghkeeran Little (Co. Westmeath), on Lough Ree, the western boundary of Clann Cholmáin (Sheehan 2008, 291), and it is also likely that there was economic advantage for the Southern Uí Néill from the presence of the documented *longphoirt* on the Liffey, Boyne and Glyde.

The Vikings strategic choice of location on the Liffey brought them into direct contact with the kingdoms of Mide, Brega and Laigin. They fought against, and allied with, the dominant 9th-century kings and dynasties: Máel Sechnaill of Clann Cholmáin, Áed Finnliath of Cenél nEógain, and Flann Sinna of Clann Cholmáin. They maximised internal dynastic power struggles to their advantage, most notably in their alliance with Síl nÁedo Sláine kings of Northern Brega against Clann Cholmáin, and sometimes these agreements were sealed by marriage. It was this interplay between political, economic and social relations that was to manifest itself more strongly in the 10th century.

902–917: 'Driven from Ireland'?

In 896, as noted above, Flannacán son of Cellach, king of Northern Brega, was killed by the Vikings. His son, Máel Finnia, was to have revenge in 902:

> The heathens were driven from Ireland, i.e. from the fortress of Áth Cliath, by Máel Finnia son of Flannacán with the men of Brega and by Cerball son of Muiricán, with the Laigin; and they abandoned a good number of their ships, and escaped half dead after they had been wounded and broken (AU).

This joint effort by the kings of Brega and Laigin to expel the Vikings has been traditionally taken as a watershed in Viking studies in Ireland, given its reported success in the annals. It is worth pondering, however, why Flann Sinna, king of the Clann Cholmáin and king of Tara, did not take part in this dramatic action. It is evident that he occasionally faced opposition from his sons, and this may have been a factor that occupied his attention at this time. In the late 9th century, for instance, he fought a battle against Máel Ruanaid and during the year before his death he was challenged by Donnchad and Conchobor (AU 915). It is quite possible that in 902 Máel Finnia was acting against Dublin with the approval of Flann Sinna. Indeed, it also seems likely that Flann Sinna assumed the role of overlord of Dublin following Máel Finnia's death in 903. His relations with Northern Brega were strengthened by the marriage of his daughter Lígach to its next king Máel Mithig (Dobbs 1930, 312, 336). Though Flann's overlordship of Dublin is not noted in the annals, there may be some supporting evidence for it in the archaeological evidence.

Kenny (1987, 516), in an analysis of the Clann Cholmáin hoards from Lough Ennell, suggests they may evidence a 'residual Viking presence' at Dublin after the events of 902. This presence may have been composed largely of traders and craftsmen, now operating under the control of Irish kings. Excavations at Temple Bar West have indeed demonstrated that there was no break in the occupation of Dublin post-902, despite the annalistic record that 'the heathens were driven from Ireland', and Simpson (2010, 420–1) has interpreted this as evidence that the expulsion was confined to Dublin's ruling elite.

A reflection of the impact of the momentous downfall of Viking Dublin in 902, and the involvement of Northern Brega in this occurrence and its consequences, may be evidenced in the large coin hoard from 'near Drogheda' (Co. Louth). This was deposited *c.* 905, and its Northern Brega provenance may reflect the role that Máel Finnia played in the attack on Dublin. No longer extant, it was reportedly an immense find, possibly comprising around 5,000 Kufic and York 'Cunetti' coins (Dolley 1966, 26–7, fn. 1), and it is potentially related to the massive Cuerdale hoard, from Lancashire, in terms of its penultimate background in Viking Dublin (Graham-Campbell 2011). A small mixed hoard from a ringfort at Millockstown (Co. Louth), which comprises ingot-derived hack-silver and a Kufic coin that provides a *terminus post quem* deposition of 905/06, may also relate to this scenario, as may the hoard from Leggagh, in Northern Brega, which comprised ingots and a small number of coins, deposited *c.* 915. In general, Northern Brega opposed the return of the Vikings to Dublin in 917 and its king, Máel Mithig, died at the battle of Dublin in 919. It is interesting to note that the panel featuring the Arrest of Christ in a conspicuous position on a broadly contemporary high cross in this kingdom, Muiredach's Cross, at Monasterboice (Henry 1967, pl. 79), could be interpreted as an artistic reflection of this Brega/Dublin enmity.

The earliest of the coin hoards from Northern Uí Néill, now lost, may also relate to post-902 Dublin connections. It was a substantial find that reportedly comprised 'great numbers' of Kufic coins (Vallancey 1804, 211). Provenanced only to 'Co. Derry', it was deposited *c.* 910(?), and Downham (2007, 30) has suggested that it and two further coin-dated hoards from Ulaid, both of which also contain hack-silver, may evidence contact between Northern Uí Néill and Hebridean-based exiles from Scandinavian Dublin following the events of 902. Certainly, given its Kufic content, the Co. Derry hoard may well ultimately have been assembled in Dublin as most hoards from Ireland containing coins of this type are provenanced to its region of influence (Sheehan 2000, 53, fig. 5).

The silver hoards from Mide may also, in part, be interpreted as reflecting the situation in Dublin between 902–17. All of the coin and mixed hoards from this kingdom were deposited in the 10th century, with eleven of the fourteen examples dating to after 950. It is clear, however,

Fig. 3.5 Silver hoard from Ballywillian, Lough Kinale (Co. Longford) (photograph: National Museum of Ireland).

that these latter finds do not necessarily reflect the period when silver was in greatest abundance in this kingdom. Indeed, its largest mixed hoard – that known as Dysart 4 (Ryan *et al.* 1984, 339–56, pls. 6–12) – was deposited during the first decade of the 10th century. In addition, a number of the coinless hoards, which as a rule have greater bullion-weight values than the coin hoards, were clearly deposited within the period 850–950 on the basis of the date-ranges for the types of ornamental metalwork that is found in them (fig. 3.5). If this assortment makes evident the occurrence of significant quantities of silver in Clann Cholmáin between 850 and 950, as it does, then another coinless hoard grouping may demonstrates the incidence there of even greater quantities of silver specifically during the early 10th century. This is made up of a number of very large ingot hoards from the Clann Cholmáin heartland of Lough Ennell (Co. Westmeath).

Coinless ingot hoards from Ireland could conventionally be assigned to the 10th century on the basis of the occurrence of ingots and/or ingot-derived hack-silver in at least sixteen mixed hoards, all of which are of this date. However, discoveries made over the past decade or so in Scandinavia, Britain and, now, Ireland – most notably at the central places at Kaupang, Vestfold (Norway) (Hårdh 2008), and Uppåkra, Skåne (Sweden) (Hårdh 2000), as well as at the winter camp established by the Danish 'great army' at Torksey (Lincolnshire) (Blackburn 2011), and the *longphort* at Woodstown (Sheehan forthcoming b) – have demonstrated that ingots, and hack-silver, were much more commonplace in the mid- and later 9th century than the coin-dated hoards alone would suggest. As a consequence, the date-range for coinless hoards of ingots and/or ingot-derived hack-silver may be extended rearwards to include the second half of the 9th century, and now stands at 850–1000. In the case of Clann Cholmáin, this increases the potential of the later 9th-century being included in the temporal spread of the kingdom's silver wealth. At present, however, it seems reasonably likely, based on the limited amount of chemical and lead isotopic analyses carried out by Cazalet on elements of some of the large Lough Ennell hoards (in Ryan *et al.* 1984, 356–61), that these are of early 10th-century date.

Three of the ingot hoards in question from Lough Ennell are conventional Viking-Age hoards, but the remaining three are extraordinary. The most substantial of these is the Carrick hoard, which consists of some sixty-one large ingots, together weighing over 31 kg. The Dysart 1 ingots, which number five, are actually products of the same matrix as those in the Carrick hoard, and they may well, indeed, have been produced in the same melt (Ryan *et al.* 1984, 337). Dysart 2 consists of five outstandingly large ingots of unique form, weighing just over 3kg each (Ryan *et al.* 1984, 337–8; Kelly 1991, 87). These three hoards, non-Scandinavian in character, are composed of uniquely massive Irish ingots (Graham-Campbell and Sheehan 2009, 83), and it may be plausibly assumed that these were made in Clann Cholmáin, even if the silver in them emanated from Viking Dublin. If these remarkable hoards are of early 10th-century date, as is suggested as probable here, then it seems likely that they relate to the kingship of Flann Sinna (877–916). As has been suggested above, he may have held the overlordship of Dublin during most of the 902–17 'hiatus' period and, thus, it seems probable that the main Lough Ennell bullion hoards relate to him. In overall terms, however, the great concentration of hoards in Clann Cholmáin throughout the 9th and 10th centuries suggests that this kingship effectively controlled the relationship with Dublin.

Enmities and alliances: the 10th century

Whatever about the toleration of a Viking presence at Dublin that may have occasionally proved useful during the early 10th century, it is clear from the annals that most Irish kings strongly and concertedly resisted the return of the Viking leaders. Ragnall (ON Røgnvaldr) and Sitriuc (ON Sigtryggr) were the grandsons of Ímar king of 9th-century Dublin – the dynasty of Uí Ímair – and they returned to reclaim their kingdom. There was a massive mobilisation of troops against them: Niall Glúndub son of Áed Finnliath, the Cenél nEógain king of Tara, led an alliance of Northern and Southern Uí Néill to Mag Femin in Mumu, where they battled against Ragnall and his forces, while Laigin fought against Sitriuc at Cenn Fúait (for a discussion of the inter-relationship of these two battles and battle-sites see Etchingham 2010). After his success at Cenn Fúait, Sitriuc proceeded to Dublin where, as stated in CS 917, 'Áth Cliath was taken by force by the foreigners from the men of Ireland'.

In 918, while Niall Glúndub continued to wage war against the newly arrived Vikings, Máel Mithig son of Flannacán, tried a different tactic. AU states that he went over to the Vikings to defend Northern Brega from them. Whether he attempted to form an alliance with them, or possibly with one band of Vikings against another, the annals tell that this availed him not. As high-king of Ireland, it was Niall Glúndub who once again gathered the troops in 919 to launch a massive attack on Dublin. He was accompanied, amongst others, by Conchobar grandson of Máel Seachnaill, of Southern Uí Néill, Máel Mithig son of Flannacán, king of Northern Brega, and Cellach son of Fogartach, king of Southern Brega. The Irish were no match for the Vikings on this occasion, and Niall Glúndub was slain along with many others. The following year, Donnchadh son of Flann Sinna, of Southern Uí Néill, defeated the Vikings in Ciannachta Brega (AFM *s.a.* 918).

For the first half of the 10th century the main concern of the Dublin dynasty was to maintain links with and hold the Viking kingdom of York (Smyth 1975–9; Downham 2007). Ragnall, king of Waterford, left Ireland and took the kingship there in 919. When Sitriuc graduated to this kingship in 921 Gofraid (ON Guðrøðr) took over the kingship of Dublin. In 927, the annals relate that Gofraid abandoned Dublin and went over-seas, but as Smyth (1975–9, 23) points out, he departed, like his brothers before him, to take the kingship of York. These Dublin connections with York and Anglo-Saxon England may be reflected in the hoard evidence. For instance, one of Dublin's seven coin hoards, from Glasnevin, was deposited *c.* 927 and has been linked with the expulsion of the Hiberno-Scandinavian dynasty from York (Dolley 1966, 28). While relating hoards to specific historically-attested episodes may often be a problematic approach, this is a reasonably persuasive proposal given that a number of mixed hoards from Britain containing Hiberno-Scandinavian silver artefacts, including those from Bossall/Flaxton and the Vale of York, both in Yorkshire (Graham-Campbell 2001, 212–17; Ager and Williams 2010), were also deposited *c.* 927–8 and, thus, collectively, these finds may belong to a trans-Irish Sea hoarding horizon related to this event. Both of the mixed hoards provenanced to Dublin, one being from 'Co. Dublin' and the second from 'near Dublin', could also relate to this phase. The former, deposited *c.* 935, contained in addition to its coins, most of which are Anglo-Saxon pennies, an ingot and two hack-silver fragments of 'Permian' rings, while the latter, which comprised ingot-derived hack-silver and two coins, one Kufic and one Anglo-Saxon, was deposited in the early to mid-10th century (Blackburn 2007, 146–7).

In 935, Amlaíb son of Gofraid sacked Lagore and Knowth, the two royal centres of Brega (AU 935), while the following year Dublin Vikings plundered Clonmacnoise (Co. Offaly) and stayed for two nights at this important ecclesiastical settlement which was under the patronage of Southern Uí Néill (AU 936). These attacks, on Brega and across the territory of Southern Uí Néill, must be interpreted as a clear attempt by Amlaíb to assert himself over his neighbours during the period following the death of his father. Donnchadh son of Flann Sinna, and king of Tara, burned Dublin in revenge (CS *s.a.* 935). Amlaíb attacked Kilcullen the following year, which prompted Donnchadh to lay siege to Dublin, and he was joined in this venture by his northern counterpart, Muirchertach son of Niall Glúndub, king of Ailech. The annals tells us that they ravaged from Dublin to Mullaghmast (Co. Kildare), which may imply that even the combined forces of the two most powerful Irish kings of the period were unable to take the town on this occasion (AU). Muirchertach was to pay for his involvement, for the following year the Vikings captured him in an attack on Ailech, but a ransom was paid and he was freed (CS *s.a.* 939).

Muirchertach had many encounters with the Vikings: in 926, he killed Alpthann (ON Hálfdan) son of Gofraid, and defeated the Vikings of Strangford Lough at Linn Duachaill. The final battle route was led by Gofraid, who had left Dublin to come to the assistance of his son (AU). The Strangford Lough Vikings caused further problems for Muirchertach when they attacked Armagh in 933. The raid was led by Amlaíb son of Gofraid, who then joined forces with Matudán son of Áed, king of Ulaid, and plundered as far as Co. Monaghan in an obvious attack on Northern Uí Néill. However, resistance was strong and Muirchertach defeated them. Earlier that year, Muirchertach had fought off an attack from his cousin, Fergal son of Domnall, accompanied by his sister's son, Sicfrith son of Uathmarán (AU). The adoption of this Norse personal name suggests an alliance between the Vikings and this branch of the family. In the 10th century, Vikings were employed by rival branches within the Cenél nEógain, and by their subjects. Interaction between Muirchertach and the Vikings, both those in the north of Ireland and Dublin, may explain the presence of a number of hoards in the Inishowen area.

The four non-numismatic hoards from Inishowen, previously mentioned, exhibit features in common, suggesting that they may represent a shared hoarding horizon: for example, each contains Hiberno-Scandinavian broad-band arm-rings, they contain few ingots and little or no hack-silver, and no coins, and at least two of the four finds appear to have been buried in ringforts. Graham-Campbell (1988, 109–10) interpreted them as relating to the presence of a Scandinavian fleet, led by Accolb (ON Helgólfr), in the Inishowen region during the early 920s (AU 921), and suggested that they were deposited during this period. The equation of these hoards with the activities of this Viking leader is supported by Ó Floinn (1995, 101–3), who presents additional literary evidence relating to it, and suggests that the hoards are representative of Viking bullion that was acquired by local rulers during the campaign. This is an appealing proposal, though it should be borne in mind, given the difficulties involved in closely dating them, that relating hoards that contain only non-numismatic material to particular historically-attested events is problematical. In the case of these four hoards, however, the fact that they seem to form a related and broadly contemporary group certainly leaves open the possibility that they may have been acquired and deposited by Northern Uí Néill resulting from the same historical cause or factor. Thus, they may indeed relate to Accolb and his ill-fated expedition, but they could equally be associated with any of the connections that existed between Northern Uí Néill and Viking Dublin, or indeed between Northern Uí Néill and Southern Uí Néill, during this period.

Another grouping of hoards in Northern Uí Néill is formed by five finds from within the kingdom of Airgialla. Four of these are from the vicinity of Armagh, a concentration that may be explained by the close association of this important ecclesiastical centre with the Uí Néill dynasty as well as its primacy within the early medieval Irish Church. It is recorded that Northern Uí Néill kings, including Áed Finnliath, were buried there, and Áed also kept a residence (*domus*) at Armagh (AU 870). The four finds comprise a small coin hoard provenanced to 'near Armagh', deposited *c.* 965, a lost coinless hoard, also provenanced only to 'near Armagh', which comprised two arm-rings most probably of late 9th or 10th century date, a coinless hoard of broad-band arm-rings from Emy, on the Monaghan side of the River Blackwater, and a large coinless from Tynan, some 12 km from Armagh, comprising six arm-rings and one large arm-ring fragment, which is likely to date to the first half of the 10th century.[3] Like the Inishowen hoards, the three coinless finds exhibit features in common – containing arm-rings, no ingots, little or no hack-silver – suggesting that they may also represent a shared hoarding horizon.

In 941, Muirchertach returned from a raid on the Hebrides and he brought with him a fleet. Almost immediately he went on a circuit of Ireland, exacting tribute from a number of kingdoms: AU record that he plundered Mide, Uí Fhailgi, Osraige, Déisi, and brought Cellachán, king of Caisel, in submission to Donnchad, reigning king of Tara. AFM preserves a tradition that this circuit also included Dublin, where he took away Sitriuc, but this is based on a 12th-century poem written in his honour during the kingship of his descendant, Muirchertach son of Lochlainn (Ó Corráin 2000).

Amlaíb son of Gofraid, king of Dublin, died in 941 and was succeeded by his brother Blacáire and subsequently by Amlaíb Cúarán. These kings fought for control of the town for much of the 940s. Doherty (1998, 301) suggests that the epithet, Old Irish *cúarán*, meaning 'shoe or sandal', indicates that Amblaíb was Irish-speaking, and may have been inaugurated, and attempted to rule, in an Irish fashion. During his initial reign he was more concerned to gain control of York than he was with Dublin. In 943, Muirchertach is killed by Blacáire son of Gofraid (AU). For two centuries the kingship of Tara had alternated between Clann Cholmáin of Southern Uí Néill and Cenél nEógain of Northern Uí Néill, but the death of Muirchertach allowed for the rise of Ruaidrí ua Canannáin of the rival Northern Uí Néill dynasty of Cenél Conaill. This rise may be connected with lost hoard from Cor, from the western coastline of Cenél Conaill, which, based on the recorded details, appears to have been fully comprised of ingot derived hack-silver. This makes it unique in the Northern Uí Néill context, given that each of the other non-numismatic hoards from this kingdom is dominated by complete ornaments. Because of its potentially broad date-range the Cor hoard cannot be tied down to any historically-recorded event, even if its provenance within Cenél Conaill may be suggestive of a connection with the alliance, against Muirchertach, of the Cenél Conaill with a Dublin fleet in Lough Foyle in 943 (AFM *s.a.* 941) and the subsequent rise of Ruaidrí ua Canannáin.

The death of Donnchadh Donn, king of Tara, in 944, allowed Congalach son of Máel Mithig, king of Northern Brega, to take advantage of the weakness of the Clann Cholmáin dynasty and become the first Síl nÁedo Sláine king to hold the kingship of Tara in over two centuries. It seems that part of Congalach's campaign involved subjugating the kingdom of Dublin. In 944, he launched a major attack on the town, accompanied by Braen son of Máel Morda of Laigin: AU records they 'took away valuables, and treasure, and much booty'. The raid receives a rather more elaborate account in AFM:

> The destruction of Áth-cliath by the Irish, i.e. by Conghalach son of Máel Mithig, heir apparent to the sovereignty of Ireland; Braen son of Máel Morda, King of Laigin; Ceallach son of Faelán, heir of Laigin. The destruction brought upon it was this, i.e. its houses, divisions, ships, and all other structures, were burned; its women, boys, and plebeians, were carried into bondage. It was totally destroyed, from four to one man, by killing and drowning, burning and capturing, excepting a small number who fled in a few ships, and reached Deilginis (AFM *s.a.* 942).

AFM, though they contain many unique and important entries, are a 17th-century compilation and at times they must be used with caution, however, this description of 10th-century Dublin as divided into plots has been confirmed by archaeological excavations in the city, particularly in Fishamble Street (Wallace 2000; see also Boyd, this volume). The raid probably occurred while Blacáire son of Gofraid, held the kingship. However, Ó Corráin (2012, 31) suggests that taking control of Dublin in this way bolstered Congalach's claim to the kingship of Tara and that, for the years immediately after, Amlaíb Cúarán served as a subordinate ally. Swift (2008, 27) argues that Congalach's fortunes were considerably improved by this attack and the resources he acquired from it funded his other campaigns: for instance, in 945 he took the hostages of Connacht (CS 945), in 949 he raided Mumu (AU), and in 951 he put a fleet on the Shannon (AFM *s.a.* 949). In 945, Blacáire gave up the kingdom of Dublin and Amlaíb succeeded him as king. Congalach and Amlaíb cemented their alliance by defeating a band of Ruaidrí ua Canannáin's followers in Conaille (AU 945). Ruaidrí was to even the score two years later at Slane, when he defeated Congalach and Amlaíb (AU). AFM relate that Congalach attacked Dublin after the battle, perhaps to re-enforce his authority over the town (*s.a.* 945). In any case, Amlaíb left for York and Blacáire resumed the kingship. Congalach does not seem to have continued his alliance with Dublin while it was under Blacáire, in fact, he plundered the town again in 948. He killed Blacáire and again the annals imply that Congalach had a significant victory; 1,600 Vikings were reportedly killed or taken captive (AU 948). Ten years

earlier the combined forces of Northern and Southern Uí Néíll had been unable to achieve the
same result. The rivalry between Blacáire and Amlaíb for control of Dublin may have meant
that different factions of Viking Dublin aligned themselves with different Irish kings. At least
one faction was with Congalach when he defeated Ruaidrí ua Canannáin in 950. AU neglects
to mention Congalach, and the foreigners are held solely responsible for Ruaidrí's death (AU).
AFM record that the Gofraid son of Sitriuc, fled from the battle, and Woolf (2002, 40) suggests
that he may have supported Ruaidrí. Though it is equally possible that the AU account is correct,
and that Ruaidrí having plundered Brega for six months had effectively subdued Congalach.

In the early 950's, Amlaíb Cuarán lost his fight to hold the kingdom of York and his return
to Dublin marks a concentration of his efforts in Ireland, which resulted in the economic
development of the town and the expansion of the kingdom. A curious indication of the extent
of Amlaíb's power and control is found in 954, when Domnall ua Néill, king of Cenél nEógain,
plundered Brega 'by the consent of the foreigners' (*s.a.* AFM 952). The implication of this record
is that Dublin might have been expected to support Brega in defence of its territory, because of
the former alliance between Congalach and Amlaíb, but did not do so. A near-contemporary
hoard, comprising ingots and Anglo-Saxon coins, was deposited *c.* 953 at Monasterboice (Co.
Louth), a Fir Arda Ciannachta church with royal associations that was patronised by Brega
kings, and this AFM entry may provide the broad context for this hoard. According to the
Banshenchus, a 12th-century text listing the mothers and wives of kings in Irish literature and
history, Dúnlaith, daughter of Muirchertach and sister of Domnall ua Néill, was married to
Amlaíb Cúarán (Dobbs 1930, 314, 337–8; 1931, 188, 227). The marriage may date to this
period (Swift 2008, 32). In 956, Congalach was killed by the foreigners of Dublin and Laigin.
The account of his death in the annals is interesting. Having just plundered Laigin, Congalach
proceeded to hold Óenach Cholmáin, an assembly which must have been the traditional
prerogative of the north Laigin kings (AFM *s.a.* 954). Not only did he display his newfound
position of dominance in this audacious manner, but he was killed in Tech Griunn (OI *tech*,
'house') while he was evidently receiving his royal subordinates. According to AFM, word had
been sent to Dublin and Amlaíb son of Gofraid, led an ambush on the king.[4]

Perhaps Congalach and his kingship have been underestimated, in particular in the context
of his relationship with Dublin. In the later 10th century, Máel Sechnaill, king of Mide, and
Brian Bóruma, king of Mumu, attempted to control Dublin and placed the exaction of tribute
from the kingdom on a more regular footing, but it seems that Congalach may have been
the first Irish king to maximise Dublin's potential in terms of military support and economic
advantage in the 940s. Allying with Dublin was a tradition that was continued by Congalach's
son, Domnall. Along with Amlaíb Cúarán, he defeated Domnall ua Néill, king of Tara, at the
battle of Mona in 970 (AU). This union, in common cause against the power of Northern Uí
Néill, was sealed by the marriage of Domnall to Ragnailt, daughter of Amlaíb (Dobbs 1930,
314, 337; 1931, 188, 227). Amlaíb and Domnall may have come to a very particular kind of
arrangement, for at the height of Amlaíb's power it seems the Vikings may have had bases at
a number of monastic settlements in Brega and surrounding territories. This is evidenced in
AFM where it is reported that the church sites at Louth, Dromiskin and Monsterboice were
plundered by Muirchertach son of Domnall, king of Ailech, and that the raids were 'against the
foreigners'. It notes that many of these were slain and that, at Monasterboice, 'three hundred
of them were burned in one house' (*s.a* 968). Ó Floinn (1998, 164) has suggested that these
Vikings may have been Christian Scandinavian residents at these monastic settlements, while

Downham (2003–4, 240) proposed that they represent Amlaíb's troops who were billeted here to protect Brega. Whatever the exact meaning of these entries, the implication is clear: that an attack on Brega was an attack on Amlaíb! In 977, Muirchertach son of Domnall of the Northern Uí Néill, and Congalach son of Domnall, were killed by Amlaíb (AU). Woolf (2002, 43) suggests that Congalach may have been killed as a peremptory strike in favour of Amlaíb's grandson, Muirchertach, the son of Ragnailt and Domnall son of Congalach. Indeed, Muirchertach and the Vikings of Dublin, presumably including some of his cousins, raided Domnach Patraic in 995 (AU).

It is notable that the depositions of no less than five of the eight Viking-Age silver hoards on record from Northern Brega – those from Monasterboice and Smarmore (both Co. Louth), and Fennor, Knowth and an unlocalised find from 'Co. Meath' (all from Co. Meath) – fall within the twenty-five year period commencing 945. This date-range neatly falls within the period 944–77, when the kingship of Brega was held by Congalach (944–56) and Domnall (956–77). Congalach, who also held the kingship of Tara, was interchangeably an ally and opponent of Amlaíb Cúarán, with whom he fought against the Northern Uí Néill during the mid- to late 940s, while Amlaíb allied with Domnall against the same opponents in 970. It may be the case that these five hoards are archaeological manifestations of this Dublin Viking king's relationship with Northern Brega. The two earlier coin hoards, from Fennor and Knowth, were deposited *c*. 945(?) and *c*. 950(?) respectively. These are from adjoining locations in the Boyne Valley, separated only by the river, and are both very small hoards of Anglo-Saxon coins. The Knowth find was discovered during the archaeological excavation of a souterrain that formed part of *Cnogba*, the royal capital of Northern Brega (Kenny 2012), from where other archaeological evidence for connections with Hiberno-Scandinavian Dublin has been identified, including a number of houses which resemble Dublin's Type 1 buildings (Wallace 1992, 71–2; see also Boyd, this volume). This is a predictable context for the hoard, given the royal status of the site, as has also been suggested above for the Monasterboice hoard of ingots and coins, deposited *c*. 953. Each of these three hoards was deposited during the reign of Congalach. The remaining two were deposited over a short period, *c*. 965–70, during the supremacy of Domnall, with both of them dating specifically to the period when it appears Dublin Vikings were in close alliance with him and may have been actually resident in Northern Brega. The Smarmore coin hoard was deposited *c*. 965, while the 'Co. Meath' find is composed of Anglo-Saxon coins and a single Kufic issue. Deposited *c*. 970, this is the latest hoard-occurrence of a Kufic coin in Ireland though, as it was a dirham of Hārūn-al-Rashīd (Dolley 1960, 43), and it had clearly been in circulation for a long period before the hoard's Anglo-Saxon element was even minted. Together, these mid- to late 10th century Northern Brega finds comprise coins, ingots and/or hack-silver, and this is precisely what one would expect to find in circulation in Dublin at this time. This suggests that the Northern Brega's relationship with the Viking settlement of Dublin was one focused on the political/economic sphere rather than one based on tribute and gift-exchange, which would manifest itself in a different way archaeologically. This association of the two kingships also appears to have involved the marriage of Domnall to Ragnailt, Amlaíb's daughter.

Amlaíb Cúarán sealed many of his alliances with other Irish dynasties by marriage. In essence, the dominant kings who competed for power in mid- to late 10th century Ireland were connected in one way or another, by marriage, through the kingdom of Dublin. This may be viewed as a Viking-age variation of six degrees of separation, though in this case Amlaíb, rather than Kevin Bacon, is the central character. He married Dúnliath, daughter of Muirchertach of Cenél nEógain, of Northern Uí Néill, and they had a son, Glún Iairn. Dúnliath also married Domnall, king of the Clann Cholmáin of Southern Uí Néill, an alliance which produced another son, Máel Sechnaill. He married Máel Muire, Amlaíb's daughter (*The Annals of Clonmacnoise* (hereafter AClon), *s.a.*1014). Another of Amlaíb's daughters, Ragnailt, was married to Domnall son of Congalach, of Síl nÁedo Sláine of Northern Brega, and their son was Muirchertach. In addition, and to add further complication, Amlaíb married Gormlaith, daughter of Murchad son of Finn, king of Uí Fáeláin, and their son was Sitriuc Silkenbeard. Sitriuc married Sláine, daughter of Brian Bóruma, to whom his mother had also been married; there is a tradition that Gormlaith was also married to Máel Sechnaill (AFM *s.a.* 1030; Ní Bhrolcháin 1982; Connon 2000). This tangled web of marriage alliances reflects the military, economic and social significance of the position that the kingdom of Dublin had come to occupy. The two dominant kings of the late 10th century, Máel Sechnaill, of Mide, and Brian Bóruma, of Mumu, were only too keen to maximise the town's potential.

In 975, Máel Sechnaill launched his first attack on Dublin and 'cut down the wood of the foreigners', Tomar's Wood, on the north side of the Liffey (*The Annals of Tigernach* (hereafter ATig)). Later, in 995, in another raid on Dublin he took away the ring of Thor and the sword of Carlus (ATig). It seems he understood the full implications of these types of actions, asserting himself by demeaning the status of important emblems of Viking Dublin. Domnall ua Néill, king of Tara, died in 980 and, in what could be read as the actions of the new king, Máel Sechnaill inflicted a crushing defeat on the Vikings of Dublin and their allies, who came from the Isles, at the Battle of Tara (AU). CS relate that Máel Sechnaill brought away many hostages, including Domnall Claen of Laigin and those of Uí Néill, which suggests that Dublin held sway over Mide for a time. ATig calls it; 'the end of the Babylonian captivity of Ireland'. Woolf (2002, 43) argues that this battle represented Amlaíb's attempt to claim the kingship of Tara for himself, and through his network of political and familial links with the dynasties of Clann Cholmáin and Síl nÁedo Sláine he may have felt justified in this bid for power. After the defeat, he retired to Iona, where he died a year later (AU).

In the years after the battle, Máel Sechnaill seems to have had an arrangement with Glún Iairn, his half-brother. Following Glún Iairn's death, in 989, Máel Sechnaill laid siege to Dublin for twenty nights (ATig). Clarke (1990–2, 111) suggests this action may imply that he was acting as kingmaker, attempting to control which of Amlaíb's sons was to succeed Glún Iairn. ATig informs us that Máel Sechnaill exacted an ounce of gold from every *garda* in Dublin. It is possible that these garths, from ON *garrða*, are represented by the division of urban space into plots, though Holm (forthcoming) proposes that the term is more likely to represent the division of the town into taxable units. This tax was to be paid every Christmas, and it is clear that the exaction of wealth from Dublin was now placed on a different footing. No longer content to exact wealth from the town by occasional raids and hostage taking, the Irish kings, led by Máel Sechnaill, instituted a more regular and formal arrangement.

Three Dublin hoards – two from Castle Street, deposited *c.* 991 and *c.* 995, both in the town, and one from Clondalkin, deposited *c.* 997 – belong to the period following 989. The two later finds, which are large by the standards of Ireland's Viking-Age coin hoards, may be regarded as archaeological reflections of the great wealth of late 10th-century Dublin that is also intimated by the heavy tribute imposed on it by Máel Sechnaill. Two mixed hoards from the heartland of Clann Cholmáin – from Ladestown, on Lough Ennell, and an localized place called 'Marl Valley', near Mullingar – may also, in terms of their location, date and nature, be potentially connected to Máel Sechnaill's Dublin tribute. The Ladestown hoard comprises ingots, ornament derived hack-silver and two coins, which provide a *terminus post quem* of 979 for the find, while the Marl Valley find, which is only partly extant, comprised over a hundred coins as well as a gold ring and a number of silver ornaments and ingots; the surviving coins indicate a deposition date of *c.* 986.

It is curious to note that there are no silver hoards on record from Southern Brega apart from those in modern Co. Dublin, which it has been argued above are likely to relate culturally, politically and economically to Viking Dublin and Dyflinarskirí rather than to this Southern Uí Néill kingdom. In fact, the only recorded silver find from Southern Brega, an arm-ring fragment, was found during excavations at Lagore, its royal capital. This apparent dearth of silver suggests that Southern Brega had a very different relationship with Dublin than did Northern Brega and Mide, the other Southern Uí Néill kingdoms, both of which have yielded significant quantities of hoards. It is interesting to note that there are few references to hostility between the Vikings and Southern Brega. One of them concerns the death of Beólan Litil, who was killed by Ímar of Limerick (*Annals of Inisfallen* (hereafter AI), 969), and the occurrence of his Norse nickname may be a reflection of the level of cultural interaction between Southern Brega and Dublin. This is also apparently evident in a poem composed by Cináed ua hArtacáin, in which he associates Amlaíb Cúarán with the ecclesiastical site at Skreen, important because of its proximity to Tara, the seat of the high-kingship. Cináed was a member of the Clann Chernaig Sotail dynasty, from whom the kings of Southern Brega were chosen, and Bhreathnach suggests these connections represent Amlaíb's attempt to gain a foothold in the area (Bhreathnach 1999).

The two late 10th-century coin hoards from Northern Uí Néill, a small deposit of Anglo-Saxon coins from Carrowen, at the base of the Inishowen peninsula, deposited *c.* 970, and another small find from 'near Armagh', deposited *c.* 965(?), reflect a continuation of the apparent connections of the earlier coinless hoards with the royal and ecclesiastical centres at Ailech and Armagh. The recently discovered ornament hoard from Lurgabrack (Co. Donegal), which dates to between the mid-10th and mid-11th centuries, consists only of 'ring-money', a specific type of silver ring that is characteristic of Scotland's Viking-Age hoards. As such it suggests a continuation of the earlier linkage between Northern Uí Néill and Scandinavian Scotland that is evidenced by Muirchertach's raiding in the Hebrides. Indeed, it is of interest to note that the find-spot of this hoard is located only a few kilometres west of Rinnaraw, Sheephaven Bay, where Fanning excavated a cashel containing a Viking-Age house with parallels in the Scottish Isles (Comber 2006; Boyd 2009, 279–80).

In the early 10th century, Niall Glúndub, as king of Tara, did his best, both in 917 and 919, to prevent the return of the dynasty of Uí Ímair to Ireland, but to no avail. And this set the trend for the first half of the 10th century; the Irish were no match for the Vikings, particularly those based at Dublin. Donnchadh Donn, Clann Cholmáin king of Tara, managed to defeat them in Brega in 920, and in the 930s he was the first Irish king to attack Dublin in over twenty years. Clarke (1988, 19) suggested that the kingship of Máel Sechnaill, Clann Cholmáin king of Tara, has been underestimated, and that the transition from Viking to Hiberno-Norse Dublin could be attributed to him more than to any other historical figure, Brian Bóruma included. But perhaps the real 10th-century innovators had in fact been the kings of Northern Brega – Congalach, who held the kingship of Tara, and Domnall, who never attained the same position as his father, though his death notice claims that he was eligible: *rígdomna Temrach* (ATig). Congalach had led two very successful attacks on the town in the 940s, and in both cases he brought away much booty and many hostages. These successes may well have funded his campaign for the kingship of Tara. Domnall likewise recognised the benefit of having Amlaíb, and Dublin, on his side, particularly in his resistance to the power of Northern Uí Néill. However, Máel Sechnaill was probably the most successful of the 10th-century Irish kings; he raided the town on a number of occasions, and won two major battles against the Dublin Vikings, in 980 and 989. In 997, when Máel Sechnaill was forced to recognise the growing power of Brian Bóruma, the two kings divided Ireland between them; Máel Sechnaill was to be king of Leth Cuinn and Brian of Leth Moga, but most significantly Brian was given the real prize, control of Dublin (AI).

Conclusion

An analysis of the broad distributional patterns of Ireland's Viking-Age silver hoards shows that most of them, whether considering the numbers of individual find-spots or their combined bullion weight value, are to be found in the kingdoms of Mumu, Southern Uí Néill and Northern Uí Néill and that the amounts of silver represented in them is large compared to that on record from Viking Dublin and its hinterland. While it is not possible to identify a context for many of these finds, this analysis indicates that there are particular associations between important groupings of hoards and certain secular and ecclesiastical centres which are associated with the dominant dynasties of Northern and Southern Uí Néill. Bearing in mind that it is difficult and perhaps unwise to associate hoard depositions with specific events recorded in the annals, it is nevertheless possible to show that there are certain periods when trends in the historical record are reflected in the depositions, contents and contexts of hoards. These trends appear evident in times when certain Irish kings, and their kingdoms, were in closest contact with Viking Dublin. Notably, in the early 10th century there is a significant concentration of hoards in Clann Cholmáin when Flann Sinna was king of Tara. The nature and location of some of these finds, particularly those from Lough Ennell, may reflect the tribute one would expect in the context of the period when the Viking elite were in exile. Association between Dublin and Northern Uí Néill is most keenly reflected in the concentration of hoards around royal Ailech and the Inishowen peninsula, as well as around Armagh. Though they are largely difficult to date closely, the distinct nature of these ornament finds may indicate that they represent status gift exchange in these regions remote from Dublin. In the mid- to late 10th century, a grouping of hoards in Northern Brega may reflect the innovative relationship that Congalach and his son Domnall had with Dublin – a connection that may be expressed in the more economic nature of these hoards. The hoards from the time of Máel Sechnaill, Clann Cholmáin king of Tara, may be evidence of his dominance over Dublin in the late 10th century and may be interpreted as an archaeological reflection of the manner by which he exacted tribute from the town.

Acknowledgments

The authors wish to thank Nick Hogan, Department of Archaeology, for preparing figs. 3.1–3; Dr Kevin Murray, Department of Early and Medieval Irish, and Professor Emeritus Donnchadh Ó Corráin, Department of History, University College Cork, for reading a draft version of this chapter; and Eamonn Kelly and Maeve Sikora, National Museum of Ireland, for permission to refer to the new hoard from Lurgabrack (Co. Donegal).

Notes

1   Published references to the individual Viking-Age hoards noted in this chapter are not normally cited. For references see Blackburn and Pagan 'Checklist of coin hoards from the British Isles, *c.* 450-1180', http://www.fitzmuseum.cam.ac.uk/coins/hoards/; Graham-Campbell (1976, Appendices B-D); and Sheehan (1998, Appendix).

2   Annal referencing: all references to events recorded in AU are to the corrected date found in the Mac Airt and Mac Niocaill (1983) edition. References to other annals, such as AFM, are generally corrected where possible with *sub anno* given in parenthesis.

3   The exceptional find from Shanmullagh, on the River Blackwater, which comprises Hiberno-Scandinavian silver as well as insular metalwork (Bourke 1993, 24–39) is not included here given its nature as an assemblage rather than a hoard.

4   Swift (2008, 51), following Todd, suggests that this is a slip for Amlaíb Cúarán son of Sitriuc, and it is possible that AFM confused the two kings.

Bibliography

Ager, B. and Williams, G. (2010) *The Vale of York Hoard*. London, British Museum Press.

Blackburn, M. A. S. (2007) Currency under the Vikings. Part 3: Ireland, Wales, Isle of Man and Scotland in the ninth and tenth centuries. *British Numismatic Journal* 77, 119–49.

Blackburn, M. A. S. (2011) The Viking winter camp at Torksey, 872–3. In M. A. S. Blackburn *Viking Coinage and Currency in the British Isles*, 221–64. British Numismatic Society, Special Publication 7. London, Spink.

Boyd, R. (2009) The Irish Viking Age: a discussion of architecture, settlement patterns and identity. *Viking and Medieval Scandinavia* 5, 271–94.

Bradley, J. (2009) Some reflections on the problem of Scandinavian settlement in the hinterland of Dublin during the ninth century. In J. Bradley, A. J. Fletcher and A. Simms (eds) *Dublin in the Medieval world: studies in honour of Howard B. Clarke*, 39–62. Dublin, Four Courts Press.

Bhreathnach, E. (1999) Columban churches in Brega and Leinster: relations with the Norse and the Anglo-Normans. *Journal of the Royal Society Antiquaries of Ireland* 129, 37–69.

Bourke, C. (1993) *Patrick: the archaeology of a saint*. Belfast, HMSO.

Clarke, H. B. (1988) Gaelic, Viking and Hiberno-Norse Dublin. In A. Cosgrove (ed.) *Dublin through the Ages*, 4–24. Dublin, College Press.

Clarke, H. B. (1990–2) The bloodied eagle: the Vikings and the development of Dublin, 841–1014. *Irish Sword* 18, 91–119.

Comber, M. (2006) Tom Fanning's excavations at Rinnarawcashel, Portnablagh, Co. Donegal. *Proceedings of the Royal Irish Academy* 106 C, 67–124.

Connon, A. (2000) The *Banshenchas* and the Uí Néill queens of Tara. In A. P. Smyth (ed.) *Seanchas: studies in early and medieval Irish archaeology, history and literature in honour of Francis J. Byrne*, 98–108. Dublin, Four Courts Press.

Dobbs, M. E. (ed. and trans.) (1930 and 1931) The Ban-Shenchus. *Revue Celtique* 47, 282–339; 48, 163–234.

Doherty, C. (1998) The Vikings in Ireland: a review. In H. B. Clarke, M. Ní Mhaonaigh and R. Ó Floinn (eds) *Ireland and Scandinavia in the Early Viking Age*, 288–330. Dublin, Four Courts Press.

Doherty, C. (2000) Cluain Dolcáin: a brief note. In A. P. Smyth (ed.) *Seanchas: studies in early and medieval Irish archaeology, history and literature in honour of Francis J. Byrne*, 182–8. Dublin, Four Courts Press.

Dolley, R. H. M. (1960) A hoard of tenth-century Anglo-Saxon coins from Glendalough. *Journal of the Royal Society of Antiquaries of Ireland* 90, 41–7.

Dolley, R. H. M. (1966) *Hiberno-Norse Coins in the British Museum*. Oxford, Oxford University Press.

Downham, C. E. (2003–4) The Vikings in Southern Uí Néill to 1014. *Peritia* 17–18, 233–55.

Downham, C. E. (2007) *Viking Kings of Britain and Ireland: the dynasty of Ívarr to A.D. 1014*. Edinburgh, Dunedin Academic Press.

Etchingham, C. (2010) The battle of Cenn Fúait. *Peritia* 21, 208–32.

Graham-Campbell, J. (1976) The Viking-Age silver hoards of Ireland. In B. Almqvist and D. Greene (eds) *Proceedings of the Seventh Viking Congress, Dublin 1973*, 31–74. Dublin, Royal Irish Academy.

Graham-Campbell, J. (1988) A Viking-age silver hoard from near Raphoe, Co. Donegal. In P. F. Wallace and G. Mac Niocaill (eds) *Keimelia: studies in medieval archaeology and history in memory of Tom Delaney*, 102–11. Galway, Galway University Press.

Graham-Campbell, J. (1998) The Early Viking Age in the Irish Sea area. In H. B. Clarke, M. Ní Mhaonaigh and R. Ó Floinn (eds) *Scandinavia and Ireland in the Early Viking Age*, 104–30. Dublin, Four Courts Press.

Graham-Campbell, J. (2001) The northern hoards: from Cuerdale to Bossal/Flaxton. In N. J. Higham and D. H. Hill (eds) *Edward the Elder 899–924*, 212–29. London, Routledge.

Graham-Campbell, J. (2011) *The Cuerdale Hoard and Related Viking-Age Silver and Gold from Britain and Ireland in the British Museum*. London, British Museum Press.

Graham-Campbell, J. and Sheehan, J. (2009) Viking-Age gold and silver from Irish crannogs and other watery places. *Journal of Irish Archaeology* 18, 77–93.

Gullbekk, S. H. (2011) Norway: commodity money, silver and coins. In J. Graham-Campbell, S. M. Sindbæk and G. Williams (eds) *Silver Economies, Monetisation and Society in Scandinavia AD 800–1100*, 89–107. Aarhus, Aarhus University Press.

Halpin, A. (2008) *Weapons and Warfare in Viking and Medieval Dublin*. Medieval Dublin Excavations 1962–81, ser. B, vol. 9. Dublin, National Museum of Ireland.

Hårdh, B. (2000) Uppåkra – a centre in South Sweden in the 1st millennium AD. *Antiquity* 74 (285), 640–8.

Hårdh, B. (2008) Hacksilver and ingots. In D. Skre (ed.) *Means of Exchange: dealing with silver in the Viking Age*, 95–118. Kaupang Excavation Project Publication Series, 2, Norske Oldfunn XXIII. Aarhus, Aarhus University Press.

Hennessy, W. M. (ed. and trans.) (1866) *Chronicum Scotorum: A Chronicle of Irish Affairs, from the earliest times to A.D. 1135, with a supplement containing the events from 1141 to 1150*. Roll Series 46. London, Longman.

Henry, F. (1967) *Irish Art During the Viking Invasions (800–1200 A.D.)*. London, Methuen.

Holm, P. (forthcoming) Manning and paying the Hiberno-Norse Dublin fleet. In E. Purcell, P. MacCotter, J. Nyan and J. Sheehan (eds) *Clerics, Kings and Vikings: essays on medieval Ireland*. Dublin, Four Courts Press.

Kelly, E. P. (1991) Observations on Irish lake dwellings. In C. Karkov and R. Farrell (eds) *Studies in Insular Art and Archaeology*, 81–92. American Early Medieval Studies 1. Ohio, Oxford Press.

Kelly, E. P. (2007) Catalogue of finds from Lough Derravarragh in the NMI. In A. O'Sullivan, R. Sands and E. P. Kelly *Coolure Demesne Crannog, Lough Derravarragh: an introduction to its archaeology and landscapes*, 93–109. Bray, Wordwell.

Kenny, M. (1987) The geographical distribution of Irish Viking-Age coin hoards. *Proceedings of the Royal Irish Academy* 87 C, 507–25.

Kenny, M. (2012) Coins, tokens and related numismatic material. In G. Eogan, *Excavations at Knowth 5: the archaeology of Knowth in the first and second millennia AD*, 518–26. Dublin, Royal Irish Academy.

Mac Airt, S. (ed. and trans.) (1951) *The Annals of Inisfallen*. Dublin, Dublin Institute for Advanced Studies.

Mac Airt, S. and Mac Niocaill, G. (ed. and trans.) (1983) *The Annals of Ulster (to A.D. 1131)*. Dublin, Dublin Institute for Advanced Studies.

MacCotter, P. (2008) *Medieval Ireland: territorial, political and economic divisions*. Dublin, Four Courts Press.

Murphy, D. (ed.) (1896) *The Annals of Clonmacnoise*. Dublin, Royal Society of Antiquaries of Ireland.

Ní Bhrolcháin, M. (1982) The manuscript tradition of the Banshenchas. *Ériu* 33, 109–35.

Ó Corráin, D. (1997) Ireland, Wales, Man and the Hebrides. In P. Sawyer (ed.) *The Oxford Illustrated History of the Vikings*, 83–109. Oxford, Oxford University Press.

Ó Corráin, D. (2000) Muirchertach Mac Lochlainn and the Circuit of Ireland. In A. P. Smyth (ed.) *Senchas: studies in early and medieval Irish archaeology, history, and literature in honour of Francis John Byrne*, 238–50. Dublin, Four Courts Press.

Ó Corráin, D. (2012) Vikings and Ireland. Unpublished article available *www.ucc.ie./celt*.

O'Donovan, J. (ed. and trans.) (1856) *Annala Rioghachta Eireann: Annals of the Kingdom of Ireland by the Four Masters, from the earliest period to the year 1616* (7 vols). Dublin, Hodges and Smith.

Ó Floinn, R. (1995) Sandhills, silver and shrines – fine metalwork of the medieval period from Donegal. In W. Nolan, L. Ronayne and M. Dunlevy (eds) *Donegal History and Society: interdisciplinary essays on the history of an Irish county*, 85–148. Dublin, Geography Publications.

Ó Floinn, R. (1998) The archaeology of the early Viking Age in Ireland. In H. B. Clarke, M. Ní Mhaonaigh and R. Ó Floinn (eds) *Scandinavia and Ireland in the Early Viking Age*, 131–65. Dublin, Four Courts Press

Purcell, E. (1995) *A reconsideration of the Ballinderry game board*. Unpublished M.Phil thesis, Department of Archaeology, University College Dublin.

Radner, J. N. (ed. and trans.) (1978) *Fragmentary Annals of Ireland*. Dublin, Dublin Institute for Advanced Studies.

Ryan, M., Ó Floinn, R., Lowrick, N., Kenny M. and Cazalet, P. (1984) Six silver finds of the Viking period from the vicinity of Lough Ennell, Co. Westmeath. *Peritia* 3, 334–81.

Sheehan, J. (1998) Early Viking-Age silver hoards from Ireland and their Scandinavian elements. In H. B. Clarke, M. Ní Mhaonaigh and R. Ó Floinn (eds) *Scandinavia and Ireland in the Early Viking Age*, 166–202. Dublin, Four Courts Press.

Sheehan, J. (2000) Ireland's early Viking-Age silver hoards: components, structure and classification. In S. Stummann Hansen and K. Randsborg (eds) *Vikings in the West*, 49–63. *Acta Archaeologica (Supplementa II)* 71. Copenhagen, Munksgaard.

Sheehan, J. (2004). Social and economic integration in Viking-Age Ireland: the evidence of the hoards. In J. Hines, A. Lane and M. Redknap (eds) *Land, Sea and Home: proceedings of a conference on Viking-period settlement, at Cardiff, July 2001*, 177–88. Society for Medieval Archaeology Monograph 20. Leeds, Maney.

Sheehan, J. (2008) The *longphort* in Viking Age Ireland. *Acta Archaeologica* 79, 282–95.

Sheehan, J. (forthcoming a) Weighty matters: silver in Viking-Age Ireland.

Sheehan, J. (forthcoming b) The Woodstown silver, in context. In I. Russell and M. F. Hurley (eds) *Woodstown: a Viking-Age settlement in County Waterford*.

Simpson, L. (2010) The first phase of Viking activity in Ireland: the evidence from Dublin. In J. Sheehan and D. Ó Corráin (eds) *The Viking Age: Ireland and the West. Proceedings of the Fifteenth Viking Congress, Cork 2005*, 418–29. Dublin, Four Courts Press.

Skre, D. (2011) Commodity money, silver and coinage in Viking-Age Scandinavia. In J. Graham-Campbell, S. M. Sindbæk and G. Williams (eds) *Silver Economies, Monetisation and Society in Scandinavia AD 800–1100*, 63–88. Aarhus, Aarhus University Press.

Smyth, A. P. (1975–9) *Scandinavian York and Dublin; the history and archaeology of two related Viking kingdoms* (2 vols). Dublin, Templekieran Press.

Stokes, W. (ed. and trans.) (1895–7) The Annals of Tigernach. *Revue Celtique* 16, 374–419; 17, 6–33, 116–263, 337–420; 18, 9–59, 150–303, 374–91 (reprinted (2 vols) (1993), Felinfach, Llanerch).

Swift, C. (2008) The early history of Knowth. In F. J. Byrne, W. Jenkins, G. Kenny and C. Swift, *Historical Knowth and its Hinterland*, 5–53. Excavations at Knowth 4. Dublin, Royal Irish Academy.

Thornton, D. (1996) Clann Eruilb: Irish or Scandinavian? *Irish Historical Studies* 30, 161–6.

Vallancey, C. (1804) On the money of the ancient Irish. *Collectanea de Rebus Hibernicis* vi, pt.i, 197–212.

Wallace, P. F. (1992) *The Viking Age Buildings of Dublin*. Medieval Dublin Excavations 1962–81, ser. A, vol. 1. Dublin, Royal Irish Academy.

Wallace, P. F. (2000) *Garrda and airbeada*: the plot thickens in Viking Dublin. In A. P. Smyth (ed.)

Seanchas: studies in early and medieval Irish archaeology, history and literature in honour of Francis J. Byrne, 261–74. Dublin, Four Courts Press.

Walsh, A. (1998) A summary classification of Viking swords in Ireland. In H. B. Clarke, M. Ní Mhaonaigh and R. Ó Floinn (eds) *Scandinavia and Ireland in the Early Viking Age,* 222–35. Dublin, Four Courts Press.

Woolf, A. (2002) Amlaíb Cuarán and the Gael, 941–81. In S. Duffy (ed.) *Medieval Dublin III*, 34–43. Dublin, Four Courts Press.

BEYOND *LONGPHUIRT*? LIFE AND DEATH IN EARLY VIKING-AGE IRELAND

Stephen H. Harrison

This chapter reassesses current archaeological approaches to Viking settlement in 9th-century Ireland. Settlements of this date are usually called *longphuirt* and are often linked to a specific earthwork form. There has been comparatively little research on the character of these settlements, which are still viewed as almost exclusively military in form and function. This chapter uses new evidence from Woodstown (Co. Waterford) to argue that whatever their relationship to Old Irish terminology, some of these early medieval nucleated settlements were far more complex than has previously been thought.

Introduction: the historical debate

Few terms pertaining to the early Viking Age have generated more debate among modern commentators than the Old Irish *longphort*. In origin, it is a compound word formed from two Latin loan-words, [*navis*] *longa*, meaning '[war]ship', and *portus*, a 'harbour' or 'haven' (Glare 2006, 1042). Despite its military origin, the Old Irish *long* rapidly came to mean any 'ship' (indeed, it remains the most common term used in modern Irish), while *port* came to mean not just a 'bank' or 'shore', but a 'place' or indeed 'stead, abode' (Quin 1983, 440, 497). Thus, there is no obvious reason why a *longphort* – in its most neutral translation a 'ship-place' – should describe a purely military base or settlement. Nonetheless, on the rare occasions when the word is used in the *Annals of Ulster* between 841 and 917, it seems to refer to a military encampment, and specifically to a site established by Scandinavian groups in Ireland (Moore 1988, 31). In the majority of cases, the word was linked to the Viking base at Dublin, but in AD 866 it was applied to all 'the strongholds of the foreigners' (*longphuirt Gaill*) in the north of Ireland (Mac Airt and Mac Niocaill 1983, 321–2), suggesting that it had a wider contemporary currency. In 917, on the other hand, it was used in the context of a battle at an unidentified site called *Topar Glethrach*, where it seems to denote a temporary base or stronghold associated with a military campaign (Mac Airt and Mac Niocaill 1983, 366–7). This latter meaning seems to have become dominant soon afterwards, with the word usually interpreted as 'camp, encampment [or] temporary stronghold'. Yet later use of the word to refer to permanent high-status dwellings may represent little more than literary flourish, although it perhaps implies that these sites were defended in some way (Quin 1983, 440). At some unknown but relatively early date, the word's nautical origins were clearly forgotten, and it was consistently applied to sites miles from any navigable water. Similarly, if the word ever had any specific associations with Scandinavian or Hiberno-Norse groups, this was also soon forgotten (Bhreathnach 1998, 36–7).

Historians and linguists, pointing to the shifting meaning of the word *longphort*, are sceptical that it was ever systematically applied to sites with a specific morphology that might be identified in the Irish landscape. Archaeologists, on the other hand, have more or less enthusiastically adopted the term in the sense in which it was at least sporadically used in the 9th century, referring to a Scandinavian base with nautical associations that was (presumably!) fortified. Within this context, these sites have been variously described as defended ship enclosures, shore fortresses, strongholds and/or trading stations (Wallace 1990, 72). All of these terms reflect historical and archaeological assumptions as much as, or more than, linguistic accuracy. While a detailed study of the use of the word among modern scholars is beyond the present study, it was used by Ryan (1990, 114) as early as 1949, but was popularised more recently by Clarke (1990, 65) and Wallace (1990, 70–80). As the earliest settlement evidence from his excavations at Wood Quay dated from *c.* 900, Wallace (1985, 107–8) proposed that this 10th-century *dún* (fortress) was preceded by an earlier *longphort* at another site in the area. This *longphort* phase, which lasted from the settlement's foundation in 841 to the (temporary) expulsion of its elite in 902, soon gained currency and remains central to chronological divisions of the city's history today. Given the importance of Dublin to Irish Viking studies, some modern commentators have effectively treated the *longphort* as a general chronological phase as well as a physical phenomenon, describing a 9th-century period of predominantly 'military' activity that is thought to contrast sharply with the 'urban' characteristics of Hiberno-Norse settlement from the 10th century onwards, however simplistic this division may be (Clarke 1998, 354).

Longphuirt: archaeological approaches

Discussion of the *longphort* at Dublin has focused almost exclusively on its site. In 1976, Graham-Campbell (1976, 40) proposed that it must have been situated somewhere close to the 9th-century cemetery at Kilmainham-Islandbridge, some 2 km west of Wood Quay. More recently, Clarke (1998, 346–8) has argued for two distinct *longphuirt* at Dublin, the most important of which was situated at Ussher's Island, immediately west of the site of the ancient *Áth Cliath*, the name given to the settlement in the majority of contemporary Irish sources. Simpson (2005, 54–9), on the other hand, has used new archaeological evidence to demonstrate that there was 9th-century 'Viking' activity in the area around the confluence of the Liffey and its tributary, the Poddle, a short distance to the east of Wood Quay, and suggests that this area was the site of the *longphort* (see also Halpin 2005, 102–4). Simpson (2005, 27–9) also noted strong similarities between late 9th-century levels at Temple Bar and mid-10th century levels at Wood Quay, but nonetheless emphasised the military character of the earlier settlement, and more specifically the associated graves from South Great George's Street. Before these recent discoveries, discussion of the *longphort* phase was essentially confined to relatively simplistic interpretations of the grave-goods found at Kilmainham-Islandbridge and elsewhere (*e.g.* Ó Cróinín 1995, 242), which emphasised the settlement's military character. With the exception of Wallace's (1990, 70) tentative suggestion that the site may have consisted of a fortification surrounded by an open settlement, little thought has been given to site morphology.

The question of the physical character of *longphuirt* was first raised in the 1980s, when

Fanning (1983) cut a series of trial trenches through a promontory fort at Ballaghkearan Little (Co. Westmeath), in the (apparently unsuccessful) hope of identifying 'Viking' settlement there. Just over a decade later, Etchingham (1994, 123) suggested that a hilltop fortification at Rathturtle (Co. Wicklow) was potentially 'Viking'. Most recent research, however, has been spearheaded by Kelly, who was the first to propose a specific morphology for *longphuirt*. In 1999, Maas and he examined a site at Dunrally (Co. Laois), a place-name thought since the 19th century to derive from *Dún Rothlaibh*, 'the fort of Rodolf' (Kelly and Maas 1999, 137). The destruction of a *longphort Rothlaibh* is recorded in the *Annals of the Four Masters s.a.* 860 (*recte* 862) (O'Donovan 1851, i, 496–7) and it has been proposed that the earthworks at this site, situated at the confluence of the River Barrow and the smaller River Glasha, correspond to this fortification. A bank and ditch enclose a roughly D-shaped area, 360 by 150 m, the straight side of which opens on to the water, an arrangement that would theoretically allow for the protection of 'the biggest of Viking fleets' (Kelly and Maas 1999, 138). It can be compared to a D-shaped banked enclosure that was constructed at Repton (Derbyshire), apparently when the 'great army' was overwintering at the site in AD 873–4 (Biddle and Kjølbye-Biddle 2001, 57–60), a decade after the abandonment of Dunrally. In 1998, Kelly, this time in collaboration with O'Donovan, published a brief note on another D-shaped enclosure at Athlunkard (Co. Clare) (Kelly and O'Donovan 1998, 13–16). Here, a 'Viking' connection was suggested by the place-name (*Áth Longphuirt*, 'the ford of the *longphort*') rather than by documentary sources, and the enclosure is considerably smaller, at just 75 by 30 m. As at Dunrally, however, the site is situated at the confluence of two streams, and a number of potentially 'Scandinavian' artefacts have been found in the locality. Kelly and Maas (1999, 141) have also linked an earthwork called Lisnaran, at Annagassan (Co. Louth) to *Linn Duachail*, the only specific site other than Dublin to have been called a *longphort* in the 9th-century *Annals of Ulster* (Mac Airt and Mac Niocaill 1983, 298–9). Here, however, the morphology of the site is a little different, with the circular earthwork of Lisnaran adjoining a D-shaped island in the River Glyde. Recently, this model has been revised by Kelly and Clinton (*pers. comm.*), who have conducted trial excavations on a ditch and bank system some distance to the north of Lisnaran, which effectively fortified a substantial area between the River Glyde and the adjacent coast. This area is now interpreted as the *longphort*. Kelly (2009) has also suggested that a site at Knoxpark (Co. Sligo), previously interpreted as an inland promontory fort with an associated late Iron Age/early medieval cemetery, is actually another example of a *longphort*. It will be noted that the sites identified by Kelly and others, while generally characterised by D-shaped enclosures, vary considerably in size and shape, and there has been some debate as to whether these generally unexcavated sites are typical of Viking-Age *longphuirt*, or indeed are of Viking-Age date at all. Ó Floinn (1998, 162–4), for example, argues that as consummate opportunists, many Viking groups must simply have reutilised the banks and ditches which surrounded so many early medieval settlement sites in Ireland, particularly monastic sites, rather than constructing their own earthworks. In 968, for example, a *longphort* was established at the monastic site of Emly (Co. Tipperary) for just two days (Mac Airt 1944, 158–9). There would have been no time for any major construction at the site.

The Woodstown evidence

Between 2003 and 2007, a series of opportunities arose to investigate parts of a roughly D-shaped enclosure beside the River Suir in Co. Waterford. The first three investigations, comprising initial testing, assessment and targeted excavation, were carried out in advance of the construction of the N25 Waterford (city) bypass (O'Brien and Russell 2005, 114), while the fourth excavation, part of a supplementary research project, was carried out following a decision to move the proposed road to avoid the site, which was declared a National Monument in 2005 (O'Brien *et al*. 2005, 19). Initially interpreted as a prehistoric enclosure, excavations at Woodstown produced a wealth of artefacts, many of which were of 'Scandinavian' or at least 'Hiberno-Norse' character and dated from the 9th or early 10th centuries. The site, technically 'Woodstown 6', promises to provide new insights, if not to *longphuirt* in particular, then certainly to nucleated settlements of the period.

Each of the four archaeological investigations led to the submission of an appropriate report, but the first three were not intended for formal publication. The fourth (Russell *et al*. 2007), which includes a summary of the first three investigations, is available online at the Dept of Environment, Heritage and Local Government webpage. Although two provisional reports on Woodstown had been published at the time of composition (O'Brien and Russell 2005; O'Brien *et al*. 2005), the online report forms the primary source for the present, discursive chapter.

Given the scale and complexity of the Woodstown site, and the fact that interpretations of it have changed considerably since its discovery in 2003, a brief summary is provided here. Woodstown is situated approximately 6 km west of the modern city of Waterford, on the southeast bank of the Suir, which enters the sea at Waterford Harbour. The site is situated immediately northeast of the Killoteran stream, a much smaller river which flows into the Suir through a low-lying, marshy area. The construction in the 19th century of the Waterford-Lismore-Dungarvan railway, which follows the south bank of the Suir at this point, seems to have destroyed any surviving evidence of the site's waterfront area. Survey failed to reveal any archaeological remains within the river itself, but this may be the result of heavy silting (O'Brien and Russell 2005, 111, 117).

The site is enclosed by the remains of two roughly parallel ditches, which extend northeast from the Killoteran stream, crossing two modern fields (called fields 22 and 23 in unpublished reports) before curving north to the edge of the railway cutting (fig. 4.1). The resulting enclosed area is some 400 m long and up to 160 m wide, being widest at its southwest end. A distinct kink in the line of the ditches corresponding to a modern field boundary led some early reports to suggest that there were two adjacent enclosures. Geophysical prospecting has also identified some outlying features, notably a 'satellite enclosure' in the northeast field (O'Brien *et al*. 2005, 15–17). The site was originally open to the Killoteran stream, and while the railway cutting has destroyed any surviving evidence, it is thought that the site was also open to the River Suir.

The earliest testing phase at the site was carried out in April 2003, and involved the excavation of 29 trenches, each 2 m wide, arranged in a herringbone pattern across the site. A substantial number of features were noted beneath the ploughsoil, and selective excavation was carried out within sections of twelve of these trenches between August and September 2003 in an assessment phase (O'Brien *et al*. 2005, 31–3). At this point, it was still believed that the site was of prehistoric date, albeit with some early medieval activity, and it was decided to preserve the site *in situ*, under the proposed road. To facilitate drainage into the Suir, however, it was necessary to excavate two culverts beneath the road, one at the northern end of the site and the other at the boundary between the two modern fields. Unexpectedly, archaeological excavation of the 20 by 60 m northern trench (culvert one) revealed a remarkable concentration of finds and a furnished grave which contained weapons of Viking-Age date. Extensive metal detection

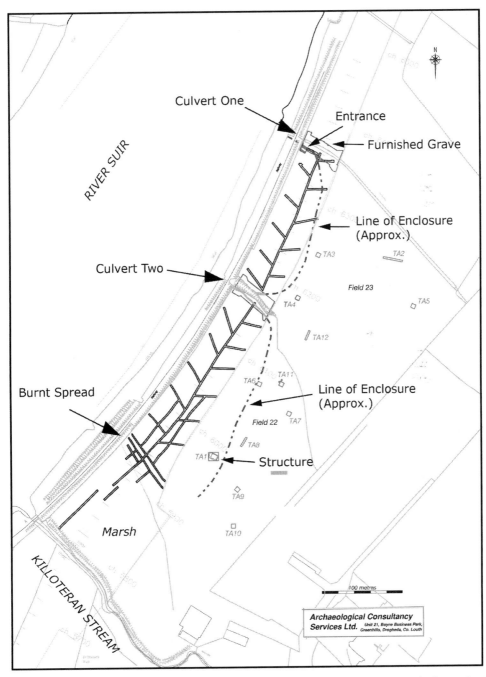

Fig. 4.1 Simplified plan of Woodstown 6, showing locations of features discussed in text. The 'herringbone' trenches of the first and second phases of excavation are clearly visible, as are the trenches (TA) of the latest phase. Culverts one and two are labelled (after an original drawing supplied by ACS Ltd, modified by the author).

of the spoil from culvert one, culvert two and the earlier test trenches also took place at this time, although plans to excavate the features exposed in culvert two were abandoned as the full scale and importance of the site became clear (O'Brien and Russell 2005, 117). Following the decision to declare the site a National Monument, in 2007 a supplementary research project targeted a number of areas within and around the enclosure, perhaps most notably the remains of a substantial structure, consisting of a 0.8 m wide slot trench enclosing a 10.4 by 7.1 m sub-rectangular area (Russell *et al.* 2007, 80–2). Despite four successive campaigns, less than 10% of the site within the original road-take has been tested, and perhaps 5% of the site has been archaeologically resolved (O'Brien and Russell 2005, 117).

The rectilinear structure excavated in 2007 clearly survived because of the depth of its slot trench, cut up to 0.7 m into the underlying subsoil. Here, as elsewhere on the site, ploughing to a depth of up to 0.4 m had destroyed almost all habitation levels and disturbed all those artefacts not associated with particularly deep features, *i.e.* pits and ditches. While it remains possible that some habitation levels may survive in other parts of the site, these cannot presently be identified. By the end of October 2004, 5,308 finds had been recovered from Woodstown (McNamara 2005, 126) and a further 699 were recovered in 2007 (Russell *et al.* 2007, 77). Of this total of 6,007 finds, *c.* 5,146 were recovered from the plough zone, with no more than 13% coming from archaeologically secure contexts. Some 750 artefacts are of post-medieval date, but Woodstown remains one of the most productive unwaterlogged early medieval sites ever excavated in Ireland, a statistic which is all the more remarkable when it is realised that acidic soil conditions resulted in almost no bone preservation.

Interpreting Woodstown

The most substantial features on the site are undoubtedly the two parallel ditches, both of which extended into culvert one. Here, excavation established that the smaller, inner ditch was backfilled before, or more probably during, the construction of the larger, outer ditch (Russell *et al.* 2007, 13). This outer ditch was up to 4 m wide and 1.48 m deep and had a series of fills (O'Brien *et al.* 2005, 43–5). A series of stake holes in the backfill of the inner ditch have been interpreted as the remains of an internal palisade, presumably defensive. The cutting also revealed a 7.5 m wide entrance feature. While its surface seems to have been metalled, no traces of posts or other potential defensive structures were identified during the excavation (O'Brien *et al.* 2005, 49–50).

The date of this outer ditch, which is central to discussion of the date of the site as a whole, has been the subject of considerable debate. Previous publications have relied on a series of radiocarbon dates from levels close to the base of the outer ditch to date its excavation to some point in the 5th, 6th or 7th century. As a result, it has been suggested that Woodstown represents an indigenous Irish enclosed site, possibly monastic, which was reoccupied in the early Viking Age, to which period the majority of artefacts from the site can be dated (O'Brien *et al.* 2005, 43–5; O'Brien and Russell 2005, 119–20). However, detailed research and a series of additional radiocarbon dates associated with the 2007 supplementary research project have demonstrated that the radiocarbon dates, based on oak samples, are almost certainly the result of the 'old wood' effect, whereby results reflect the date of growth rather than the date of felling (Taylor 1987, 23). One in particular comes from a ditch level *above* a fill containing charred grain, which produced calibrated radiocarbon dates of AD 780–990 and AD 883–1014, both calculated to two standard deviations (Russell *et al.* 2007, 20–1). While none of the finds from the lowest level of either ditch preclude deposition at an earlier date, they are entirely compatible with Viking-Age activity. Thus, the latest research indicates that the Viking-Age settlement was established on a site which had not previously been enclosed, and which has not yet produced any secure evidence for earlier occupation. The reasons for the backfilling of one ditch and the construction of another just outside it are not presently understood, but it may be noted that the aforementioned kink in these ditches at the boundary between the two fields (fig. 4.1) also suggests two phases of activity at this site. As this latter feature has not been subject to excavation, however, it cannot be directly related to the ditches exposed in culvert one, on the opposite side of the northeastern field 23.

Culvert one also revealed the remains of a 'Viking' grave approximately 22 m outside the entrance feature. While the acidic soil had removed all traces of the body and its upper levels had been disturbed by ploughing, the grave was remarkably well-furnished, at least by insular standards. The grave goods included a (broken) sword, spearhead, axehead, and shield boss, as well as a ringed pin, whetstone, knife, and some other small artefacts (O'Brien and Russell 2005, 121–2). While of a rare type, the sword hilt suggests a deposition date in the 9th century, which would make it broadly contemporary with the ditch, the majority of finds recovered from the topsoil, and indeed the major phase of occupation at the site.

The Woodstown grave is presently one of only a handful of 'Viking' graves from Britain and Ireland that can be directly linked to a contemporary settlement, and the site is exceptional in other ways too, particularly in the number and quality of its finds. While few other Viking-Age sites have been subject to similar, exhaustive sieving and metal detection, it is difficult to believe that such a rich material culture was common to all settlements in the period. While analysis is ongoing, finds include high-status artefacts, notably a group of *c.* 38 fragments of silver, pieces of weapons, beads and mounts. There are also more mundane artefacts such as nails and rivets, of which *c.* 1,663 examples have been recovered; not all date from the early medieval period, but 566 have been identified as 'possibly Viking Age or medieval' and associated with boat repair at the site (J. Bill *pers. comm.*). This was far from the only manufacturing activity at the site, with particularly good evidence for metalworking. No less than 140 smithing hearth 'cakes' were found spread across the site, and there is also evidence for metalworking within the (outer) ditch exposed in culvert one (Russell *et al.* 2007, 36). Most metalworking seems to have involved iron, but there is more limited evidence for the working of copper alloy, silver and lead (McNamara 2005, 126). Excavations at the rectilinear structure produced no less than 47 crucible fragments, as well as a substantial number of rotary sharpening stones (elsewhere burnishing stones), finds which point to extensive metalworking in the area (Russell *et al.* 2007, 78). While metalworking evidence was found across the site, it seems to have been focused in the southwestern field, close to the Killoteran stream. Here, too, an extensive spread of heat-shattered stones was partially investigated, and found to seal older features (Russell *et al.* 2007, 12). Charcoal associated with this potential dumping area has produced a radiocarbon date of AD 870–1010, calibrated to two standard deviations (Russell *et al.* 2007, 148). Although no structural evidence has been located in the northeastern field, finds from this area seem to have been more domestic in character, including spindle whorls and other small artefacts (McNamara 2005, 126). It should be stressed, however, that there seems to have been considerable spatial overlap between areas of 'industrial' and 'domestic' activity at the site.

Woodstown: form, function and identity

Long before the various on-site investigations were complete, debate on Woodstown was well under way. This has focused almost exclusively on whether or not the site is a *longphort* in the archaeological sense. It now seems clear that activity at the site was focused in the 9th century, albeit with some material that may be slightly earlier or later, but with no secure evidence for activity before *c.* 750 or after *c.* 1000. This places the site firmly in the early Viking Age, and potentially the mid-late 9th century, when Dublin was enjoying its *longphort* phase and the term is most frequently used to refer to 'Viking' sites in the Irish annals (above). A subtler question relates to the ethnicity of the site's occupants. Were they 'Vikings', or at least of Scandinavian origin? Today, archaeologists are (justifiably!) wary of drawing direct links between material culture and ethnicity in any period, and in the case of the Irish Viking Age, in particular, it has been argued that there is no real difference between 'Irish' and 'Hiberno-Norse' material culture (Bradley 1988, 60). Woodstown, however, has produced a number of features, artefacts and assemblages that are not directly paralleled on any known Irish site, and they strongly suggest that at least some of the individuals living at the site had a lifestyle that was distinctive within the early medieval Irish *milieu*.

Perhaps the most obvious of these is the furnished burial. While excavations over the last 20 years have made it increasingly clear that small artefacts occasionally made their way into Irish graves in the medieval period, these are normally small items such as dress-fasteners, of little intrinsic worth. The deposition of weapons in graves, on the other hand, is essentially unknown in this period or the preceding Iron Age, with the one exception of the 9th and early 10th centuries – the early Viking Age (Harrison 2001, 61–2). While Halsall (2000, 263–4) has argued that comparable English graves need not necessarily represent 'Scandinavians', the fact remains that the Woodstown burial was created by people who were at least broadly familiar with an inhumation rite found in most areas of Viking settlement in these islands, and particularly common in Norway itself. Even if they were not themselves Scandinavian, at least some of Woodstown's inhabitants were clearly aligning themselves with that funerary tradition. The fact that only one grave of this type has been found at Woodstown does not in itself indicate these 'Vikings' were in the minority at the site. Across Britain and Ireland, approximately three of every four 'Viking' burial sites are represented by single graves (Harrison 2008, 68). The prominent position of the Woodstown grave relative to the entrance feature, combined with the deposition of all three 'Viking' weapons (Solberg 1985, 66–7), points to a burial of some considerable importance.

Within the enclosure, many of the finds also point to Scandinavian associations. While almost nothing is known of Irish wooden boat-building traditions before the Viking Age (Pochin Mould 2001), rivets are rarely, if ever, found on contemporary Irish sites, but are relatively common in 10th- and 11th-century levels at Dublin, a site with strong Hiberno-Norse associations (McGrail 1993, 45–7). The Woodstown rivets point to maritime activity at the site, which would not be out of place in other parts of the Scandinavian world.

Another striking artefact group from Woodstown is the lead weight assemblage. A total of 215 have now been recovered from the site, with weights apparently focused at 11 and 22 g (McNamara 2005, 127; Russell *et al.* 2007, 78). Again, the only comparable assemblage comes from Hiberno-Norse Dublin, where 'at least two hundred' examples have been found (Wallace 1987, 212). Away from the Hiberno-Norse towns, lead is a rare find on contemporary sites in

Ireland, and weights of any type are essentially unknown. Silver, on the other hand, was widely used (or at least hoarded) by Irish groups during the Viking Age, but the introduction of large quantities of the metal to Ireland is closely associated with Scandinavian activity (Sheehan 2004, 178, 181). Two Kufic coins from Woodstown point to the importation of at least some silver, presumably along Scandinavian communication routes (McNamara 2005, 128; Russell *et al.* 2007, 78). More importantly, the overwhelming majority of the 38 silver artefacts from Woodstown is hack-silver, fragments cut from larger artefacts, presumably in the course of trade or exchange. Both the weights and size of the hack-silver fragments imply the regular and perhaps repeated exchange of relatively small quantities of bullion at the site (Russell *et al.* 2007, 34–5). Across Ireland generally, hack-silver hoards are rather rare (Sheehan 2004, 187).

It would be a mistake, however, to view Woodstown as an entirely 'Scandinavian' site. Many artefacts have strong Irish or insular connections. Even some of the grave-goods, notably the ringed pin and the shield boss, are of insular origin, and other artefacts and assemblages are in no way atypical of contemporary Irish sites. While it might be argued that the Woodstown assemblage is distinctive because of the site's economy rather than the putative ethnicity of its inhabitants, there are clear parallels between Woodstown and other known insular Scandinavian sites of the 9th century, from Dublin to Torksey (Lincolnshire) (Blackburn 2002). This must indicate that these sites operated within a similar ethnic, as well as socio-economic, *milieu*.

Those commentators who have been keenest to identify Woodstown as a *longphort* have, of course, emphasised its 'military' rather than its 'economic' characteristics, most notably its defences and the associated 'warrior' grave. To see the rite of weapon burial as exclusively military is, however, problematic: while it is no coincidence that weapons were symbols of power in this period, those buried in this way were no 'mere' Vikings. Graves such as that at Woodstown represent respected members of essentially settled communities with a vested interest in preserving local social hierarchies and other distinctions (Harrison 2008, 103–4). Evidence for Woodstown's defences is also problematic. Enclosed sites were virtually unknown in contemporary Scandinavia, and (with the obvious exception of the Irish ringfort) seem to have been rare in 9th- and even 10th-century insular contexts. As Wallace (1985, 109–10) has pointed out in the case of Dublin, defensive banks and ditches may be a feature of the insular rather than the Scandinavian world. More specifically, it will be noted that even Woodstown's outer ditch was never particularly substantial, seems to have silted up relatively quickly, and was used as a shelter for a metalworking hearth at much the same time that the site was in use (Russell *et al.* 2007, 31–2). Whatever the reasons for the ditch's construction, defence does not seem to have been a priority for much of the period when the site was occupied.

Of course, none of this evidence negates the possibility that Woodstown functioned as a base for a group of Viking raiders who sought to exploit the Suir valley from a site located on the border between the Irish kingdoms of the Déisi and Osraige (Russell *et al.* 2007, 6). It does, however, point to a site with a far more complex socio-economic character than is normally assumed for *longphuirt*. While the site's metalworkers may well have served a military elite, their presence transforms our understanding of the site, which was clearly much more than a simple defended camp. There is also clear evidence that Woodstown operated within an economic framework that extended far beyond the immediate area, at least on occasion. At a more local level, the weights and hack-silver point to a complex exchange mechanism within the site that clearly went beyond the reward of loyal warriors and included the regular transfer of small quantities of silver. Whatever the influence of the excavation's recovery strategy on find numbers and types, their quantity and quality leaves no doubt that the settlement was exceptionally wealthy, at least by the standards of the 9th century. If the ultimate source of this wealth was, as many have suggested, raiding or tribute, then at least some of this new-found affluence was exchanged at a local level, and alternative or related models of wealth creation and exchange cannot be ruled out, at least using archaeological evidence.

Woodstown: *a longphort?*

Was Woodstown a *longphort*? Given the presence of boat rivets, the 'Viking' character of much of its material culture, and indeed its morphology, a refusal to designate this site as a *longhphort* would essentially rob the word of any intrinsic meaning. If, however, all sites called *longphuirt* in the 9th and early 10th centuries functioned as similar centres of production and exchange, then there is a need for a radical revision of our interpretation not just of these sites but of our understanding of the period as a whole, for the exchange of wealth would then be radically more extensive and complex than has previously been believed. In reality, the term *longphort* was almost certainly applied to a wide range of sites from the very beginning, with Dublin, Woodstown and perhaps a handful of others representing (semi-)permanent sites at the apex of a phenomenon which included sites of varying sizes, forms, and military or economic significance. Nonetheless, the fact that such an important site as Woodstown does not seem to be recorded in any surviving Irish annals provides food for thought for all those seeking to reconcile historical and archaeological evidence.

Ultimately, splitting hairs on *longphuirt* and the relevance of the term to Woodstown may represent something of an intellectual *impasse* which detracts from a series of more interesting questions raised by the site, specifically its relationship to broader settlement trends and exchange mechanisms within these islands. In 1998, Clarke (1998, 379) suggested that while the 'Vikings' undoubtedly created Ireland's first recognisable towns, this process occurred much later than is generally thought, in the later 10th century at the earliest. Before this date, insular trade outside England was focused on small nucleated settlements, not necessarily with fixed populations (Clarke 1998, 339-43). In a related article, Griffiths (1992, 64–5) has pointed to a series of 'coastal trading sites' and other non-urban exchange points around the Irish Sea. As a nucleated site of considerable economic importance with direct sea access, Woodstown must have been related to these other sites in some way. Comparison with Meols, on the Wirral peninsula, may be every bit as significant as comparisons to Repton let alone Emly (Co. Tipperary) (above). Woodstown can also be compared to many of these sites because activity ceased there in the 10th century, when a whole series of new exchange centres were established around the Irish Sea (Griffiths 1992, 65). Under these circumstances, there can be little doubt that its decline is more or less directly linked to the developing importance of Waterford, some 5 km downstream.

Despite its ultimate failure, however, Woodstown was clearly an important centre in the early Viking Age, and represents one of the most important discoveries of the last 30 years, not just in Ireland but further afield. The present *longphort* debate has focused discussion on the site's morphology and alleged military character. While these are self-evidently important aspects of the site, they have detracted attention from its clear economic significance, and from some of the subtleties of its material culture, which its excavators and other commentators are only beginning to address. Whatever its classification, this evidence points to the complexity of life, and indeed death, in a nucleated settlement established in 9th-century Ireland.

Acknowledgements

Thanks to Ian Russell, director of the Woodstown excavations, ACS Ltd, the National Roads Authority and DoEHLG for their support in producing this paper, which is based on publicly available information. Dr. E. Bhreathnach was kind enough to read an early draft of this paper. This paper was prepared while the author was an IRCHSS post-doctoral fellow at the School of Archaeology, UCD.

Bibliography

Biddle, M. and Kjølbye-Biddle, B. (2001) Repton and the 'great heathen army', 873–4. In J. Graham-Campbell, R. A. Hall, J. Jesch and D. N. Parsons (eds) *Vikings and the Danelaw: select papers from the proceedings of the thirteenth Viking Congress, 21–30 August 1997*, 45–96. Oxford, Oxbow.

Blackburn, M. A. S. (2002) Finds from the Anglo-Scandinavian site of Torksey, Lincolnshire. In R. Kiersnowski, S. K. Kuczynski, M. Meclewska and M. Mielczarek (eds) *Moneta Mediævalis: studia numizmatyczne i historyczne ofiarowane Professorowi Stanislawowi Sucholdolskiemu*, 89–101. Warsaw, DiG.

Bradley, J. (1988) The interpretation of Scandinavian settlement in Ireland. In J. Bradley (ed.) *Settlement and Society in Medieval Ireland: studies presented to F. X. Martin OSA*, 49–78. Kilkenny, Boethius.

Bhreathnach, E. (1998) Saint Patrick, Vikings and *Inber Dée – Longphort* in the early Irish literary tradition. *Wicklow Archaeology and History* 1, 36–40.

Clarke, H. B. (1990) The topographical development of early medieval Dublin. In H. B. Clarke (ed.) *Medieval Dublin: the making of a metropolis*, 52–69. Dublin, Four Courts Press.

Clarke, H. B. (1998) Proto-towns and towns in Ireland and Britain. In H. B. Clarke, M. Ní Mhaonaigh and R. Ó Floinn (eds) *Ireland and Scandinavia in the Early Viking Age*, 331–80. Dublin, Four Courts Press.

Etchingham, C. (1994) Evidence for Scandinavian settlement in County Wicklow. In K. Hannigan and W. Nolan (eds) *Wicklow: history and society. Interdisciplinary essays on the history of an Irish county*, 113–38. Dublin, Geography Publications.

Fanning, T. (1983) Co. Westmeath. Ballaghkearan Little, Athlone (N073445). Medieval Britain and Ireland in 1982. *Medieval Archaeology* 27, 221.

Glare, P. G. W. (ed.) (2006) *Oxford Latin Dictionary*. Oxford, Oxford University Press.

Graham-Campbell, J. (1976) The Viking Age silver hoards of Ireland. In B. Almqvist and D. Greene (eds) *Proceedings of the Seventh Viking Congress*, 39–74. Dublin, Royal Irish Academy.

Griffiths, D. (1992) The coastal trading ports of the Irish Sea. In J. Graham-Campbell (ed.) *Viking Treasure from the North West: the Cuerdale hoard in its context*, 63–72. Liverpool, Liverpool Museum.

Halpin, A. (2005) Development phases in Hiberno-Norse Dublin: a tale of two cities. In S. Duffy (ed.) *Medieval Dublin VI*, 94–113. Dublin, Four Courts Press.

Halsall, G. (2000) The Viking presence in England? The burial evidence reconsidered. In D. M. Hadley and J. D. Richards (eds) *Cultures in Contact: Scandinavian settlement in England in the ninth and tenth centuries*, 259–76. Turnhout, Brepols.

Harrison, S. H. (2001) Viking graves and grave-goods in Ireland. In A. C. Larsen (ed.) *The Vikings in Ireland*, 61–75. Roskilde, Viking Ship Museum.

Harrison, S. H. (2008) *Furnished Insular Scandinavian Burial. Artefacts and landscape in the early Viking Age*. Unpublished PhD thesis, Trinity College Dublin.

Kelly, E. P. (2009) Re-evaluation of a supposed inland promontory fort. Knoxpark, Co. Sligo: Iron Age fortress or Viking stronghold? In G. Cooney, K. Becker, J. Coles, M. Ryan and S. Sievers (eds) *Relics of Old Decency: archaeological studies in later prehistory: Festschrift for Barry Raftery*, 485–97. Bray, Wordwell.

Kelly, E. P. and O'Donovan, E. (1998) A Viking longphort near Athlunkard, Co. Clare. *Archaeology Ireland* 12, 13–16.

Kelly, E. P. and Maas, J. (1999) The Vikings and the Kingdom of Laois. In P. G. Lane and W. Nolan (eds) *Laois: History and Society. Interdisciplinary essays on the history of an Irish county*, 123–60. Dublin, Geography Publications.

Mac Airt, S. (ed.) (1944) *The Annals of Inisfallen (MS. Rawlinson B.503)*. Dublin, Dublin Institute for Advanced Studies.

Mac Airt, S. and Mac Niocaill, G. (ed. and trans.) (1983) *The Annals of Ulster (to A.D. 1131)*. Dublin, Dublin Institute for Advanced Studies.

McGrail, S. (1993) *Medieval Boat and Ship Timbers from Dublin*. Medieval Dublin excavations 1962–81 B.3. Dublin, Royal Irish Academy.

McNamara, S. (2005) Woodstown 6: the finds. In J. O'Sullivan and M. Stanley (eds) *Recent Archaeological Discoveries on National Road Schemes 2004*, 125–30. National Roads Authority, Dublin.

Moore, E. (1988) *Longphort* and *Dúnad* in early medieval Ireland. *Trowel* 1, 31–2. Dublin, University College Dublin Archaeological Society.

O'Brien, R. and Russell, I. (2005) The Hiberno-Scandinavian site of Woodstown 6, Co. Waterford. In J. O'Sullivan and M. Stanley (eds) *Recent Archaeological Discoveries on National Road Schemes 2004*, 111–24. Dublin, National Roads Authority.

O'Brien, R., Quinney, P. and Russell, I. (2005) Preliminary report on the archaeological excavation and finds retrieval strategy of the Hiberno-Scandinavian site of Woodstown 6, County Waterford. *Decies* 61, 13–122.

Ó Cróinín, D. (1995) *Early Medieval Ireland 400–1200*. London, Longman.

O'Donovan, J. (ed. and trans.) (1848 & 1851) *Annals of the Kingdom of Ireland by the Four Masters from the Earliest Period to the Year 1616* (7 vols). Dublin, Hodges and Smith.

Ó Floinn, R. (1998) The archaeology of the early Viking Age in Ireland. In H. B. Clarke, M. Ní Mhaonaigh and R. Ó Floinn (eds) *Ireland and Scandinavia in the Early Viking Age*, 131–65. Dublin, Four Courts Press.

Pochin Mould, D. (2001) The sailing ships of ancient Ireland. *Archaeology Ireland* 15.1, 15–18.

Quin, E. G. (ed.) (1983) *Dictionary of the Irish Language based on Old and Middle Irish Materials: compact edition*. Dublin, Royal Irish Academy.

Russell, I., Harrison, S. H., Nicholls, J., Kinsella, J., McNamara, S. and O'Hare, M. (2007) *Woodstown 6 Supplementary Research Project*. Unpublished Report, ACS Ltd for DoEHLG (available at http://www.environ.ie/en/Publications/Heritage/NationalMonuments).

Ryan, J. (1990) Pre-Norman Dublin. In H. B. Clarke (ed.) *Medieval Dublin: the making of a metropolis*, 110–27. Blackrock, Four Courts Press.

Sheehan, J. (2004) Social and economic integration in Viking-Age Ireland: the evidence from hoards. In J. Hines, A. Lane and M. Redknap (eds) *Land, Sea and Home: proceedings of a conference on Viking-period settlement, at Cardiff, July 2001*, 177–88. Society for Medieval Archaeology Monograph 20. Leeds, Maney.

Simpson, L. (2005) Viking warrior burials in Dublin: is this the *longphort*? In S. Duffy (ed.) *Medieval Dublin VI*, 11–62. Dublin, Four Courts Press.

Solberg, B. (1985) Social status in the Merovingian and Viking periods in Norway from archaeological and historical sources. *Norwegian Archaeological Review* 18, 61–76.

Taylor, R. E. (1987) *Radiocarbon Dating: an archaeological perspective*. Orlando, Academic.

Wallace, P. F. (1985) The archaeology of Viking Dublin. In H. B. Clarke and A. Simms (eds.) *The Comparative History of Urban Origins in Non-Roman Europe*, 103–45. British Archaeological Reports International Series 255(i). Oxford, British Archaeological Reports.

Wallace, P. F. (1987) The economy and commerce of Viking Age Dublin. In K. Düwel, H. Jankuhn, H. Siems and D. Timpe (eds) *Untersuchungen zu Handel und Verkehr der vor- und frühgeschichtlichen Zeit in Mittel- und Nordeuropa*, 200–45. Göttingen, Vandenhoeck and Ruprecht.

Wallace, P. F. (1990) The origins of Dublin. In H. B. Clarke (ed.) *Medieval Dublin: the making of a metropolis*, 70–97. Dublin, Four Courts Press.

5

FROM COUNTRY TO TOWN: SOCIAL TRANSITIONS IN VIKING-AGE HOUSING

Rebecca Boyd

This chapter considers how daily life can be explored through the architecture of Viking-Age towns in Ireland. Most previous work on this urban architecture has focused on construction styles or classification of the architecture, rather than delving into how the people who lived there used the houses as their homes. The life of the household was contained within the plot, which acted as both home and workplace. This chapter considers how the plot boundaries may have acted as fixed points of reference for the household, creating a sense of place and links to the past. The so-called Hiberno-Norse Type 1 house is the main building in each plot, but attention is paid to the other buildings and features in the plot as key locations in the daily life of the household. Finally, the chapter explores the role of women in the Viking-Age town and considers how their daily work sustained the family and was of central, if subconscious, importance within the home. The chapter focuses primarily on Dublin, because it has the most extensive archaeological evidence, but supporting evidence is drawn from other Viking-Age towns such as Waterford, York and Lincoln.

Much of the supporting evidence in this chapter comes from the surviving historical and literary sources. These texts give an astonishingly detailed view of daily life during the early medieval and Viking periods, but the nature of these documents should be acknowledged. The laws represent the ideal standards of society, to which all members of society must aspire, while the sagas and literary tales were mass entertainment. Accordingly, neither can be accepted as mirror images of reality and the very existence of the laws implies that real life did not always meet those standards. In addition, both the Irish and Icelandic sources depict a rural way of life, not an urban one (Kelly 1988, 6–7). Finally, there is a significant chronological discontinuity between all these sources. The Irish laws date from 6th- to 10th-century Ireland, while the Icelandic sagas purport to represent the 9th and 10th centuries but were not transcribed until the 13th and 14th centuries. These chronological gaps make it very difficult to transfer implications from the texts to the Viking Age, but it is possible to draw some cautious inferences about the way society may have been organised in the Viking Age.

A sense of place

The occupants of the first town in Ireland – Dublin – must have felt that they were in unfamiliar territory in the middle of the 9th century. The town was a new phenomenon, and while it was close to existing monastic and secular sites, it was not associated with either of them (Simpson 1999, 5). There is some evidence for 8th-century settlement at Temple Bar West, but this was overlain by plough marks indicating that this land had returned to agricultural use (Simpson 1999, 9–12) before becoming the site of the town. The new townspeople were encountering a new way of life, and the new town had not yet acquired its own past. The most enduring and striking features of the Irish Viking-Age towns are the distinct property plots that contained each household. Permanent plot boundaries have been excavated in the earliest levels of Dublin, Waterford, Wexford and Cork. These boundaries are usually indicated by the remains of post-and-wattle fences, which were repaired and rebuilt on the same lines for centuries (Wallace 2005, 24). Even if no physical fence remains, it is possible to read the boundaries of properties through the site stratigraphy. Wallace (2000, 263) rightly identifies these boundaries as 'the very essence of town life'. Biddle (1976, 100) identified houses and urban plots as two of the key characteristics of urbanism in Anglo-Saxon England, and this view has dominated subsequent studies of urbanism. Wallace argues that understanding the boundaries is crucial to understanding how the people of the Viking-Age towns related to each other. It is possible that the plot boundaries helped to re-create and then maintain a sense of place for the townspeople, and that they allowed them to establish their own past and create a sense of belonging in this new settlement.

Easthope (2004, 131–2) defines place as 'a very influential force in one's life' that provides one with 'a sense of belonging and comfort'. Both native Irish and Scandinavian patterns of settlement had been to establish farmsteads and homes and then for successive generations to re-build on the same site (for example, see Lynn 1994; Hamerow 2002; Munch *et al.* 2003). This created settlement continuity and links to the past in both societies, which new townspeople, whether of Irish or Scandinavian descent, would have found lacking in the early decades of Dublin. Easthope (2004, 130) distinguishes between a conscious awareness of place – a sense of place – and an unselfconscious feeling of being comfortable in your place – rootedness. The creation and maintenance of the plot boundaries indicates an awareness of place and a deliberate attempt to create a new sense of place and a feeling of belonging, as well as a claim to the land. Once established, the positions of the plot boundaries virtually never changed and their original lines were faithfully curated. One gets the impression that the changing of boundary lines was not 'allowed'. Simpson (2006, 113) suggests that there was nothing special about the fixed nature of these boundaries, but it is exactly this unchanging nature that makes these boundaries remarkable. Wallace (2000, 265) suggests that the boundaries may have been imposed by a civic authority, but there is little to indicate the existence of such an authority in Viking-Age Dublin. Moreover, the fact that these boundary 'rules' are almost never breached implies that the whole of society accepted and agreed upon them, rather than that they were imposed upon an unwilling populace. There must have been a remarkable level of social cohesion to allow the boundaries to last.

Their remarkable nature is illustrated by the only two cases in which boundaries were significantly altered, both of which occurred at Temple Bar West. This site provides the earliest habitation evidence, and also demonstrates continuity of settlement through the supposed abandonment of Dublin in the early 10th century. One of the most remarkable features of Temple Bar West is a wholesale re-orientation of the domestic settlement in the early 10th century (fig. 5.1). The 9th-century settlement was laid out on the eastern side of the site and

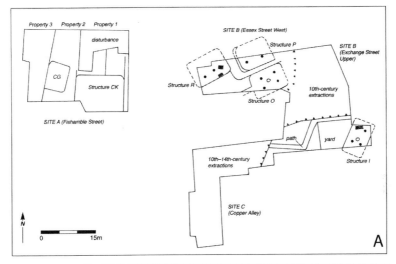

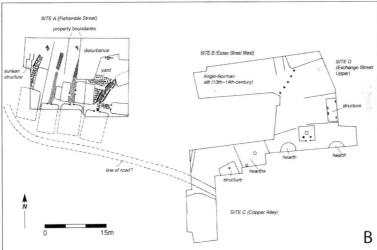

Fig. 5.1 These plans show the change in property orientations at Temple Bar West. A illustrates the early properties oriented along an east-west axis on the east of the site. B demonstrates the movement of properties to the west of the site and the amalgamated familial plot 5/6 is visible at the right of Site A (reproduced from Simpson 1999, figs 10 and 16; permission to reproduce granted by Linzi Simpson).

had property plots oriented in an east-west direction. However, in Level 7 (early 10th century), the east of the site was converted to industrial use, the housing moved to the west and seven new north-south oriented properties were established. The excavator associates this with the return of Viking power in AD 917 and suggests it represents an 'urban renewal' of the existing settlement (Simpson 2002, 832). If the property boundaries did act as a connection to the past, it is possible to suggest that this re-orientation was not only an 'urban renewal' but also a disconnection from the past. It is somewhat ironic, then, that after this dramatic re-orientation the social status of the residents of Temple Bar West diminished; the houses were less well made, lower quality materials were used for repairs, and the artefacts found are of a poorer quality.

The other example comes from Level 12 (spanning the mid-11th to 12th centuries) of the site where four of the north-south plots were adjusted (Simpson 2002, 599–638). Plot 4 was widened by over one metre, while plots 5, 6, and 7 were amalgamated to form a single substantial household. It seems that there were close relationships between the households in plots 5 and 6 from Level 7 onwards when the main house on each plot shared not only the same foundation deposit but also boundary fences (Simpson 2002, 296). Simpson (1999, 30) suggests that this decision to reorganise property boundaries was a family choice, perhaps a result of marriage. It implies long-term, probably familial, occupation of the same property plots and neighbourhood. The local scale of this alteration contrasts strongly with the Level 7 re-orientation, which affected the entire neighbourhood. These are the only two examples of boundary alterations in the Irish Viking-Age towns, and even when construction styles change, as they do in 12th-century Waterford (Hurley *et al.* 1997, 106), the boundaries do not change. Similarly in York (England) (Hall 1994, 64), the introduction of sill beam construction in the late 10th century did not result in boundary movement. Excavations at Flaxengate in Lincoln also demonstrated continuity of boundaries throughout the Anglo-Scandinavian period (Perring 1981).

The initial establishment of the boundaries created a 'sense of place' in the new town, marked out new settlements, and helped the new townspeople to belong in their new environment. It was the maintenance of those boundaries over centuries that fostered the development of 'rootedness' in the towns, and allowed their descendants to feel at home.

Buildings ordering movement

While the plot boundaries played an important social role in establishing continuity within the townscape, they were also very practical. They were barriers restricting the movement of people and animals and they distinguished and separated one household from the next. In the Irish countryside, privacy in and around the home was highly valued (Ó Corráin 1983, 250), and an 8th-century legal text, the *Crith Gablach*, notes fines assigned to breaches of privacy. These range from one cow, for looking into another's house, up to 5 *séts*, for crossing the courtyard or opening the door to the house (a *sét* is a unit of fixed value, equivalent to half a milch cow; Kelly 1988, 10). There was an acceptable code of behaviour in relation to other people's property, but this code applied in the countryside where people lived in relative isolation. In the towns, people were living only a few metres away from each other with neighbours on all sides. In

Fig. 5.2 (opposite) The Hiberno-Norse building typology. A) Type 1 and Type 5; B) Type 2; C) Type 3 (all from Fishamble Street, Dublin); D-E) Type 4 (from Peter Street, Waterford, and Temple Bar West, Dublin); F) Type 6; G) Type 7 (both from Peter Street, Waterford) (A-C reproduced from Wallace 1992, figs 84, 101 and 114; permission to reproduce granted by National Museum of Ireland. D, F-G reproduced from Hurley et al. 1997, figs 6.2, 6.65 and 6.115; permission to reproduce granted by Maurice Hurley and Orla Scully. E reproduced from Simpson 1999, fig. 9; permission to reproduce granted by Linzi Simpson).

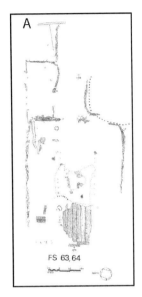

FS 63,64

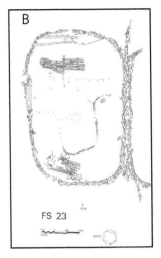

FS 23

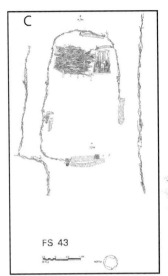

FS 43

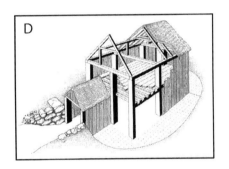

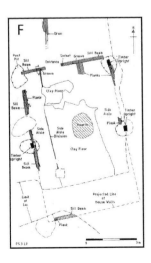

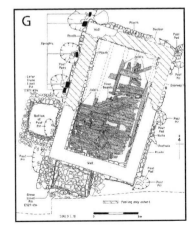

Rebecca Boyd

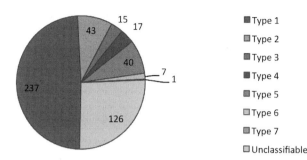

■ Type 1
□ Type 2
■ Type 3
■ Type 4
□ Type 5
□ Type 6
■ Type 7
□ Unclassifiable

Fig. 5.3 This chart shows the current known totals for each category of the Hiberno-Norse building typology. There are 486 structures in total, but the Type 4, 6, and 7 buildings are 12th century and later in date. 126 structures are not classifiable to type.

this context, the plot boundaries may have been social barriers between households, creating an illusion of household privacy and allowing the townspeople to live in close proximity. The height of the boundary fences may have helped to maintain a degree of visual separation. Ó Corráin (1983) explores the legal references to fencing in the *Bretha Comaithchesa* ('The Judgements of Neighbourhood'), in particular to the types of fences erected between the lands of inheriting kinsmen. This legal text from the late 7th century states that fences of stone, post-and-wattle, or oak must be maintained at a height of 12 fists or 1.8 metres (one fist is 6 inches, or 15 centimetres). Most reconstruction drawings of urban landscapes depict the fences at waist height but there is no archaeological evidence for or against doing so. If the urban fences were closer in height to the rural boundaries, this would increase the illusion of privacy between the plots, allowing each household a greater feeling of seclusion.

There are seven different types of building found in the Viking-Age plots and these are categorised in the Hiberno-Norse Building Typology (fig. 5.2) (Wallace 2005). Figure 5.3 provides the most recent breakdown of numbers of building in each class. Types 1, 2, 3, and 5 are all post-and-wattle buildings, while Type 4, 6, and 7 are sunken-floored houses, sill-beam houses, and stone houses respectively. Most attention has been focused on the rectangular Type 1 house, which is the main residential building. This is the most commonly excavated building type, and has an average floor area of 40m² which is divided into three longitudinal strips by free standing roof supports which dominate the interior of these buildings. There is a central hearth and raised bedding platforms against the side walls, whilst each end wall usually features a doorway. Types 4, 6, and 7 appear from the middle of the 12th century onwards and fall outside the focus of this chapter. The Type 1 house is always placed end-on to the street in each plot, but beyond this there are no rules for laying out the space. Each plot could contain a combination of outbuildings and other features such as middens, wells, cesspits, pathways and kitchen gardens. These outbuildings are generally categorised as Type 2 or Type 3 buildings (smaller houses interpreted as additional living space) (also see McAlister, this volume), or as Type 5 structures. This miscellaneous Type 5 class includes animal pens, storage sheds, workshops and huts but it is misleadingly simple and conceals the full variety of functions, and occupations that existed in each plot.

Common to almost every plot are the pathways that create safe passage across damp or subsiding ground and link the different areas in the plots (Wallace 2000, 272). These well-built stone, timber and wattle paths often remain in existence over two or three phases of housing within the plot. The buildings themselves were in a constant cycle of repair, abandonment, destruction and rebuilding. Estimates of the lifespan of the Type 1 house vary from 15 to 30 years, while the average life expectancy in this period was roughly 30–40 years. In contrast, the paths could remain in use for anything from 45 to 60 years; the average Dubliner may have seen his home rebuilt three times in his life, but the pathways through the plot may not have changed at all. In addition, there is some evidence that the function of outbuildings could also change. Analyses at Temple Bar West tell us that at least one structure was originally used as an animal pen and was subsequently occupied by people (Reilly 2003, 47–8). In this environment of change, the movements from the main house to, around, and through the yard and outbuildings were constants in the daily life of the household.

As the main residence, the Type 1 house would be used on a continuous basis, but the other elements of the plot may have been used much less often, depending on their functions. Cesspits would have been used very regularly, and animals kept within the plot would have needed daily care; these may have been the most commonly visited features on each plot. On the other hand, storage huts may have been left unused for days or weeks at a time, if they were only required seasonally (although given the limited space in the urban landscape, it is unlikely that many buildings were used on an irregular basis). Workshops also may not have been required on a daily basis as craft production may not have been a daily activity. Hall (1994, 106) has suggested that bone comb production at Coppergate (York) was undertaken by itinerant combmakers, because there was insufficient debris to suggest permanent full-time working and because the debris was concentrated around the main house rather than in a dedicated workshop (see also Ashby, this volume). Preliminary analyses of artefacts and debris suggests that there were workshops in Temple Bar West, such as structure Q – a probable smithy – and AU, which may be a wood workshop (Simpson 2002). The presence of such dedicated buildings implies a more permanent commitment to these crafts, and makes it less likely that – at least in these plots – there were itinerant craftsmen. Rather, the occupants of these plots were sufficiently well established in their craft to make a significant investment through the reservation of dedicated craft spaces.

With the exception of Reilly's (2003) work at Temple Bar West, there have been no targeted studies of any of these ancillary buildings and their functions remain unclear. One building in need of closer analysis is the Type 2 house, which is usually interpreted as residential because of its hearths and wattle flooring. It is usually viewed as sub-ordinate to the Type 1 house because of its smaller size and location behind the main house. Indeed, the doorways of the two buildings are often aligned towards each other with paths leading directly between them clearly indicating close connections. Suggestions about who lived in the Type 2 house have included women giving birth, the infirm or elderly, or children (Wallace 1992, 15; see also McAlister, this volume). However, not every Type 1 house was associated with a Type 2 house, suggesting that not every household required one and that, therefore, its function was not one shared across society. Almost half of the Type 2 houses contain hearths, which would make it unlikely that in these houses children would have been left there unsupervised – fire is a constant danger in a wooden building. One possibility is that these houses were intended for persons of some importance. I have suggested elsewhere that some of these buildings may have been provided with their own access routes, which would allow the resident to receive guests without the knowledge of those who lived in the main house (Boyd 2009). The presence of hearths in some Type 2 houses may lend extra weight to this argument that the resident was someone of a relatively high social status. Householders must provide food and drink to visitors and passers-by, or be fined and suffer a slight to their honour (Kelly 1988, 139–40). If the occupant of a Type 2 house had their own hearth they could offer hospitality to their guests on their own terms, and without the intervention of the rest of the household.

The household

The documentary sources suggest that the standard family grouping across Ireland and Scandinavia was relatively similar and probably consisted of the immediate family (parents and children) and the extended family (grandparents, aunts and uncles, cousins). Fosterage was common in early medieval Ireland, and apparently also occurred among Scandinavian families (Valante 2008, 90–4), so households may have included children or young adults who were not blood-relations. Noble or higher-status households would have included retainers such as warriors, advisors, and servants (Kelly 1988, 65). Slavery was common, and whilst royal households and many farmsteads would have included slaves (Valante 2008, 87), it is uncertain to what extent slaves were present in the towns. There may also have been different types of households that were not kin-based (Brink 2008, 28); perhaps groups of warriors living in barracks (Christiansen 2006, 52–8), or priests living on their own or with a housekeeper. Overall, there seem to be considerable similarities between these idealised families, and, at a practical level, the transition from a Scandinavian or an Irish household to an urban Hiberno-Scandinavian household was probably relatively simple, at least in terms of the people that it contained. It is impossible to explore how all the different people within that household may have experienced daily life in this chapter. Instead, the remainder of this chapter will explore how women may have experienced life in the towns.

A woman's life

Integrated readings of the archaeology and the texts such as those provided by Jesch (1991), McAlister (2003) and Dommasnes (2008) paint a much clearer picture of women's life in the Viking Age than either type of evidence can do on its own. The typical Scandinavian housewife took charge of the care and sustenance of the house and the household, as illustrated by the grave goods she was provided with for the afterlife in some graves (Jesch 1991, 9–41): keys show her in charge of the food chests and of feeding her household; tools demonstrate her daily work, most often in textile production or cooking; the weights and balances indicate her role in trade and her function in looking after the wealth of the household. The number of furnished female graves represents only a tiny proportion of the original female population of Scandinavia (Dommasnes 1982), but the presence of all these items in non-funerary contexts lends weight to interpretations of these grave goods as relatively realistic impressions of daily life. According to the medieval documentary sources, women kept possession of their own goods in marriage, and the presence of runestones paid for by women and commemorating women indicate that they had some economic standing (Christiansen 2006, 17–21). If her husband passed away, she could act as head of household, usually in trust for a son or other male figure, or, if the marriage failed, she could return to her own family with her goods. During the Viking Age, women enjoyed a relative degree of freedom in their daily life, but the introduction of Christianity curtailed this somewhat after the 10th century, relegating women to a place of lesser status (Jesch 1991, 204).

There are as yet no studies of women's lives in Viking-Age Ireland that integrate the archaeological and literary evidence, and also reconcile the Scandinavian and other foreign influences on the Irish woman. There are only a few female furnished Viking-Age graves in Ireland, but the picture they paint is, unsurprisingly, very similar to that found in women's furnished graves in Scandinavia. The historical sources can provide some insight into native Irish women's daily activities (McAlister 2003, 149–54; O'Sullivan 2008, 243–4). These included farm work, tending animals, housework, food production, textile production and childcare, as well as caring for the sick and elderly. In some regards, the Irish woman was freer than her Scandinavian counterpart, in that she could instigate divorce proceedings. Very occasionally, she could also achieve high status as a female poet, builder, physician, or holy woman. In reality, her 'independent legal capacity' was limited and Irish women in the 6th to 9th centuries belonged to their nearest male kin (Kelly 1988, 75–6). The 9th-century *Trecheng Breth Féne* ('The Triads of Ireland') is a compilation of proverbs and gnomic material and describes women's three best attributes as 'a steady tongue, a steady virtue, a steady housewifery' (Kelly 1988, 69). However, the adoption of Christianity in the early medieval period may have helped to improve the Irish woman's place in society, slowly allowing her to gain more equality over the centuries (Kelly 1988, 77).

These images seem to portray a clear image of Scandinavian and Irish womanhood, however this may be misleading. The texts vary considerably in date, from the 6th to the 14th centuries, and just how reflective these idealised depictions are of reality is debatable. Another issue to consider is the differing influences of the Christian Church in both societies – Ireland accepted Christianity in the 5th century, but 9th-century Scandinavia was, by and large, pagan (although the men who transcribed the Icelandic sagas in the 14th century were Christian). One must wonder how these opposite ideologies met and reconciled themselves in the Hiberno-Scandinavian milieu, not just in terms of women's roles, but how the rest of society reacted to these new ideas.

A woman's work

At a basic level much of the daily work of women on both sides of the North Sea must have been very similar. This work can be characterised as maintenance activities, 'the basic tasks … that regulate and stabilize social life' (Gonzáles-Marcén *et al.* 2008, 3), such as care giving, food preparation, cooking, textile production, medical care, hygiene, and child rearing. Maintenance activities are highly specialised activities, which must be learned and passed on to the next generations. They do not occur in isolation and require close contacts between those who possess these skills and those who must learn them, making these activities very sociable. The importance of maintenance activities has been downplayed in traditional historical and archaeological interpretations (Gonzáles-Marcén *et al.* 2008, 4), yet while they are not dramatic or startling activities, without them society will not survive (Gonzáles-Marcén *et al.* 2008, 8). In fact, Dommasnes (2008, 94) has argued that, without women's innovations in the development of sailcloth and waterproof textiles, the Viking Age would not have happened.

Textile production was a critical maintenance activity in Viking-Age Scandinavia (Dommasnes 2008, 95), and it is one of the most archaeologically visible crafts, through finds on both urban and rural sites of tools and of scraps of cloth, wool and garments. The farms described in sagas were often provided with buildings known as *dyngja*, women's buildings specifically associated with textile production (Milek 2006, 237). It has been suggested that Icelandic pit houses and Scandinavian sunken-floored huts are the archaeological remains of *dyngja* (Milek 2006, 236–40; Andersson 2007, 24). These sunken-floored buildings have prominent hearths and large numbers of apparently random postholes in the floor, and they consistently contain spindle whorls, loom weights and other weaving related implements.

Detailed artefact distributions are not published for any of the Irish excavations, but there is no apparent concentration of spindle whorls, loom weights or other weaving tools in any building known to this writer. Nor do any of the sunken-floored buildings (Hiberno-Norse Type 4 buildings) resemble the *dyngja*. The Irish laws make no mention of gender-specific buildings, either male or female, and, given the detail of these texts, it is unlikely that they would not have mentioned such buildings if they did exist. McAlister (2003, 154) has stated that textile production was a significant component of women's work in Ireland, but, as yet, there is no evidence to show that it was organised in the same way as on Scandinavian, or Icelandic, rural settlements. Walton Rogers (1997) carried out detailed analysis of the textile production at Coppergate in York, while work at Lincoln has also identified evidence for textile production (Stocker 2003). However, the conclusions are contrasting – Walton Rogers argues that the production at Coppergate was Anglo-Saxon in origin (Walton Rogers 1997, 1821–2), while Stocker (2003, 287) indicates that textile workers in Lincoln used a Scandinavian-style horizontal loom. Until further work is undertaken on the methods of textile production in the Irish towns, it is difficult to come to any definite conclusion about just who was producing textiles.

As yet, there is little evidence to show that Scandinavian women made up a significant proportion of the population of the Irish towns. There are few typically Scandinavian female graves in Ireland, which may imply that there were relatively few Scandinavian women present. It seems likely that the majority of women in the Viking-Age towns were of native descent, while the men were of native or foreign descent. If so, it is possible that these women were continuing to live and work using their own traditions, methods and ideologies. However, in a mixed environment like the Hiberno-Scandinavian towns, it may be as valuable to look for evidence of fusion of such traditions, rather than to search for the signs of an ethnically distinct Scandinavian or Irish identity. O'Sullivan (2008, 236–8) has identified a practice of depositing broken quernstones in Irish roundhouses as a way of attaching importance to food production and food producers – women. This may indicate that food production was an especially significant maintenance activity in early medieval Ireland. Brink (2008, 26–7) has also identified that hospitality was a key responsibility and providing generous hospitality was a method of establishing one's place in early Scandinavian society. In the towns, then, food production may have been an area where the maintenance activities of all members of society overlapped.

Our understanding of how food was acquired, stored, processed and consumed in towns is limited, but quernstones are present in occupation deposits implying that some food processing did occur. At FS72 in Fishamble Street, Dublin, two quernstones were excavated in post-abandonment layers, but, as they were not placed on the house floors, they cannot be seen as closing deposits. Inside the house, the hearth is the focus for food-related activities. During cooking, food and food waste was stored in small hollows scooped out of the floor around the hearth (Geraghty 1996, 69). Small postholes around the edge of the hearth indicate the use of cooking cranes, while stone, timber and clay kerbs could be used to section off parts of the hearth for different purposes (for example, in HSB/1, High Street, Dublin and FS88, Fishamble Street). The hearth is placed in the middle of the house and its significance lies in this central location. It dominates the house and is the feature around which other activity and movement must rotate.

The person in charge of the hearth not only ensures that the household is fed, but also plays a role in control of the access to and through the building because of their location at its heart (Boyd 2009). This positioning both physically and conceptually re-emphasises the importance of the hearth, and, by extension, indicates the importance within the household of those who prepared the food – the women. Returning to the Type 2 houses, this provides additional support for the theory that the occupants of houses that were provided with hearths were important. Famine was a constant threat in the countryside (Ó Corráin 2005, 578), and more so in these towns, because the townspeople were no longer self-sufficient. Instead, they had to rely on other people to supply their food. Food production and food security may have been becoming a more pressing issue in the towns, leading to a growth in the social importance of food-related maintenance activities. Food production is also an activity that all households must engage in, and it may have been a maintenance activity where different ethnic groups could engage with each other creating a common ground.

Social networks and change

The perpetuation of maintenance activities depends on large social networks enacting these activities on a regular basis (Gonzáles-Marcén *et al.* 2008, 4–5). This creates a cycle of learning, repetition, and teaching in which one generation instructs the next. In the countryside, each household had a relatively small social network of neighbours, family members and occasional visitors. Most people stayed close to home and only the learned and noble classes could travel freely around the country (Kelly 1988, 4–5). Dommasnes (2008, 94) argues that change to the practices of maintenance activities can have a beneficial effect on society, and that change is often detected through the 'slow and patient work' of those involved in maintenance activities. Within these small networks, there were fewer opportunities for outside influences to affect society, and change happened very slowly. Increases in social networks result in greater opportunities for modification of, and change in, daily life. The new towns were filled with strange and foreign traders, visitors, products, materials, and ideas. The social network of an urban household was much larger than a rural network and included more people but also greater influence from these people, both natives and foreigners.

In Ireland, these enlarged social networks resulted in the development of the Hiberno-Scandinavian material culture. This fusion of Irish, Scandinavian, and other elements is most obviously expressed in the art styles of 10th- to 12th-century urban Ireland, but is also visible in other elements such as language (see Wallace 2008 for the most recent discussion of this hybrid culture). There was rapid change in the Viking-Age town, but not in its architecture – the Type 1 house dominated the townscapes for four centuries. Even when a new construction style was introduced – sill beam construction – the three-aisled division remained in use, despite the absence of the roof supports, which were the original cause of that tri-partite division (Hurley *et al.* 1997, 106). Judith Flanders' study of the Victorian house notes a similar architectural stagnation in the mid-19th century and she suggests that this desire for a stable and unchanging home environment was a reaction to the 'dynamism … [and] … rapid technological change' of the world outside the home (Flanders 2004, xxi). This description could equally be applied to the world of the Viking-Age towns and relates to Easthope's observations about place. Easthope (2004, 133) concludes that when the world outside the home is in a state of change, the need and desire for a sense of belonging and place increases. The fast pace of change in the Irish towns and in Irish society may have been exactly why the townspeople sought to establish some continuity and stability by conserving their architecture and maintaining their sense of place through curating the established plot boundaries.

Conclusions

Houses are vital in understanding daily life because they are where daily life is enacted. The discussion began by exploring the social roles that the constant and unchanging boundaries played not only in separating household units, but also in creating a sense of place in urban settlements. These boundaries may, in an atmosphere of constant change and rebuilding of individual houses, also have acted as a connection to the past, linking generations of families through their stability. Changes in plot boundaries are very unusual, and when they do occur may mark a conscious decision to break with the past, as seen at Level 7 in Temple Bar West, or to change the future of individual households, as in Level 12. The family and household structures of both Ireland and Scandinavia seem to have been relatively close, but women probably experienced much the same work in their daily lives. Women's work consisted of maintenance activities geared towards sustaining the life of the household by feeding, clothing, and caring for the family. In the towns, it is possible that maintenance activities related to food production were important because the townspeople were no longer self-sufficient and they represented an arena where women from different backgrounds could interact.

The Viking era was a period of rapid change and is most obviously expressed in the speedy adoption and development of an urban way of life. The fixed plot boundaries and continued dominance of post-and-wattle architecture for four centuries in Ireland may have been a conscious reaction to this rate of change and a way of maintaining a sense of place and continuity for the townspeople.

Bibliography

Andersson, E. B. (2007) Textile tools and production during the Viking Age. In C. Gillis and M.-L. B. Nosch (eds) *Ancient Textiles, Production, Craft and Society*, 17–25. Oxford, Oxbow.

Biddle, M. (1976) Towns. In D. M. Wilson (ed.) *The Archaeology of Anglo-Saxon England*, 99–150. London, Methuen and Co.

Boyd, R. (2009) The Irish Viking Age: a discussion of architecture, settlement patterns and identity. *Viking and Medieval Scandinavia* 5, 271–94.

Brink, S. (2008) *Lord and Lady – Bryti and Deigja: some historical and etymological aspects of family, patronage and slavery in early Scandinavia and Anglo-Saxon England.* London, Viking Society for Northern Research.

Christiansen, E. (2006) *The Norsemen in the Viking Age.* Oxford, Blackwell.

Dommasnes, L. H. (1982) Late Iron Age in western Norway: female roles and ranks as deduced from an analysis of burial customs. *Norwegian Archaeological Review* 15, 70–84.

Dommasnes, L. H. (2008) 'Spun on a wheel were women's hearts': women between ideology and life in the Nordic past. In S. Montón-Subías and M. Sánchez-Romero (eds) *Engendering Social Dynamics: the archaeology of maintenance activities*, 87–95. British Archaeological Reports International Series 1862. Oxford, Archaeopress.

Easthope, H. (2004) A place called home. *Housing, Theory and Society* 21, 128–38.

Flanders, J. (2004) *The Victorian House: domestic life from childbirth to deathbed.* London, Harper-Collins.

Geraghty, S. (1996) *Viking Dublin: botanical evidence from Fishamble St, Dublin.* Dublin, Royal Irish Academy.

Gonzáles-Marcén, P., Montón-Subías, S. and Picazo, M. (2008) Towards an archaeology of maintenance activities. In S. Montón-Subías and M. Sánchez-Romero (eds) *Engendering Social Dynamics: the archaeology of maintenance activities*, 3–8. British Archaeological Reports International Series 1862. Oxford, Archaeopress.

Hall, R. A. (1994) *Viking Age York*. London, B.T. Batsford.

Hamerow, H. (2002) *Early Medieval Settlements: the archaeology of rural communities in north-west Europe 400–900*. Oxford, Oxford University Press.

Hurley, M. F., Scully, O. M. B. and McCutcheon, S. W. J. (eds) (1997) *Late Viking Age and Medieval Waterford: excavations 1986–1992*. Waterford, Waterford Corporation.

Jesch, J. (1991) *Women in the Viking Age*. Woodbridge, Boydell.

Kelly, F. (1988) *A Guide to Early Irish Law*. Dublin, Dublin Institute for Advanced Studies.

Lynn, C. J. (1994) Houses in rural Ireland A.D. 500–1000. *Ulster Journal of Archaeology* 57, 81–94.

McAlister, D. (2003) All in the family: archaeological evidence of Viking and Hiberno-Scandinavian women and children in Ireland. In J. Augusteijn, M. A. Lyons and D. MacMahon (eds) *Irish History: a research yearbook, number 2*, 148–61. Dublin, Four Courts Press.

Milek, K. B. (2006) *Houses and Households in Early Icelandic Society: geoarchaeology and the interpretation of social space*. Unpublished PhD thesis, University of Cambridge.

Munch, G. S., Johansen, O. S. and Roesdahl, E. (2003) *Borg in Lofoten: a chieftain's farm in north Norway*. Trondheim, Tapir Academic Press.

O'Sullivan, A. (2008) Early medieval houses in Ireland: social identity and dwelling spaces. *Peritia* 20, 225–56.

Ó Corráin, D. (1983) Some legal references to fences and fencing in early historic Ireland. In T. Reeves-Smyth and F. Hamond (eds) *Landscape Archaeology in Ireland*, 247–51. British Archaeological Reports British Series 116. Oxford, British Archaeological Reports.

Ó Corráin, D. (2005) Ireland *c*. 800: aspects of society. In D. Ó Cróinín (ed.) *A New History of Ireland 1: prehistoric and early Ireland*, 549–607. Oxford, Oxford University Press.

Perring, D. (1981) *Early Medieval Occupation at Flaxengate, Lincoln*. The Archaeology of Lincoln 9 (1). London, Council for British Archaeology.

Reilly, E. (2003) The contribution of insect remains to the understanding of the environment of Viking Age and medieval Dublin. In S. Duffy (ed.) *Medieval Dublin IV*, 40–62. Dublin, Four Courts Press.

Simpson, L. (1999) *Director's First Findings, Temple Bar West*. Dublin, Temple Bar Properties.

Simpson, L. (2002) *Excavations at Essex St. West/Temple Bar West*. Unpublished Margaret Gowen and Co. Report.

Simpson, L. (2006) John Rocque's map of Dublin (1756): a modern source for medieval historians. In S. Duffy (ed.) *Medieval Dublin VII*, 113–51. Dublin, Four Courts Press.

Stocker, D. (ed.) (2003) *The City by the Pool: assessing the archaeology of the City of Lincoln*. Lincoln Archaeological Studies 10. Oxford, Oxbow.

Valante, M. A. (2008) *The Vikings in Ireland: settlement, trade and urbanisation*. Dublin, Four Courts Press.

Wallace, P. F. (1992) *The Viking Age Buildings of Dublin*. Medieval Dublin Excavations 1962–81, ser. A, vol. 1. Dublin, Royal Irish Academy.

Wallace, P. F. (2000) *Garrda* and *airbeada*: the plot thickens in medieval Dublin. In A. P. Smyth (ed.) *Seanchas: studies in early medieval and Irish archaeology, history and literature in honour of Francis J. Byrne*, 261–74. Dublin, Four Courts Press.

Wallace, P. F. (2005) The archaeology of Ireland's Viking Age towns. In D. Ó Cróinín (ed.) *A New History of Ireland 1: prehistoric and early Ireland*, 814–42. Oxford, Oxford University Press.

Wallace, P. F. (2008) Irish archaeology and the recognition of ethnic difference in Viking Dublin. In J. Habu, C. Fawcett and J. M. Matsunaga (eds) *Evaluating Multiple Narratives: beyond nationalist, colonialist, imperialist archaeologies*, 166–83. New York, Springer.

Walton Rogers, P. (1997) *Textile Production at 16–22 Coppergate*. The Archaeology of York 17 (11). York, Council for British Archaeology.

CHILDHOOD IN VIKING AND HIBERNO-SCANDINAVIAN DUBLIN, 800–1100

Deirdre McAlister

This chapter examines the evidence for the daily lives of children in Viking and Hiberno-Scandinavian Dublin. The themes of environment, socialisation and play are discussed in order to explore how children created their own cultural worlds, which intersected with – but were also distinct from – the adult world (Lillehammer 1989; 2000). The material and cultural world of children can be traced through the study of the nature and distribution of objects that belonged to children, such as toys (Sofaer-Derevenski 1994; Baxter 2005). Toys are given both significance and meaning by the children who play with them, and, as Crawford (2009, 57) has argued, 'given that children engaged with material culture in object play, it is imperative to identify their toys in the past if children's culture, and its relationship with adult culture, is to be understood'. Interaction between children and the adult world can also be examined through analysis of artefacts that represent labour production and socialisation. Finally, analysis of the range of artefacts buried with children allows for exploration of the ways in which childhood identity and experience were interrelated with other identities, such as class and gender.

'Finding' children in the archaeological record

There is little doubt that traces of the lives of children can be found in the archaeological record, even if our capacity to identify them is, as yet, still somewhat limited. As Mizoguchi (2000, 141) has argued, 'talking about children in the milieu of archaeological discourse is currently as contentious as talking about gender used to be. This is predominantly because children are often deemed to be invisible, or difficult to recognize archaeologically … however it is simply not accurate to state that children cannot be seen in archaeological material'. Nevertheless, childhood is not widely studied by archaeologists (Park 2005, 53). There are a number of reasons for this, but Hirschfeld (2002, 612) has argued that the lack of child-focused scholarship has principally been the result of a cultural mindset that overestimates the role of adults in cultural learning, and underestimates the contribution of children in cultural reproduction. He also states that there has traditionally been a lack of appreciation of 'the scope and force of children's culture, particularly in shaping adult culture' (Hirschfeld 2002, 612). Another reason why childhood studies have been sidelined in archaeology is the persistent belief that 'we already understand what childhood is all about' (Park 2005, 54). Park (2005, 54) argues that this belief is unfounded:

Ethnographic research demonstrates that childhood can be defined differently from culture to culture, and therefore the experience of being a child undoubtedly varies as well. And if synchronic variation is possible, then so of course is variation over time. Hence there is the need for an archaeology of childhood, in which at least one goal should be to explore how and why childhood varied.

In similar vein, Finlay (2000) has lamented the fact that 'the child as a subject is still largely a neglected category of analysis in archaeology, especially in Ireland', and has observed a tendency to conflate infants and adolescents into a unitary class called 'the child'; such categories need to be disaggregated.

Those few archaeological studies of children and childhood across the Scandinavian diaspora have typically focused on artefacts that can be confidently identified as relating to children. Examples include feeding vessels found in children's graves, such as that made from a stick twined with bronze wire and a horn from a child's grave on Gotland (Denmark) (Rundkvist 2003, 62), and an alder wood 'suckle cup' from 11th-century Lund (Sweden) (Engberg-Ekman 2001, 72). A toddler's chair or 'high-chair', dating to *c.* 1050, was found at Lund (Roesdahl and Wilson 1992, 376), indicating that furniture specific to children existed in Viking-Age Scandinavia. This deduction is reinforced by the sagas, albeit of a later date, which refer occasionally to child-related furniture, such as cradles (Press 1899, 85; Jochens 1996, 40). Miniature versions of adult artefacts have also sometimes been associated with children. For example, among the many steatite objects from Jarlshof (Shetland) were a tiny bowl and miniature quern carved from local steatite, which Ritchie (2003) has argued were probably toys.

A number of sites across the Scandinavian diaspora have yielded miniature wooden and bone animals that appear to have been children's playthings. Numerous miniature horses (discussed further below) have been found, and Brisbane (1992, 173) also cites a number of wooden birds, a dog, a seal and a beaver among the finds from Novgorod. A small toy duck carved from elk or moose antler, excavated at Birka (Sweden), has been dated to between the 8th and 10th century. This object may have been attached to a stick in a manner similar to the wooden toy horses from Kvívik in the Faroes (Graham-Campbell 1980, 26). Spinning tops are also known from Dublin, Waterford and numerous Scandinavian sites outside of Ireland (McAlister 2009, 310–11). It is likely that Viking-Age children also played with items such as dolls; however, archaeological evidence for such playthings remains slim. Dolls may have been constructed from organic materials, such as fabric or straw, which are unlikely to survive in the archaeological record. This is confirmed by the Old Norse term for doll, '*dokka*', a term that could also be used to refer to a 'bundle'. However, an intact early medieval doll is known from Uppsala in Sweden (McAlister 2009, 326), whilst a carved wooden anthropomorphic figure that may be a doll was excavated from Hólar in Skagafjörður (Iceland) (Callow 2006, 67). A number of 'crudely carved' wooden objects that may be dolls have furthermore been identified in 12th- to 13th-century contexts in Bergen (Norway), whilst early 12th-century wooden pegs with the ends carved in the form of a human head, interpreted as possible dolls, have been found at Trondheim (Norway) (Long 1975, 25). Six examples of wooden dolls have also been identified from Novgorod (Brisbane 1992, 173). Linguistic evidence suggests that Viking-Age dolls played a similar role to modern dolls. The word *leika* in its neuter form means 'a plaything, a doll or a toy', and in its feminine form was used to denote a young girl or maiden living in the same home as the person using the expression, while sisters who live together are called *leikur* ('play-sisters'), and parents could call their foster-daughter their *leika* (Cleasby and Vigfusson 1874; Rydberg 1907, 366).

The Scandinavian sagas provide some indications of the nature of children's play and the locations in which it took place. While these are later in date than the focus of the present study, they nonetheless provide useful insights, which have potential cross-cultural resonance. In her discussion of play in the sagas, Hansen (2004, 6) has pointed out that while games are not necessarily confined to children, children are often described as playing games. These games sometimes required specific artefacts, or toys, some of which can be recognised archaeologically, although the evidently important *places* of play are more elusive in the archaeological record. Hansen (2004, 6) cites an example from *Bolla þáttur Bollasonar*, in which Ólafr, when seven or eight years old, 'went from the farm to play and build himself a house, as it is customary for children to do'. In the saga of *Olaf Haraldson*, Asta's young sons are said to have built houses and barns in their play, as well as 'sailing' ships of wood in small pools (Monson and Smith 1980, 280), while in *Njáls Saga* there are references to female children playing on a rainy day on the floor inside the house (Dasent 1861, 1). Other games that leave no archaeological trace include the role-playing games in which both boys and girls engaged in *Njáls Saga* and *Finnboga saga* (Dasent 1861, 16; Hansen 2004, 5). Finally, the saga of Bishop Guðmundr the Good, composed shortly after his death in 1237, describes the young Guðmundr playing the role of a bishop officiating at a make-believe church and altar with a child-sized mitre, staff and gown. He was playing with his cousin, Ogmundr, who was later renowned for his skill and bravery as a warrior, who is said to have wielded battle-axe, shield and other weapons in their games (Ciklamini 2004, 60). Despite the difficulties of identifying the presence of children in the archaeological record, beyond the existence of toys, as Lewis (2009, 9) has argued, there may, nonetheless, be subtle evidence for the presence of children:

> It is conceivable that small items, or badly drawn or sculpted figures in the archaeological record, were used and created by children ... it is time to start considering the potential of identifying childhood spaces, where ... children are viewed as independent agents within their own social space.

This chapter takes up this challenge.

Toys and functional miniatures in the Viking Age: cultural artefacts and the process of socialisation

Toys are a useful category of material culture to consider in an archaeological study of children and socialisation, as they are typically used exclusively or primarily by children (Baxter 2005, 41). Yet they are often dismissed as curiosities, or oversimplified and not examined in context as cultural objects. Utilising toys as a means of accessing children and/or childhood in the past certainly presents its own set of difficulties, as it can lead to the separation of the child from what is perceived as the more 'serious' adult world (Lillehammer 1989, 98–100). However, approaching children's toys as meaningful tools within the socialisation process provides an opportunity to study situated learning and the acquisition of technical competence (Baxter 2005, 12). They also provide a method of identifying children's behaviour within the archaeological record. As Sofaer-Derevenski (1994, 13) has stated, 'the multiple meanings associated with toys do not assume a binary opposition and separate the adult and child worlds, but they are the way in which interactions between them take place'. Toys are not simply a means by which adults enculturate children into the adult world, but they can also be 'contentious objects in dialogues of control and resistance' (Baxter 2005, 22). Indeed, Baxter (2005, 41) has described toys as encapsulating both the 'imperial practices of adults' and the 'native practices of children'.

As today, many toys in the past are miniaturized versions of adult objects, and, as Wileman (2005, 28) points out, their use by children is often in imitative explorations of the adult world. In such contexts, toys are not only to be understood as items of play but also of education and socialisation. Indeed, in some cases, toys can be used in an adult manner, for example, in processes of manufacture and production (see below). However, it is important to remember that children interact with and redesign toys through new ways, ignore toys that do not suit them, and of course create toys from non-toy objects (Wilkie 2000, 102; Wileman 2005, 28; Crawford 2009). Toys can be items manufactured specifically for children to play with but toys can also be any object, whatever its primary function, that a child plays with (Crawford 2009, 67).

Identifying children's artefacts

One of the problems in identifying toys in the archaeological record is that a small object did not necessarily belong to a child. Miniature votive or religious objects are found throughout the Scandinavian diaspora and often take the form of small statues of Scandinavian gods (such as Freyr or Odin), or miniature hammers that symbolize Thor (Gräslund 1992, 190–1). Tiny weapons were often strung around the neck and could take the form of miniature swords and spears, such as the Viking-Age examples from Uppsala (Sweden). On the other hand, not all miniature objects necessarily had a ritual function, and, as the preceding discussion demonstrates, the existence of toys certainly is attested in the written record for both Ireland and Scandinavia (McAlister 2009).

As children would have grown up in a family environment, they would have imitated their parents from an early age. In this process of socialisation, both toys and miniature versions of adult work equipment were crucial. The distinction between toys and miniature versions of adult work equipment is fluid, but examples of miniature household artefacts, such as millstones and quernstones, support the idea that children began to contribute to labour processes at a young age. Miniature quernstones and millstones are of limited distribution in the archaeological record, with fourteen from Shetland and eight from the vicinity of Trondheim (Hansen and Larsen 2000, 112–13). It is only recently that the significance and distribution of such miniatures has begun to be investigated in their social context. Hansen and Larsen (2000, 108) examined the corpus of these miniature quernstones and millstones and categorised them on the basis of features similar to 'normal size' quernstones and millstones in order to define these objects as 'model or toy quern- or millstone'. Hansen and Larsen (2000, 113) identified fourteen objects from Shetland of Viking to medieval date that may be miniature quernstones and millstones, including four quernstones, seven millstones, and three objects for which it was not possible to determine whether they were quernstones or millstones. Eleven of the fourteen objects were made from soapstone, two of sandstone, and one of mica schist (the latter being the preferred material for 'adult' size quernstones or millstones).

A miniature quernstone has been also noted from the Irish royal site of Lagore (Co. Meath), and although it is unstratified, and thus undated, it is similar in form to the Shetland and Scandinavian miniatures (Hencken 1950, 175; Hansen and Larsen 2000, 115; McAlister 2009, 283). Could this be indicative of trade links or other contact with Scandinavian Shetland? Certainly there are other objects found at Lagore that represent probable trade links with Hiberno-Scandinavian Dublin, such as combs (Hencken 1950, 184–90; Dunlevy 1988,

341–422) and spearheads (Edwards 1990, 90). There was certainly a strong export trade of steatite objects from Shetland to trading ports such as Dublin. However, while the majority of the Shetland examples are constructed from steatite (soapstone), the example from Lagore is made from shale and may, instead, represent local toy manufacturing, perhaps influenced by contacts with Shetland.

The preponderance of stones made from different material from the 'normal size' objects is notable, as is the lack of wear marks indicating usage. While the mica-schist stone could conceivably have served the same purpose as the 'adult-size' quernstones and made a contribution to household labour, the soapstone examples could not have been used in actual household production because the stone was unsuitable for grinding, and so they appear to be 'toys'. Yet whether they were toys or work items, these miniature querns and millstones must undoubtedly have played a part in socialising children into the roles they would be expected to adopt as adults, in particular in an agrarian subsistence economy. Hansen and Larsen (2000, 120) argue that the appearance of miniature quernstones and millstones in Shetland (and, indeed, the area around Trondheim) may be explained by the importance of grain growing in a subsistence economy (Shetland and the Trondheim area were the most northerly areas where grain growing played an important role). They argue that 'to the communities on the edge – Shetland and Middle Norway – agriculture became extremely important in order to maintain their social structure and identity. Therefore, this identity was expressed symbolically, in e.g., the production of miniature quern and millstones' (Hansen and Larsen 2000, 120). This evidence suggests, then, that children were fundamental to the processes of identity-formation in these regions.

Toys from Viking-Age Dublin

Excavations in Dublin have yielded many artefacts that may have been utilised in children's play, including possible musical instruments such as toggles, so-called 'buzz-disks' and string rattles (Hall 1994, 104; Hurley *et al.* 1997, 675–6, 685; McAlister 2009, 305–10; Wallace 1988, 17). Child-sized bone skates were recovered from the excavations at Wood Quay in Dublin (Wallace 1988, 17), indicating that children were encouraged to learn at an early age how to master this means of travel, as well as, presumably, of play. A large number of small bronze bells, both round and hexagonal, are known from 'Viking' contexts in the British Isles, some of which are specifically associated with children through their deposition in child burials. For example, four bells were excavated at Peel Castle on the Isle of Man, including a hexagonal copper-alloy bell from a 9th- to 10th-century child's grave (Graham-Campbell 1998, 123–4; Batey 1988, 214). The interpretation of these bells as rattles or playthings of high-status children is supported by a reference in the 13th-century *Völsung Saga*. The text refers to two royal children playing with a gold ball-like object with a golden ring attached to it, which appears to resemble some of the bells from Birka (Byock 1990, 45). In addition, a small number of wooden toys have been found in Dublin. The possible role of these miniature boats/ships, swords and horses in the process of socialisation in Viking-Age Dublin will stand central to the following discussion.

Boats and ships

The sea was of obvious importance during the Viking Age, and, therefore, it is perhaps not surprising that a number of small finely carved miniature wooden boats have been discovered in Dublin, of a type found widely across the Scandinavian diaspora, including Greenland, the Faroe Islands, Hedeby, Trondheim, Bergen, Vestfold and Oslo (Hansen and Larsen 2000, 115; McAlister 2009, 302–4). Toy boats have also been identified from Danzig (Poland) and from Sweden (where they are often constructed from bark) (McAlister 2009, 303). These miniature boats were carved in various levels of detail, often so accurate that different types of ships can be distinguished. While they are often described as 'models', the interpretation of these objects as children's toys is supported by the literary sources, which make reference to children playing with toy boats and ships. For example, a 14th-century Icelandic tale (detailing events from the end of the 10th to the middle of the 11th century) describes how 'the Norwegian's son had for a playing a ship' and that he had brought the toy with him from Norway (Hansen 2004, 6; Roach 2008, 315).

Small wooden ships and boats have been excavated at Winetavern Street and Fishamble Street in Dublin (Christensen 1988, 24). A total of five miniature ships and boats dating from the 10th to the 13th century have been identified in the Dublin material. One example from Winetavern Street is a Viking-style 10th-century boat, found in a pit wrapped in a pillow or *palisse* of bracken and hay, presumably for protection (Mitchell 1987, 30–1, plate V). Later examples include a 12th-century example from Winetavern Street, which in its present fragmentary state measures 11.1 cm in length and is of clear Norse type. It is missing its stern, but the keel and stepping as well as circular holes along the side for fastening a pair of shrouds indicate that there was originally a mast and rigging (Christensen 1988, 19–20). A nearly intact miniature boat of 12th- to 13th-century date, measuring 36 cm in length, was also excavated from Winetavern Street (Christensen 1988). The boat is well made and its maker appears to have had good knowledge of contemporary ship building. It is carved from a solid piece of wood, and has a damaged raised prow, intact stern, and shallow keel. The hole in the side of the ship for the attachment of a steering oar can be clearly seen, and the stepping for the mast in the bottom of the ship is slightly off centre (National Museum of Ireland 1973, 44). The rudder fastening is paralleled on a toy ship from Norway, and it has a number of shared characteristics with northern Norwegian boats of more recent date (Christensen 1988, 20). A number of miniature ships/boats were also identified at Fishamble Street (Christensen 1988, 24), including one 11th-century example. Measuring 30.9 cm long, the object is described as having incised faint scrolls that may be serpents on the better preserved prow (Lang 1988, 79–80, fig. 94). The ship was excavated from the south internal partition of a house, its location strengthening the suggestion that it was, indeed, a toy.

Christensen (1988, 24) has argued that the Dublin vessels are toy sailing models of real vessels which were most likely originally rigged and furnished with sails in order to be raced on a pond or river. The majority of the Dublin miniatures appear to resemble contemporary sailing vessels of the period (for further discussion see Christensen 1988, 19–25). Small stem-tops and masts are also known from the Bryggen excavations in Bergen (Herteig 1961, fig. 58), and bronze miniature weather vanes, probably fittings for some of the toy boats, have been recovered from graves and settlement sites (Graham-Campbell 1980, 80–1). A number of possible 'toy paddles' are also known from the archaeological record. While no toy ships or boats are known from this period in England, Egan (1998, 11) has suggested that a number of later medieval tiny metal anchors found in the Thames may well represent the remains of later toy wooden boats that were lost in the river.

0   5

cm

Fig. 6.1 One of the toy swords from Novgorod (Russia) (drawn by Letty ten Harkel, after Noonan 1997, 153).

Swords

The finding of an unadorned partial miniature wooden sword near a pathway to a house at Fishamble Street, measuring 23.7 cm, offers further proof that children imitated the behaviour of the adult community (Lang 1988, 79). While children presumably also played with 'swords' made of sticks – which would be impossible to deduce even if the sticks survived in the archaeological record – the very fact that toy swords were modelled closely on their adult counterparts – and in such large quantities – suggests that they were used to socialise children into the values of the adult community. The Fishamble example corresponds to Peterson's Type O, which represents over a quarter of 'adult-sized' Viking-Age swords from Ireland, and is the most common sword type found in Norway (Walsh 1998, 229). Other small swords from the Irish archaeological record include a 10th-century iron 'Viking' sword from Lough Gur (Co. Limerick), where a Viking army established a base in 926. The sword is 54 cm in length and the width of the blade is 4 cm. The blade shows evidence of damascening on both sides up to the lower crossbar (Bøe 1940, 86). The shortness and very narrow grip of the sword suggests that it was manufactured for a child (British Museum no. 1864, 1–27, 3; Barry Ager *pers. comm.*). Child-sized swords are not yet known from the native Irish archaeological context, but literary evidence suggests that Irish children did have swords of their own (McAlister 2009, 270, 281).

Child-sized swords made from both iron and wood are also known from Sweden, and range in date from the 8th century to the later medieval period. The vast majority appear to have been modelled upon their adult counterparts, suggesting that children (presumably male?) were being socialised into the practice of using a sword whilst becoming familiar with specific types of sword common to their geographical region. Over 116 child-sized wooden swords are also known from the excavations at Novgorod, as well as five daggers, fourteen bows and a number of arrows of miniature proportions (fig. 6.1). These miniature weapons are constructed with such accuracy that they, too, can be directly compared with their metal adult counterparts. The Novgorod swords date from the 10th to the 14th centuries, with the majority dating to the 10th to 12th centuries (Brisbane 1992, 175). Interestingly, a sharp decline has been noted in the range of toys available to the children of Novgorod in the period *c.* 1150–1250, which may be attributable to the widespread death of children in this period due to famines recorded in the *Chronicles of Novgorod* (Brisbane 1992, 173).

Horses

The horse was an animal of great importance in Scandinavian society, both for transport and

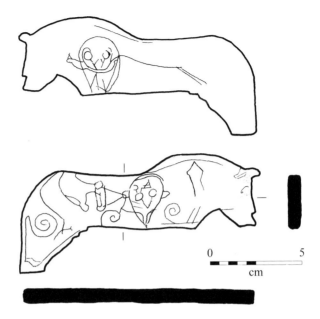

Fig. 6.2: Schematic drawing of toy horse from Fishamble Street, Dublin, showing possible child's drawing of spirals and anthropomorphic figures (drawn by Letty ten Harkel, after Gardeła 2012, 237 (fig. 1)).

for agriculture. As Sikora (2003, 93) notes, 'as a possession, it was a sign of status and, perhaps because of this, the horse became a central element of Nordic – that is Scandinavian – religion and funerary practices'. Burials of men, women and children with horses and horse-related paraphernalia have been found across the Scandinavian diaspora, including male burials with horses at Athlumney (Co. Meath), Islandbridge (Co. Kildare) and Cloghermore Cave (Co. Kerry) (Connolly *et al.* 2005). Horses accompanying the burials of children or young people have been identified in Iceland, the British Isles and a number of the Scandinavian countries (for discussion, see Sikora 2003), but not yet in Ireland, with the possible exception of a burial containing a female and a child with the animal bone and the lower jaw of a pony from Cloghermore Cave (Connolly and Coyne 2000, 18–19; Connolly *et al.* 2005, 164). The significance of horses in Viking society is reflected in the widespread occurrence of wooden horses as children's playthings. Examples have been found at Trondheim, Kvívik (Roesdahl and Wilson 1992, 231, 310), Hólar in Skagafjörður (Iceland) (Callow 2006, 67), Östergötland (Sweden) (National Historical Museum Sweden no. SHM:B9:9 VL SR), Staraja Ladoga (Russia) (Roesdahl and Wilson 1992, 301), and on the Baltic island of Wollin, while there are over seventy examples – both with and without saddles – from Novgorod (Kolchin 1989; Brisbane 1992, 173). Across the Viking diaspora, most of the wooden horses that have been found are roughly 12.5 cm long, suggesting that this object type was remarkably homogenous.

A small wooden horse was recovered from Fishamble Street in Dublin (fig. 6.2). It measures 12 cm in length, and was dated, on the basis of associated coins, to between 1000 and 1025. The horse has faint traces of an eye, with spirals on the belly and joints and there are incised human faces on either side of the object. These drawings of male human figures bear a remarkable resemblance to other Norse representations of human figures, such as the man carved on the cross in St Andrew's church, Middleton (Yorkshire) and on the Gotlandic picture stones and Viking-Age Scandinavian runestones. Eyes, ears and beard are highly defined in the drawing on the Fishamble Street horse, as is what may be a cone-shaped hat or a conical helmet, and these rather prominent triangular shapes on the horse are indicative of a splayed nose guard. Could the drawings on the Fishamble Street horse represent an attempt to copy the established 'adult' images of men? Are they a rare example of a child's artistic expression?

Miniature horses made of other materials have been found, and these also seem likely to have been toys. Examples include a miniature ceramic horse from Bergen, which appears to have been part of a larger group of toys that include rattles as well as miniature pots, horses and jugs (Herteig 1961, 28–9, 31). The Icelandic sagas confirm that toy horses were played with by children, in particular very young children. *Viga Glums Saga* describes two children aged four and six playing with a little brass horse. The younger child asks the older to lend him the toy, and the older child then gifts it to him, responding that 'looking to my age, it is more fit for your plaything than mine' (Head 1866), suggesting that small horses were not considered to be appropriate toys for older children. A number of small bronze horses similar to the type mentioned in *Viga Glums Saga* are known in the archaeological record. These objects are often termed *messingarhestr* (brass horses), and have sometimes been interpreted as weights, although examples from Shetland (Paton 1936–7, 93), Kosvig (Norway),[1] Bergen (Bergen National Museum no. BNM: B6764), Þingvellir (Iceland) (Callow 2006, 66–7) and Lincolnshire in England (United Kingdom Detector Finds Database no. 13841) have been interpreted as children's objects.

Discussion

The striking similarity among the child-sized weapons, ships and horses found throughout the Viking world suggests a remarkable cultural and geographical consistency in the importance of swords, horses and ships and boats in the material culture of children. The swords, toy horses and small ships discussed above all appear to relate to the socialisation of male children. The historical and literary sources confirm the importance of 'adult-sized' swords, horses and ships as an important part of Scandinavian masculine identity, and boat burials, horses and swords are often found as part of male Viking warrior grave assemblages. It is also interesting to note the continued importance of the ship in Hiberno-Scandinavian Dublin, which was the major maritime port in Ireland, and from where at least four toy ships are known. The male children of Hiberno-Scandinavian Dublin would have seen the adult male community as traders, merchants, craftsmen, as well as sea-faring members of the warrior class. As such, the accoutrements of these roles would have been imitated in their play culture.

Children in the household

The house was central to the lives of infants and children in the Viking Age. As mentioned previously, children sometimes transformed their domestic space for the purposes of play and both the poetic *Eddas* (c. 1220) and the sagas suggest that there were defined spaces for the birthing process, known as *kvinna hús* or 'women's quarters', which were separate from the main house or *skáli* (Jochens 1995, 80).[2] Examples of such structures have been sought in the archaeological record. While it is difficult to ascertain the exact use of domestic space, the layout of the so-called Type 2 houses from Dublin suggests that at least some may have been used as birthing spaces, nurseries or sleeping areas for children (see also Boyd, this volume and fig. 5.2). Unlike the other house types identified at Dublin, walking was restricted within the

Type 2 houses and they had single entrances and were snug spaces with soft bedding, creating a comfortable space. The houses were devoid of paving and much of the floor space was covered with woven mats, which was a material used in the bedding side aisles of the Type 1 houses. Various suggestions have been made about their function, including the possibility that they were used as accommodation for the infirm (Wallace 1992, 15), or that these buildings served as weaving areas, a craft that is traditionally associated with women in both occupation and religious rituals (McAlister 2009, 127–30, 134–8). Type 2 houses have also, however, been identified at Limerick, London, York (Wallace 1992, 15) and Waterford, where their small size along with the presence of frequently insulated walls, bedding material and their ancillary position to the larger Type 1 houses combined 'to create a picture of comfortable sleeping quarters' (Hurley 1992, 65).

While only Wallace (1992, 36) has – to my knowledge – suggested that these Type 2 houses may have been used for and by children, the fact that these houses were devoid of paving or hard floors, the lack of evidence for food production in the hearths and their location near pathways connecting them to the larger Type 1 'main residences' supports their interpretation as sleeping quarters. However, the fact that some of the Type 2 houses were devoid of any evidence of a hearth may suggest that these structures served a seasonal function, as the lack of fire during the cold Dublin winter would not have made for comfortable sleeping. The Waterford examples, however, normally did have hearths, but they were small and did not contain evidence for cooking. In Waterford there was usually only one Type 2 house associated with each Type 1 house, and the Type 2 houses were frequently connected on one side to a pathway leading to the back door of the larger Type 1 house (Hurley 1998, 168–9). If children did use these spaces, it reveals not only a significant investment in the rearing and comfort of children in Viking-Age Dublin, but, interestingly, also a degree of separation of children from the main living areas of the house. Despite such a distinction between the worlds of adults and children, the close location of the Type 2 houses to the larger 'main' houses may suggest that it was mainly young children who were kept separate, yet close by. As Boyd (this volume) has observed, it probably would not have been advisable to leave young children entirely unattended given the hazards of fire in those Type 2 houses in which hearths were present.

Dressing the children of Viking-Age Dublin

The recovery of child-sized clothing, footwear and jewellery from a variety of sites in Dublin and elsewhere permits further insights into the ways in which children were socialised. It appears that children were provided with attire that was similar to that of adults. Textile finds from Dublin and Waterford indicate that female children wore caps resembling those worn by women. One silk cap from the early to mid-10th-century levels at Fishamble Street, similar in both pattern and material to the silk caps excavated at York and Lincoln, appears to have had a secondary use by a child. This deduction is based on the contrast between the lightweight, veil-like weave of the fabric, and the 'make do and mend' quality of the later repairs, which, according to Wincott-Heckett (2003, 47) may represent the passing on of a treasured silk piece to a child. At York, a number of early 11th-century pieces of linen were identified as being part of a young child's smock (Walton Rogers 1989, 348) and a child's silk tabby headdress similar to those worn by adults was also identified (Wincott-Heckett 2003, 51).

Contrary to the Dublin evidence, depictions on Scandinavian stone sculptures suggest that children sometimes wore clothing different from that of adults. For example, a 9th-century picture stone from Ardre on Gotland, which is possibly one of the oldest images of a Scandinavian child, depicts a child wearing what appears to be a short skirt-like shift cinched in at the waist and belling out slightly at the knees (Lindquist 2001, 27). This costume is unlike that in which adults are depicted. Evidence from an 11th-century runestone raised to a child who died very young in Torsätra in Uppland (Sweden) furthermore suggests that children wore special clothing for their christening. The inscription records that 'Unna had this stone raised to his son Östen, who died in christening robes, God help his soul'. Thus, alongside the archaeological finds suggesting that children were dressed similarly to adults, we need to acknowledge that they may also sometimes have had distinctive clothing, especially for rites of passage.

A number of children's boots and shoes were recovered from Dublin, in particular from the High Street and Winetavern Street excavations. The finds indicate that a range of styles were available in children's footwear, many of which are also reflected in the adult styles. Most footwear was made from calfskin or goatskin and most was laced at the ankle. Legs and feet could be covered with thick wool leggings or socks over which leather shoes were worn. The typical shoe type during the Viking Age was the leather turn-shoe, which was worn by men, women and children alike (Ewing 2006, 58). Archaeology confirms that low-cut shoes were in fashion in Ireland in the Hiberno-Scandinavian period (Hall *et al.* 2003, 81–8). The population of Dublin was unique in that low shoes were typically worn, and these were usually laced with thongs and were without heels in preference to the high bootees that were fashionable in Viking towns outside of Ireland (Wallace 1988, 11).

Like clothing, children's jewellery was also similar to that worn by adults. Two objects that may represent children's bracelets are known from the excavations at Wood Quay. These include a small lead-alloy bracelet from Winetavern Street and a copper-alloy example from St John's Lane. Similar 'adult-sized' copper-alloy bracelets are also known from the Dublin excavations. However, there were also differences between children's and adult jewellery, in particular with respect to its value. In emphasising the beauty and poise of Gudrun, the author of *Laxdæla Saga* describes her as being such a woman of state that whatever other women wore in the way of finery of dress was looked upon as children's 'gewgaws' (trinkets) compared to hers (Press 1899, 95).

Education in Viking-Age Dublin

If there is evidence for material culture manufactured *for* children, and it is possible to identify such objects in the material record, is it possible, then, to go a step further and identify evidence for material culture manufactured *by* children? It may be, as Lewis (above) has proposed, that objects that display a rougher or simpler execution are representative of children's attempts at manufacture or design, as seen, for example, in some of the miniature steatite lamps from Scandinavian and medieval Scotland and the aforementioned decoration on the Fishamble Street horse (McAlister 2009, 291–3). The Dublin excavations produced a remarkable assortment of what are known as trial or motif pieces and it is highly likely that some of these objects were used in the training of apprentice artists and jewellers (Graham-Campbell and Kidd 1980, 150), some of whom may have been very young. Such motif pieces are found on stone, bone, wood and antler in both rural and urban, native and Hiberno-Scandinavian contexts (O'Meadhra 1987).

There are between five and six thousand extant runic inscriptions from the Scandinavian world, with the vast majority dating to the late Viking Age (Sawyer and Sawyer 1993, 67). Although it is unclear when people learnt to write during the Viking period, there is a strong likelihood that at least some runic inscriptions were made by children, for example those on children's toys (Olofsson 2008, 178). It has also been argued that some of the runestones from Bergen represent the work of children. Dating between the late 12th and 15th centuries, many of the stones appear to demonstrate a pedagogical context, with a more practiced hand carving out the runes on one side, and a learner trying to copy the inscription onto the other side (Hagland and Lorentzen 1997; Spurkland and Van der Hoek 2005, 177). Of the fourteen runic inscriptions known from Ireland, the rune-inscribed cattle scapula from a mid-11th-century house site at Christchurch Place, Dublin, may represent *barneregler*, or children's rhymes (Barnes *et al.* 1997, 33). Like some of the Bergen runes, the carvings appear to have been executed by two different people with differing degrees of expertise, perhaps representing a student and a teacher. The inscription also contains repeated runes carved multiple times, suggesting that the carver was practicing the *fuþark* (alphabet). The 24 runic characters upon this cattle scapula have been identified as being too 'untidy' to be ornamental, yet appear to have a clear and precise purpose (Barnes *et al.* 1997, 32–3). It is possible, therefore, that the inscription represents archaeological evidence of a young person learning to write (Knirk 1994).

Burial treatment of children in Viking-Age Dublin

A final category of evidence that can be drawn upon to reconstruct the social identities of children during this period is burial evidence. Christiansen (2002, 40) has argued that the Viking Age witnessed the emergence of specifically child-oriented grave goods, such as small ornaments and mirrors. The small bronze bell in a child's grave at Peel Castle on the Isle of Man (see above) was located around the neck of the child along with a number of beads and a small copper-alloy ring (Freke 2002, 94–5). Batey (1988, 214) has suggested that the original context of another example of a bronze bell was from disturbed inhumations from the early Christian St Patrick's chapel near West Nappin, Jurby (Isle of Man). Only one interment of a child has so far been identified with certainty in Viking-Age Dublin. The Fishamble Street excavations unearthed a late 9th-century burial of a five to six year-old child. The burial was accompanied by the skull of a cow, in a practice that mirrored the deposition of animal bones in some adult graves, including two adult burials from Islandbridge, which contained the jawbone of a cow and an ox, and a horse tooth, respectively (Bøe 1940, 59–60).[3] The jaw of the animal found in the Fishamble Street burial was found in a closed position, indicating that the flesh was intact at the time of burial. The head was separated from the rest of the body, perhaps in a sacrificial manner similar to the practice of placing ritually sacrificed swords and shields in adult male burials, examples of which have been identified in the British Isles and Scandinavia.

The possibility of another child's burial from Dublin emerges from the discovery of a diminutive bronze axe, measuring 14.4 × 4.4 cm at Islandbridge (Bøe 1940, 53), although, like most of the artefacts from this site, its precise location was not recorded. It has been suggested that the Dublin axe is a 'stick pin', or brooch, from an adult costume due to its very small size (O'Brien 1998, 211). However, the possibility that it was, instead, associated with a child is raised by the fact that similar small axes have been found in children's graves in Iceland, mainly in those aged under ten years (Pétursdóttir 2007, 63). Axes are common Viking-Age grave goods across the Scandinavian diaspora, found almost exclusively in the graves of adult males (although a small number have been found in female graves), and the literary evidence supports the idea that small axes could be associated with children. For example, *Grettis Saga* describes Þorbjorn and his son harvesting hay in a meadow when the father places his shield and sword momentarily by a bundle of hay, but the boy keeps hold of his small axe (Jochens 1996, 109). As Iceland was uninhabited before Scandinavians arrived from Norway, Scotland and Ireland, and miniature axes are not known from child burials in Scandinavia, their presence in child burials in Iceland and perhaps also Dublin may reflect a developing insular practice. It is difficult to establish the context of the small corpus of children's burials in Viking-Age Dublin. However, as Hadley and Hemer (2011, 72) have stated:

> In migrant situations, children's graves may offer opportunities for communities to experiment as the burials of children are less constrained by social convention than are those of adults, and this certainly appears to be true of Scandinavian burials in Britain.

They also suggest that children on the cusp of social adulthood were immensely important during the processes of acculturation and that their deaths sometimes needed to be ameliorated with distinctive funerary rites.

Conclusions

By identifying particular objects that can be identified as the material culture of childhood, and studying their distribution in the archaeological record, it becomes possible to trace the activities of children through time and space. The evidence indicates that children were active participants in the environment, and had a material culture of their own which was remarkably consistent throughout the Viking diaspora and reflected aspects of the adult world. The range of objects associated with children includes items indicating social status, such as swords and other weaponry, horses and miniature ships, all of which were important material possessions within the adult male world. In rural contexts, miniature quernstones and millstones, both with and without wear marks, have been identified, indicating that children would be trained in the use of these objects from an early age, either through play or through real contribution to household labour, although such items have not, as yet, been identified in the urban archaeological record and this may be a significant pattern. The suggestion that children were very much part of the adult world is strengthened by the evidence for children's clothing, which seems to have been largely identical to adult clothing, with the possible exception of the clothing of young children. What is more, burial evidence also suggests that certain children enjoyed similar status and even held similar responsibilities to adults. Evidence from the literary sources, however, suggests that there were also playthings that were 'age appropriate', such as balls. Finally, the evidence from the Type 2 houses, if indeed they were children's spaces, also suggests that children were kept separate from the adult world when they were very young.

Whether it is possible to distinguish between urban and rural childhood remains uncertain. While the vast majority of the artefacts discussed here come from urban contexts, it is important to note that this may very well be down to differential survival; certainly much of the survival of the Dublin material is because of waterlogged conditions which created good organic preservation of the Viking and Hiberno-Scandinavian layers. In addition, until the last ten years or so, urban areas tended to be more of a focus for excavation. Nonetheless, there are certainly some contrasts evident in the material culture of children: the miniature quernstones and millstones reflect the importance of grain growing in rural subsistence areas, whilst the toy boats from the 'urban' centres reflect the importance of seafaring and mercantile activities of the settlers. As such, children's play made an important contribution to the integration of the Viking settlers into Irish society.

Nevertheless, toys played an important role in the process of adaptation to the new colonial lands. The burial evidence confirms this. The processes of migration and changing understandings of identity placed a greater emphasis on power and status than age or gender, resulting in the similar treatment of children and adults in terms of funerary practices (McAlister 2009; Hadley and Hemer 2011).

Some of the artefacts discussed in this article such as the toy horses, swords and ships and boats demonstrate a remarkable consistency over several centuries and across the Scandinavian diaspora. One of the reasons for this may simply be the continuing importance of these symbols in 'adult' society. Other artefacts may have been influenced by the need to adapt to the new colonial lands, as in the case with the miniature quern and millstones, which reflect the importance of grain growing in rural subsistence areas. However, recent excavations and research has the potential to provide further evidence, as long as children remain a focus of academic inquiry into the past.

Notes

1   For a photograph of this object, see https://picasaweb.google.com/stylegar/Oldsaker#50261 59615606136386.
2   These spaces were areas into which men could not enter without being utterly emasculated and shamed, except in the case of the most virile of heroes. For example, Helgi Hundingsbana was able to hide disguised as a maid in the *kvenna hús*, but for any lesser man such an act would have been regarded as cowardice, and the man who braved the *dyngja* would have been labelled as *níðingr* and *ragrmann* simply because the location was so strongly associated with women's activity and central role in the society as weavers (*Helgakviða Hundingsbana* II 1–5).
3   Stephen Harrison (2001, 74) has argued that the circumstances of the excavations of the Viking graves at Kilmainham/Islandbridge means it is likely that many more such animal depositions with human remains may have been missed.

Bibliography

Barnes, M., Hagland, J. R. and Page, R. I. (1997) *The runic inscriptions of Viking Age Dublin, National Museum of Ireland. Medieval Dublin excavations 1962–81*. Series B, vol. 5. Dublin, Royal Irish Academy.

Batey, C. (1988) A Viking-Age bell from Freswick Links, Caithness. *Medieval Archaeology* 32, 213–16.

Baxter, J. E. (2005) *The Archaeology of Childhood: children, gender, and material culture*. Walnut Creek, Altamira Press.

Bøe, J. (1940) *Norse Antiquities in Ireland, Volume III of Viking Antiquities in Great Britain and Ireland*. Oslo, Aschehoug and Co.

Brisbane, M. (ed.) (1992) *The Archaeology of Novgorod, Russia: recent results from the town and its hinterland*. Society for Medieval Archaeology Monograph 13. Lincoln, Society for Medieval Archaeology.

Byock, J. (trans.) (1990) *The Saga of the Volsungs. The Norse epic of Sigurd the dragon slayer*. California, University of California Press.

Callow, C. (2006) First steps towards an archaeology of children in Iceland. *Archaeologia Islandica* 5, 55–96.

Christensen, A. E. (1988) Ship graffiti and models. In P. Wallace (ed.) *Miscellanea 1, Medieval Dublin Excavations 1962–81*, Series B, ii, 13–26. Dublin, Royal Irish Academy.

Christiansen, E. (2002) *The Norsemen in the Viking Age*. Oxford, Blackwell.

Ciklamini, M. (2004) Sainthood in the making: the arduous path of Guðmundr the Good, Iceland's uncanonized saint. *Alvíssmál: Forschungen zur mittelalterlichen Kultur Skandinaviens* 11, 55–74.

Cleasby, R. and Vigfusson, G. (1874) *An Icelandic-English Dictionary*. Oxford, Clarendon Press.

Connolly, M. and Coyne, F. (2000) Cloghermore Cave, the Lee Valhalla. *Archaeology Ireland* 14 (4), no. 54, 16–19.

Connolly, M., Coyne, F. and Lynch, L. (2005) *Underworld, Death and Burial in Cloghermore Cave, County Kerry*. Wordwell, Bray.

Crawford, S. (2009) The archaeology of play things: theorizing a toy stage in the 'biography' of objects. *Childhood in the Past* 2, 55–70.

Dasent, G. W. (1861) (trans.) *The Story of Burnt Njal, or Life in Iceland at the End of the Tenth Century*. Edinburgh, Edmonston and Douglas.

Dunlevy, M. (1988) A classification of Irish combs. *Proceedings of the Royal Irish Academy* 88 C, 341–422.

Edwards, N. (1990) *The Archaeology of Early Medieval Ireland*. Philadelphia, Routledge.

Egan, G. (1998) Miniature toys of medieval childhood. *British Archaeology* 35, 10–11.

Engberg-Ekman, M. (ed.) (2001) *Destination Viking, Western Viking route*. Västervik, North Sea Viking Legacy.

Ewing, T. (2006) *Viking Clothing*. Stroud, Tempus.

Finlay, N. (2000) Cradle and grave, death and the archaeology of childhood. Unpublished paper presented at Archaeology Ireland Conference, *Answers from the Grave, the Archaeology of Death*, University College Dublin.

Freke, D. (ed.) (2002) *Excavations on St. Patrick's Isle, Peel, Isle of Man, 1982–88*: prehistoric, Viking, medieval and later. Liverpool, Liverpool University Press.

Gardeła, L. (2012) What the Vikings did for fun? Sports and pastimes in medieval northern Europe. *World Archaeology* 44 (2), 234–47.

Graham-Campbell, J. (1980) *Viking Artefacts: a select catalogue*. London, British Museum.

Graham-Campbell, J. (1998) The early Viking Age in the Irish Sea area. In H. B. Clarke, M. Ní Mhaonaigh and R. Ó Floinn (eds) *Ireland and Scandinavia in the Early Viking Age*, 102–28. Dublin, Four Courts Press.

Graham-Campbell, J. and Kidd, D. (1980) *The Vikings*. London, British Museum.

Gräslund, A. S. (1992) Thor's hammers, pendant crosses and other amulets. In E. Roesdahl and D. Wilson (eds) *From Viking to Crusader: the Scandinavians and Europe 800–1200*, 190–1. Sweden, Rizzoli.

Hadley, D. M. and Hemer, K. A. (2011) Microcosms of migration: children and early medieval population movement. *Childhood in the Past* 4, 63–78.

Hagland, J. R. and Lorentzen, R. T. (1997) Skrift med runer i lys av forsking på tidig skriving hos barn. In S. Nyström (ed.) *Runor och ABC, elva förläsningar från ett symposium i Stockholm våren 1995*, 43–78. Stockholm, Riksantikvarieämbetet Stockholms medeltidsmuseum.

Hall, R. A. (1994) *Viking Age York*. Manchester, Batsford Ltd.

Hall, R. A., Mould, Q., Carlisle, I. and Cameron, E. (2003) *Craft, Industry and Everyday Life: leather and leatherworking in Anglo-Scandinavian and medieval York*. The Archaeology of York 17. York, Council for British Archaeology.

Hansen, A. (2004) Childhood in early Icelandic society: representations of children in the Icelandic Sagas. In S. Würth, T. Jonuks and A. Kristinsson (eds) *Sagas and Societies. International conference at Borgarnes, Iceland, September 5–9, 2002*. University of Tübingen, electronic book (http://w210. ub.uni-tuebingen.de/dbt/volltexte/2004/1057/pdf/3_anna-1.pdf) (12 May, 2007).

Hansen, S. and Larsen, A. (2000) Miniature quern- and millstones from Shetland's Scandinavian past. *Acta Archaeologica* 71, 105–21.

Harrison, S. (2001) Viking graves and grave-goods in Ireland. In A. C. Larsen (ed.) *The Vikings in Ireland*, 61–75. Roskilde, Viking Ship Museum.

Head, E. (trans.) (1866) *The story of Vigaglum, translated from the Icelandic, with notes and an Introduction*. London, Williams and Norgate.

Hencken, H. (1950) Lagore crannog: an Irish royal residence of the seventh to tenth century AD. *Proceedings of the Royal Irish Academy* 23, section c, 1–248.

Herteig, A. (1961) *Bryggen I Bergen*. Bergen, Greig.

Hirschfeld, L. (2002) Why don't anthropologists like children? *American Anthropologist* 104 (22), 611–27.

Hurley, M. F. (1992) Late Viking Age settlement in Waterford city. In W. Nolan and T. P. Power (eds) *Waterford History and Society*, 49–72. Dublin, Geography Publications.

Hurley, M. (1998) Viking Age towns: archaeological evidence from Waterford and Cork. In M. Monk and J. Sheehan (eds) *Early Medieval Munster: archaeology, history and society*, 164–78. Cork, Cork University Press.

Hurley, M., Scully, O. M. B. and McCutcheon, S. W. J. (eds) (1997) *Late Viking Age and Medieval Waterford*. Waterford, Waterford Corporation.

Jochens, J. (1995) *Women in Old Norse Society*. Cornell, Cornell University Press.

Jochens, J. (1996) *Old Norse Images of Women*. Philadelphia, University of Pennsylvania Press.

Knirk, J. (1994) Learning to write with runes in medieval Norway. In I. Lindell (ed.) *Medeltida skrift- och språkkultur. Nordisk medeltidsliteracy i ett diglossiskt och digrafiskt perspektiv II. Nio föreläsningar från ett symposium i Stockholm våren 1992*, 169–212. Runica et Mediævalia Opuscula 2. Stockholm, Stockholms Universitet.

Kolchin, B. A. (1989) *Wooden Artefacts from Medieval Novgorod*. British Archaeological Reports International Series S495i and ii. Oxford, Archaeopress.

Lang, J. T. (1988) *Viking-Age Decorated Wood: a study of its ornament and style*. Medieval Dublin Excavations 1962–81, series b, vol. i. Dublin, Royal Irish Academy.

Lewis, C. (2009) Children's play in the later medieval countryside. *Childhood in the Past* 2, 86–109.

Lillehammer, G. (1989) A child is born: the child's world in an archaeological perspective. *Norwegian Archaeological Review* 22 (2), 89–105.

Lillehammer, G. (2000) The world of children. In J. Sofaer-Derevenski (ed.) *Children and Material Culture*. London, Routledge.

Lindquist, M. (2001) Concerning the existence of children. *Viking Heritage Magazine* 1, 27.

Long, C. (1975) Excavations in the medieval city of Trondheim. *Medieval Archaeology* 19, 1–32.

McAlister, D. (2009) *Gender, Age and Visibility: the archaeology of women and children in Ireland 700–1200*. Unpublished PhD thesis, National University of Ireland, Maynooth.

Mitchell, G. F. (1987) *Archaeology and Environment in Early Dublin*. Medieval Dublin Excavations 1962–1981, series c, vol. 1. Dublin, Royal Irish Academy.

Mizoguchi, K. (2000) The child as a node of past, present, and future. In J. Sofaer-Derevenski (ed.) *Children and Material Culture*, 141–50. London, Routledge.

Monson, E. and Smith, A. H. (ed. and trans.) (1980) *Heimskringla or the Lives of the Norse Kings*. New York, Dover Publications.

National Museum of Ireland (1973) *Viking and Medieval Dublin: National Museum excavations 1962–73: catalogue of exhibition*. Dublin, National Museum of Ireland.

Noonan, T. (1997) Scandinavians in European Russia. In P. Sawyer (ed.) *The Oxford Illustrated History of the Vikings*, 134–55. Oxford, Oxford University Press.

O'Brien, E. (1998) The location and context of Viking burials at Kilmainham and Islandbridge, Dublin. In H. B. Clarke, M. Ní Mhaonaigh and R. Ó Floinn (eds) *Ireland and Scandinavia in the Early Viking Age*, 201–18. Dublin, Four Courts Press.

Olofsson, Å. (2008) Early writing among ancient Vikings and today's pre-schoolers: a cognitive developmental perspective on reading acquisition and alphabets as effective artifacts. *Paedagogica Historica* 44 (1–2), 167–78.

O'Meadhra, U. (1987) *Motif pieces from Ireland: early Christian, Viking and Romanesque art*. Thesis and Papers in North European Archaeology 17. Stockholm, Almqvist and Wiksell International.

Park, R. (2005) Growing up North: exploring the archaeology of childhood in the Thule and Dorset cultures of Arctic Canada. In J. E. Baxter (ed.) *Children in Action: perspectives on the archaeology of childhood*, 53–64. Archaeological Papers of the American Anthropological Association 15. Berkeley, University of California Press.

Paton, R. (1936–7) An unpublished Scottish gold coin. *Proceedings of the Society of Antiquaries of Scotland* 71, 92–7.

Pétursdóttir, Þ. (2007) *Deyr fé, deyja frændr*: re-animating mortuary remains from Viking Age Iceland. Unpublished MA thesis, Faculty of Social Sciences, University of Tromsø.

Press, M. (trans.) (1899) *The Laxdaela Saga*. London, Penguin.

Ritchie, A. (2003) Great sites: Jarlshof. *British Archaeology* 69, 20–3.

Roach, A. (2008) Model boats in the context of maritime history and archaeology. *International Journal of Nautical Archaeology* 37 (2), 313–34.

Roesdahl, E. and Wilson, D. (1992) *From Viking to Crusader: the Scandinavians and Europe 800–1200*. London, Rizzoli.

Rundkvist, M. (2003) *Barshalder 2. Studies of late Iron Age Gotland*. Stockholm, Elanders Gotab.

Rydberg, V. (1907) *Teutonic Mythology: gods and goddesses of the Northland* (3 vols). Copenhagen, Norrœna Society.

Sawyer, B. and Sawyer, P. (1993) *Medieval Scandinavia: from conversion to Reformation* c. *800–1500*. London, University of Minnesota Press.

Sikora, M. (2003) Diversity in Viking Age horse burial: a comparative study of Norway, Iceland, Scotland and Ireland. *Journal of Irish Archaeology* 12–13, 86–95.

Sofaer-Derevenski, J. (1994) Where are the children? Accessing children in the past. *Archaeological Review from Cambridge* 13 (2), 7–20.

Spurkland, T. and Van der Hoek, B. (2005) *Norwegian Runes and Runic Inscriptions*. Woodbridge, Boydell.

Wallace, P. (1988) *Aspects of Viking Dublin 1–6*. Dublin, National Museum of Dublin.

Wallace, P. (1992) *The Viking Age Buildings of Dublin*. Medieval Dublin excavations, 1962–81. Series A. Vol. 1 and 2. Dublin, Royal Irish Academy.

Walsh, A. (1998) A summary classification of Viking-Age swords in Ireland. In H. B. Clarke, M. Ní Mhaonaigh and R. Ó Floinn (eds) *Ireland and Scandinavia in the Early Viking Age*, 222–35. Dublin, Four Courts Press.

Walton Rogers, P. (1989) *Textiles, Cordage and Raw Fibre from 16–22 Coppergate*. The Archaeology of York 17 (5). London, Council for British Archaeology.

Wileman, J. (2005) *Hide and Seek: the archaeology of childhood*. Stroud, Tempus.

Wilkie, L. (2000) Not merely child's play: creating a historical archaeology of children and childhood. In J. Sofaer-Derevenski (ed.) *Children and Material Culture*, 100–14. New York, Routledge.

Wincott-Heckett, E. (2003) *Viking Age Headcoverings from Dublin*. Medieval Dublin Excavations 1962–81, series B, vol. 6. Dublin, Royal Irish Academy.

7

WHITHER THE WARRIOR
IN VIKING-AGE TOWNS?

D. M. Hadley

Analysis of the construction and articulation of gender identities has become fundamental to historical and archaeological studies of early medieval society (*e.g.* Nelson 1997; van Houts 1999; Stoodley 1999; Brubaker and Smith 2004; Coon 2010). However, the gendered dimensions of the Scandinavian raiding and settlement in Britain and Ireland remain under-explored. A handful of studies have addressed the experiences and identities of women in the areas of Scandinavian settlement (Fell 1984; Jesch 1991; Kershaw 2009; see also Boyd, this volume), but the explicit discussion of masculinity has scarcely begun (for an isolated exception see Hadley 2008). This scholarly neglect is surprising on three counts. First, there is now an extensive body of scholarship on early medieval masculinity, which provides a context for understanding masculinity in the Viking Age (*e.g.* the various contributions to Lees 1994; Hadley 1999; Murray 1999; Cullum and Lewis 2004). Second, there have been a number of studies by literary scholars of the Scandinavian sources for the Viking Age – including sagas, poetry and runic inscriptions – in which masculinity is central (*e.g.* Jesch 2001; Jakobsson 2007; Phelpstead 2007). Third, the study of much of the Scandinavian impact on the British Isles has long been about the activities and behaviour of men, even if the construction of masculinity has not been explicitly articulated. This chapter draws on written, archaeological and material culture evidence to explore the construction and renegotiation of masculinity in urban settlements in England and Ireland in the wake of Scandinavian settlement. The focus is on the manner in which masculine warrior identities and ideals were transformed in the wake of settlement, and, in particular, on the contexts in which the symbolism of warfare remained relevant during the processes of settlement and acculturation.

Masculinity in the Viking Age

Insights into the masculine ideals and warrior culture of Scandinavia in the 9th and 10th centuries are principally to be gleaned from later written sources. There have been a number of studies of the attributes of masculinity presented in the sagas of the 12th to 14th centuries (*e.g.* Clover 1993; Jakobsson 2007; Phelpstead 2007), but these are widely regarded as problematic sources for understanding the historical realities of earlier centuries, given the late date at which they were written down and the undoubted influence of Christian ideals on the texts (*e.g.* Pálsson

1992). More reliable evidence for the period under discussion in this chapter can be derived from runestones and skaldic verse, which were the basis of an extended study of the nature of Viking-Age masculinity published a decade ago by Judith Jesch (2001). The runestones date to between the late 10th and early 12th century, with the vast majority surviving from Sweden. They incorporate inscriptions that record property inheritance and commemorate the dead, occasionally revealing something of their experiences and status (Sawyer 2003). Although skaldic poems principally survive in manuscripts of the 13th or 14th century, many were evidently composed at an earlier date. It is thought that the strict metre of skaldic poetry helped to maintain the integrity of poems over time, and the later written versions may, therefore, represent quite faithfully much earlier versions (Jesch 2001, 21–33). While the sources studied by Jesch span a broad time period, and were created in variety of geographical and cultural contexts, they have sufficient in common for it to be permissible to draw on this literary corpus to understand something of masculine attributes and experiences in Viking-Age Scandinavia. In turn, this provides a framework for understanding aspects of masculine identity among at least some of those Scandinavian men who settled in the towns of England and Ireland.

Jesch's analysis of this commemorative repertoire has revealed an array of characteristics associated with Scandinavian men. The term 'viking' apparently had positive connotations when employed on runestones, as at least fifteen record individuals with the personal name *Víkingr*, while on three further occasions the common noun *víkingr* is associated with individuals who had travelled, although whether for war or trade is unclear (Jesch 2001, 44–9). In contrast, in the skaldic poetry the term *víkingr* is often used pejoratively of enemies and wrongdoers (Jesch 2001, 49–54). This contrasting usage of the term *víkingr* may reflect something of the contemporary ambivalence towards the behaviour it encapsulates. Yet, whatever the connotations of *víkingr* behaviour, it is apparent that travel was a major element. The importance of sea-faring to Scandinavian men is emphasised in both sources of evidence, and the skaldic poetry, in particular, employs a rich array of terminology for both the various elements of ships and constructional techniques (Jesch 2001, 120–71; see also McAlister, this volume).

In the skaldic poetry there is a notable emphasis on the leader of the group, especially in accounts of preparing and launching the ship, and on some occasions he is also described as rowing the ship, all undertakings that could not possibly have been the work of one man (Jesch 2001, 171–8). Yet, the poetry simultaneously emphasises the importance of the warrior group to success in battle, as do many runic inscriptions (Jesch 2001, 180–203). The support of this group for each member was reinforced by oaths of loyalty and expectations that the wider group would not be betrayed by any of its members (Jesch 2001, 258–65). The term used to capture this expectation was *drengr*, which was used far more commonly than *víkingr* to describe Scandinavian men (Jesch 2001, 216–32). While this term has proven notoriously difficult to translate precisely, *drengr* evidently referred to groups of men, whether warriors or merchants, captured an expectation of loyalty and had an exclusive quality. According to Jesch (2001, 22), '*drengr* belongs to the vocabulary of the in-group'.

In recent work, Neil Price has sought to understand what it was that bound Viking armies together. He has drawn inspiration from studies of early modern piracy, characterised by an emphasis on the 'hydrarchy', an 18th-century term that described the powerful bonds that enabled dispersed groups to exert control over vast maritime areas. Price (*pers. comm.*) has examined archaeological evidence for the appearance of Viking warriors, including traces of clothing, the eye make-up and skin decoration applied to the body, and dental modification.

The unity of Viking armies must also have been reinforced by their ships, which had distinctive appearances and were often assigned names. For example, skaldic poems record the names of several ships that belonged to Óláfr Tryggvason, including *Trana* ('Crane'), *Ormr inn skammi* ('The Short Serpent') and, most famously, *Ormr inn langi* ('The Long Serpent') (Jesch 2001, 120–71; Crumlin-Pedersen 1997). That Viking armies were held together by shared values, manifest in their appearance as well as their behaviour, may help to explain how these raiding groups could remain active for years, if not decades.

The skaldic poetry records that the successful warrior could be relied upon not to flee the conflict. He would also kill many and provide corpses on which the beasts of battle – eagles, ravens and wolves – would feast: 'Óláfr's avenger, you provided the stuff of poetry … You cause the hawks of Hlokk [i.e. eagle or raven] to drink the liquid of corpses' (Jesch 2001, 252). It has been argued that the beast of battle imagery served to prepare the warriors for the task that awaited them on the battlefield, and that it was part of the training they received: 'War becomes poetry. By this means one can forget how unpleasant it really was and be psychologically prepared for the next time' (Jesch 2010, 171–2). In this way, the skalds were central to the effectiveness of the warrior group (Jesch 2010, 172).

Skaldic poetry and runic inscriptions cannot be confidently used to uncover real lived experience among Scandinavian men who fought and settled in England and Ireland in the 9th and 10th centuries. Nonetheless, they provide a framework for understanding aspects of Viking-Age warfare that many of those who subsequently settled may have experienced. The remainder of this chapter explores the extent to which the masculine ideals evident in the runic inscriptions and skaldic poetry were manifest in the towns of England and Ireland in the 9th and 10th centuries, the contexts in which an emphasis of martial ability occurs and the reasons for its select appearance.

Remaining a warrior in England and Ireland

If comradeship, loyalty, martial ability and the glorification of violence had all been important during the period of raiding, then such attributes are unlikely to have been lightly abandoned, even if transformations in behaviour were inevitable in the wake of settlement. Certainly, battles continued to be waged even after particular regions of England and Ireland had been conquered and settled by Scandinavians in the second half of the 9th century; thus, the reality, as well as the imagery, of warfare continued to be central to the experiences of many of the Scandinavian men who settled (Hadley 2006, 28–71; Ó Cróinín 1995, 238–56). Written accounts occasionally suggest something of the violence of these encounters, although they are, on the whole, not as evocative as the skaldic corpus (Jesch 2010, 169–70). For example, a poem incorporated in the *Anglo-Saxon Chronicle* records a battle that took place in 937 at *Brunanburh* – a location that has not been conclusively identified – at which the West Saxon forces defeated Óláfr Guthfrithsson, who had been leader of a Viking army in Ireland, and his allies, Constantine, king of Alba, and Owein, king of Strathclyde. It describes the battlefield as 'dark with the blood of men' and littered with the bodies of 'many a man destroyed by the spears, many a northern warrior shot above his shield', left behind after their comrades fled. The poem is, however, more concerned with the symbolic value of the victory for reinforcing the dynastic pretensions of the West Saxon lineage, than in evoking the horrors of battle (Whitelock 1961, 69–70).

There are other indications that violence could be used in a highly symbolic fashion, both to reinforce victory in battle and to proclaim new regimes. For example, an entry in the *Annals of Ulster* for 862 refers to the Scandinavians despoiling the ancient burial mounds at Newgrange, Knowth and Dowth (Co. Meath), and in the following year one of the Irish kings of Meath, Conchobor son of Donnchad, was 'put to death in water at Cluain Iraird' by Óláfr, leader of a Scandinavian army. Shortly before this event, Óláfr had allied with the other king of Meath, Lorcan, and the manner of the death of the latter's rival (Conchobor) was doubtless intended to carry symbolic weight and to serve local, as well as Scandinavian, political interests (Mac Airt and Mac Niocaill 1983, 318–21; Downham 2007, 20).

Viking armies fought over long periods of time and wide geographical areas, which suggests that Scandinavian leaders must have been effective at binding together groups of warriors, including, on occasions, those of local origins. For example, in 853 the *Annals of Ulster* record the arrival in Ireland of the aforementioned Óláfr, and both the Irish and other Scandinavians are said to have submitted to him. Over the following decades war was waged across Britain and Ireland by Óláfr and his associates, including Ívarr and Ásl (Mac Airt and Mac Niocaill 1983, 312–13), who various contemporary and later sources suggest were his brothers (Downham 2007, 16). Aside from fighting in Ireland, Óláfr and Ívarr also waged war and took captives in northern Britain, notably besieging Dumbarton Rock, the stronghold of the Strathclyde Britons, for four months in 870 (Mac Airt and Mac Niocaill 1983, 326–7). Ívarr was, furthermore, one of the leaders of the so-called 'great army' that ravaged England in the 860s, along with another brother, Hálfdan. Members of the dynasty of Ívarr played a leading role in the politics of England until the mid-10th century and of Ireland until the early 11th century (this dynasty is discussed at length in Downham 2007).

Warrior groups were doubtless bound together by a range of factors, including the apparently formidable reputation of their leaders; Ívarr was, indeed, sufficiently prominent for the *Annals of Ulster* to proclaim him 'king of the Northmen of all Ireland and Britain' upon his death in 873 (Mac Airt and Mac Niocaill 1983, 328–9). Repeated successes in battle must have generated considerable portable wealth with which followers could be rewarded. The large hoard deposited at Cuerdale (Lancashire) *c.* 905, which contained Anglo-Saxon, continental and Arabic coins, hacksilver and jewellery, has been interpreted as an army pay-chest. It was found close to what must have been the major routeway between Dublin and York (Graham-Campbell 1992a, 1–15), and was perhaps gathered together in the years after the Scandinavians were driven out of Dublin in 902 in order to facilitate a return to Dublin (Graham-Campbell 1992b, 114). This capacity to generate wealth (which presumably was not invariably subsequently lost!), along with an apparent ability to negotiate the contemporary political landscape, must have cemented the reputation of certain warrior leaders (Hadley 2006, 28–71; Downham 2007, 11–120).

Nonetheless, rivalries did emerge within the Scandinavian armies, and unity of purpose may have been a fragile commodity. Indeed, several members of the dynasty of Ívarr apparently died in Ireland at the hands of a relative. These included Ásl who was killed in 867 'by kinsmen in patricide' according to the *Annals of Ulster*, and Eysteinn, son of Óláfr, who was killed by Hálfdan in 875, while Hálfdan himself died in battle in 877 between rival groups of Scandinavians at Strangford Lough (Co. Down) (Mac Airt and Mac Niocaill 1983, 322–3, 330–3; Downham 2007, 16, 24). Moreover, defeat in battle must have challenged the unity of warrior groups, and threatened the maintenance of the rituals of the war band. Written sources provide occasional insights into the implications of military failure. For example, besieged to the point of starvation in a fortress on the banks of the River Severn at Buttington (Wales) in 893, a Viking army apparently resorted to eating its horses, both symbols of military status and practical necessities for a raiding party (Whitelock 1961, 56). Aside from sullying the reputations of their leaders, the price of defeat for the Scandinavians must sometimes have been symbolically reinforced by lack of any appropriate burial provision, as bodies were abandoned at the site of battle or disposed of by their enemies. The descriptions of the dead left behind on the 'field of slaughter' at *Brunanburh*, among them Constantine's son, may recall a common occurrence, and the aftermath of defeat may have been terrible indeed as the bodies were descended upon by scavengers:

> They left behind them the dusky-coated one, the black raven with its horned beak, to share the corpses, and the dun-coated, white-tailed eagle, the greedy war-hawk, to enjoy the carrion, and that grey beast, the wolf of the forest (Whitelock 1961, 70).

The consequences of defeat have been dramatically demonstrated by the recent excavation of a mass burial of Scandinavians at Ridgeway Hill near Weymouth (Dorset). Radiocarbon dating places the deposit between 890 and 1030 AD, while the application of stable isotope analysis has revealed that the dead were mainly from Norway and Sweden, with one individual likely to have been from the Arctic circle. The disorderly deposit comprised the decapitated remains of over 50 adult males, which had been thrown into a ditch, with the skulls stacked together nearby. The lack of general wound trauma has suggested that these men had been executed, rather than having died in battle (Boyle 2011; Chenery and Evans 2011); indeed, the location of the deposit, near to the parish boundary and to prehistoric barrows, is reminiscent of the locations of Anglo-Saxon execution cemeteries (Reynolds 2009, 203–34). The lack of dress-accessories has led to speculation that the men were stripped naked before they were executed, which was doubtless intended to compound the shame of defeat. Not only were members of the Scandinavian army apparently prevented from retrieving their dead and providing them with funerary rituals appropriate to their status and experiences, but these Scandinavian men were seemingly killed and disposed of in a manner deliberately chosen to carry significant symbolic weight within Anglo-Saxon society. A mass burial excavated in the grounds of St John's college, Oxford may provide another insight into the fate of Scandinavian raiders. The deposit contained at least 35 individuals, all male (bar two unsexed juveniles), the majority in the age range of 16 to 25 years, with peri-mortem weapon injuries, some of whom had been burned, and who had been dumped in the top of a ditch. Radiocarbon dating suggests that these burials date to the 10th century and stable isotope evidence for dietary profiles tentatively indicated that the individuals were likely to be of Scandinavian origin, and it has been concluded that this deposit is also likely to represent a group of executed Scandinavian raiders (Pollard *et al.* 2012). Evidently, then, for some of those Scandinavian men who set out on a *víkingr* adventure, doubtless enthused by the values expressed in the skaldic poetry, the reality was sometimes quite different, and very grim.

Warriors in death

When the Scandinavians were in a position to bury their own dead, burial furnished with weaponry was evidently one option for Scandinavian men (Ó Floinn 1998; Graham-Campbell 2001). This may have served to help ameliorate the loss of a warrior in battle. For example, the most elaborately furnished warrior burial at Repton (Derbyshire) was provided for a man who had apparently met a very violent end (Biddle and Kjølbye–Biddle 2002, 60–5). While the corpus of warrior burials is not extensive in either England or Ireland, nonetheless, there are some

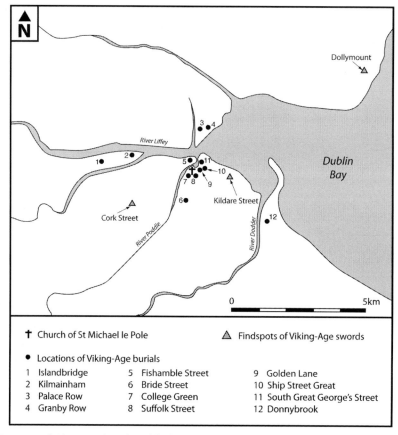

Fig. 7.1 Locations of Viking-Age burials and find spots of Viking-Age swords in Dublin (drawn by Oliver Jessop).

potentially significant differences in the prevalence of such burials in the two regions. Warrior burials have rarely been found in urban contexts in England. The few examples currently known are two poorly recorded burials accompanied by weapons from Nottingham (Nottinghamshire), a burial accompanied by a sword at Thetford (Norfolk) and a male accompanied by horse and sword at Reading (Berkshire) (Graham-Campbell 2001, 105–6, 114–15). Burials containing weaponry seem, in contrast, to be more common in urban contexts in Ireland, especially Dublin where weapon burials have been found at several locations (fig. 7.1). For example, at Bride Street a skeleton accompanied by a sword, spearhead and shield boss was found in 1860 (Ó Floinn 1998, 144), at least two furnished burials have been excavated at College Green, from which the grave goods included two swords, four spearheads, a shield-boss and a copper-alloy buckle, while at least one further furnished burial was excavated close by in the mid-19th century at Suffolk Street (Ó Floinn 1998, 135–6; Harrison 2010). To the south-east of the city centre at Donnybrook a burial excavated in 1879 was accompanied by a sword, spearhead and arrowheads (Hall 1978). At Palace Row, to the north of the River Liffey, late 18th-century accounts suggest the discovery of a furnished burial, including a sword and shield-boss, while at around the same time a sword, spearheads and iron rivets were found in association with human remains nearby at Granby Row (Ó Floinn 1998, 134, 139). The discovery of swords at a number of locations in and around Dublin, including Cork Street, Kildare Street and Dollymount, may indicate the locations of further weapon burials (Ó Floinn 1998, 132, 134). At Kilmainham and Islandbridge, *c.* 2 km to the west of the town, burials accompanied by a range of artefacts including swords, shield bosses, weighing-scales and hammers have been excavated (O'Brien 1998).

Raghnall Ó Floinn (1998, 137) has suggested that the burial arrangements at Dublin were similar to those in broadly contemporary Scandinavian settlements, with a multiplicity of burial sites strung out around the waterways and other routeways into the settlement. More recently, excavations have revealed burials within the settlement area as well (Simpson 2005). For example, furnished burials have been excavated at South Great George's Street, one accompanied by a shield boss and a knife, and another with fragments of a shield boss (Simpson 2005, 38–44), and excavations at Golden Lane have uncovered the lower half of a burial containing a spearhead, buckle, strap-end, knife and two lead weights (O'Donovan 2006). At Ship Street Great the truncated burial of a male accompanied by a glass bead, silver finger-rings and a decorated square iron disk has been excavated. Given that they were found in the area of the cervical vertebrae, these artefacts had possibly been part of a necklace, while a fragment of a sword found nearby is thought to have been another of the grave goods from this burial (Simpson 2005, 32–3).

Many of the furnished burials excavated in Dublin were located at existing burial sites or notable landscape features. For example, there are earlier unfurnished cist burials at Islandbridge, while the burials at Bride Street, Ship Street Great and Golden Lane were close to the location of the church of St Michael le Pole, and they may have been inserted into, or buried immediately adjacent to, an existing cemetery (Simpson 2005, 34; Simpson 2010, 426). Similarly, the furnished burials at Kilmainham were located near to the site of Cell Maignenn, believed to have been an early ecclesiastical foundation associated with a 6th- or 7th-century saint, St Maigniu (O'Brien 1998, 217–18). The weapon burial excavated at Donnybrook in 1879 also appears to have been inserted into a pre-existing cemetery, as a contemporary report stated that it had been interred with the remains of some 6–700 other individuals (Hall 1978). The disorderly disposition of some of the remains led Richard Hall (1978, 73) to interpret the deposit as the product of 'an indiscriminate massacre' of the Irish, who were subsequently interred with a Scandinavian warrior. However, Elizabeth O'Brien (1992) has since offered a more prosaic account of what was encountered in the 1870s, suggesting that this was probably a long-lived indigenous burial ground, with later generations of burial disturbing earlier remains, into which a Scandinavian warrior burial was inserted. The burials excavated in 1817–18 at College Green were close to the location of a large mound levelled in 1685, in a district known as Hoggen Green (from Old Norse *haugr*, 'mound'). It is believed that these burials, and those at Suffolk Street (see above), were near to, rather than within, the mound, which is thought to have been of prehistoric origins (Ó Floinn 1998, 135; Harrison 2010).

The interment of the Scandinavian dead in or near existing burial grounds suggests something of the potential for human remains to have been used symbolically in the processes of conquest and settlement. It must surely have been a conscious decision to appropriate existing ritual locations, which must have had a powerful impact on local communities. While furnished burials of females are certainly also known, they are less numerous, and the emphasis on warrior display suggests that this reuse of existing ritual places was intimately linked with expressions of masculine lordship.

In this respect the contrast between Dublin and York – the two towns in which significant numbers of Viking-Age burials have been excavated – is striking. Burials of the 9th and 10th centuries excavated at York Minster, where burial had been taking place since the 7th century, were not accompanied by extensive arrays of grave goods, still less weapon assemblages. Nonetheless, it seems certain that Scandinavians were buried near the Minster, given the Scandinavian influence evident on stone sculptures from the cemetery (Lang 1991, 55–9, 69–78). The role of successive archbishops in the political life of York may have influenced the burial strategies of the Scandinavians, among other aspects of their behaviour (for discussion of the numismatic evidence, see below). For example, it was presumably with archiepiscopal acquiescence that Guthred, a Scandinavian leader who had been supported by the religious community of St Cuthbert, was given burial in York 'in the superior church' in the 890s (Campbell 1962, 51). Large numbers of burials of 9th- or 10th-century date have been excavated adjacent to churches elsewhere in York (Buckberry 2007), but furnished graves are rare (Wenham *et al.* 1987, 83), and weapon burials of a type encountered in Dublin are unknown.

Not only are burials accompanied by weaponry more numerous in Dublin than in any of its English counterparts, but there is also other evidence for an emphasis on warrior culture and violence, as well as an awareness of the symbolic potential of human remains. Barra O'Donnabhain (2010) has recently suggested that human remains excavated in the Fishamble area of the city in the 1970s betoken a symbolic use of human remains in the construction of the identity of the town. Of the seventeen skulls found scattered along Fishamble Street in 10th- and 11th-century levels, eleven were certainly adult males, four were unsexed, and there was also one female and one juvenile. Six of the skulls showed evidence of trauma – either cut marks or blunt force trauma – and two had the cervical vertebrae still attached, of which one has evidence of cut marks on these vertebrae. The characteristics of this assemblage have been interpreted as providing evidence for decapitation, and a hole in one skull may suggest that it had been displayed on a pole (O'Donnabhain 2010, 274–5). The Irish annals provide accounts of the Irish decapitating their victims, and occasionally removing heads from the battleground and subsequently displaying them. For example, the *Annals of Ulster* record that in 866:

> Aed son of Niall plundered all the strongholds of the foreigners, in the territory of the north … and took away their heads, their flocks and their herds from camp by battle. A victory was gained over them at Loch Febail and twelve score heads taken thereby (Mac Airt and Mac Niocaill 1983, 320–1).

The Scandinavians also understood the symbolic resonances of decapitation, linking disembodied heads, at least according to later medieval sources, with prophetic powers. Given these attitudes towards decapitation, O'Donnabhain (2010, 281) concluded that 'vanquished foes could concurrently have been perceived as respected adversaries, while graphic warnings to potential enemies or dissidents could also have been understood as apotropaic talismans'.

Does the contrasting funerary record suggest that the Scandinavian warrior ideal was more significant in Irish towns than in their English counterparts? The paucity of weapon burials from English towns could, of course, merely reflect the limitations of the archaeological record, but the possibility that it is a genuinely significant pattern is reinforced by the fact that the warrior imagery incorporated into 10th-century stone funerary sculptures from northern England is also overwhelmingly found in rural environments, not in towns (Hadley 2008, 278) (fig. 7.2). Some churches in urban settings – such as St Mark's, Lincoln, and the Minster and St Mary Bishophill Senior in York – certainly have unusually large numbers of funerary monuments, but warrior images scarcely feature among this sculptural repertoire. David Stocker (2000, 186–91, 200–7; and this volume) has argued that such concentrations of urban funerary monuments can be accounted for by the presence of a sizeable merchant elite, expressing aspects of their identity through funerary display. Such mercantile social competition appears to have found no use for warrior imagery. Indeed, as Letty ten Harkel argues elsewhere in this volume, the suggestion that military status was not highly prized in at least some urban contexts is reinforced by the paucity of decorative horse harness accessories from towns, notably Lincoln.

What accounts for the apparently greater extent of furnished burial in urban contexts in Ireland? That the settlers in Ireland were from regions of Scandinavia in which furnished burial was more extensively practiced is a possibility, but given the evidence for the strong connections between the Scandinavian raiders and settlers in both Ireland and England (*e.g.* Downham 2007) this seems unlikely to be a significant factor. Nor can we imagine that the mercantile groups were less in evidence in Dublin than in English towns. It may be that there was a more protracted period

Fig. 7.2 Sculpture from Weston (Yorkshire), depicting a warrior with a sword in one hand, accompanied by a woman (height: 22cm). The image was carved in the 10th century on the arm of an earlier cross-shaft. Sculptures from northern England showing warrior imagery are overwhelmingly to be found in rural settings (drawn by Oliver Jessop).

of furnished burial in Dublin; indeed, some potentially very early radiocarbon dates have been generated from the burials at Ship Street Great and South Great George's Street, although doubt about the interpretation of the results remains, and on balance the late 8th-/early 9th-century radiocarbon dates seem unreliable (Griffiths 2010, 75–6). That the settlers took longer to adapt to indigenous funerary practices in Ireland seems plausible, and such a deduction is reinforced by other indications of the differing degrees of integration and acculturation of the settlers in the two regions. While there is certainly much to debate about the degree to which the melding of Scandinavian and English styles and iconography on jewellery, dress-accessories (Leahy and Paterson 2001), coinage (Blackburn 2001; 2004) and stone sculpture (Bailey 1996, 77–94) betokens acculturation, such artefactual evidence does, at least, exist in 9th- and 10th-century England, whereas a similar fusion of indigenous and Scandinavian styles of material culture is scarcely known in Ireland (Abrams 2010, 2). At the same time, it is apparent that Scandinavian rulers in England quickly adapted to existing styles of rule, minting coins in local style that displayed ecclesiastical influences (see below) (fig. 7.3). In this broader context, then, it may not be coincidental that distinctive burial practices should be more numerous in the urban centres of Ireland than in England. In general, Scandinavian material culture is rare outside of urban environments in Ireland. This need not betoken an absence of Scandinavian activity in rural contexts, as silver hoards of Scandinavian character are widely known (Sheehan 2004), but it does indicate that Dublin, in particular, was a focal point for overt expressions of Scandinavian

Fig. 7.3 Coins minted in York in the early 10th century. Coins 1, 4 and 5 are silver pennies of St Peter, the latter two with a sword and a sword and mallet, respectively. Coin 2 has a bust of the king, while coin 3 incorporates a bow and a hammer; both were minted for Ragnall (from Blackburn 2004) (copyright Fitzwilliam Museum, University of Cambridge).

identity, among which masculine displays were particularly prominent. Recent discoveries at Woodstown (Co. Waterford), including a male burial accompanied by a sword, spearhead, axe-head, shield-boss, ring-headed pin, whetstone and knife, suggest that a similar emphasis on warrior display may await discovery in the *longphoirt* where Viking armies spent the winter, and apparently also engaged in trade and manufacture (Harrison, this volume).

Coinage and the language of battle: ambivalent attitudes

The extent to which the Scandinavian elite were capable of expressing their authority in English terms is strikingly demonstrated by the coinage minted for Scandinavian rulers in York in the 890s. This was overtly Christian in nature, incorporating an array of different types of crosses and Latin inscriptions containing Biblical references (Blackburn 2004, 329). Nonetheless, the ethos of the battle retained its significance in elite display, and was articulated in the early 10th-century coinage incorporating depictions of weaponry such as a sword, hammer, and bow and arrow, and symbols of the battleground, including a banner of the type raised by armies in battle, and the raven, a carrion bird (Blackburn 2004, 334–7) (fig. 7.3). However, this imagery was typically combined with Christian symbols, most obviously a cross, while the coins almost invariably incorporated Latin inscriptions, in which the Scandinavian ruler, if he is named, is presented in Latin as 'Rex'. The importance of warfare and martial success were, then, linked to expressions of Christian kingship. Indeed, some of the martial imagery itself may have had Christian resonances: for example, the banner was usually topped with a cross, and in Northumbria the raven was also associated with St Oswald (d. 642) (Blackburn 2004, 336).

It seems to have been in the context of regime change that innovative battle-related imagery was incorporated into the coinage minted in York (Hadley 2008, 278). The arrival in York *c.* 919 of Ragnall, who had been active elsewhere in the British Isles, prompted various innovations in coin design including the incorporation of a bust of the king on one issue, and a glove that has been interpreted as the iron glove of Thor on another, while a third issue combined a Thor's hammer with a bow and arrow (Blackburn 2004, 334) (fig. 7.3). The coinage of Óláfr

Guthfrithsson, who seized York after the death of King Athelstan in 939, featured a raven, and the name of this king was presented, not in Latin, as on all previous coinage minted in York for Scandinavian rulers, but in Old Norse as 'ANLAF CVNVNC' (Blackburn 2004, 336). In the light of the foregoing discussion about the emphasis on Scandinavian warrior display in Dublin, it may not be coincidence that rulers who had just arrived from Dublin should have emphasized both their Scandinavian identity and the imagery of the battlefield on their coinage, which was a new medium of display for these rulers.

Fig. 7.4 Coin minted in the name of St Edmund. This coin was minted somewhere in East Anglia, by the moneyer Oviæs. It was found in a hoard recovered at Morley St Peter (Norfolk) (SCBI 26 East Anglian 23 (EMC 1026.0023)) (reproduced with kind permission of the Sylloge of Coins of the British Isles).

The coinage minted for Scandinavian rulers in other English towns presents a complex relationship with military success through the depiction of saints who were known for having died violently. For example, the coinage minted at various locations in East Anglia and the east Midlands (thought to include Norwich (Norfolk), Stamford (Lincolnshire) and *Sceldfor* (possibly Shelford, Cambridgeshire)) that commemorated St Edmund, made reference to a king who had been killed by a Scandinavian army in 869 (Whitelock 1961, 46) (fig. 7.4). The poor literacy on the coinage suggests that it was minted for Scandinavian rulers (Blackburn 2001, 139). How this king came to be venerated by Scandinavians on coins in little over a generation can partly be explained by the fact that by 880 Guthrum, a Scandinavian king who had converted to Christianity and taken the baptismal name of Æthelstan, had settled in East Anglia. Some time afterwards he entered into a written treaty with King Alfred of Wessex, which formalised relationships between their realms, and he appears to have sought to reign in the manner of an Anglo-Saxon king, minting coins modelled on those of Alfred or incorporating his Old English baptismal name (Keynes and Lapidge 1983, 171–2; Kershaw 2000). These developments may have provided the circumstances in which an earlier Christian king might have emerged as worthy of veneration, and association with Edmund undoubtedly served to promote a sense of continuity with the earlier regime.

The details of the cult of St Edmund may provide further clues to his appeal for both the Scandinavians and the local population. The broadly contemporary accounts provided by the *Anglo-Saxon Chronicle* and Asser's *Life of King Alfred* provide little detail about the death of the king, although they leave open the possibility that he died on the battlefield (Whitelock 1961, 50; Phelpstead 2009, 30–1). In contrast, later written sources suggest that Edmund had refused to take up arms against the raiders as he did not wish to shed blood, and that he had consequently died a particularly gruesome death, tied to a tree, tortured and then beheaded (Winterbottom 1972, 65–87). It is, however, unclear whether these late 10th-century accounts of Edmund's death are based on knowledge of the actual events or simply adopt hagiographical conventions, which expected martyrdom to conform to particular tropes (Phelpstead 2009, 31–3). Yet, oral tradition clearly underpins the earliest written account of the martyrdom of Edmund by Abbo of Fleury, written when resident at the monastery of Ramsey (Huntingdonshire) in the 980s (Cubitt 2000, 63–4). He had apparently learned of Edmund's fate from Archbishop Dunstan, who had heard the tale at the court of King Athelstan in the early 10th century from an elderly man who had allegedly been Edmund's arms-bearer on the day he died. The East Anglian people had, according to this account, gathered up Edmund's remains and taken them to a local church,

Fig. 7.5 Coin minted in Lincoln in the name of St Martin; moneyer uncertain (SCBI 4 (Copenhagen 1), 620 (EMC 1004.0620)) (reproduced with kind permission of the Sylloge of Coins of the British Isles).

before they were translated to the more important church at Bury St Edmunds (Suffolk). The cries of Edmund's head led to its location beneath a thorn tree, where it was found guarded by a wolf. Importantly, as Catherine Cubitt (2000, 64) has observed, lay veneration of the cult appears to have emerged before it received official ecclesiastical recognition; the early actors in the creation of the cult were layman, while the story of Edmund's head has popular religious connotations. The miracles that were soon associated with Edmund's body may have held a powerful appeal, at least for those Scandinavians who had accepted Christianity, as a sign of a Christian ruler whose powers were able to transcend death (Christie 2005, 145–55).

Intriguingly, as Cubitt (2000, 63–4) has pointed out, the early miracles associated with Edmund were not related to healing, as is often the case with saints, but rather to vengeance. In one miracle an arrogant noble, Leofstan, demands to see Edmund's body, and as a result becomes insane and meets a horrible death. In another miracle, thieves were prevented by the saint from breaking into his shrine. They were subsequently condemned to death by Bishop Theodred, although he had to retract this order on the grounds that a priest should not be responsible for shedding blood. Cubitt (2000, 64) suggests that this 'may reflect lay pleasure at the come-uppance of a harsh prelate'. The account of Edmund's death and of Bishop Theodred's intervention contrast the king's refusal to shed blood with the willingness of the bishop to condone bloodshed, and Cubitt (2000, 64) sees in this a reflection of the ideals of late 10th-century reformed monasticism, which condemned bloodshed by ecclesiastics. Yet, while the account may not have reflected accurately the concerns of the late 9th century, the story of Edmund, nonetheless, captures a sense of the competing attributes of lay and ecclesiastical lordship. It is, moreover, grounded in violent clashes between Scandinavian and English armies. In these contexts, it may not be too fanciful to suggest that the St Edmund coins, minted in a variety of locations, may have articulated tensions revolving around competing contemporary forms of masculine lordship.

The power of another saint who had rejected the battlefield may have been harnessed in the coinage issued in Lincoln in the name of St Martin in the early 10th century (Stewart 1967; Stocker, this volume) (fig. 7.5). Martin was a 4th-century Roman soldier, who refused to fight on account of his Christian faith. He was widely known across early medieval Europe, and many miracles were associated with him (Stancliffe 1983). This saint may have been chosen because of the existence of a church dedicated to St Martin in Lincoln, but this cannot be confirmed, and it is worth allowing for the fact that the undoubted popularity of this saint in both Frankia and Ireland may have influenced the choice by Scandinavian rulers who had encountered St Martin elsewhere (Stancliffe 1983; Mullins 2009; Stocker, this volume). It is notable that while he was renowned for rejection of weaponry, the coins minted in the name of St Martin incorporated a sword, which must have been, at least partly, influenced by similar imagery on broadly contemporary coins in York. While it is difficult to be certain which of his attributes prompted his inclusion on coinage minted for a Scandinavian ruler, that he was renowned for his rejection of weaponry and for refusing to fight is striking at a time when success in military encounters was a principal source of claims to authority. With both the St Edmund and St Martin coinage we can see the promotion of individuals in the urban mints of England whose status and reputation did not primarily rest on military prowess; elite masculinity was evidently understood, and accepted, as a multi-faceted identity in the Viking Age.

Conclusions

Battle-hardened warriors responded to the demands of settlement in diverse ways. While the warrior ethos retained its resonance, notably in the burial rites employed in Dublin, it is apparent that in the urban centres of England and Ireland it was modified in the wake of settlement. Transformations in Scandinavian elite behaviour, especially in England, seem to have been prompted by encounters with other forms of masculine ideal, notably those of the Church and of Christian kingship, and societies in which death at the hands of pagans could be presented as glorious martyrdom. Analysis of the imagery incorporated into the coinage minted in English towns for Scandinavian rulers suggests that the martial ethos of Scandinavian society was harnessed but modified in the process, in large part, it seems, because of the importance of the Church to the establishment of Scandinavian lordship. In contrast, in Ireland, there is little material or written evidence that the Church supported and articulated Scandinavian rule in the late 9th and early 10th century (Abrams 2010).

There is much that Dublin, in particular, had in common with English towns, with respect to evidence for trade and manufacture, but the ways in which elite status was expressed differed considerably, even though the same elite groups moved frequently between Dublin and York. In England, warrior imagery is more evident in the rural environment than it is in the seemingly more complex socio-political melting pot of the towns. Warrior ideology and imagery did not, of course, cease to be relevant upon settlement in England and Ireland, but they are unevenly identifiable in the urban archaeological record. This may tell us less about differences in the nature of urbanism between the two regions than about the contrasting levels of ecclesiastical influence on displays of lordship.

This chapter has focussed on the processes of settlement in urban environments, and the symbolic responses to them, among warrior groups. However, it is important to note that this group and its experiences were not common to all of the Scandinavian settlers. Men whose priority was manufacture or trade also settled (see ten Harkel and Ashby, this volume), as did women and children (Hadley and Hemer 2011; Boyd, this volume; McAlister, this volume). While this wider community may have bought into the warrior ideology in their conceptions of their communities, they did not actively share in it, and this may have, ultimately, been another factor in the transformation of the warrior ethos.

Acknowledgements

I am grateful to Letty ten Harkel for her feedback on this chapter. I would also like to thank Oliver Jessop for the drawings, and Adrian Popescu, Lynda Clark and Rory Naismith for their assistance with securing permissions for reproduction of photographs.

Bibliography

Abrams, L. (2010) Conversion and the Church in Viking-Age Ireland. In J. Sheehan and D. Ó Corráin (eds) *The Viking Age. Ireland and the West*, 1–10. Dublin, Four Courts Press.

Bailey, R. N. (1996) *England's Earliest Sculptors*. Toronto, Pontifical Institute of Medieval Studies.

Biddle, M. and Kjølbye-Biddle, B. (2001) Repton and the 'great heathen army', 873–4. In J. Graham-Campbell, R. A. Hall, J. Jesch and D. N. Parsons (eds) *Vikings and the Danelaw: select papers from the proceedings of the thirteenth Viking Congress, 21–30 August 1997*, 45–96. Oxford, Oxbow.

Blackburn, M. A. S. (2001) Expansion and control: aspects of Anglo-Scandinavian minting south of the Humber. In J. Graham-Campbell, R. A. Hall, J. Jesch and D. N. Parsons (eds) *Vikings and the Danelaw: select papers from the proceedings of the thirteenth Viking Congress, 21–30 August 1997*, 125–42. Oxford, Oxbow.

Blackburn, M. A. S. (2004) The coinage of Scandinavian York. In R. A. Hall (ed.) *Aspects of Anglo-Scandinavian York*, 325–49. York, York Archaeological Trust.

Boyle, A. (2011) Human remains. In *Weymouth Relief Road Mass Burial. Ridgeway Hill, Dorset. Post-Excavation Assessment and Project Design*. Unpublished report, Oxford Archaeology.

Brubaker, L. and Smith, J. M. H. (eds) (2004) *Gender in the Early Medieval World: East and West, 300–900*. Cambridge, Cambridge University Press.

Buckberry, J. (2007) On sacred ground: social identity and churchyard burial in Lincolnshire and Yorkshire, *c.* 700–1100. In S. Semple and H. Williams (eds) *Early Medieval Mortuary Practices*, 117–29. Anglo-Saxon Studies in Archaeology and History 14. Oxford, Oxford University Committee for Archaeology.

Campbell, A. (ed. and trans.) (1962) *The Chronicle of Æthelweard*. Edinburgh, Edinburgh University Press.

Chenery, C. and Evans, J. (2011) Isotope analysis. In *Weymouth Relief Road Mass Burial. Ridgeway Hill, Dorset. Post-Excavation Assessment and Project Design*. Unpublished report, Oxford Archaeology.

Christie, E. (2004) Self-mastery and submission: holiness and masculinity in the Lives of Anglo-Saxon martyr kings. In P. Cullum and K. Lewis (eds) *Holiness and Masculinity in the Middle Ages*, 143–57. Cardiff, University of Wales Press.

Clover, C. (1993) Regardless of sex: men, women and power in early northern Europe. *Speculum* 68, 1–28.

Coon, L. (2010) *Dark Age Bodies. Gender and monastic practice in the early medieval West*. Philadelphia, University of Pennsylvania Press.

Crumlin-Pedersen, O. (1997) *Viking-Age Ships and Shipbuilding in Hedeby/Haithabu and Schleswig*. Schleswig and Roskilde, Wikinger Museum Haithabu and The Viking Ship Museum in Roskilde.

Cubitt, C. (2000) Sites and sanctity: revisiting the cult of murdered and martyred Anglo-Saxon royal saints. *Early Medieval Europe* 9 (1), 53–83.

Cullum, P. and Lewis, K. (eds) (2004) *Holiness and Masculinity in the Middle Ages*. Cardiff, University of Wales Press.

Downham, C. E. (2007) *Viking Kings of Britain and Ireland. The dynasty of Ívarr to A.D. 1014*. Edinburgh, Dunedin Academic Press.

Fell, C. (1984) *Women in Anglo-Saxon England*. London, British Museum.

Graham-Campbell, J. (1992a) The Cuerdale hoard: a Viking and Victorian treasure. In J. Graham-Campbell (ed.) *Viking Treasure from the North West. The Cuerdale hoard in its context*, 1–14. Liverpool, Liverpool Museum.

Graham-Campbell, J. (1992b) The Cuerdale hoard: comparisons and context. In J. Graham-Campbell (ed.) *Viking Treasure from the North West. The Cuerdale hoard in its context*, 107–15. Liverpool, Liverpool Museum.

Graham-Campbell, J. (2001) Pagan Scandinavian burial in the central and southern Danelaw. In J. Graham-Campbell, R. A. Hall, J. Jesch and D. N. Parsons (eds) *Vikings and the Danelaw: select papers from the proceedings of the thirteenth Viking Congress, 21–30 August 1997*, 105–23. Oxford, Oxbow.

Griffiths, D. (2010) *Vikings of the Irish Sea. Conflict and assimilation AD 790–1050*. Stroud, The History Press.

Hadley, D. M. (ed.) (1999) *Masculinity in Medieval Europe*. London, Longman.

Hadley, D. M. (2006) *The Vikings in England: settlement, society and culture*. Manchester, Manchester University Press.

Hadley, D. M. (2008) Warriors, heroes and companions: negotiating masculinity in Viking-Age England. *Anglo-Saxon Studies in Archaeology and History* 15, 270–84.

Hadley, D. M. and Hemer, K. A. (2011) Microcosms of migration: children and early medieval population movement. *Childhood in the Past* 4, 63–78.

Hall, R. A. (1978) A Viking-Age grave at Donnybrook, Co. Dublin. *Medieval Archaeology* 22, 64–83.

Harrison, S. H. (2010) The Suffolk Street sword: further notes on the College Green cemetery, Dublin. In J. Sheehan and D. Ó Corráin (eds) *The Viking Age. Ireland and the West*, 136–44. Dublin, Four Courts Press.

Jakobsson, A. (2007) Masculinity and politics in Njáls saga. *Viator* 38 (1), 191–225.

Jesch, J. (1991) *Women in the Viking Age*. Woodbridge, Boydell.

Jesch, J. (2001) *Ships and Men in the Late Viking Age: the vocabulary of runic inscriptions and skaldic verse*. Woodbridge, Boydell.

Jesch, J. (2010) The warrior ideal in the late Viking Age. In J. Sheehan and D. Ó Corráin (eds) *The Viking Age. Ireland and the West*, 165–73. Dublin, Four Courts Press.

Kershaw, J. (2009) Culture and gender in the Danelaw: Scandinavian and Anglo-Scandinavian brooches. *Viking and Medieval Scandinavia* 5, 295–325.

Kershaw, P. (2000) The Alfred-Guthrum treaty: scripting accommodation and interaction in Viking Age England. In D. M. Hadley and J. D. Richards (eds) *Cultures in Contact: Scandinavian settlement in England in the ninth and tenth centuries*, 43–64. Turnhout, Brepols.

Keynes, S. and Lapidge, M. (ed. and trans.) (1983) *Alfred the Great. Asser's Life of King Alfred and other contemporary sources*. Harmondsworth, Penguin.

Lang, J. (1991) *Corpus of Anglo-Saxon Stone Sculpture, Volume 3: York and Eastern Yorkshire*. Oxford, Oxford University Press.

Leahy, K. and Paterson, C. (2001) New light on the Viking presence in Lincolnshire: the artefactual evidence. In J. Graham-Campbell, R. A. Hall, J. Jesch and D. N. Parsons (eds) *Vikings and the Danelaw: select papers from the proceedings of the thirteenth Viking Congress, 21–30 August 1997*, 181–202. Oxford, Oxbow.

Lees, C. (ed.) (1994) *Medieval Masculinities: regarding men in the Middle Ages*. Minneapolis, University of Minnesota Press.

Mac Airt, S. and Mac Niocaill, G. (ed. and trans.) (1983) *The Annals of Ulster (to A.D. 1131)*. Dublin, Dublin Institute for Advanced Studies.

Mullins, J. (2009) Trouble at the white house: Anglo-Irish relations and the cult of St Martin. In J. Graham-Campbell and M. Ryan (eds) *Anglo-Saxon/Irish Relations before the Vikings*, 113–27. Oxford, Oxford University Press.

Murray, J. (ed.) (1999) *Conflicted Identities and Multiple Masculinities: men in the medieval West*. New York, Garland Press.

Nelson, J. L. (1997) Family, gender and sexuality. In M. Bentley (ed.) *Companion to Historiography*, 153–78. London, Routledge.

O'Brien, E. (1992) A reassessment of the 'great sepulchral mound' containing a Viking burial at Donnybrook, Dublin. *Medieval Archaeology* 36, 170–3.

O'Brien, E. (1998) The location and context of Viking burials at Kilmainham and Islandbridge, Dublin. In H. B. Clarke, M. Ní Mhaonaigh and R. Ó Floinn (eds) *Ireland and Scandinavia in the Early Viking Age*, 203–21. Dublin, Irish Academic.

Ó Cróinín, D. (1995) *Early Medieval Ireland, 400–1200*. London, Longman.

O'Donnabhain, B. (2010) Culture clashes? The human remains from the Wood Quay excavations. In J. Sheehan and D. Ó Corráin (eds) *The Viking Age. Ireland and the West*, 271–82. Dublin, Four Courts Press.

O'Donovan, E. (2006) The Irish, the Vikings and the English: new archaeological evidence from excavations at Golden Lane, Dublin. In S. Duffy (ed.) *Medieval Dublin VIII*, 36–130. Dublin, Four Courts Press.

Ó Floinn, R. (1998) The archaeology of the early Viking Age in Ireland. In H. B. Clarke, M. Ní Mhaonaigh and R. Ó Floinn (eds) *Ireland and Scandinavia in the Early Viking Age*, 131–65. Dublin, Irish Academic.

Pálsson, G. (ed.) (1992) *From Sagas to Society: comparative approaches to early Iceland*. Enfield Lock, Hisarlik.

Phelpstead, C. (2007) Size matters: penile problems in sagas of Icelanders. *Exemplaria* 19 (3), 420–37.

Phelpstead, C. (2009) King, martyr and virgin: *imitatio Christi* in Ælfric's Life of St Edmund. In A. Bale (ed.) *St Edmund, King and Martyr: changing images of a medieval saint*, 24–44. Woodbridge, Boydell.

Pollard, A. M., Ditchfield, P., Piva, E., Wallis, S., Falys, C. and Ford, S. (2012) 'Sprouting like cockle amongst the wheat': the St Brice's Day massacre and the isotopic analysis of human bones from St John's College, Oxford. *Oxford Journal of Archaeology* 31 (1), 83–102.

Reynolds, A. (2009) *Anglo-Saxon Deviant Burial Customs*. Oxford, Oxford University Press.

Sawyer, B. (2003) *The Viking-Age Rune-Stones: custom and commemoration in early medieval Scandinavia*. Oxford, Oxford University Press.

Sheehan, J. (2004) Social and economic integration in Viking-Age Ireland: the evidence of the hoards. In J. Hines, A. Lane and M. Redknap (eds) *Land, Sea and Home: proceedings of a conference on Viking-period settlement, at Cardiff, July 2001*, 177–88. Society for Medieval Archaeology Monograph 20. Leeds, Maney.

Simpson, L. (2005) Viking warrior burials in Dublin: is this the *longphort*? In S. Duffy (ed.) *Medieval Dublin VI*, 11–62. Dublin, Four Courts Press.

Simpson, L. (2010) The first phase of Viking activity in Ireland: archaeological evidence from Dublin. In J. Sheehan and D. Ó Corráin (eds) *The Viking Age. Ireland and the West*, 418–29. Dublin, Four Courts Press.

Stancliffe, C. (1983) *St Martin and his Hagiographer: history and miracle in Sulpicius Severus*. Oxford, Clarendon Press.

Stewart, I. (1967) The St Martin coinage of Lincoln. *British Numismatic Journal* 36, 46–54.

Stocker, D. (2000) Monuments and merchants: irregularities in the distribution of stone sculpture in Lincolnshire and Yorkshire in the tenth century. In D. M. Hadley and J. D. Richards (eds) *Cultures in Contact: Scandinavian settlement in England in the ninth and tenth centuries*, 179–212. Turnhout, Brepols.

Stoodley, N. (1999) *The Spindle and the Spear: a critical enquiry into the construction and meaning of gender in the early Anglo-Saxon burial rite*. British Archaeology Research Reports British Series 288. Oxford, Archaeopress.

Van Houts, E. (1999) *Memory and Gender in Medieval Europe, 900–1200*. Basingstoke, Macmillan.

Wenham, L., Hall, R. A., Briden, C. and Stocker, D. (1987) *St Mary Bishophill Junior and St Mary Castlegate*. York, York Archaeological Trust.

Whitelock, D. (1961) *The Anglo-Saxon Chronicle*. London, Eyre and Spottiswoode.

Winterbottom, M. (1972) *Three Lives of English Saints*. Toronto, Toronto Centre for Medieval Studies.

8

ARISTOCRATS, BURGHERS AND THEIR MARKETS: PATTERNS IN THE FOUNDATION OF LINCOLN'S URBAN CHURCHES

David Stocker

For archaeologists, dealing with history through material culture, definitions of what distinguishes a town from other forms of settlement have been easier to find, perhaps, than they have been for colleagues dealing with history constructed from documentary sources. Archaeologists have preferred an economic rather than a legalistic definition, along the lines that a settlement rises to 'urban' status when a significant proportion of the economic activity in the town is directed, not towards agriculture, but towards trades and services that facilitate agricultural production within a zone around the settlement. Thus towns are fundamentally about trade and manufacture, the buying and selling of goods (see Perring 2002, ch. 2). This chapter takes a similarly economic and functionalist approach to a particular aspect of urban life that might have been thought relatively immune from influences of the market: the urban church. It concludes that the facilitation of commerce was a major factor in the foundation of urban churches, just as it was in the foundation of the towns themselves.

In the East Midlands, post-Roman towns are rightly thought of as Anglo-Scandinavian monuments. None of the region's towns has adequate evidence for 'urban life' prior to this period. Enclosures at Leicester and Stamford may have been occupied by the Church before the late 9th century, and such occupation has been demonstrated by excavation at Northampton and Derby (though not yet at Nottingham). Yet this should come as no surprise. All such towns were significant locations in the landscape that would have been prestigious holdings in any age. Anglo-Saxon lords frequently marked their ownership of such locations by sponsoring a church (*e.g.* Sawyer 1981). The Church was present in pre-Viking Lincoln also. But, again, no satisfactory evidence has yet been brought forward to demonstrate that 'urban life' was present alongside any ecclesiastical presence.

By the end of the 10th century, however, many of the Danelaw towns were flourishing and their number continued to grow. It has seemed to some writers that the great towns of eastern England acquired a superfluity of churches during this initial flush of urbanisation (Morris 1989, fig. 38). These were all parochial churches, the outcome of ecclesiastical reforms in the 10th century that harnessed church structures to those of the emerging lesser aristocracy and gentry in the countryside in the long drawn-out process of manorialisation (Stocker and Everson

2006). Such parochial churches were also founded in considerable numbers in the new towns of the Danelaw: Norwich had at least 46 by 1086, York 40, Oxford and Thetford some 20 apiece, Ipswich *c.* 15, Stamford 14, Leicester 9 and Northampton 9 (Morris 1989, 168*ff*, table 2).

The major urban centre based in and around the one-time Roman walled enclosures at Lincoln is a notable example of this ecclesiastical hyper-activity. Anglo-Scandinavian settlement here has been explored in a number of excavations (Vince 2003a; 2003b). It seems quite clear that Lincoln was amongst those early towns containing large numbers of churches founded before the early 12th century: at least 32 were documented by that date (Vince 2003a; Morris 1989, 168*ff*), and we should probably presume that the documents understate the total number founded before that date. It is this great number of church sites, and the quantity of archaeological detail now available for use in comparing them, that makes Lincoln a good candidate for this study of urban church foundation in the 10th and 11th centuries.

Lincoln's archaeology has been well studied. The general history of the Church in the early town was expertly explored by Sir Francis Hill (1948), whilst subsequent studies of individual churches (*e.g.* Gilmour and Stocker 1986) have added further archaeological detail to the general picture. Studies by Paul Everson and this author, based around Lincoln's surviving early monumental sculpture have also suggested that there may be distinctions between different types of church foundation within the town (Everson and Stocker 1999; Stocker 2000; Stocker and Everson 2001; Stocker and Everson 2006, 74–5). Between 1999 and 2003, a research, synthesis and mapping project was undertaken, generating a complete three-dimensional narrative for the city. The Lincoln Archaeological Research Assessment (LARA), exploiting the capacity of GIS to provide access to databases in three dimensions, 'characterised' the archaeology of the city (both standing and buried) in over 500 Research Agenda Zones (RAZs). These RAZs are grouped into seven 'Eras', which are organised according to principal subdivisions visible in the record of Lincoln's material culture. Thus, the Anglo-Scandinavian period (taken here to mean *c.* 875 to *c.* 1100) forms part of Era 9 (*The High Medieval Era, c. 850-c.1350*). This Era is divided into about 140 RAZs, one of which (9.60) includes the sites of 46 parochial churches (fig. 8.1).

Each RAZ entry contains: first, a brief statement of the state of current knowledge of the church and its churchyard; second, indications of topics and themes that might be explored in future research; and, finally, an indication of the RAZ boundary's reliability. The 2003 version of LARA was published as a disc accompanying *The City by the Pool* (ed. Stocker 2003), and is now available at heritageconnectlincoln.com. This chapter will therefore not provide detailed accounts or references for the churches discussed, which can be found within the LARA database.

This chapter draws these various pieces of work together to judge whether or not we can suggest a chronological sequence of foundation for the parochial churches of Lincoln, and whether or not we can distinguish between foundations of differing character. Capitalising on the spatial mapping undertaken for LARA, and on the research that went into the preparation of the RAZ texts for RAZ 9.60, it will explore a single research question: 'what can we say about the origins of the city's parochial churches?' LARA reveals that we can trace the approximate locations of all of the city's 46 medieval parochial churches and, in many cases, we can identify the boundaries of their churchyards. In all but a few cases, we find that parts of churchyard boundaries have survived through the city's period of population contraction and economic decline during the 14th and 15th centuries, and through the Reformation, and were represented on the city's earliest mapping (Mills and Wheeler 2004).

The map published in 1842 by the local surveyor J. S. Padley is particularly useful (Mills and

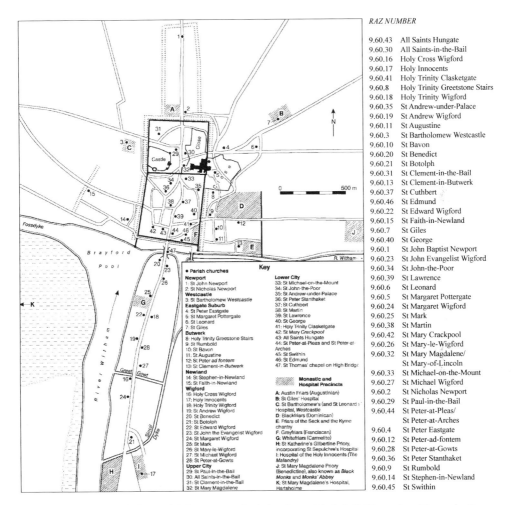

Fig. 8.1 Map and list of all Lincoln's known parochial churches, with their RAZ numbers (drawn by Dave Watt; copyright English Heritage).

Wheeler 2004, 44–57) (fig. 8.2). Lincoln's marked decline after the collapse of its cloth industry in the late 13th century, and the remarkable stasis that followed between the 14th and 18th centuries, means that Padley's map depicts a very similar city to Speed's 1610 map. In respect of the boundaries of property-plots owned by institutions (including former churchyards), Padley's map offers a near-approximation of 13th-century topography. Figures 8.3, 8.4, 8.5 and 8.7, therefore, are extracts from Padley's 1842 map of the 46 churchyard locations identified in LARA, drawn to the same uniform scale and including their local property boundaries. Such mapping of churchyard sites alongside their surrounding properties provides the starting point for this present characterisation and discussion of Lincoln's parish churches.

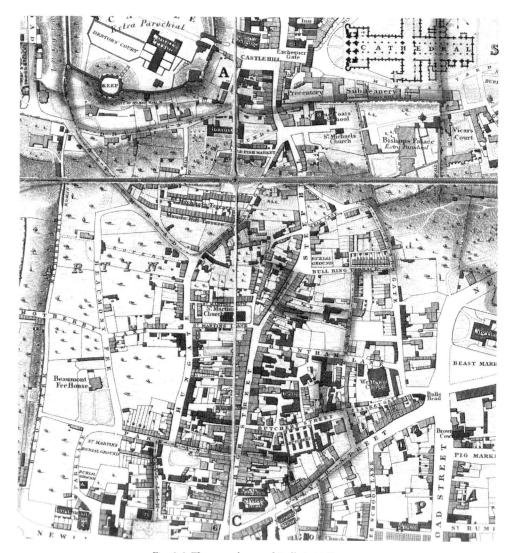

Fig. 8.2 The central part of Padley's 1842 map.

A preliminary characterisation of the churchyard locations of Lincoln on grounds of urban topography

Taking a morphological study of the parochial churchyards of Lincoln as a starting point, by superimposing the LARA information on Padley's 1842 map, Lincoln's parochial churchyards are seen to fall into one of four categories (figs 8.3, 8.4, 8.5 and 8.7): churchyards located within 'strip plots'; churchyards located at the junctions of streets and lanes; churchyards located within the public open space of markets; and churchyards located within religious precincts, rural, or unknown topographies. These four broad categories, or variations on them, have been

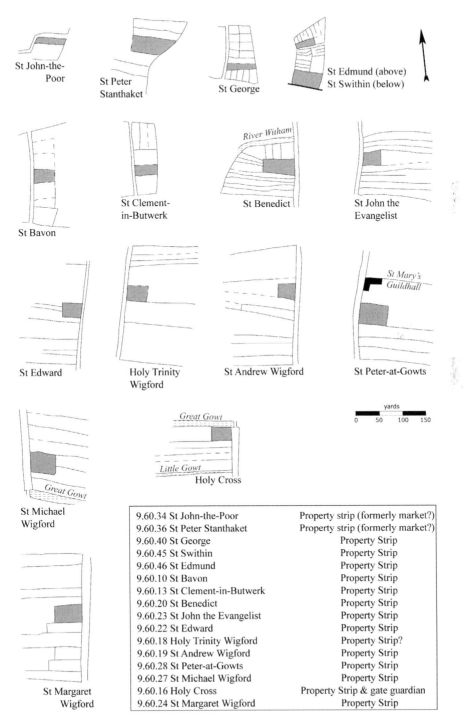

Fig. 8.3 Map and list of churchyards in 'burgage plot locations' (drawn by Letty ten Harkel).

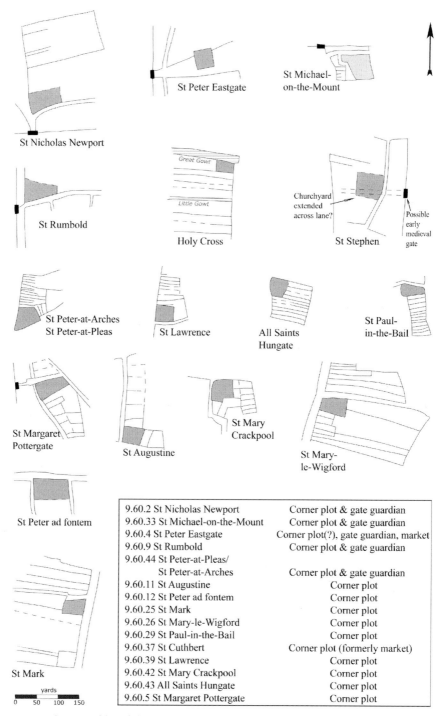

Fig. 8.4 Map and list of churchyards in 'corner plot locations' (drawn by Letty ten Harkel).

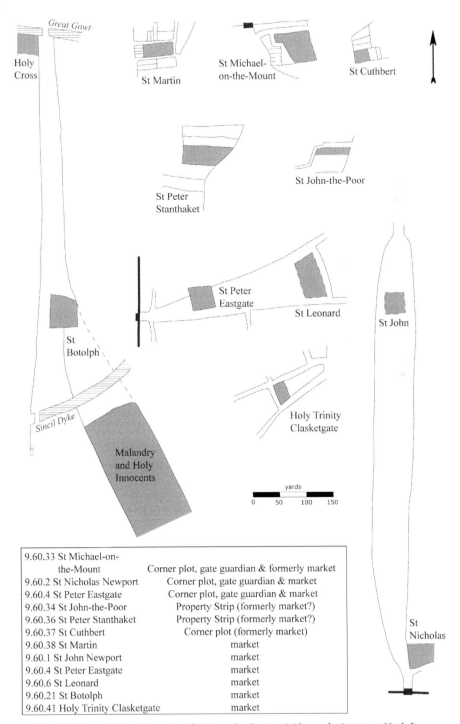

9.60.33 St Michael-on-the-Mount	Corner plot, gate guardian & formerly market
9.60.2 St Nicholas Newport	Corner plot, gate guardian & market
9.60.4 St Peter Eastgate	Corner plot, gate guardian & market
9.60.34 St John-the-Poor	Property Strip (formerly market?)
9.60.36 St Peter Stanthaket	Property Strip (formerly market?)
9.60.37 St Cuthbert	Corner plot (formerly market)
9.60.38 St Martin	market
9.60.1 St John Newport	market
9.60.4 St Peter Eastgate	market
9.60.6 St Leonard	market
9.60.21 St Botolph	market
9.60.41 Holy Trinity Clasketgate	market

Fig. 8.5 Map and list of churchyards in 'market locations' (drawn by Letty ten Harkel).

noted in many English towns (Palliser *et al.* 2000, 178–81). Later in this chapter, some of these simple topographical categories will be further sub-divided, and it will be argued that an effort to view these typological categories against more complex socio-economic considerations will yield more substantial results. First, however, the range of churchyard-location types mentioned above will be presented.

Churches established within 'strip plots'

The largest and most straightforward topographical category is a group of rectilinear churchyards that were fitted into a sequence of long thin property strips, extending away from the street (fig. 8.3). These strips are presumed to represent burgage plots, and the link between them and burgage-hold has been established, especially in the Bail (Jones *et al.* 1984–96; Vince 2003a, *passim*). There may be as many as sixteen churchyards in such locations. As fig. 8.3 shows, the long, narrow, plots in question are a variety of lengths and widths (there is certainly no such thing as a uniform burgage plot size in Lincoln) but, of greater interest, is the comparison between the length and widths of churchyard plots compared with those that surround them.

Although many boundaries shown on Padley's map are likely to be of medieval date, especially those defining former churchyards, many of the property boundaries mapped in 1842 will be the result of complex processes involving both amalgamations and subdivisions of medieval strips. This means that we cannot be categorical about any individual case but, even so, we can state with some confidence that, for example, the churchyard of St Peter-at-Gowts was cut out of the corner of a larger rectilinear property, most of which survived as a large single property until the early 20th century. The remainder of this property block was occupied by the palatial 12th-century townhouse known as St Mary's Guildhall (Stocker 1991). This topographical co-location strongly suggests that the owner of the plot that eventually contained St Mary's Guildhall made ecclesiastical provision for an urban estate centre here, by creating a small churchyard in one corner of the plot. Although its northern boundary remains unknown we might also suggest that the churchyard of Holy Trinity Wigford was cut out of a similarly large property block. Perhaps a second lord, with an urban estate based around this plot, was providing a parochial church for his estate centre in the same manner? This model of church foundation, more closely resembling the provision of churches within rural manorial *curiae* (as at Willingthorpe below), might also explain why certain other churchyards seem to disrupt the pattern of property strips extending back from High Street in the Wigford suburb (St Edward, St Andrew and St Michael, for example). In such cases we might be able to suggest the presence of a resident, or occasionally resident, lord; and indeed during the Reformation, the Sutton family claimed to have been the founders, and therefore the owners, of St Andrew in just this manner (Hill 1948, 166–7; 1956, 55, 58; Stocker 1990; 1999).

In cases such as St Bavon, St Clement-in-*Butwerk*, and St George, however, the churchyards appear to have been founded on properties of very similar size to those around them, a feature which has been explained in towns like Chichester through the observation that the dead from such parishes must have been buried at the Cathedral as there is no room on the plot for a burial-ground (Morris 1989, 195–6). There is no hint of such arrangements in Lincoln, however, and churchyards apparently consisting of two or more plots combined, giving more space for burial, are more frequently seen (St John Evangelist and St Edmund look like double plots, whilst the churchyard of St Benedict – and perhaps also St Swithin – apparently occupy three). This latter group might be contrasted, then, with those sites apparently cut out of larger plots, as they are perhaps less likely to have been associated with a lordly residence. In such cases, we might be safer presuming that the owner of the church has merely allocated one subdivision, or multiples of such subdivisions, of his urban estate for a church to service his tenants holding the adjacent strips.

Vince (2003a, 205–7, 260–64, fig. 9.83 RAZ 9.22) interprets two such churchyards (St John-the-Poor and St Peter *Stanthaket*) as occupying strips adjoining the earliest market place on the hillside below the Upper City south gate. Like the extent of the market place with which they were associated, the date of their foundation remains uncertain, but these churches may be later than those churches founded within the market space itself (St Martin and perhaps St Cuthbert, below) and could date from the period when the market place was filled-in with permanent buildings (a process which began in the mid-11th century). It is also possible, however, that both churches might have represented religious institutions within the early 'open' market place (like St Martin and St Cuthbert) and were merely 'tidied up' at this late date and fitted into a new, regular, layout of property plots. In the new regularised layout of market streets, however, St John's continued to service the fish market, held in the open space to the north of the churchyard, whilst the fell market continued to be held in St Peter's churchyard until it was pushed into *Parchmingate* outside in 1223 (Hill 1948, 154).

Although St Peter and St John might belong more comfortably below with the group of market churches, they might be compared with St Margaret Wigford. Here, too, a churchyard was established within a run of property blocks extending back from a market. But in this case, we can suggest that the market was founded in the late 10th or early 11th century, and its western side (containing St Margaret's) was re-developed into property plots prior to *c.* 1100.

Just to the north of St Margaret, the church of Holy Cross Wigford also sits within a run of property strips between the Great and Little Gowts. But the sequence of development proposed by Vince (2003a, 243–7; RAZ 9.51.4) for the development of Wigford suggests that the Great Gowt, which formed the northern boundary of Holy Cross churchyard, was, for a time in the late 10th and early 11th century, the southern boundary ditch of the Anglo-Scandinavian city. Holy Cross, then, once sat as a 'gate-guardian'; in the same relationship to the southern entrance to the city as St Nicholas Newport and a number of others (below).

Churches established at the junctions of streets and lanes

Approximately thirteen churchyards appear to be sited at the junctions of streets (fig. 8.4), but these corner locations clearly represent a variety of circumstances of foundation. The list includes St Nicholas Newport, St Rumbold and St Michael-on-the-Mount, all of which are close to gates through city walls, and the corners on which they stand are the junctions of roads leading to the gates themselves. Like Holy Cross Wigford, they are gate-guardians. The locations of all three adjacent to, but outside the gates of, the walled city has occasionally led to their being considered 'early' foundations (on the basis of continental models of churches founded over the graves of early Christian saints in extra-mural Roman and sub-Roman graveyards; Biddle 1986; Morris 1989, 29–45), but in other circumstances the dedications to St Nicholas and St Rumbold, at least, might suggest relatively late dates of foundation, and neither has produced any early evidence. This group of gate-guardians might also have once included St Peter Eastgate, not least because of the suitability of its dedication, though the later medieval churchyard depicted in 1842 is some distance to the east of the road junction outside the Upper East Gate. Like several other gate-guardian churchyards, St Peter's also became associated with a market place. In this case, indeed, we have evidence that its west tower dated from *c*. 1100 and its nave was probably earlier (Stocker and Everson 2006, 205), though evidence for a date before *c*. 1000 is lacking.

St Michael-on-the-Mount is evidently a gate-guardian and might also be a candidate for an early foundation. It is one of the few Lincoln churches mentioned in *Domesday Book* (Foster and Longley 1924, 204; Owen 1988–9, 105–11), and St Michael dedications are sometimes an indicator of ancient foundations (Morris 1989, 52–6). The adjacent properties seen on Padley's map might also conceal the church's prominence in the early townscape. This plot pattern could have arisen, however, in two entirely different ways, resulting in contrasting views regarding the churchyard's origins. First, the plot layout might suggest that it was established on a 'rear plot'; the large churchyard fronting onto the minor road approaching the rear door of the Bishop's Palace (presuming that the road existed prior to the 12th century), but with no frontage onto the Steep Hill, implying that it was already occupied when the churchyard was established. But alternatively St Michael's might have been a more ancient feature in the local topography, originally with an even larger churchyard, fronting onto both Steep Hill and the secondary lane. Certainly a cloth market was held within the churchyard until 1223, when it was relocated by civic order (Hill 1948, 154). As the city expanded and the open market in this area was replaced by permanent property plots, street front locations such as those parts of St Michael's churchyard facing Steep Hill could have been colonised by 'rows', perhaps erected by the owners of St Michael themselves.

The group of churchyards in the gate-guardian class might be extended to include that containing the twin churches of St Peter Arches and St Peter-at-Pleas, even though they are located inside, rather than outside, the gate itself. Here, however, stronger evidence for an early foundation date has been brought forward and together they represent a plausible pre-Viking church site, though describing their original setting as urban would be incorrect (Gem 1993; Jones 2003, 137; Vince 2003b, 156). Such an assessment must imply that the churchyard predates the property boundaries by which the churchyard was surrounded by 1842, and indeed the shape of the churchyard is not conformable with the adjacent properties: it does not extend as far east as those to the north and it extends further south than those to its east.

Something similar might also be said of St Lawrence, where the known churchyard boundaries are not conformable with the adjacent property plots either; possibly implying an early foundation for this church also. It might be relevant that Pope Vitalian sent relics of St Lawrence to King Oswiu of Northumbria in the mid-7th century (Colgrave and Mynors 1969, 321), an event which might represent interest in this saint in Northumbria prior to the 9th century. We know from excavation that St Paul-in-the-Bail was also established before the 10th century, and Vince's analysis of the block pattern of the Upper City shows that its churchyard was laid out earlier than the property blocks within which it sat. Although on the corner at the north end of a row of burgage plots, nevertheless St Paul's churchyard extended much further west than their back lane. Vince made a closely-argued case that the row of plots to the south of St Paul's were laid out only in the 12th century, whereas excavations at the churchyard itself show ecclesiastical occupation extending back to the 7th century, if not before (Vince 2003a, 209–14 and fig. 9.54).

The topography of Wigford, with its long straight road along a causeway cannot have encouraged the foundation of churches at corners, yet it is notable that churchyards were established at junctions of both known medieval lanes extending east and west from the High Street: St Mary-le-Wigford and St Mark. It is also true, however, that there were many small – mostly nameless – passageways between the properties extending back from High Street to the watercourses on both sides. These two churches have been linked previously, however, in a quantification study of Anglo-Saxon sculpture (Stocker 2000), and St Mark's has been extensively excavated (Gilmour and Stocker 1986), demonstrating that there was no meaningful post-Roman activity on the site prior to the layout of the churchyard in the later 10th century.

The 'corner churches' also include a small group of churchyard sites located in the town's 'back-lands'. Padley's map leaves us in some doubt about the shape of the plots around St Peter-*ad-Fontem*, although research shows that it was bounded by both *Bagerholmegate* and *Lyme Lane*, but St Augustine, also in *Butwerk*, appears to sit within a corner plot of similar extent to those facing the nameless east-west road onto which it fronts. Similarly the plots in which the two 'back-land' churches west of High Street sit (All Saints Hungate and St Mary *Crackpool*) also seem to conform to the layout of private properties to either side. These 'back-land' churchyard plots are relatively large compared with their equivalents in more central locations; a result, perhaps, of there being less intense pressure on space in these parts, and it is possible that such reduced pressure on land might result in churchyards being more frequently located at corners.

Churches established within the public open space of markets

Vince's (2003a, 260–4) analysis of Anglo-Scandinavian Lincoln has shown a town replete with markets, large and small. Some of these presumed market spaces are large and well documented, others are smaller and less written about, whilst several have been identified on topographical grounds alone. It is clear, however, that all but the latest of the city's market places were legitimated by the presence of a church (fig. 8.5).

In Vince's view, the earliest of these markets is likely to have been located in the area of open ground spilling down the hillside, away from the south wall of the Roman fortress and towards the built-up area on the north bank of the river, with its landing places and manufacturing establishments. There is no documentary evidence for this early market, which pottery evidence suggests originated in the late 9th century, but critical evidence is provided by a rare coinage minted in Lincoln and dedicated to St Martin. These coins imitate the well-known St Peter's coinage of York, where it is presumed that they indicate that the market within which the coinage was used was under the patronage of St Peter (Stewart 1967; Mossop 1970; Blackburn *et al.* 1983, 13–14;

Fig. 8.6 St Martin's church in a detail from a view from the northeast, made in c. 1784 (by S. H. Grimm). The view looks across the area of the early hillside market, which had reverted to an area of sparse occupation by the 18th century. The inset shows one of the rare 'St Martin's' coins from the early Lincoln mint (Mossop 1970, plate I/7).

Blackburn 2004, 332–5). The equivalent St Martin coins of Lincoln, presumably demonstrate, therefore, that the early market here was under the patronage of St Martin. Consequently, it is satisfying to discover that the longest-lived of the churches within this early fan-shaped market place on the steeper part of the Lincoln hillside was dedicated to St Martin (fig. 8.6). Within this early market we can imagine an irregular open space on the steep hillside, on the edge of the occupied area, populated by traders' booths extending north, east and west of St Martin's churchyard, probably as far as the former Roman wall lines. But excavations have shown that the market space became filled up with permanent buildings during the late 11th and 12th centuries and the open market space with its presumed rows of traders' booths developed into a street network, with specialised goods being sold in different streets. St Martin's churchyard itself, and the streets around, became the hay market, for example. At this stage, St Martin's churchyard, although clearly earlier in the townscape than the property plots around it, probably acquired a row of properties along its western side. As we have seen, something similar might also have occurred at St Michael's, by the gate leading to this same market.

Like St Martin, St Cuthbert might also have started life as a foundation within the open early market space on the steepest parts of the hillside, only to become engulfed by property plots when that open market area was tidied-up into streets. At that stage St Cuthbert became a corner plot in a group of properties that faced westwards onto the corn market and southwards onto Bullring Lane.

The early fan-shaped market on the hill side, of course, was outside the south gate of the Upper Roman defences, which may have been re-used as a 'reserved' or military enclosure by the Vikings at Lincoln from the 9th century (the 'burh') and will be considered in greater detail later (Stocker 2004, 15–16; Parsons 2004). The city's other markets were also often established at the approaches to the city's defences. The largest and earliest of these is thought to be outside the southern boundary of the city. This was a huge funnel-shaped space extending southwards from the Great Gowt bridge. Traders in this space will have had access to as many as four parochial churches, although it is unlikely that all were founded at the same time as the market. We have already seen that Holy Cross might have been a gate-guardian, but we have also seen that St Margaret Wigford churchyard is clearly located within a layout of the property plots leading back from the market's western boundary, perhaps only developed once the market itself had been firmly established.

Indeed, the row of plots containing St Margaret's churchyard might date from the period after the market place had been truncated, as this huge southern market was evidently cut down in size by the construction of the Sincil Dyke right across it. Although once thought a Roman canal, it is now widely agreed to be of medieval origin: whereas it is unlikely to have been laid out prior to the Great Gowt in the late 10th or early 11th century, it was there by *c.* 1100 (RAZ 9.51.5). St Margaret's churchyard and its associated properties were perhaps established, then, in the mid- or later 11th century.

St Botolph's churchyard, on the other hand, like St Martin's, St John Baptist and St Leonard's, was located partly, if not wholly, within the open space of the market. It was an 'island-church'. St Botolph, of course, became a favourite dedication associated with travellers, but he was also associated with great markets, as at Boston, no doubt because the traders travelled to and from them (Morris 1989, 217–19). Lincoln's St Botolph had several characteristics, such as its size and cruciform plan, which has led to speculation that the church was an early or a senior foundation within the city's ecclesiastical hierarchy, but the church's location at the heart of

Lincoln's greatest later medieval market probably accounts for many of its distinctive qualities. Further south still, alongside the great southern market space was the parochial church of Holy Innocents, which might also have originated as an island-church; but evidence is absent, as it was assimilated into the Malandry Hospital in the 12th century (below).

In order of foundation date, Lincoln's next-oldest markets are probably those outside the east and north gates of the upper Roman enclosure, marked by the churches of St Peter Eastgate and St Leonard's and St Nicholas' and St John Baptist. Although the markets they served were markedly different in shape, in terms of ecclesiastical provision they were remarkably similar. Both had gate-guardians close to the town wall, and both were provided with a subordinate island-church towards the farthest end of the market area. In both cases, trading seems to have been largely between the two churches, and around the island-churches themselves. We know that the city's early market was under the patronage of St Martin – its own island-church – and we can speculate that the southern market was under St Botolph's patronage, similarly an island-church. Consequently those to north and east of the Upper City were probably also under the patronage of the island-churches of St John and St Leonard respectively. Indeed, some evidence that the Newport Market was dedicated to St John occurs in the 14th century, when the fair here was focused around his feast on 24 June (Vince 2003a, 227). The date of establishment of these markets (and therefore the likely date of establishment of the churches of St John and St Leonard) is not precisely known, but there is a persistent tradition that the northern market was established when the Upper City was defined as a castle in 1068, and this tradition might recall a foundation date shortly after the Conquest (*e.g.* Abell and Chambers 1936, 36). The dedication of the gate-guardian to St Nicholas, however, might suggest an even later foundation. Although in existence since the 4th century, the cult of St Nicholas received a great boost in England *c.* 1100, following Anselm's attendance at the re-enshrinement of the saint at Bari in 1095 (Farmer 1997, 364–5). Furthermore, it is a dedication frequently associated both with markets and travellers (Jones 2004, 7 and note; Keene 1985). St John is probably even later in date than St Nicholas, as its minimal parish was clearly 'cut-out' of the older church's possessions. A date around 1100 would also be appropriate if the eastern market was indeed dedicated to Leonard; sometimes said to be the favourite 'Norman' saint, his spectacularly successful cult was launched in 1103 (Farmer 1997, 303–4).

The only market inside the walls associated with a single church is the *Clew* – or thread – market just inside the lower gate in the eastern walls. Here, on a constrained triangle of land between Clasketgate and Silver Street, there once existed an island-church dedicated to the Holy Trinity about which little is known except that it was associated with the market place itself. The church was probably established at the same date as the market, but it is uncertain when this occurred. The earliest reference to the name recorded by Cameron (1985, 114) is in 1271–2. The very specific nature of the trade here might suggest that the market dates from the period of concentration of traders when the great market on the hillside was regularised from the mid 11th century onwards. If so, Holy Trinity might date from the late 11th or early 12th centuries.

By the time the large new market was laid out on partly reclaimed land at Newland, outside the Lower City's west gate, however, no church was established within or alongside it. This probably suggests that Newland market dates from a period when new parochial foundations were much more difficult to achieve: *i.e.* a period after the early 12th century (Morris 1989, 177). It seems, however, to have been present by 1182 (Cameron 1985, 85), and there is no record of any church here subsequently, apart from a cross, later known as Buttercross.

Churches established within precinct, rural, or unknown locations

The remaining churchyards identifiable on Padley's map do not conform to a simple morphological grouping (fig. 8.7), but they can be grouped together in other ways. Three outlying parochial churches were, for example, subsequently included within the precincts of the later medieval ecclesiastical institutions, which over-wrote their original topographical setting (St Bartholomew, St Giles and Holy Innocents). All three churches were located on the edges of the built-up area, but documentary sources suggest that all three pre-dated the institutions of which they later became parts. St Giles (typically a dedication of the later 11th and 12th centuries; Morris 1989, 226) and St Bartholomew might originally have fallen into the 'strip plot' category, though St Bartholomew might have also played a role as gate-guardian for the western gate of the Upper City, even though located someway from the gate itself. We have already noted that Holy Innocents might have been an island-church, originally within the southern market.

St Faith-in-Newland, on the other hand, owes its origin to the Bishop's manor of Willingthorpe, and seems to have been located within the manorial curia (RAZ 9.32.1 and 2). The settlement itself might belong to the chain of spring-line nucleated villages at the foot of the cliff to the north and, if so, its church might be a foundation of the later 10th century (Everson and Stocker 1999, 76–9; Stocker and Everson 2006, 67–9). Furthermore, if the church was located within the manorial curia, then the founder of the church was probably the manorial lord. By *Domesday*, this formerly rural settlement not only belonged to the Bishop, but the parish already contained burgage plots, indicating that the urban area extended this far westwards. If St Faith was indeed originally established within the manorial curia by its owner, to serve his household and the people of the estate based there, it should bear comparison with St Peter-at-Gowts, the main difference being the legal status of the lordly estate.

Also on Lincoln's western side, lay the churchyard of St Stephen Newland. Although the 1842 map offers little useful topographical information, it is possible that St Stephen's was established prior to the reorganisation of the street pattern in Newland, as it lies on the presumed original line of *Midhergate* (Vince 2003a, 228–30) close to where this hypothesised road would have emerged from the walled area. St Stephen's, then, might be another gate-guardian. Streets in this area were reorganised to accommodate the Newland market place of the mid-12th century (above) and, consequently, St Stephen's should date from before that date.

Although we can only guess at the local topography within which the churchyards of Holy Trinity Greetstone Stairs and St Andrew-under-Palace were founded, they were evidently located in back-streets, and the 1842 map helps little in interpreting the two remaining Bail churches (St Clement's and All Saints) as, although we know the general area of their churchyards, both disappeared during the medieval period. The early Bail churches are exceptional within the city, however, and they are discussed as a group below.

The final Bail church, St Mary Magdalen, is also exceptional. As mapped by Padley it seems an excellent surviving example of a church placed within a single burgage plot (fig. 8.8). St Mary's is not included within this category, however, because it has only occupied this burgage-plot location since the end of the 13th century (Srawley 1966; Jones *et al.* 1987, 73–4). Previously the church was co-located within the Cathedral, and as far as we know, the burgage plot that it has occupied subsequently was originally in secular uses. Before the cathedral itself was established here in 1073, this was the site of the minster church of St Mary-of-Lincoln, which presumably also had parochial responsibilities. Padley's map adds nothing to our understanding

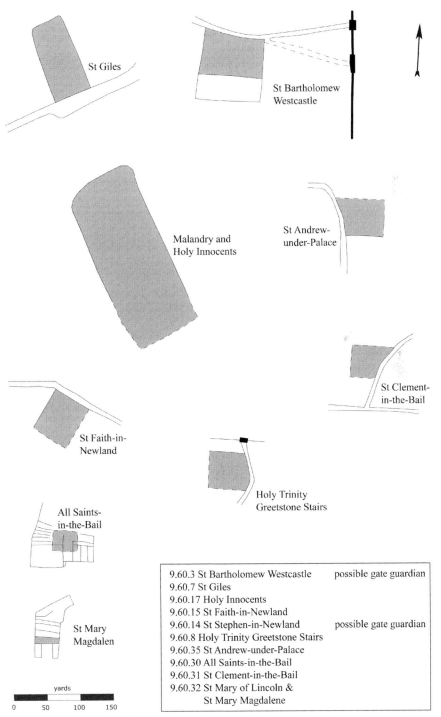

St Giles

St Bartholomew
Westcastle

Malandry and
Holy Innocents

St Andrew-
under-Palace

St Clement-
in-the-Bail

St Faith-in-
Newland

Holy Trinity
Greetstone Stairs

All Saints-
in-the-Bail

St Mary
Magdalen

yards

0   50   100   150

9.60.3 St Bartholomew Westcastle	possible gate guardian
9.60.7 St Giles	
9.60.17 Holy Innocents	
9.60.15 St Faith-in-Newland	
9.60.14 St Stephen-in-Newland	possible gate guardian
9.60.8 Holy Trinity Greetstone Stairs	
9.60.35 St Andrew-under-Palace	
9.60.30 All Saints-in-the-Bail	
9.60.31 St Clement-in-the-Bail	
9.60.32 St Mary of Lincoln & St Mary Magdalene	

Fig. 8.7 Map and list of churchyards in 'other locations' (drawn by Letty ten Harkel).

Fig. 8.8 St Mary Magdalen, from the southwest c. 1800 (detail of a view by an unnamed artist in the Local Studies Collection, Lincoln Central Library; courtesy of Lincolnshire County Council).

of its original topographical setting but, along with the other Bail churches, St Mary-of-Lincoln will figure in our consideration of the proprietorial category of churches in the following section.

Beyond topography: the role of the market in urban church foundation

There has been much discussion about those Lincoln churches that might have been founded prior to the revitalisation of the town itself in the late 9th and 10th centuries (Everson and Stocker 1999; Gem 1993; Stocker 1993; Vince 2003a). No conclusion has yet been reached regarding the date of the first church of St Paul-in-the-Bail, but it is clear that there was an established ecclesiastical presence here prior to the 10th century. We have seen that the same may also be true in the case of the two St Peters in the Lower City, and perhaps St Lawrence might also have been in existence prior to the late 9th century. These churchyards, then, may pre-date the expansion of the town from its late 9th- and early 10th-century focus south of the market on the hillside. The final potentially pre-Viking church site (St Mary's Priory) need not concern us here, as it was always outside the urban area and was not a parochial church (RAZ 8.1; 9.55).

Churches were evidently founded thick and fast in the two centuries following the Anglo-

Scandinavian 're-foundation' of Lincoln in *c.* 875, and the existence of at least 32 of those in fig. 8.1 is recorded in documentary sources by *c.* 1110 (Morris 1989, 169, 173). Amongst these new urban foundations, outside the upper walled enclosure, it is perhaps St Martin's that has the strongest claim to priority. Set on an 'island' near the south-west corner of the great market on the hill side, the coinage issue probably indicates not just its existence, but its seniority, in the early 10th century. The Frankish dedication is a surprise, however, for a church associated so clearly through the St Martin's coinage with the Hiberno-Norse of York. St Martin's principal cult site at Tours was attacked by Norsemen (of uncertain origin) in 853, but its revival in the early 10th century 'can hardly have been unconnected' with Norse activity (Sawyer 1997, 46), and it is worth asking whether the apparent dedication of Lincoln's early market to St Martin might suggest some level of trade with the Loire. Given the close similarity between the St Martin coinage and contemporary coinages from York (Blackburn 2006; also see Sawyer 1998), it has been suggested that the Lincoln coins were minted under the authority of York. If this is true then we see here an ascendant Viking kingdom based in York establishing a new market at a trading hub near its southern border, perhaps hoping to attract Frankish merchants. The foundation of both market and church, then, seems to be further evidence that Lindsey was not re-conquered by Edward the Elder in 918 but that it remained under the control of York until 944 (Everson and Stocker 1999, 80–4; Stocker and Everson 2001). The alternative explanation for the Frankish dedication, that the church and/or the market were earlier than the mid 9th century and that they represent a period of pre-Viking trading, lacks any corroborative evidence.

Like St Martin, the church of St Cuthbert may also have been an island-church within this early market place, and both would be comparable with many other 10th- and 11th-century foundations in urban markets across England (Morris 1989, 212). St Cuthbert's dedication suggests a somewhat later foundation date than St Martin, belonging to a group of Lincoln church dedications with foundations in the mid- or late 10th century (others include St Swithin, St Edward King and Martyr, St Edmund and St Rumbold). All of these saints have been associated with the period of resurgence of Wessex rule in the Danelaw at this date (Rollason 1989; Fell 1978; Vince 2003a, 234). To this list of saints favoured by the house of Wessex we might add St Augustine, first Archbishop of Canterbury, who was culted at this time for similar reasons (Thacker 1999, 384); perhaps also St Benedict, whose cult might have received a boost following Aethelwold's monastic reforms; and Holy Cross, to which a cult based at Abingdon (Oxfordshire) flourished in the mid- to late 10th century (Thacker 1988, 59–63). This group of presumed later 10th-century church foundations do not, however, share a single churchyard topography. St Cuthbert's, then, could have been founded in the second half of the 10th century as an island-church within an already thriving open market, but its topographical setting would have more in common with St Leonard, which we suspect is *c.* 1100 in date, than with other members of this late 10th-century group. Similarly, five of the remainder were established in strip plots whilst two are on corner plots, again indicating that their local topographical location is not related to the date of their foundation.

Although this group of potentially later 10th-century churches does not include all those within what Vince (2003a, figs 9.37 and 9.38) considered to be the contemporary urban area, nevertheless they do sit within its boundaries. These apparently later 10th-century dedications, then, might be seen to form a second phase of urban growth, expressed through an intensification of trade in the hillside market, and expansion at the periphery of the settlement, not just eastwards into western *Butwerk*, but southwards into 'Upper' Wigford.

This development of the city southwards down Wigford is of particular interest as Vince (2003a, 196, 235–42) suggested that it might have been stimulated in part by the Fossdyke's construction or re-opening, linking Lincoln to the Trent at Torksey. This suggestion is based on the sudden appearance of pottery types imported from western kilns, but it was confirmed by the excavations at St Mark's, in Upper Wigford, which indicated a church established in the second half of the 10th century. St Mark's is also one of only two Lincoln churches that have produced exceptional quantities of graveyard monuments, of cheap but numerous types. It has been suggested that such concentrations might be associated with trading settlements (Stocker 2000). The same study also suggested that St Mark's was a candidate for a church foundation of the type documented at St Mary Castlegate York, Holy Trinity Norwich and St Martin's Vintry and All Hallows-the-Great, both in London (Morris 1989, 173; Schofield 1994, 35). The other potential Lincoln example of this type of collective foundation is St Mary-le-Wigford, which stands immediately to the north. Both St Mary and St Mark sit within corner plots, but they are the only churches with comparable sculpture evidence, rendering it unlikely that all other Lincoln churches with this local topography were mercantile foundations.

The 'corner-plot' group also contains gate-guardians, both pre-Viking examples (like St Peter-at-Arches and St Peter-at-Pleas) and later ones, like St Peter-*ad-Fontem* (below). The phase of late 10th-century expansion down 'Upper Wigford', which was bounded to the south by the Great Gowts, also included the churches of St Peter-at-Gowts and Holy Trinity Wigford, which our plot analysis suggests were cut out of larger, and presumptively lordly, properties. Such churchyards are more likely to represent a 'private' lordly initiative, aimed at religious provision for a lordly household, rather than the coming together of a merchant community, as seems to have been the case at St Olave's, York and St George's, Oxford (Morris 1989, 171–2, 204–5).

As possible appurtenances of lordly households, it may be more appropriate to consider churches such as St Peter-at-Gowts alongside the four Anglo-Scandinavian churches in the Bail: St Clement, St Paul, All Saints and St Mary-of-Lincoln. During some 20 years of analysis of archaeological findings in the Bail, it was concluded that the whole of the area within the wall of the upper Roman city was a 'reserved area' in the century or two prior to the Norman Conquest. All available archaeological evidence points towards the Norman conquerors adopting the entire area within the Roman wall as their 'castle' (Vince 2003a, 170–9; Stocker 2004). *Domesday Book* reports that 166 houses were made 'waste' by the creation of Lincoln's castle but, following Roffe's research on Stamford and elsewhere (Mahany and Roffe 1982), we believe that this entry does not imply the physical destruction of actual houses, but merely that a taxable area equivalent to this number of houses was lost to the King, through the castle's foundation. It is possible, therefore, that *Domesday* does *not* record that the upper walled enclosure of the Anglo-Saxon city was merely an extension of the urban houses of the commercial settlement at the bottom of the hill. The way is open instead for a reconsideration of the character of the area within the Roman walls during the Anglo-Scandinavian period. There is nothing in the archaeological record to refute the suggestion that the Upper City was primarily a fortress, rather than an urban centre at this time, indeed it has frequently been identified as the 'burh' of Lincoln, established by the Vikings in the later 9th century (Parsons 2004; Stocker 2004; forthcoming).

If the Bail was occupied only by a small number of high-status dwellings in the Anglo-Scandinavian period, as we believe, a detailed case can be made that the four known churches belong to the households of the four principal lords known to have held property in Lincoln at the Conquest: the Earl of Northumbria, the Earl of Mercia, the Bishop of Dorchester and the Sheriff of Lincolnshire. Furthermore, within this distribution, we can suggest that the church of All Saints belonged to the Earl of Northumbria, and was presumably in close proximity to his hall. That of St Mary clearly belonged to the Bishop of Dorchester, who we might also suggest had a residence here. St Paul-in-the-Bail was the Earl of Mercia's church, and therefore, by elimination, St Clement-in-the-Bail would have been associated with the Sheriff's hall. The suggestion, then, is that the Bail was essentially divided into four quarters, each with its church associated with the hall of its respective lord (Stocker forthcoming).

Returning to Wigford, although St Peter-at-Gowts and Holy Trinity might fall into similar categories to the Bail churches, the slight majority of churches in Upper Wigford fall into the category of churchyards established within single or multiple strip properties (St Benedict, St John Evangelist, St Edward, St Andrew, St Michael-at-Gowts). The presumption that such churches represent the division of a unit within an urban estate set aside for the church, when the remainder of the property was divided into plots for tenants, is widely held (Morris 1989, 192–209) and is certainly not challenged by this Lincoln evidence. The widths and orientation of these strip plots in Wigford often change along the same lines as post-medieval parish boundaries, and it is a fair assumption that each orthogonal group of plots represented a single urban estate, with its church and parish. Unfortunately the original thirteen 11th-century parish churches of Wigford were reduced to five in 1549, and several former parishes were divided up amongst those that continued, so reconstructing original 11th-century parishes is far from straightforward. At St Mark's, where this exercise was attempted, it was thought that its original parish (before its amalgamation with part of St Edward in 1549) might have amounted to no more than a dozen plots and probably fewer (Gilmour and Stocker 1986, 4–6).

The dedication to St Clement of one of the Bail churches might indicate a foundation date in the reign of Cnut (Crawford 2008, 119–26), but the second dedication to St Clement-in-*Butwerk*, can be dated more reliably to the generation between 1066 and 1086. St Clement-in-*Butwerk* has been reliably identified in LARA as one of the two churches mentioned in *Domesday Book* as having been founded by Colsuain on his urban estate, built between these years on new ground and containing 36 houses (Foster and Longley 1924, 7, no.21; Vince 2003a, 230–2). These churches not only marked an extension to the urban area at this date, but they also marked the high-water mark of the town's urban expansion to the east: the town never grew further east than this, and the area had returned to agricultural uses by the 14th century. Yet, despite this documentary evidence that they owe their origin to the same lordly initiative, churchyard topography places them within two different categories. St Peter's might have been a corner plot, whereas St Clement's was more clearly a single unit in a regular row of properties. This reinforces the conclusion that local circumstances dictate churchyard topography and not the date of the foundation or the status of the lord involved.

In this *Butwerk* case, however, one might question why Colsuain thought it necessary to found two churches on a single urban estate, although it is true that, at 35 houses, this would be a large population to be served by a single urban church, if the dozen or so served by St Mark's was typical. Crawford (2008, 124–6) has suggested that a St Clement dedication in this location is not unusual at this time, but a dedication to St Peter perhaps stands out as a little old-fashioned. Indeed, although the parochial church was clearly founded in the 11th century, St Peter's might still represent a pre-existing cult site associated with the well of its soubriquet and it is possible that Colsuain was merely bringing a pre-existing 'chapel' into the parochial system.

Secondary Characterisation of Lincoln's Parochial Churches	
Pre-urban churchyard sites	St Paul-in-the-Bail
	St Peter Arches & St Peter-at-Pleas
	St Lawrence?
Churchyards associated with lordly enclosures	St Paul-in-the-Bail
	St Clement-in-the-Bail
	All Saints-in-the-Bail
	St Mary-of-Lincoln
	Holy Trinity Wigford?
	St Andrew Wigford?
	St Faith
	St Peter-at-Gowts
Churchyards established within urban estates	All Saints Hungate
	St Augustine
	St Bavon
	St Benedict
	St Clement-in-*Butwerk*
	St Edmund
	St Edward Wigford
	St George
	St John Evangelist Wigford
	St Margaret Wigford
	St Mary *Crackpool*
	St Peter-*ad-fontem*
	St Swithin
Churchyards established as 'gate-guardians'	Holy Cross Wigford
	St Margaret Pottergate?
	St Michael-on-the-Mount
	St Nicholas Newport
	St Peter Eastgate
	St Rumbold
	St Stephen?
Churchyards established as market islands	Holy Trinity Clasketgate
	St Botolph
	St Cuthbert?
	St John Baptist
	St Leonard
	St Martin
Collaborative group foundations	St Mark Wigford
	St Mary-le-Wigford
Unallocated	Holy Innocents
	Holy Trinity Greetstone
	St Andrew-under-Palace
	St Bartholomew *Westcastle*
	St Giles
	St John-the-Poor
	St Peter *Stanthaket*

Fig. 8.9 Revised characterisation of church sites into more useful categories.

A similar date, between the mid-11th century and *c.* 1100 has been suggested above for the churchyard of St Margaret in Lower Wigford on the basis of its local topography, and, along with Colsuain's expansion to the east, the expansion of Lower Wigford to the south may represent a contemporary phase of post-Conquest development. If so, we have also seen that it is likely to have included the markets outside the north and east gates of the Upper City, which were perhaps both laid out at this moment, with their island-churches and the Norman dedication of St Leonard. When compared with the island-churches of St Cuthbert and St Martin, whose foundations may have dated from as much as two centuries earlier, however, it is clear that the needs of the market place dictated the location of the church, not the date, nor the personal diktat of a specific lord. These needs would have included not just the visual symbolism of the church validating the market place but also practical considerations such as the need to swear oaths, store money and write and witness documents (Jones 2004), indeed it may be that some churches played the role of secular assembly room, as in Winchester, which was later occupied by dedicated guildhalls (Morris 1989, 213).

It seems, then, that the real value of our characterisation of the local topographies of Lincoln churchyards is not to explore an association between the roles of particular groups within society in these foundations, but rather to identify the specific functions leading to the foundation of the churches in the first place. Thus our topographical characterisation of 'strip plot', 'corner plot' and 'market' might be replaced with a more complex, more functional, subdivision. Instead we can divide the churches up into: 'pre-existing church site', 'lordly enclosure', 'urban estate', 'gate-guardian', 'island-church' and the two suggested examples of 'collaborative foundations' (fig. 8.9).

Conclusion

The current generalisation for the foundation of urban churches suggests that most were, like many in the countryside, founded within the context of feudal lordship, based around a manorial estate centre. Recent work in rural Lincolnshire has suggested, however, that this was not always simply a matter of a lord imposing a church to suit himself within his manorial *curia*. A variety of church-foundation types were identified, and some of these show the community's active if not predominant participation (Stocker and Everson 2006, 58–70). The present study shows that the pattern of the establishment of urban churches was similarly complex. Some of the categories in fig. 8.9 do indicate lordly involvement in church foundation within their own residential properties, much in the same way as lords founded churches within their manors in the countryside. But many more were founded as part of a bargain between new urban tenants and their lords, whereby one of the lord's new urban strips was devoted, not to the generation of rents, but to the provision of a church for the occupants of the other plots. Such a plot would not be considered a complete commercial loss by the lord, of course, as the church would still bring in money through various ecclesiastical dues, but would these payments have represented a comparable income to the rent due on a normal tenancy? In some such cases, perhaps, a corner plot might attract more payments of *soulscot*, through having greater space available in its burial ground than it would as a standard tenement, and this might have made this location popular amongst landlords. A similar impulse might lie behind the establishment of the gate-guardians, in that prayers and offerings were a necessary part of every journey, and such churches were well placed to encourage offerings to saints associated with travel, like St Botolph and St Nicholas. A lord responsible for a market place, on the other hand, might have been forced to build a church because this was regarded, by the traders at the market, as a necessary facility, both spiritually and practically. The same lord, owning a hall in one part of the city, holding a group of burgage plots in a second part and sponsoring a market in a third, then, might well found three entirely different types of churches. What we can say, however, is that few of these lordly foundations in Lincoln can have been very profitable, as very few of them were retained in private hands beyond the early 12th century; the only churches which were not eventually swept up to become part of the support for the Precentor in the new cathedral, a process which started early in the reign of Henry I and continued until the mid 12th century, were those either associated with the halls of the great magnates (like St Paul-in-the-Bail, and possibly St Clement-in-the-Bail) or belonging to other religious institutions (such as St Bartholomew) (Hill 1948, 144–5).

Finally, we need to consider how typical (or atypical) generalisations regarding Lincoln might be of other Danelaw towns. A superficial glance at most such towns reveals many churches that seem to be set within agglomerations of burgage plots, apparently demonstrating the ubiquity of this type of foundation. Equally, across Danelaw towns, corner plots also appear popular. But Northampton, Norwich, Oxford, Stamford and York also have churches associated with probable early market sites. Oxford's great open fair-ground outside the north gate is still marked by churches at either end (St Mary Magdalene and St Giles), for example, whilst at York, the market space outside the eastern gate of the former walled enclosure, now occupied by the block of 'infill' tenements between Shambles and Colliergate, appears to have had churches placed at either end of it (Holy Trinity or Christchurch King's Square and St Crux). To the southwest, the market known as Pavement was evidently dominated by the island church of All Saints, which stood in its midst. This market place, however, may also have been overlooked by the church of St Peter the Little, which has yet to be satisfactorily investigated (Wilson and Mee 1998, 146). St Peter's attracts our attention in this context particularly, because of the York coinage series, already mentioned above, dedicated to St Peter. We have already noted that these coins have been taken as evidence that the market at York was under the patronage of St Peter, but it has always been presumed that the church in question was that which preceded today's Minster. Is it possible, though, that the church of St Peter, under whose benign influence the Anglo-Scandinavian market was held, was actually that at Pavement, and that the St Peter in question was actually St Peter the Less? The answer to this question has important consequences for Anglo-Scandinavian archaeology, of course, as the south side of this market was lined with the tenements excavated at Coppergate, established on this site at the start of the 10th century, more or less contemporaneously with the coin issue (Hall and Hunter-Mann 2002; Hall 2004). It seems likely, therefore, that the results extracted from our detailed study of Lincoln are indeed more widely applicable. Further study might reveal, not just the influences of landowners on church foundations, but the relationship between the Church and the establishment of the new market economy.

Acknowledgements

I am extremely grateful to Graham Fairclough who read an early draft of this paper. Several of the major contextual points derive from discussions with him. Paul Everson was, as always, a helpful critic, as was Richard Morris, and I am also grateful to Dawn Hadley for her comments on the draft. In addition to commenting helpfully on the text, Letty ten Harkel put great effort into the excellent drawings with which it is illustrated. Without her work the illustrations would not serve adequately to support the argument.

Bibliography

Abell, E. I. and Chambers, J. D. (1936) *The Story of Lincoln: an introduction to the history of the city.* Lincoln, Lincoln Education Committee.

Biddle, M. (1986) Archaeology, architecture and the cult of Saints in Anglo-Saxon England. In L. A. S. Butler and R. K. Morris (eds) *The Anglo-Saxon Church: papers on history, architecture, and archaeology in honour of Dr H. M. Taylor*, 1–31. Council for British Archaeology Research Report 60. London, Council for British Archaeology.

Blackburn, M. A. S. (2004) The coinage of Scandinavian York. In R. A. Hall (ed.) *Aspects of Anglo-Scandinavian York*, 325–49. The Archaeology of York 8 (4). York, Council for British Archaeology.

Blackburn, M. A. S. (2006). Presidential Address 2005: currency under the Vikings. Part 2: the two Scandinavian kingdoms of the Danelaw, *c.* 895–954. *The British Numismatic Journal* 76, 204–26.

Blackburn, M. A. S., Colyer, C., and Dolley, M. (1983) *Early Medieval Coins from Lincoln and its Shire c. 770–1100.* The Archaeology of Lincoln 6 (1). London, Council for British Archaeology.

Cameron, K. (1985) *The Place-Names of Lincolnshire Part 1: the place-names of the county of the City of Lincoln.* Cambridge, English Place-Name Society.

Colgrave, B. and Mynors, R. A. B. (eds) (1969) *Bede's Ecclesiastical History of the English People.* Oxford, Oxford University Press.

Crawford, B. (2008) *The Churches dedicated to St Clement in Medieval England: a hagio-geography of the seafarer's saint in 11th-century North Europe.* St Petersburg, Axioma.

Everson, P. and Stocker, D. (1999) *Corpus of Anglo-Saxon Stone Sculpture Volume 5: Lincolnshire.* Oxford, Oxford University Press.

Farmer, D. (1997, 4th edn) *The Oxford Dictionary of Saints.* Oxford, Oxford University Press.

Fell, C. E. (1978) Edward King and Martyr and the Anglo-Saxon hagiographic tradition. In D. Hill (ed.) *Ethelred the Unready: papers from the millenary conference*, 5–14. British Archaeological Reports British Series 59. Oxford, British Archaeological Reports.

Foster, C. W. and Longley, T. (1924) *The Lincolnshire Domesday and the Lindsey Survey.* Publications of the Lincoln Record Society 19. Lincoln, Lincoln Record Society.

Gem, R. (1993) The episcopal churches of Lindsey in the early 9th century. In A. Vince (ed.) *Pre-Viking Lindsey*, 101–22. Lincoln Archaeological Studies 1. Lincoln, City of Lincoln Archaeology Unit.

Gilmour, B. J. J. and Stocker, D. A. (1986) *St Mark's Church and Cemetery.* Archaeology of Lincoln 13 (1). London, Council for British Archaeology for the Trust for Lincolnshire Archaeology.

Hall, R. A. and Hunter-Mann, K. (2002) *Medieval Urbanism in Coppergate: refining a townscape.* The Archaeology of York 10 (6). York, Council for British Archaeology.

Hall, R. A. (ed.) (2004) *Aspects of Anglo-Scandinavian York.* The Archaeology of York 8 (4). York, Council for British Archaeology.

Hill, F. (1948) *Medieval Lincoln.* Cambridge, Cambridge University Press.

Hill, F. (1956) *Tudor and Stuart Lincoln.* Cambridge, Cambridge University Press.

Jones, M. (2003) The *Colonia* era: the archaeological account. In D. Stocker (ed.) *The City by the Pool: assessing the archaeology of the City of Lincoln*, 56–138. Oxford, Oxbow.

Jones, G. (2004) The market place: form, location and antecedents. In S. Pinches, M. Whalley and D. Postles (eds) *The Market Place and the Place of the Market*, 1–18. Leicester, Friends of the Centre for English Local History.

Jones, S. R., Major, K. and Varley, J. (1984) *Survey of Ancient Houses 1: Priorygate to Pottergate.* Lincoln, Lincoln Civic Trust.

Jones, S. R., Major, K. and Varley, J. (1987) *Survey of Ancient Houses 2: houses to the south and west of the Minster*. Lincoln, Lincoln Civic Trust.

Jones, S. R., Major, K. and Varley, J. (1990) *Survey of Ancient Houses 3: houses in Eastgate, Priorygate, and James Street*. Lincoln, Lincoln Civic Trust.

Jones, S. R., Major, K., Varley, J. and Johnson, C. (1996) *Survey of Ancient Houses 4: houses in the Bail: Steep Hill, Castle Hill, and Bailgate*. Lincoln, Lincoln Civic Trust.

Keene, D. J. (1985) Introduction to the medieval churches of Winchester. *Bulletin of the Council for British Archaeology Churches Committee* 24, 21–4.

Mahany, C. and Roffe, D. (1982) Stamford: the development of an Anglo-Scandinavian borough. In R. A. Brown (ed.) *Anglo-Norman Studies V: proceedings of the Battle Conference*, 198–219.

Mills, D. R. and Wheeler, R. C. (2004) *Historic Town Plans of Lincoln 1610–1920*. Publications of the Lincoln Record Society 92. Lincoln, Lincoln Record Society.

Morris, R. (1989) *Churches in the Landscape*. London, Dent.

Mossop, H. R. (1970) *The Lincoln Mint c. 890–1279*. Newcastle-upon-Tyne, Corbitt and Hunter Ltd.

Owen, A. E. B. (1988–9) Carlton, Reston and Saint Michael: a reconsideration. *Nomina* 12, 105–11.

Palliser, D., Slater, T. R. and Dennison, P. (2000) The topography of towns 600–1300. In D. Palliser (ed.) *The Cambridge Urban History of Britain Volume 1: 600–1540*, 153–86. Cambridge, Cambridge University Press.

Parsons, D. (2004) Urban castles and late Anglo-Saxon towns. In P. Lindley (ed.) *The Early History of Lincoln Castle*, 30–40. Occasional Papers in Lincolnshire History and Archaeology 12. Lincoln, Society for Lincolnshire History and Archaeology.

Perring, D. (2002) *Town and Country in England: frameworks for archaeological research*. Council for British Archaeology Research Report 134. York, Council for British Archaeology.

Rollason, D. (1989) St Cuthbert and Wessex: the evidence of Cambridge, Corpus Christi College MS 183. In G. Bonner, D. Rollason and C. Stancliffe (eds) *St Cuthbert: his cult and his community to AD 1200*, 413–24. Woodbridge, Boydell.

Sawyer, P. (1981) Fairs and markets in early medieval England. In N. Skyum-Nielsen and N. Lund (eds) *Danish Medieval History: new currents*, 153–68. Copenhagen, Museum Tusculanum Press.

Sawyer, P. (1997) *The Oxford Illustrated History of the Vikings*. Oxford, Oxford University Press.

Sawyer, P. (1998) *Anglo-Saxon Lincolnshire*. The History of Lincolnshire 3. Lincoln, Society for Lincolnshire History and Archaeology.

Schofield, J. (1994) Saxon and medieval parish churches in the City of London. *Transactions of the London and Middlesex Archaeology Society* 45, 23–145.

Srawley, J. H. (ed.) (1966) *The Book of John de Schalby*. Lincoln Minster Pamphlets 2. Lincoln, Lincoln Cathedral.

Stewart, I. (1967) The St Martin coins of Lincoln. *British Numismatic Journal* 36, 46–54.

Stocker, D. (1990) The archaeology of the Reformation in Lincoln: a case study in the redistribution of building materials in the mid sixteenth century. *Lincolnshire History and Archaeology* 25, 18–32.

Stocker, D. (1991) *St. Mary's Guildhall, Lincoln: the survey and excavation of a medieval building complex*. The Archaeology of Lincoln 12 (1). London, Council for British Archaeology.

Stocker, D. (1993) The early Church in Lincolnshire: a study of the sites and their significance. In A. Vince (ed.) *Pre-Viking Lindsey*, 101–22. Lincoln Archaeological Studies 1. Lincoln, City of Lincoln Archaeology Unit.

Stocker, D. (1999) '*A Very Goodly House Longging to Sutton...*': a reconstruction of John of Gaunt's palace, Lincoln. *Lincolnshire History and Archaeology* 34, 5–15.

Stocker, D. (2000) Monuments and merchants: irregularities in the distribution of stone sculpture in Lincolnshire and Yorkshire in the tenth century. In D. M. Hadley and J. Richards (eds) *Cultures in Contact: Scandinavian settlement in England in the ninth and tenth centuries*, 179–212. Turnhout, Brepols.

Stocker, D. (ed.) (2003) *The City by the Pool: assessing the archaeology of the City of Lincoln*. Oxford, Oxbow.

Stocker, D. (2004) The two early castles of Lincoln. In P. Lindley (ed.) *The Early History of Lincoln*

Castle, 9–22. Occasional Papers in Lincolnshire History and Archaeology 12. Lincoln, Society for Lincolnshire History and Archaeology.

Stocker, D. (forthcoming) Lincoln's Upper City before the Conquest. In P. Dixon and D. Stocker (eds) *Lincoln before St Hugh*.

Stocker, D. and Everson, P. (2001) Five Towns funerals: decoding diversity in Danelaw stone sculpture. In J. Graham-Campbell, R. A. Hall, J. Jesch and D. N. Parsons (eds) *Vikings and the Danelaw: select papers from the proceedings of the thirteenth Viking Congress, Nottingham and York, 21–30 August 1997*, 223–34. Oxford, Oxbow.

Stocker, D. and Everson, P. (2006) *Summoning St Michael: early Romanesque towers in Lincolnshire*. Oxford, Oxbow.

Thacker, A. (1988) Aethelwold and Abingdon. In B. Yorke (ed.) *Bishop Aethelwold: his career and influence*, 43–64. Woodbridge, Boydell.

Thacker, A. (1999) In Gregory's shadow? The pre-Conquest Cult of St Augustine. In R. Gameson (ed.) *St Augustine and the Conversion of England*, 374–90. Stroud, Sutton.

Vince, A. (2003a) The new town: Lincoln in the high medieval era (*c.* 850–*c.* 1350). The archaeological account. In D. Stocker (ed.) *The City by the Pool: assessing the archaeology of the City of Lincoln*, 159–295. Oxford, Oxbow.

Vince, A. (2003b) Lincoln in the early medieval era, between the 5th and 9th centuries. The archaeological account. In D. Stocker (ed.) *The City by the Pool: assessing the archaeology of the City of Lincoln*, 141–56. Oxford, Oxbow.

Wilson, B. and Mee, F. (1998) *The Medieval Parish Churches of York: the pictorial evidence*. The Archaeology of York Supplementary Series 1. York, York Archaeological Trust.

9

MORE THAN JUST MEAT: ANIMALS IN VIKING-AGE TOWNS

Kristopher Poole

Anyone living in a modern city could be forgiven for forgetting the central role that animals played in past societies. With food now often produced and transported from hundreds of miles away, the closest many people get to encounters with animals are as pets, pests (such as rats and mice), as garden birds, or while visiting the zoo. Given this, it is easy to overlook the sheer ubiquity of animals in peoples' daily lives in Viking-Age England and Ireland. Whether as living animals, food, raw materials, iconography, or simply as beings that were 'good to think with' (Lévi-Strauss 1964), they inhabited both the physical and mental worlds of human beings. However, social position, whether based on ethnicity, status, age, religion or gender, would have played a major role in determining a person's working tasks, and hence the nature of contact between people and animals. This interaction between people and their worlds in turn affected how people perceived themselves and their relations with others (Löfgren 1985). Bearing this in mind, the growth of towns in Viking-Age England and Ireland can be seen as one of the most significant processes in the history of both countries in terms of the impact that it had on peoples' quotidian existence. The establishment of these permanent settlements created central places in which substantial numbers of people were involved in non-agricultural occupations, and relied in large part on their surrounding hinterlands for sustenance. In this way, people became distanced from the rhythms of farming life, their interactions with most domestic animals limited to use of body-parts (meals, waste), raw materials, and objects. At the same time, these urban centres provided new ecosystems, which led to people being brought into closer contact with animals that thrive in such environments.

This chapter uses animal bone data synthesised from thirteen rural and 45 urban Viking-Age assemblages excavated within England (Poole 2011), along with comparative data from Ireland, to explore the effects of urbanisation upon human-animal relationships. It is important to study both the urban and the rural context due to the close links that existed between them (Vince 1994, 117), with changes in the hinterland likely impacting on the town, and *vice versa*. Animal remains are especially useful in this context because they can represent physical evidence of human-animal relations. Whilst such aspects as species representation, kill-off and body-part patterns have largely been used to reconstruct economic systems, this chapter will demonstrate how this information can also be used to elucidate social aspects of life in Viking-Age towns. It does so by considering not just consumption, but also the preceding processes of breeding, raising and working with animals, for all carry significant social meaning (Knight 2005, 5). In the case of domestic species, people often had a continuous daily association with individual animals, leading to a high level of mutual familiarity. Before considering the changes in these relationships resulting specifically from urbanisation, this chapter will first assess what impact Scandinavian influence had on human-animal interactions, including dietary preferences and the cultural and religious importance accorded to certain animals.

Animals and Scandinavian influence

The apparent cultural importance of cattle within the Scandinavian world (Lucas and McGovern 2007, 23) has, in previous studies, been used to explore Scandinavian influence on animal husbandry in Viking-Age England and Ireland, through discussion of the relative frequency of cattle bones in zooarchaeological assemblages (O'Connor 1989; Poole 2008; Sykes 2007). Relative frequencies of cattle are, indeed, overall higher for northern and eastern England than the south and west of the country during this period, but such a pattern seems to have been in place before the arrival of Scandinavian settlers (Poole 2008, 105; Sykes 2007, 29). It would seem, then, that, at a very general level, the Scandinavian incomers had little impact on the frequencies of animals kept in this country. There are a number of reasons why this could be so, including the coarse resolution used for analysis, meaning that shifts in localised patterns of animal husbandry are overlooked (Pluciennik 1996, 43). However, attention also needs to be given to the suitability of the criteria used to determine Scandinavian influence. This is especially so because patterns of farming seem to have varied widely across the Scandinavian world, making it impossible to identify a single 'Scandinavian' model of animal husbandry (O'Connor 2010, 13; Poole 2008, 104–5). Moreover, given that the most socially significant animals are often the least well represented in animal bone assemblages (Sykes 2007, 9), even where cattle are not the most frequently represented species in an assemblage, this does not divest them of cultural importance. As such, quantification is not just the end product of analysis, and we must bear in mind the difference between live and dead cattle. In societies where cattle represent a unit of wealth, as in much of the early medieval world, the cattle are valued for themselves, and not just as food resources (Abbink 2003; Russell 1998, 44).

Apart from animal bones, other sources of evidence can inform about the use of animal products and cultural factors in Viking-Age towns in England. Most of the fleece types recovered from Coppergate, York were of a 'Hairy Type' typical of Norse sites in northern Britain, Greenland and Shetland (Walton Rogers 2007, 13). A similar range of fleece types were identified in preserved textiles from late 9th- to late 10th-century London, but 'Hairy' fleeces made up a much smaller part of the sample than at York (Pritchard 1984, 48–50). Therefore, although this fleece type was not restricted to northern and eastern England, the evidence does suggest a significant difference in the raw material, and hence the types of sheep, available, between York and London. Apart from one Roman sample from *Vindolanda*, a Roman fort and *vicus* a few miles behind Hadrian's Wall not far from Hexham (Northumberland), there is no evidence for 'Hairy' wools in Britain until the 9th century (Walton Rogers 2007, 13). This is interesting in light of Ryder's (1981, 21) suggestion that the region in which the black-faced, horned type of sheep emerged roughly corresponds with the Danelaw, and that the existence of similar sheep in Denmark might suggest a Scandinavian introduction of particular types of sheep.

As well as providing a means of subsistence, animals and plants are integral parts of people's environment, and often closely associated with different landscapes (Evans and Yarwood 1995,

141). By bringing particular animal and plant types with them, settlers would, in effect, have brought part of their landscape with them, helping in the adjustment to new surroundings. As with species proportions, it is difficult to test this zooarchaeologically due to a dearth of measurements from sites that have both mid-Saxon and Viking-Age levels. One exception is Flixborough (Lincolnshire), where average cattle and sheep size remained very similar between the mid-8th and late 10th century, with no suggestion of animals being imported from overseas during this time (Dobney *et al.* 2007, 148–78). Even so, this is just one site, and it is not necessarily the case that, for example, particularly woolly sheep would have been larger than another sheep type. Genetic studies provide another way of considering this issue: at Fishamble Street, Dublin, the cattle were genetically more similar to modern 'old' breeds of Britain and Ireland than to those of Scandinavia. This suggests that, in this case, cattle were not being imported (McHugh *et al.* 1999); existing stock seem to have sufficed for Dublin's inhabitants. Given the potential insight to be gleaned, it would be interesting to see a similar approach applied to animals from Viking-Age England.

More evidence for Scandinavian attitudes to animals is indicated by the barrow cemetery at Heath Wood, Ingleby (Derbyshire), where many of the cremation burials contained both human and animal bone (horse, cattle, sheep/goat, pig and dog) (Bond and Worley 2006, 96). These animals may have served as food offerings or displays of wealth. It is also possible that the mixing of humans and animals through cremation was linked to shamanistic beliefs in which human and animal identities were perceived as fluid, with the animal seen as a guardian, helping the person move into the next world (Danielsson 2007; Williams 2005). The choice of guardian may well have been linked to the interactions that person had with animals in life: what better companion than a species, or a particular individual of that species, with which a person had close links/interactions? Such overt statements of Scandinavian identity are otherwise rare in England in the 9th century, with an apparent willingness by settlers to adopt local burial practices, if not necessarily the ideology behind them (Hadley 2006, 263).

Within the towns themselves, direct zooarchaeological evidence of Scandinavian influence is also scarce. Given the religious significance of horses and horse-flesh consumption within parts of Scandinavia, the tendency for butchered horse bones to be identified in areas of the Danelaw (including in towns), more than elsewhere in England, has been suggested to be linked to the presence of Scandinavian settlers (Poole 2008, 110). Other evidence for beliefs is perhaps indicated by the two bear claw bones recovered from Coppergate, York (O'Connor 1989), which likely came from an imported bearskin, given that bears were probably extinct in England by this time (Hammon 2010). The find is interesting in light of the links between wearing animal skins and shamanic beliefs in Scandinavian sources (Pluskowski 2006, 113), although in the absence of any clear evidence of a Scandinavian presence at Coppergate (Richards 2004, 90), we must be cautious of such an interpretation. Other evidence of Scandinavian trade routes, especially with the eastern Mediterranean, is found in the form of a pheasant bone from Viking-Age Lincoln and peacock remains from Viking-Age Thetford (Norfolk), both non-native species that were probably deliberately imported as exotica (Poole 2010a). In summary, whilst there are hints that Scandinavian settlement did have some effects on human-animal interactions, this may have been minimal. Arguably, much greater lifestyle adjustments were effected by the development of towns, and it is to the nature of such changes that this chapter now turns, beginning with wild animal exploitation, before considering the involvement of towns in food production and craft specialisation.

The call of the wild

In Viking-Age towns, wild species make up only 0.7% of the animal remains, indicating little reliance on non-domestic food sources. Most of the red deer and roe deer remains from urban sites are antler, often shed, and so do not represent good evidence for venison consumption, or contact with wild species. Additional dietary protein could have been obtained from the rivers in and around towns; fish bone data indicate a predominance of freshwater and estuarine species, but this changes around the turn of the 11th century, with a major shift towards marine species (Barrett *et al.* 2004). This change is particularly marked at urban centres, and was potentially linked to the concentration of population at these sites creating demand for fish (especially during fasting periods), which surpassed the potential quantities of freshwater and estuarine fish available (Barrett *et al.* 2004, 630). Lesser availability of fresh water and estuarine fish may in part have been caused by the elite-imposed restrictions on these fish; both groups are particularly well represented on elite sites of this period, whilst charter evidence indicates concern with securing control over these resources (Sykes 2007, 58–60). Wild birds also provided a very small part of the diet within towns (0.3% of the total bone fragments). As commerce within towns grew, the rise of professional fowlers, such as that mentioned in Aelfric's *Colloquy* (Crossley-Holland 1999, 223–4), would have helped vary the urban diet, as at Coppergate, York, which witnessed greater diversity in bird species during the late 10th to early 11th century (O'Connor 1989, 193). A trend towards increased consumption of wild species is also true of England in general at this time, although they tend to be most frequent on elite and ecclesiastical sites (Poole 2011).

Other species with which urban dwellers may have come into more contact, but were not considered food, are probably under-represented archaeologically, especially smaller animals on sites where sieving was not employed during excavation. Recovery of small bird bones from thrushes, blackbirds, sparrows and chaffinches show that many of these bird species, familiar even to the modern city-dweller, were attracted to these places. Other species, such as corvids (crow family), may have been particularly drawn to these centres; their bones are present in 28.3% of urban assemblages (Poole 2011) but they would probably have been seen around most towns. Throughout history, corvids have commonly been presented in negative ways, but in Viking-Age towns, as in later medieval urban centres, their ability to help control refuse levels may have been recognised (Ratcliffe 1997, 16), and so attitudes of urban dwellers may have been largely ambivalent towards them. In contrast, species such as rats and mice would have been seen as pests, with mice sharing buildings with humans, but rats perhaps exploiting the fringes of towns (O'Connor 1989, 189). Having considered some of the less common species within towns, attention will now focus on the domestic sphere, in particular the provision of food to urban centres.

Food production and domestic animals in towns

Whilst cattle are overall the most frequently represented of the main domesticates in Viking-Age England, sheep tend to be the most frequent on rural sites (fig. 9.1), and a greater proportion of rural assemblages of this period seem to be sheep-dominated than other site types (towns and secular/ecclesiastical elite centres) (Sykes 2006, 61–2). In contrast, cattle percentages are overall greater on urban sites than at any other site type, and a similar pattern is found in Denmark

Kristopher Poole

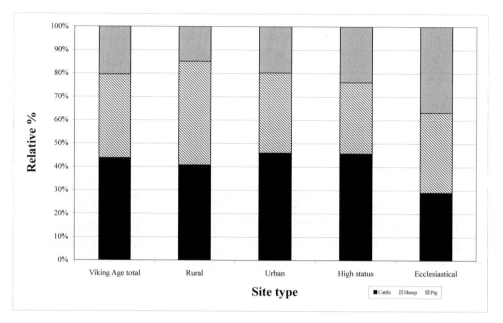

Fig. 9.1 Relative percentages of cattle, sheep and pigs (NISP) on Viking-Age sites.

and southern Sweden (Randsborg 1985, 239). This may have been because beef commanded a higher price than mutton or pork, or, alternatively, the amount of meat provided by a cattle carcass may have been too much for a small rural community to consume before it became inedible, leading to preferential export of cattle into towns (Albarella 2005, 134). The greater part of the meat consumption on rural sites, thus, seems to have consisted of mutton, in contrast to urban centres. For the proportion of cattle that remained, and were consumed, in the countryside, some of the meat could potentially have been preserved, but another way to deal with the large amount of fresh meat would have been through the holding of communal feasts, as McCormick (2002, 26) suggests for medieval Ireland.

The social significance of communal eating has been much discussed within anthropology and archaeology (Jones 2007), and is understood as serving variously to express group identity and social position and to create obligations. From documentary sources, it would seem that beef, poultry and pork were apparently considered suitable foods for feasts, whilst sheep do not seem to be mentioned (Hagen 1992, 101), perhaps indicating their status as a more everyday meat source. However, this information primarily derives from wills making provisions for funerary feasts, and so might not be relevant to other feasting contexts. We have some evidence for feasting from Old English poetry, but this tends to focus on the great halls of prominent lords (Magennis 1999), whereas it is possible that lower classes also have had their own feasts. In such cases, the consumption of an animal, which members of that community had helped breed and raise and with which they had worked, would have seen much greater symbolic importance attributed to the act of slaughter and consumption than by those people (such as urban dwellers) who played little or no part in the lives of the animals they ate.

Figs 9.2 and 9.3 present the available ageing data for cattle and sheep for Viking-Age urban

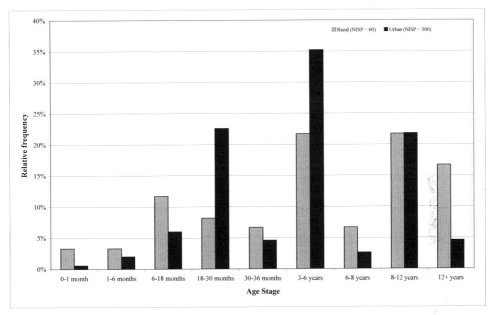

Fig. 9.2 Relative frequencies of cattle per age stage at Viking-Age rural and urban sites.

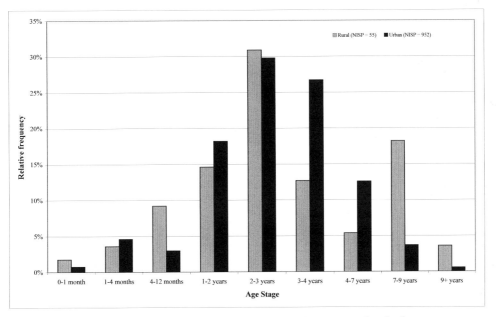

Fig. 9.3 Relative frequencies of sheep per age stage at Viking-Age rural and urban sites.

and rural sites in England. As might be expected, in both cases, the youngest animals are more frequent at rural sites, indicating that these settlements were more frequently engaged in animal breeding and raising than were urban centres. The greater number of older animals on rural sites would also equate with animals being kept for breeding, traction, dairying and wool. Urban centres, however, were not completely removed from food production; a small proportion of mandibles from cattle and sheep are from the youngest stages, which may suggest on-site breeding. The extent to which a town depended on food coming in from the surrounding area, and the amount it supplied for itself would have varied depending on size. In Winchester (Hampshire), pressure on space was so intense by the first half of the 10th century that extra-mural suburbs developed (Biddle 1976, 134). In contrast, other towns may have produced much of their food needs, as at Gloucester (Gloucestershire), where byres and agricultural activity are evident inside its walls (Astill 2000, 36). Whatever the case, when animals were imported to towns, body-part patterns indicate that they were driven in on-the-hoof and butchered there. In Dublin, the body-part data are supported by semi-digested vegetation from ruminants' stomachs, indicating the presence of live animals (McCormick 1983, 261).

Such a pull of resources to at least the larger towns seems to have affected the layout of their surroundings. This is indicated by the series of droveways to the north of London, probably existing in this period, which led from its hinterland to the meat market at Smithfield, outside the Roman walls (Vince 1990, 123). Similarly, charters of AD 923 (S1629) and 1002 (S905) refer to *Hrythera* and *Rytherceap* – 'the cattle market' – outside Canterbury's (Kent) eastern walls (Tatton-Brown 1984, 8). A town's hinterland would have been required to help feed the growing numbers of people not involved in food production, and the demands placed on the surroundings could have been considerable. O'Connor (1982, 47–8) suggests that around 500 cattle, 700 sheep and 400 pigs would have been required every year to feed the estimated 4,000 people living in Lincoln around the time of the *Domesday* survey. Some measure of this is indicated by metrical and non-metrical animal bone data from urban centres, with cattle horn cores at Coppergate, York (O'Connor 1989) and Flaxengate, Lincoln (O'Connor 1982) suggesting a fairly high degree of genetic diversity. Moreover, at Thetford, the cattle from two separate assemblages seem to have belonged to different types, indicating that even some of the smaller urban centres could draw on a number of different sources for food (Albarella 2005, 144). The drawing into urban centres of these domestic animals of varying types, with differing horn shapes, colours and fleece-types, would have created a visible, as well as a physical, expression of its status as a central place, and of the resources that it was consuming in such large numbers.

As well as meat, other animal products such as cheese and butter could have been imported into towns from their hinterlands. It seems likely that this was the case in late Anglo-Saxon London, with clause 12 of the law code *IV Æthelred* (dating to AD 991–1002) stating that 'women who deal in dairy produce (*i.e.* cheese and butter) – pay one penny a fortnight before Christmas and another penny a week before Christmas' (Robertson 1925, 73). Place-names provide further evidence: the place-name element *wīc* having been argued by Coates (1999, 96) to mean 'dependent place with a specialised commercial function', which could include trading centres (such as *Hamwic* and *Lundenwic*), as well as specialised farms. In relation to the latter, the term is frequently compounded with terms denoting domestic animals of varying kinds (*e.g.* Shapwick (Somerset) and Oxwick (Norfolk)), or particular types of animal products, frequently those derived from dairying. Such locations are often close to urban centres, such as Exeter (Devon) (Exwick and Cowick), Winchester (Weeke), Bath (Somerset) (Bathwick) (Fox 2008, 360–1), as well as Wigford, Lincoln (Steane *et al.* 2001), Chiswick (around 6 miles southwest of London) and Keswick (3 miles southwest of Norwich (Norfolk)), the latter two names meaning literally 'specialised cheese farm'.

Of the three main domesticates, pigs were probably the species with which townspeople most came into contact as living animals, as they can be fed on scraps and do not require the same amount of space as cattle and sheep. High numbers of neonatal pig bones at York suggest that households occasionally obtained a pregnant sow from rural communities, or that pigs were being bred in towns (O'Connor 1989, 17). Although pigs were strongly associated with woodland in this period (Albarella 2006, 77), it is possible that much of the pork consumed in towns was produced by townspeople themselves. We know from later medieval sources that pigs were sometimes allowed to roam the streets as a way of helping keep down waste levels, and the same may have been true of pigs in Viking-Age towns, although medieval legislation indicates that they could be a nuisance (Albarella 2006, 79). In this way, the pig could perhaps have been seen as an urban animal as much as a woodland one.

Domestic birds could also have contributed a significant proportion to the diet. Chickens were probably the most common domestic birds kept in towns (Poole 2008, 107), as they were easily kept in backyards. Some idea of chicken husbandry is evident from a mid-Saxon chicken skeleton recovered from Bishopstone (Sussex), which stable isotope analysis revealed to have had an elevated nitrogen value indicative of an omnivorous diet, suggestive of living around the settlement and eating waste food and scraps (Marshall *et al.* 2010). Percentages of mature chicken bones on urban sites range from 82–93% of the total identified chicken remains, indicating that eggs were the primary reason for keeping these birds; large quantities of egg-shell, predominantly chicken, but some of goose, were recovered at Coppergate, York (O'Connor 1989, 193). Unfortunately data are not available for rural low-status sites in this period, but at the high-status site of Bishopstone, around 72% of chicken bones were fused, a lower proportion than is generally the case in towns, suggesting a greater exploitation of chickens for meat than in urban centres. However, the tendency of urban waste to derive from people of a range of social levels may mask higher chicken consumption by some urban dwellers. Geese are the second-most common domestic birds in towns, but lack of immature goose bones on urban sites suggests that most geese were raised in rural areas before being driven into urban centres, perhaps from some distance; 18th- and 19th-century evidence suggests that flocks could cover 10 miles in one day (Serjeantson 2002, 51).

Other domestic animals may not have been considered suitable human food, but, nonetheless, formed an important part of the town environment, with cat and dog remains being recovered from 76.1% and 80.4% of urban assemblages respectively. These animals would have been part of daily life for many people, fulfilling a range of other functions such as companionship, hunting, killing vermin, and providing fur. McCormick and Murray (2007, 116) have suggested the existence in Ireland of a dichotomy between urban and rural contexts in the way cats were treated during this period: rural cats were larger and lived longer, suggesting that they were pets, while the remains of urban cats often have skinning marks indicative of commercial exploitation of their skins. In England, a number of urban sites have evidence for cat skinning, in the form of butchery marks, and a high proportion of immature cats, but ageing data are lacking from rural site reports, as is any mention of butchery; it is unclear whether this is due to absence of butchery or inadequate reporting (Poole 2011). Cats in urban contexts certainly seem to have been treated in some cases as a source of fur, the large numbers of young animals perhaps also suggesting exploitation of feral cats.

Despite the apparent existence of utilitarian attitudes towards cats within urban environments, the situation could have been much more complex. At Bishopstone (Poole 2010b), the cats were much smaller than on contemporary urban sites, whilst the majority of them were young and some had cut marks, indicating use of their fur. At least one of the cats seems to have been cared for, with isotopic evidence indicating a strong marine component (30–50%) in its diet (Marshall *et al.* 2010), probably indicative of deliberate feeding by people living at the settlement. Here, at the same site, we perhaps have feral cats, exploited as an economic resource, and possibly some cats being kept as pets. It is not difficult to imagine the same being true in urban centres, and this was probably also the case for dogs – some living in a feral state, but others kept as pets, as indicted by remains of lap dogs at the Winchester Western Suburbs (Bourdillon 2009) and Lincoln (Dobney *et al.* 1996). Thus, the evidence for cats and dogs suggests that town and country did not constitute two diametrically opposed entities during this period, but shared certain attitudes towards animals between them. Even so, in other aspects of life, such as involvement in food production, and the types of meat eaten, the two probably increasingly diverged during this period.

Butchers and biographies

As noted above, animals were probably largely driven into towns on-the-hoof, but once they arrived, they, of course, had to be slaughtered and their carcasses divided up for meat and raw materials. The apparent lack of 'typical' butchery-waste deposits (containing a preponderance of head and foot elements) in Viking-Age towns in England and Ireland has led to the suggestion that, for much of the period, specialist butchers were largely itinerant, undertaking slaughter and butchery on the consumer's premises. At Flaxengate, Lincoln (O'Connor 1982, 16), specialist butchery is not apparent until the mid-11th century, when longitudinal splitting of carcasses, a method that requires the carcass to be hoisted, became increasingly common. In York, existence of a butchers' street or quarter may be implied by the area known as the Shambles, mentioned in *Domesday Book*, if the term held the same connotations then as it had more recently (O'Connor 1989, 159). Butchery waste is, however, sometimes apparent. At Bury Road, Thetford, two 10th- to 11th-century pit zones were dominated by sheep head and lower limb elements, cattle vertebrae and lower limbs, and pig heads and lower limbs (Jessica Grimm *pers. comm.*). Coupled with butchery evidence, which demonstrated a high level of standardisation with sagitally-split vertebrae, this indicates professional butchers, and this area was possibly a 'butchery quarter'. In addition, excavations in the Smithfield area of London recovered late 11th- to mid-12th-century animal bone waste, including 'general processing waste from the meat market' (Telfer 2003, 117).

The rise of professional butchers along with markets in urban centres represents an important shift in the role of the person dividing up a carcass. In rural areas and on estates, meat was probably divided up along lines of status, gender and religion, but when meat started to be divided up and sold in the marketplace, butchers instead learnt to divide animals up into 'cuts', with corresponding prices (Symons 2002, 443–4). In contrast to rural sites, where, as noted above, meat was consumed largely from animals that the consumers had raised themselves, or high-status sites, where meat was provided as food rent or grown by the workers on the estate, in towns, the animals became transformed into commercial transactions, rather than purely social ones. Relatively large numbers of single coin finds in the 10th century suggest that coins were increasingly likely to be used in everyday transactions, making possible indirect exchanges between total strangers separated by long distances (Hinton 2005, 158, 326). The producer and the consumer thus became increasingly separated, and the biography of animals, so closely tied to the lives of rural communities, faded into the background for urban dwellers. Whilst the actual slaughter represents a close bodily engagement with the animal, adopting a standardised method of butchery leads to the removal of individuality from that creature.

The move away from full-time agricultural production towards full-time craft production would, therefore, have been significant, as people began engaging with animals not so much as living creatures, but more often as body-parts (meals, waste), raw materials and objects (see Ashby, this volume). The transformation of an entity from a live animal into food or an inanimate object is significant because, in changing form, its ability to affect people's perceptions and the uses to which it is put are altered (the same is also true of plants; see Head and Atchison 2009, 237). Certain processes, such as the manufacturing of bone tools, may even remove all trace of the animal's original species identity. Alternatively, the species may assume a new species identity, as was the case with narwhal tusks in the later medieval period, which, once imported into parts of Europe, were believed to come from unicorns (Pluskowski 2004). Unlike rural contexts, in which most people would have been involved with the various stages of food production at some stage, urban specialisation would have led to a loss of knowledge by individuals of the full range of processes in production, potentially leading to feelings of alienation (Evans 2003, 31); the person becomes separated from the typical agricultural cycle. This found its ultimate expression with the formation of professional guilds in the centuries after the Norman Conquest. Even without guilds, there was still increasing specialisation and zoning of particular craft activities in certain areas of at least the larger towns, as indicated by street names in 10th-century Winchester (such as Tanner Street and Fleshmonger Street) and York (Biddle 1976, 131), and this would have helped to create a collective identity, as particular types of urban-dwelling craftsmen, living in a setting different from that of the majority of the country's population. Differential attitudes are also evident in treatment of waste, with disposal into pits being characteristic of urban sites, whilst rural sites often used waste to manure fields (Astill and Grant 1988, 3). Therefore for many urban centres, consumption was emphasised as the last useful stage of that animal's life, but in the farming landscape, consumption was part of a cyclical process with food production.

Conclusions

Animals, whether through the presence or absence of particular species, were an important part of the formation of urban identities. Howe (2008) has demonstrated that, in contemporary rural contexts, a close sense of place was created by lived experience. In doing so, Howe highlights the importance of the tasks that people carried out in the landscape. Although he does not specifically mention them, animals were involved in many of these tasks, whether through their husbandry, slaughter or consumption, whilst wild animals would have been seen and heard, especially in the case of birdsong. Whilst towns could produce food, the sheer *scale* of food production was different from the countryside, and the majority of town-dwellers are likely to have been involved in non-agricultural occupations. This pattern would have increased as towns grew in size. As a result, many people would have had very different interactions with their surroundings than the majority who laboured in the fields. Town and country were closely linked, but towns would have begun to take on a different character than their surroundings, with different smells, sounds, and proportions of particular species. We cannot necessarily speak of a distinctive urban fauna, but some animals would have thrived in an urban environment, whilst others were mostly only present on market days or when brought in for slaughter, a process that transformed the living animal into a very different form. The potential for this animal to affect, and be affected by, human action, was therefore very much altered.

In this way, animals in Viking-Age towns represented more than just meat, but rather a different way of life, and of perceiving oneself, than had existed before. The Scandinavian influence in this process derives from the indirect stimulus they provided to urban growth, in the defended sites that they created, as well as the *burhs* set up against them (Richards 2004, 107). This would have been further aided by the possible forcible settlement of populations, or disruption in the countryside leading rural dwellers to seek new opportunities in urban centres (Hinton 1990, 92). Whilst the populaces of these towns likely consisted of people from a range of backgrounds, whether Scandinavian in origin or otherwise (Hadley 2006, 181), living alongside one another in such settings perhaps fostered a shared sense of identity. Yet the extent to which ethnicity was a factor within urban centres, and upon human-animal relationships is unclear. In seeking to understand this, we might turn to Yorke's (2003, 7) comment with regards to gender in early medieval England: even people of the same gender could have had greater distance in their lives depending on whether they were at the top or bottom ends of society, rather than any experiences due to their shared gender. Similarly, we could postulate that a person's social standing, and hence the sorts of tasks they undertook in daily life, were potentially of greater significance than notions of 'Scandinavian' and 'Saxon'. Thus, the differences between urban and rural lifestyles, which became particularly marked over time, were increasingly significant factors in the creation and maintenance of social identity.

Bibliography

Abbink, J. (2003) Love and death of cattle: the paradox in Suri attitudes toward livestock. *Ethnos* 68 (3), 341–64.

Albarella, U. (2005) Meat production and consumption in town and country. In K. Giles and C. Dyer (eds) *Town and Country in the Middle Ages: contrasts, contacts and interconnections, 1100–1500*, 131–48. Society for Medieval Archaeology Monograph 22. Leeds, Maney.

Albarella, U. (2006) Pig husbandry and pork consumption in medieval England. In C. M. Woolgar, D. Serjeantson and T. Waldron (eds) *Food in Medieval England: diet and nutrition*, 72–87. Oxford, Oxford University Press.

Astill, G. (2000) General survey 600–1300. In D. Palliser (ed.) *The Cambridge Urban History of Britain Volume 1: 600–1540*, 27–49. Cambridge, Cambridge University Press.

Astill, G. and Grant, A. (1988) The medieval countryside: approaches and perceptions. In G. Astill and A. Grant (eds) *The Countryside of Medieval England*, 1–11. Oxford, Blackwell.

Barrett, J. H., Locker, A. M. and Roberts, C. M. (2004) 'Dark Age Economics' revisited: the English fish bone evidence AD 600–1600. *Antiquity* 78 (301), 618–36.

Biddle, M. (1976) Towns. In D. M. Wilson (ed.) *The Archaeology of Anglo-Saxon England*, 99–150. London, Methuen and Co. Ltd.

Bond, J. and Worley, F. (2006) Companions in death: the roles of animals in Anglo-Saxon and Viking cremation rituals in Britain. In R. Gowland and C. Knüsel (eds) *Social Archaeology of Funerary Remains*, 89–98. Oxford, Oxbow.

Bourdillon, J. (2009) Late Saxon animal bone from the northern and eastern suburbs and the city defences. In D. Serjeantson and H. Rees (eds) *Food, Craft and Status in Saxon and Medieval Winchester: the evidence from the suburbs and city defences*, 55–81. Winchester, Winchester Museums Service.

Coates, R. (1999) New light from old wics: the progeny of Latin *vicus*. *Nomina* 22, 75–116.

Crossley-Holland, K. (1999) *The Anglo-Saxon World: an anthology.* Oxford, Oxford University Press.

Danielsson, I. B. (2007) *Masking Moments: the transitions of bodies and beings in late Iron Age Scandinavia.* Unpublished PhD thesis, University of Stockholm.

Dobney, K. M., Jacques, S. D. and Irving, B. G. (1996) *Of Butchers and Breeds: report on vertebrate remains from various sites in the City of Lincoln.* Lincoln Archaeological Studies 5. Oxford, Oxbow.

Dobney, K., Jacques, D., Barrett, J. and Johnstone, C. (2007) *Farmers, Monks and Aristocrats: the environmental archaeology of Anglo-Saxon Flixborough.* Excavations at Flixborough 3. Oxford, Oxbow.

Evans, J. G. (2003) *Environmental Archaeology and the Social Order.* London, Routledge.

Evans, N. and Yarwood, R. (1995) Livestock and landscape. *Landscape Research* 20 (3), 141–6.

Fox, H. (2008) Butter place-names and transhumance. In O. J. Padel and D. N. Parsons (eds) *A Commodity of Good Names: essays in honour of Margaret Gelling*, 352–64. Donington, Shaun Tyas.

Hadley, D. M. (2006) *The Vikings in England: settlement, society and culture.* Manchester, Manchester University Press.

Hagen, A. (1992) *A Handbook of Anglo-Saxon Food: processing and consumption.* Hockwold-cum-Wilton, Anglo-Saxon Books.

Hammon, A. (2010) The brown bear. In T. P. O'Connor and N. J. Sykes (eds) *Extinctions and Invasions: a social history of British fauna*, 95–103. Oxford, Oxbow.

Head, L. and Atchison, J. (2009) Cultural ecology: emerging human-plant geographies. *Progress in Human Geography* 33 (2), 236–45.

Hinton, D. A. (1990) *Archaeology, Economy and Society: England from the fifth to the fifteenth century.* London, Routledge.

Hinton, D. A. (2005) *Gold and Gilt, Pots and Pins: possessions and people in medieval Britain.* Oxford, Oxford University Press.

Howe, N. (2008) *Writing the Map of Anglo-Saxon England: essays in cultural geography.* London, Yale University Press.

Jones, M. (2007) *Feast: why humans share food.* Oxford, Oxford University Press.

Knight, J. (2005) Introduction. In J. Knight (ed.) *Animals in Person: cultural perspectives on human-animal intimacies*, 1–13. Oxford, Berg.

Lévi-Strauss, C. (1964) *Totemism.* London, Merlin Press.

Löfgren, O. (1985) Our friends in nature: class and animal symbolism. *Ethnos* 50, 184–213.

Lucas, G. and McGovern, T. (2007) Bloody slaughter: ritual decapitation and display at the Viking settlement of Hofstaðir, Iceland. *European Journal of Archaeology* 10 (1), 7–30.

McCormick, F. (1983) Dairying and beef production in early Christian Ireland: the faunal evidence. In T. Reeves-Smyth and F. Hammond (eds) *Landscape Archaeology in Ireland*, 253–67. British Archaeological Reports British Series 116. Oxford, Archaeopress.

McCormick, F. (2002) The distribution of meat in a hierarchical society: the Irish evidence. In P. Miracle and N. Milner (eds) *Consuming Passions and Patterns of Consumption*, 25–31. Cambridge, McDonald Institute for Archaeological Research.

McCormick, F. and Murray, E. (2007) *Knowth and the Zooarchaeology of Early Christian Ireland.* Dublin, Royal Irish Academy.

McHugh, D. E., Troy, C. S., McCormick, F., Olsaker, I., Eythórsdóttir, E. and Bradley, D. G. (1999) Early medieval cattle remains from a Scandinavian settlement in Dublin: genetic analysis and comparison with extant breeds. *Philosophical Transactions of the Royal Society of London* 354, 99–109.

Magennis, H. (1999) *Anglo-Saxon Appetites: food and drink and their consumption in Old English and related literature.* Bodmin, Four Courts Press.

Marshall, P., van der Plicht, J., Cook, G. T., Grootes, P. M., Beavan Athfield, N. and Buzinny, M. (2010) Scientific dating evidence. In G. Thomas (ed.) *The Later Anglo-Saxon Settlement at Bishopstone: a downland manor in the making*, 196–200. Council for British Archaeology Research Report 163. York, Council for British Archaeology.

O'Connor, T. P. (1982) *Animal Bones from Flaxengate, Lincoln c. 870–1500.* The Archaeology of Lincoln 18 (1). London, Council for British Archaeology.

O'Connor, T. P. (1989) *Bones from the Anglo-Scandinavian Levels at 16–22 Coppergate.* The Archaeology of York 15 (3). London, Council for British Archaeology.

O'Connor, T. P. (2010) Livestock and deadstock in early medieval Europe from the North Sea to the Baltic. *Environmental Archaeology* 15 (1), 1–15.

Pluciennik, M. (1996) A perilous but necessary search: archaeology and European identities. In J. A. Atkinson, I. Banks and J. O'Sullivan (eds) *Nationalism and Archaeology*, 35–58. Glasgow, Cruithne Press.

Pluskowski, A. (2004) Narwhals or unicorns? Exotic animals as material culture in medieval Europe. *European Journal of Archaeology* 7 (3), 291–313.

Pluskowski, A. (2006) *Wolves and the Wilderness in the Middle Ages*. Woodbridge, Boydell.

Poole, K. (2008) Living and eating in Viking-Age towns and their hinterlands. In S. Baker, M. Allen, S. Middle and K. Poole (eds) *Food and Drink in Archaeology 1: University of Nottingham Postgraduate Conference 2007*, 104–12. Totnes, Prospect Books.

Poole, K. (2010a) Bird introductions. In T. P. O'Connor and N. J. Sykes (eds) *Extinctions and Invasions: a social history of British fauna*, 156–65. Oxford, Oxbow.

Poole, K. (2010b) The mammal and bird remains. In G. Thomas (ed.) *The Later Anglo-Saxon Settlement at Bishopstone: a downland manor in the making*, 142–57. Council for British Archaeology Research Report 163. York, Council for British Archaeology.

Poole, K. (2011) *The Nature of Society in England, c. AD 410–1066*. Unpublished PhD thesis, University of Nottingham.

Pritchard, F. A. (1984) Late Saxon textiles from the City of London. *Medieval Archaeology* 28, 46–76.

Randsborg, K. (1985) Subsistence and settlement in northern temperate Europe in the first millennium A.D. In G. Barker and C. Gamble (eds) *Beyond Domestication in Prehistoric Europe in the First Millennium A.D.*, 233–65. London, Academic Press.

Ratcliffe, D. (1997) *The Raven*. London, T. and A. D. Poyser.

Richards, J. D. (2004) *Viking Age England*. Stroud, Tempus.

Robertson, A. J. (1925) *The Laws of the Kings of England from Edmund to Henry I*. Cambridge, Cambridge University Press.

Russell, N. (1998) Cattle as wealth in Neolithic Europe: where's the beef? In D. W. Bailey (ed.) *The Archaeology of Value*, 42–54. British Archaeological Reports British Series 730. Oxford, Archaeopress.

Ryder, M. L. (1981) British medieval sheep and their wool types. In D. W. Crossley (ed.) *Medieval Industry*, 16–28. Council for British Archaeology Research Report 40. London, Council for British Archaeology.

Serjeantson, D. (2002) Goose husbandry in medieval England, and the problem of ageing goose bones. *Acta Zoologica Cracoviensia* 45, 39–54.

Steane, K., Darling, M. J., Mann, J., Vince, A. and Young, J. (2001) *The Archaeology of Wigford and the Brayford Pool*. Lincoln Archaeological Studies 2. Oxford, Oxbow.

Sykes, N. J. (2006) From *Cu* and *Sceap* to *Beffe* and *Motton*. In C. M. Woolgar, D. Serjeantson and T. Waldron (eds) *Food in Medieval England: diet and nutrition*, 56–71. Oxford, Oxford University Press.

Sykes, N. J. (2007) *The Norman Conquest: a zooarchaeological perspective*. British Archaeological Reports International Series 1656. Oxford, Archaeopress.

Symons, M. (2002) Cutting up cultures. *Journal of Historical Sociology* 15 (4), 431–50.

Tatton-Brown, T. (1984) The towns of Kent. In J. Haslam (ed.) *Anglo-Saxon Towns in Southern England*, 1–36. London, Phillimore.

Telfer, A. (2003) Medieval drainage near Smithfield Market: excavations at Hosier Lane, EC1. *London Archaeologist* (summer), 115–20.

Vince, A. (1990) *Saxon London: an archaeological investigation*. London, Seaby.

Vince, A. (1994) Saxon urban economies: an archaeological perspective. In J. Rackham (ed.) *Environment and Economy in Anglo-Saxon England*, 108–19. Council for British Archaeology Research Report 89. York, Council for British Archaeology.

Walton Rogers, P. (2007) *Cloth and Clothing in Early Anglo-Saxon England, AD 450–700*. Council for British Archaeology Research Report 145. York, Council for British Archaeology.

Williams, H. (2005) Animals, ashes and ancestors. In A. Pluskowski (ed.) *Just Skin and Bones? New perspectives on human-animal relations in the historical past*, 19–40. British Archaeological Reports International Series 1410. Oxford, Archaeopress.

Yorke, B. (2003) *Nunneries and the Anglo-Saxon Royal Houses*. London, Continuum.

NO POTS PLEASE, WE'RE VIKINGS: POTTERY IN THE SOUTHERN DANELAW, 850–1000

Paul Blinkhorn

The mid- to late 9th century in England saw a major change in pottery production with the introduction of a number of wheel-thrown, kiln-fired wares that were produced on an industrial scale, the first time pottery had been made in this way since Roman times. Archaeologists have for some time known this, although the stimulus for this major change has not been greatly discussed, other than perhaps to assume this was due to the arrival of the Vikings, despite the fact that Viking society, in Scandinavia, was largely aceramic. This chapter addresses a number of outstanding questions relating to this change, and the traditional view of the origins and 'meaning' of these new pottery types. It begins with a chronological overview of the start dates of the various industries and the way in which the pottery has been interpreted in the context of changing 'ethnic' identities in Viking-Age England. The new, mass-produced pottery types of the Midlands and East Anglia (the so-called 'southern Danelaw') stand central to the discussion. Although utilitarian, these wares also had 'meaning', particularly in the expression of the identities of the people who used them. They were new pottery types for a new way of life, but they also referred back to far older allegiances and social identities.

Pottery and identity in pre-Viking England

The concept that the people of Anglo-Saxon England used material culture, particularly pottery, as a means to broadcast social information is not a new one. In the mid-19th century, pioneers of the study of the period noted regional differences in styles of early Anglo-Saxon objects, such as brooches, and linked them to different cultural identities, usually related to Bede's 'three tribes' story of the settlement of England by the Angles, Saxons and Jutes (Lucy 2000, 11). In the field of pottery studies, this approach was later developed by Myres (1969; 1977), who defined stylistic groups for early Anglo-Saxon (*c.* 5th–7th century) decorated pottery, including cremation urns, and attempted to link each type to a particular group of those Germanic peoples. Most now accept that Myres's work is fundamentally flawed, mainly due to his largely art-historical approach and excessive reliance on typology, but more recent work (Richards 1987; 1992;

Blinkhorn 1997) has indicated that there is good evidence to believe that early Anglo-Saxon pottery, at all levels from manufacture to decoration and use, was imbued with 'meaning', and that it reflected the beliefs, identities and traditions of its makers and users. We may not fully understand what the pots were saying, but they certainly spoke to the people who experienced them in the past, and they had a significance that went far beyond being just simple containers.

A good case can be made that pottery continued to be used as a medium of broadcasting social information in the middle Anglo-Saxon period (*c.* 700–850), although by then the material had purely non-funerary functions. In East Anglia, Ipswich (Suffolk) was home to what can be regarded as the first post-Roman pottery industry in England, with large-scale production of kiln-fired pottery with a highly restricted range of forms and decoration (Hurst 1976, 299; Blinkhorn in prep.). The products of this industry, known as Ipswich Ware, were not truly wheel-thrown, but built from coils of clay on a turntable, but were fired in kilns, which was a major technological step forward from the early Anglo-Saxon era, when bonfire firing appears to have been the norm. Two of these kilns have been excavated (Smedley and Owles 1963; Blinkhorn 1990). Recent work indicates that this pottery, which began to be produced in *c.* 720, was more or less the only type of ceramic used by the inhabitants of the East Anglian kingdom during the middle Anglo-Saxon period. The hand-built wares that had been common staple in the region in the early Anglo-Saxon period were extremely rare in these later assemblages in Norfolk, Suffolk and eastern Cambridgeshire (Blinkhorn in prep.). Effectively, then, Ipswich Ware was part of the social 'kit' of the inhabitants of the kingdom and, by using it, they confirmed and broadcasted their East Anglian identity. Imported wares occurred in small quantities in East Anglian ports such as Ipswich, whilst a few sherds are known mainly from high-status sites inland, but generally, East Anglians used Ipswich Ware virtually to the point of total exclusion of all other pottery types.

Elsewhere in England, such as in the *wics* of *Hamwic* (Southampton, Hampshire) and *Lundenwic* (London), local potters continued to make simple hand-built forms (*e.g.* Timby 1988; Blackmore 1988; 1989; 2003), despite the fact that, in both places, continental wheel-thrown wares and, in the case of London, large quantities of Ipswich Ware were imported. There appears to have been no attempt by potters in these places to imitate any of these technologically more advanced wares, such as jugs. This is striking, given that the Ipswich Ware and imported assemblages included large proportions of jugs, a form which was obviously desirable, as jugs form a much higher proportion of Ipswich Ware assemblages at sites located outside the East Anglian kingdom than at those within it (Blinkhorn in prep.).

Elsewhere in much of southern England, undecorated hand-built pottery continued to be made that was, to all intents and purposes, identical to that of the early Anglo-Saxon period. In the southeast Midlands and Lincolnshire at the same time, a new pottery tradition emerged in the form of Maxey-type Ware (Hurst 1976, 307), which comprised hand-built vessels in a coarse shelly limestone-tempered fabric. No evidence has been found for a manufacturing centre, but Maxey-type Ware probably came from a number of workshops, as the forms from the southeast Midlands are quite different from the Lincolnshire types, with the former having distinctive bar-lugs, and the latter simple upright triangular types. Ipswich Ware vessels, in particular jugs, were imported to the regions in which Maxey Ware was produced, but, again, the local potters made no attempt to copy the ware. This was despite the fact that – again – jugs occurred in much greater proportions here than in Ipswich Ware assemblages in East Anglia, suggesting, hence, that they were desired objects.

Much of western and south-western England appears to have been largely aceramic, in the sense that there was no local production of pottery, and the small amounts that occasionally occur are imported from relatively distant sources during the middle Anglo-Saxon period. For example, in Oxfordshire, which has produced plenty of early Anglo-Saxon pottery at sites such as Eynsham Abbey and Yarnton (Blinkhorn 2003; 2004), the only later pottery present consisted of a few sherds of Ipswich Ware and some continental imported wares and hand-made vessels, both of which appear likely to have travelled down the Thames from London together with the Ipswich Ware. A similar situation may have occurred in much of the Upper and Middle Thames Valley. For example, at Lake End Road, Maidenhead (Berkshire) (Blinkhorn 2002), a large assemblage of hand-built pottery was noted of a type that is very similar to the types found in London (*i.e.* sandy and chaff-tempered wares), along with Ipswich Ware and French imports, but there were no wares that can be said with certainty to have been locally produced. It is possible, therefore, that the only pottery being consumed in the Thames Valley came from the same sources that were supplying the *wic* of London at that time.

It appears, then, that there were distinct regional trends in the production and use of pottery in many areas of England in the middle Anglo-Saxon period, and that potters were apparently resistant to change. The pottery of East Anglia – Ipswich Ware – was very different from that of Mercia, which consisted of chaff- and sand-tempered wares, and both were different from the chalk-tempered wares produced in Wessex. The products of the Ipswich kilns are found at a fairly large number of sites in Mercia, but they are almost unknown south of the Thames. Other than in northern Kent, where Ipswich Ware occurs quite frequently, the only occurrence of Ipswich Ware from south of the Thames is a single sherd from *Hamwic*. Ipswich Ware is, in contrast, widely found north of the Thames, where it occurs as far east as Gloucestershire and as far north as north Yorkshire (Blinkhorn in prep.), while large quantities are also known from London. Thus, it seems that not only were the people of Wessex using pottery that was different from that used in Mercia, but there was also a strong resistance in Wessex to what was, perhaps, considered 'Mercian' material culture. This is particularly notable given that, at the same time, continental wares were apparently acceptable.

We do not know why the people of East Anglia chose to change dramatically the methods of manufacture and the type of pottery they used in the early 8th century. However, the transition from production and use of simple hand-built wares to Ipswich Ware, and the emergence of new vessel forms, particularly jugs, indicates a significant transformation in the expression of identity. This may be related to a crystallization of the identity of the kingdom in the face of the expansion of Mercian hegemony. Indeed, as Hadley (2001, 24) has noted in the context of Viking-Age England, 'feelings of ethnic allegiance ... may have become more prominent when mobilised in the context of political conflict, as a means of moulding an identity and a sense of community in opposition to one's enemies', and this seems equally applicable to the pre-Viking period. It was not just pottery that changed. In the 8th century, the materials from which jewellery, particularly brooches, was made changed as well, with the highest-status items generally made from silver-and-niello, rather than from gold and garnet, as had been the case in the 7th century (*e.g.* Wilson 1976, 267).

Pottery and identity in Viking-Age England

The later 9th and 10th centuries witnessed one of the most momentous events in English history. After decades of raids, the country was settled by the Scandinavians, and then effectively divided in half, with the West Saxons ruling the area of England broadly to the south of Watling Street and the River Lea, while the area to the north, which later became known as the Danelaw, came under Scandinavian control. In the 10th century, the West Saxons gradually conquered northern and eastern England, which, eventually, and for the first time, became a single political entity under one king. The period also witnessed the significant re-occupation of some of the deserted Roman towns, such as Winchester, York, Lincoln and Leicester, and the construction of 'new' settlements that developed to become towns, such as some of the West Saxon and Mercian *burhs* (*e.g.* Clarke and Ambrosiani 1991, 91).

East Anglia and the south Midlands saw a radical transformation of pottery production in the 9th and 10th centuries. New industries, based in the new urban centres, produced pottery on a scale that was unprecedented since Roman times, the fast wheel was reintroduced for the first time since the Roman period and vessel forms were inspired by continental types, which had continued Roman pottery traditions. Excavations in towns such as Thetford (Norfolk), Ipswich and Stamford (Lincolnshire) usually produce large quantities of these new ceramic types, which were also used in smaller rural settlements in the hinterlands of these towns (*e.g.* Kilmurry 1980, fig. 32). In the southern Danelaw, the uptake of these new wares appears to have been more or less universal, and the preceding pottery types – hand-built wares and Ipswich Ware – ceased to be made and used within a decade or two at the most. Despite the availability of a large data set that can be used to generate new understandings of late Anglo-Saxon society, these new wares have been largely untheorised by archaeologists. Instead, they have been used mainly as a dating tool, with most researchers' energies directed at typology and chronology (*e.g.* Kilmurry 1980). While these are fundamental and necessary areas of research, they do not engage with the material in the same manner as the original users; they may tell us 'when', but not 'why?'. Generally speaking, the literature that discusses such pottery usually dismisses it as utilitarian, as the vast majority of the products comprise simple jar forms with minimal decoration. In sum, they were boring pots for boring tasks!

Few attempts have been made to explain the wholesale change in pottery manufacture in this period, other than by making vague reference to the arrival of the Scandinavians (*e.g.* Kilmurry 1980, 195). However, this is unconvincing, as Scandinavian society was at that time largely aceramic. Moreover, it has been noted that production of at least some of these new pottery types may have started in England *before* the Scandinavian invasions (Hurst 1976, 319), although the implications of this evidence have scarcely been explored. A review of the chronology of the new pottery types is therefore long overdue, especially given the extensive ceramic assemblages that have come to light through the vast amount of excavation that has been carried out in the towns and cities of England in the last 25 years or so. A principal aim of this chapter is to establish the chronology of the start of production of these new wares, which is crucial for a clearer understanding of the reasons why they came into existence.

Chronology of production

The first formal classification of many of the late Anglo-Saxon pottery industries of the southern

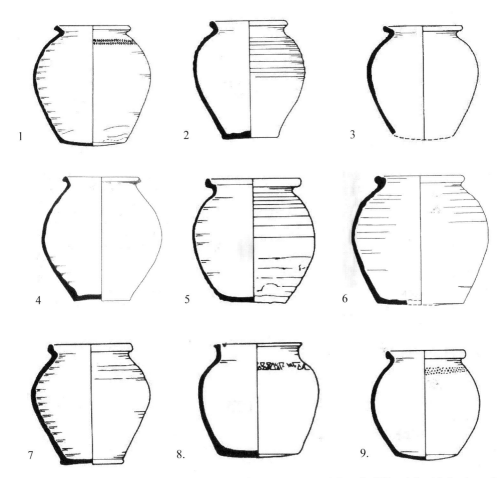

Fig. 10.1 Typical examples of wheel-thrown late Anglo-Saxon pottery: 1) Stamford Ware (after McCarthy and Brooks 1988, fig. 76, no. 111); 2) Ipswich-Thetford Ware (after McCarthy and Brooks 1988, fig 87, no. 257); 3) St. Neots Ware (after McCarthy and Brooks 1988, fig. 93, no. 317); 4) Leicester Ware (after Hurst 1976, fig. 7.23 no. 1); 5) Northampton Ware (after McCarthy and Brooks 1988, fig. 92, no. 298); 6) Nottingham-type Ware (after Young and Vince 2005, fig. 65, no. 404); 7) Norwich-Thetford Ware (after McCarthy and Brooks 1988, fig. 84, no. 207); 8) Stafford Ware (after McCarthy and Brooks 1988, fig. 111, no. 521); 9) Thetford Ware (after McCarthy and Brooks 1988, fig. 80, no. 157).

Danelaw was made in the 1950s (Hurst 1955; 1956; 1957), and the general chronologies advanced at that time still hold good. However, Hurst himself later noted that the precise date-ranges of many of the wares were uncertain due to a lack of closely dated assemblages from the chronological extremes of the periods of production (Hurst 1976, 314). This assertion is still generally applicable, as there has not subsequently been a major review of the chronology of these industries. What follows cannot be regarded as exhaustive, but will hopefully highlight some of the crucial uncertainties concerning the production of the ceramics of the 9th and 10th centuries. Figure 10.1 illustrates some of the main pottery types from this period.

Stamford Ware

The pottery industry of Stamford in Lincolnshire, which is usually given a date range of 850–1250, is well known to archaeologists (Kilmurry 1980). A number of kilns have been excavated and published, the earliest of which was excavated at Stamford Castle. A large piece of charred oak from the stokehole yielded radiocarbon dates of AD 837 ± 77 and AD 678 ± 83 (which need to be recalibrated), and the kiln itself yielded an archaeomagnetic date of AD 850 ± 50 (Kilmurry 1980, 32). The earliest products were large, glazed and/or red-painted vessels and small unpainted jars, which are virtually identical to pottery that was produced in northern France from the early 9th century onwards (Kilmurry 1980, 188–9, figs 7 and 8). The kiln, which had at least four phases of construction, was stratigraphically later than a layer which also produced red-painted Stamford Ware, leading Kilmurry (1980, 188–9) to suggest that those sherds were from pots that 'must have been fired in an earlier clamp or kiln'. Given that the scientifically-derived dates are all from the *last* firing of the structure, and it is probably not the first kiln in the area, it seems highly likely that Stamford Ware production began by the mid-9th century at the very latest, and possibly as early as 800.

Ipswich-Thetford-type Ware

Ipswich was the best equipped of the late Anglo-Saxon centres to begin the mass-production of pottery as, by the middle of the 9th century, it had been manufacturing kiln-fired pottery on a near-industrial scale for around 150 years. What is more, at least one 8th-century kiln (Blinkhorn 1990) that has been excavated is technologically the equal of those of the 9th century, and in some ways, is more sophisticated. It was a double-flue updraught kiln with a fixed firing floor, a feature lacking in some of the late Anglo-Saxon kilns from the town, which were simple ovens, with no firing floor or flues other than a row of inverted 'waster' pots from previous firings.

The new pottery produced in the town, Ipswich-Thetford ware, was different from middle Anglo-Saxon Ipswich Ware in that it was fully wheel-thrown, and while the basic functional range of forms produced was similar, the vessels had much thinner walls, and were often larger than their predecessors, with minimal – although different where it occurs – decoration. The chronology of Ipswich-Thetford Ware is a little vague. In part this is because there is a paucity of excavated coinage from Ipswich from the mid-8th to the early 10th centuries, which limits our ability to date ceramic assemblages through associated coin finds (Wade 1988, fig. 56). However, the fact that Ipswich Ware and Ipswich-Thetford Ware are often found stratified together in Ipswich, indicates that there was an overlap in their use. The latest dates of coins found with assemblages that contain only Ipswich Ware are *c.* 855, suggesting that production of this ware ceased during the mid-9th century. Ipswich-Thetford Ware was certainly being made before the end of the 9th century, as numerous pits containing this type of pottery are known from excavations beneath the town defences, which were dated to the early 10th century by related coin finds of that date, particularly the St Edmund memorial issue (Wade 1988, 97). The evidence, thus, suggests that Ipswich-Thetford Ware production had started by 860, although refinement of the chronology of this ware is still needed.

St Neots Ware

St Neots Ware was one of the first late Anglo-Saxon pottery types to be recognised as such, but the source of the material remains unknown. It is largely wheel-thrown, with a fabric containing fairly large quantities of shelly limestone. It is found in a wide belt across the Midlands and East Anglia from Worcester to Ipswich, although its main zone of usage appears to be Bedfordshire, Cambridgeshire, northern Oxfordshire and Northamptonshire. It is likely, on petrological grounds, to have been made at a number of production centres, although none have yet been found. It is usually given a date range of 850–1100, although Hurst (1976, 323) noted that the earliest examples from Cambridge, in the heartland of the East Anglian consumption area, are of early 10th-century date. At Northampton, the earliest absolute dates come from associations with St Edmund memorial pennies dated to 900–930 (Denham 1985, 55), although a few sherds were noted in contexts pre-dating those in which the coins appeared. Denham (1985, table 11), in her appraisal of St Neots Ware from Northampton, noted that the wheel-thrown late Anglo-Saxon wares do not appear to have started before 900, and comprise mainly small jars. There are also mid- to late 9th-century hand-built wares with a similar fabric that are sometimes classified as St Neots Ware, but Denham (1985) argued that these were basically regional variations on the preceding hand-built Maxey Ware. They are perhaps best regarded as an earlier tradition which utilised the same clay sources as St. Neots ware, rather than being part of the late Anglo-Saxon tradition.

At Oxford, St Neots Ware was common in the 10th century, and Mellor's (2003) examination of the pottery from a sequence of deposits at the All Saints church site showed that the earliest finds of St Neots Ware were stratigraphically somewhat later than the first Stamford Ware. Significantly, just three sherds of St Neots Ware were noted in a phase pre-dating a fire deposit (Mellor 2003, 336–7), which produced a radiocarbon date of 890–1030 at the 95% confidence level (Marshall 2003, table A2.4). It appears, therefore, that a start date of the earlier 10th century is the most appropriate for this ware.

Leicester Ware

A kiln was noted during excavations at Southgate Street in Leicester in the 1960s (Hebditch 1967–8). It was provisionally dated to the early 10th century from coin finds associated with Leicester Ware from Northampton, but more recently Leicester Ware has been noted in mid- to late 9th-century levels at Lincoln (Young and Vince 2005, 72–3), suggesting that a mid-9th-century start date is more appropriate. Curiously, the ware is extremely rare in Leicester itself, with no published sherds known other than at the kiln site, although recent, as yet unpublished, excavations in the city are said to have revealed large quantities of the material (Deborah Sawday *pers. comm.*). The exact end date is unknown, but production appears to have been rather short-lived.

Northampton Ware

A kiln was discovered in the Horsemarket area of Northampton in 1974 (Williams 1974), which appears to be the only source of the ware. It is very similar to Stamford Ware in terms of fabric, and the two cannot be separated chemically (Denham 1985, 55). The vessels were largely coil-built and wheel-finished, and consisted of jars and spouted bowls with heavily knife-trimmed bases, which are relatively crude and clumsy compared to Stamford Ware examples. The *floruit* of the industry appears to cover the period 925–75, which is based mainly on coin finds associated with Northampton Ware pottery from the St Peter's Way site in the town (Williams 1974; Denham 1985, 55).

Nottingham-type Ware

Production evidence for Nottingham-type Ware comprises a group of wasters from a stoke pit at Halifax Place, Nottingham (Nailor 1984). The material is recognisably of the Thetford Ware tradition, with grey, rouletted small jars and larger vessels with applied strips. No absolute dating was obtained, although Nailor (1984, 62) argued for a late 10th- or early 11th-century date, based on the stratigraphic evidence obtained from the excavation. More recently, an early 10th-century date for the start of production has been suggested, based mainly on typological characteristics such as roller stamping, the rim forms and the use of a former for shaping the rims. These traits are all thought to be typical of the period, and there is also an association of the material with late 9th- to early 10th-century Lincoln Wares in Lincoln (Young and Vince 2005, 74).

Norwich-Thetford-type Ware

A number of kilns have been excavated in Norwich (Atkin *et al.* 1983). The kiln from Bedford Street in the city returned an archaeomagnetic date of AD 1000 60 ± 40, while charcoal from the fill of the Lobster Lane kiln produced a radiocarbon date of AD 1180 ± 80, although these dates are nearly 30 years old and need recalibrating (Atkin *et al.* 1983, 92). It appears, thus, that production started in the mid- to late 10th century, and continued until the mid-12th century.

Stafford Ware

At least four kilns have been excavated in Stafford, although the results are yet to be fully published (Ford 1999, 16). The material has been found in Chester, where it was at first thought to have been a local product, dubbed 'Chester-type Ware', but this is now seen as a product of the Stafford kilns (Ford 1995, 29). A Stafford Ware pot containing a coin hoard of 972–3 is known from Chester, but uncalibrated radiocarbon dates from three kilns at Tipping Street in Stafford suggest that the start of the industry can be placed much earlier, before the foundation of the Æthelflaedan *burh* in 913, and perhaps even in the first half of the 9th century (Ford 1995, 18). The radiocarbon dates from Tipping Street, the main late Anglo-Saxon pottery production area in Stafford, were in the range AD 780 ± 80 and 830 ± 40, leading Ford (1995, 29) to conclude that the industry was 'fully developed' by 870/80.

Thetford Ware

A large number of kilns have been excavated in Thetford in the last 60 years or so, but the dating of the start of the industry remains problematic. The earliest products of the industry were small jars with rouletted decoration (Dallas 1993, 127), and these were generally given a start date around 925 due to a fairly large number of St Edmund memorial coins being present in the town. However, the coin sequence from Thetford is very likely to have the same shortcomings as that from Ipswich; in other words, there is a paucity of excavated coinage from the mid-8th to the early 10th centuries. Settlement in Thetford and its environs started in the early Anglo-Saxon period, and appears largely unbroken from that time onwards (*e.g.* Andrews 1995), although the early pottery kilns appear to have been largely located on previously unoccupied sites. A Northumbrian styca dated to the third decade of the 9th century was noted at the St Barnabas hospital site, where one of the kilns was located (Rogerson and Dallas 1984, 58). However, it occurred in a residual context, in a pit that contained both late Anglo-Saxon and early medieval

```
AD850--------------AD900--------------AD950--------------AD1000---------

?------Stamford Ware--------------------------------------------------------------

?------Ipswich-Thetford Ware--------------------------------------------------

?------Thetford Ware---------------------------------------------------------------

?------Stafford Ware---------------------------------------------------------------

?------Leicester Ware-----?

                              ?--St. Neots Ware----------------------------

                              ?------Northampton Ware--?

                                       ?------Nottingham Ware--------

                              ?------Norwich-Thetford Ware-
```

Fig. 10.2 Suggested chronology for the late Anglo-Saxon pottery industries of the southern Danelaw.

pottery. Significantly, no early Stamford Ware (*c.* 850–900) occurred at that site, while middle Anglo-Saxon pottery, such as Ipswich Ware, was also entirely absent. This all suggests very strongly that pottery production at the site did not start until the 10th century at the earliest.

Early finds of Thetford Ware have been made elsewhere. In Lincoln, for example, a number of sherds have been found in horizons of mid- to late 9th-century date (Young and Vince 2005, 99), so it appears possible that the industry began production before the arrival of the Scandinavian settlers. Clarification of the start-date of this industry is therefore necessary, and, in the context of this discussion and the archaeology of the period in East Anglia, extremely important.

Chronology of production: conclusions

The foregoing review of the chronology of pottery production in the southern Danelaw shows that, in the majority of cases, the dating of the late Anglo-Saxon pottery industries is rather problematic. Nonetheless, a case can be made that these industries started either before the Scandinavian settlement, or after the West Saxon conquests of the early 10th century, and that they are, either way, purely Anglo-Saxon in nature. Ipswich-Thetford Ware, Thetford Ware, Stamford Ware, Leicester Ware and Stafford Ware all appear to pre-date the Scandinavian settlements of the 870s, while St Neots Ware, Northampton Ware, Nottingham Ware and Norwich-Thetford Ware all seem to date to the early 10th century, after the West Saxon conquest of the southern Danelaw. However, none of the ceramic industries can be confidently demonstrated to have originated during the period of Scandinavian control (*i.e.* between *c.* 870 and the early 10th century) (fig. 10.2).

The stimuli for change

The new pottery industries of the mid-9th century all produced wares which, in terms of manufacture, form and decoration, are very similar to those that were in use in northern France at the time, and very different from the existing Anglo-Saxon pottery types. Such is the similarity to northern French pottery that it is very difficult to see any other source for these influences. This was first highlighted by Kilmurry (1980, 193) in her discussion of the origins of the Stamford Ware industry. Given the fact that the preceding centuries of Anglo-Saxon pottery production had been characterised by conservatism in both the method of production and the physical nature of the pots in terms of form, function and decoration, this sudden change is somewhat curious.

It can be suggested that this change was due to a wider 'Carolingianisation' of Anglo-Saxon society, which had its roots in the 8th century, well before the arrival of the Scandinavian settlers. It is well documented that Offa and Charlemagne had close links, and there is plenty of evidence, both historical and archaeological, for trade between England and the Carolingian realm in the 8th century and earlier (*e.g.* Hodges 1980, 104–30). These links appear to have stimulated a reform of the English coinage, which saw the sceatta gradually replaced by a silver penny, which was very heavily modelled on contemporary Carolingian coinages of the early part of the second half of the 8th century (Dolley 1976, 353).

Hodges (1980) has noted that many of the technological advances in 8th- and 9th-century Europe originated in the Frankish realm, such as the introduction of iron smelting furnaces, mortar-mixers, new stone building methods and the aforementioned coinage, all of which spread into Anglo-Saxon England in the 9th and 10th centuries. The implication is that the expertise and, for that matter, the experts were imported by the Anglo-Saxon elite, as they appear likely to have been responsible for the control of coinage and the construction of stone buildings, and there is a case to be made that they largely controlled the mining and manufacture of iron (Blinkhorn 1999). Certainly, there are precedents. Bede records that the 7th-century monasteries of the northeast were largely built and glazed by Franks, and Frankish shipwrights later came to England to build trade-ships for the nuns of Thanet (Kent) in the 8th century (Kelly 1992).

Thus, the manufacture of Frankish-style pottery in England can perhaps be seen as just part of this general 'Carolingianisation' of Anglo-Saxon society. In most cases, it was made in the place where the people who used it lived, and thus was part of the identity of those living there. Anglo-Saxon society was changing, with a large part of the population having to adapt to urbanism, which for most of them would have been an entirely new way of living. Pottery, and material culture in general, perhaps changed in response to this; it was a new identity for a new way of life. The stylistic uniformities of these wares proclaimed a common identity, although this identity was not that of 'being English'. Outside of those areas settled by the Scandinavians – basically the kingdom of Wessex – new pottery types were also being made, but they were quite different from the wares of the southern Danelaw in both form and technology. The following section will briefly summarise the main characteristics of the West Saxon pottery types, and provide an explanation for the differences that exist with contemporary pottery types produced in the southern Danelaw.

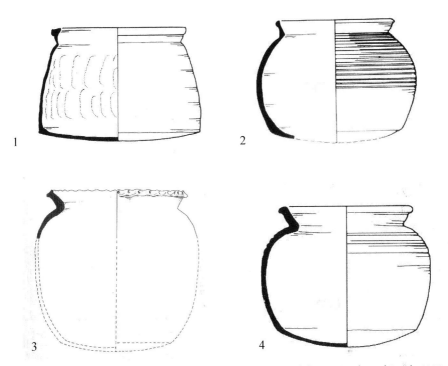

Fig. 10.3 Late Anglo-Saxon pottery from Wessex: 1) Cotswolds-type Ware (after McCarthy and Brooks 1988, fig. 167, no. 1010); 2) Portchester Ware (after McCarthy and Brooks 1988, fig. 99, no. 389); 3) Michelmersh Ware (after Hurst 1976, fig. 78.27, no. 1); 4) Cheddar Ware (after McCarthy and Brooks 1988, fig. 105, no. 429).

Late Anglo-Saxon pottery and identity

The south and west of England also witnessed the production of new pottery types in the 10th century, but these were made on a turntable, like Ipswich Ware, rather than being wheel-thrown like the pottery that was made in the *burhs* of the southern Danelaw, and occurred in a quite different range of shapes from the Thetford-type Wares. The pots were generally quite squat and baggy and usually wider than they were high, and they were, thus, quite different from the relatively tall, slightly shouldered forms of the southern Danelaw. They are instantly recognisable as different. As with some of the Danelaw types, it seems likely that these new wares were either being made just before the Viking incursions, in the mid-9th century, or came into use around the time of, or after, the construction of the *burhs* in the 10th century. Their method of manufacture and basic characteristics of form seem to have been common to many of the new types, such as Newbury Ware (Mepham 1997), Cotswolds Ware (*e.g.* Mellor 1994), and Cheddar, Portchester and Michelmersh Wares (*e.g.* Hurst 1976), with the Cotswolds-type ware probably first made in the period before the Scandinavian settlement, and the rest in the 10th century or later. The people of Wessex could easily have embraced the technology and forms of the pottery in use in the Danelaw at that time, but they chose not to, instead producing pots that were quite different (fig. 10.3).

INDUSTRY	MANU-FACTURE	FABRIC	COLOUR	FABRIC TEXTURE	GLAZE/PAINT	DECORATION	BASE
IPSWICH	FW	SANDY	GREY	SANDY	NO	FINGER-GROOVING	FLAT
THETFORD	FW	SANDY	GREY	SANDY	NO	ROULETTING	SAGGING
NORWICH	FW	SANDY	GREY	SANDY	NO	ROULETTING	FLAT
STAMFORD	FW	SANDY	BUFF/PINK	SMOOTH	GLAZE/PAINT	ROULETTING	FLAT
ST NEOTS	SW	SHELLY	BLACK/PURPLE	SOAPY	NO	ROULETTING	SAGGING
NORTHAMPTON	SW	SANDY	GREY/BUFF	SMOOTH	GLAZE/PAINT	ROULETTING	FLAT
LEICESTER	FW	SANDY	GREY	SANDY	NO	NONE	FLAT
NOTTINGHAM	FW	SANDY	BROWN	SMOOTH	?SPLASH GLAZE	ROULETTING	??????
STAFFORD	FW	SANDY	RED-BROWN	SANDY	NO	ROULETTING	?SAGGING

Fig. 10.4 Danelaw pottery parameters (FW = 'fast-wheel' manufacture; SW = 'slow-wheel' manufacture).

As was argued earlier in this chapter, in the middle Anglo-Saxon period it was possible to distinguish a West Saxon from a Mercian on the basis of the ceramics they used. Similarly, the differences between the pottery types that were in use in the southern Danelaw and Wessex in the 10th century meant that it was still possible to distinguish a West Saxon from a Mercian household. Thus, despite the fact that England was supposedly politically unified from the middle of the 10th century, the people of Wessex and Mercia appear to have continued to regard themselves as different from each other, and this difference was partly articulated through the pottery used in each region. Research by the author (2003) has suggested that the Wessex-style pottery appears to have been consumed in a wide range of sizes, whereas that of the Danelaw, specifically St Neots Ware, was used in a much narrower range, indicating that both the pottery and the way in which it was used were different. In other words, there were differences between the inhabitants of the two regions at the fundamental levels of cooking and eating.

In the southern Danelaw, where each 'urban' production centre produced a distinctive type of pottery, a case can furthermore be made that the new pottery types broadcasted a 'Mercian' identity, simultaneously proclaiming that the inhabitants were different from the people of Wessex, whilst the pottery also allowed the people of each individual town to relate their identity to that town. At a time when 'urban' life was still largely a new experience, such explicit expressions of specific 'urban' identities may have been vital as a means to combat insecurities associated with this new lifestyle. In this respect, there is no difference between the expression of *ethnic* allegiance and *urban* allegiance, both of which, as Hadley (2001, 24; see above) has suggested, may have been more prominent at a time of social unrest.

Figure 10.4 shows seven of the different parameters that make up each of the simple jars that formed the majority of the early products of the new industries. When they are examined in this way, it can clearly be seen that although the different wares are all variations on the same basic theme, they are all different. No two wares are the same; the combinations of colour, the shape of the base and/or decoration were all different, and, thus, all characteristic of specific production centres. As a result, in each of the new towns, non-local wares, and people using them, would have been easily have been recognised as being 'other', as would the people who used them. As each ware had its own identity, each town also had its own identity, even if similarities in their shape indicated that they were at the same time part of a greater whole that transcended town-specific identities.

Conclusions

The Anglo-Saxons had, by the middle of the 10th century, been using pottery as an expression of their identity for around 500 years. This chapter suggests that, in the late Anglo-Saxon period, when new wares of an essentially non-Anglo-Saxon nature began to be used in the new urban environment, they were still vehicles for expressions of identity, despite their apparently utilitarian nature. The pottery industries of the 9th and 10th centuries both acknowledged and reinforced this new way of life, whilst maintaining identities that were far older, and found their roots in the distinctions between the various Anglo-Saxon kingdoms of Mercia, East Anglia and Wessex. By the mid-10th century, England was supposedly a single nation rather than a collection of kingdoms. The pottery tells us quite a different story.

Bibliography

Andrews, P. (1995) *Excavations at Redcastle Furze, Thetford, 1988–9*. East Anglian Archaeology 72. Gressenhall, Norfolk Museums Service.

Atkin, M., Ayers, B. and Jennings, J. (1983) Thetford-type Ware production in Norwich. In P. Wade-Martins (ed.) *Waterfront Excavation and Thetford Ware Production, Norwich*, 61–97. East Anglian Archaeology 17. Gressenhall, Norfolk Archaeological Unit.

Blackmore, L. (1988) The Anglo-Saxon pottery. In R. L. Whytehead and R. Cowie with L. Blackmore, Two Middle Saxon occupation sites: excavations at Jubilee Hall and 21–22 Maiden Lane. *Transactions of the London Middlesex Archaeological Society* 39, 81–110.

Blackmore, L. (1989) The Anglo-Saxon Pottery. In R. L. Whytehead and R. Cowie with L. Blackmore, Excavations at the Peabody site, Chandos Place and the National Gallery. *Transactions of the London Middlesex Archaeological Society* 40, 71–107.

Blackmore, L. (2003) The pottery. In G. Malcolm, D. Bowsher with R. Cowie (eds) *Middle Saxon London: excavations at the Royal Opera House, 1989–99*, 225–41. Museum of London Archaeology Service Monograph 15. London, Museum of London.

Blinkhorn, P. (1990) Middle Saxon pottery from the Buttermarket kiln, Ipswich. *Medieval Ceramics* 13, 12–16.

Blinkhorn, P. (1997) Habitus, cultural identity and early Anglo-Saxon pottery. In C. G. Cumberpatch and P. Blinkhorn (eds) *Not So Much A Pot, More A Way of Life*, 113–24. Oxbow Monograph 83. Oxford, Oxbow.

Blinkhorn, P. (1999) Of cabbages and kings: production, trade and consumption in middle Saxon England. In M. Anderton (ed.) *Anglo-Saxon Trading Centres and their Hinterlands: beyond the emporia*, 4–23. Glasgow, Cruithne Press.

Blinkhorn, P. (2002) The Anglo-Saxon pottery. In S. Foreman, J. Hiller and D. Petts (eds) *Gathering the People, Settling the Land: the archaeology of a Middle Thames Landscape, Anglo-Saxon to Post-Medieval*, 35. Oxford Archaeology Thames Valley Landscape Monograph 14. Oxford, Oxford Archaeology.

Blinkhorn, P. (2003) The pottery. In A. Hardy, A. Dodd and G. D. Keevil (eds) *Aelfric's Abbey: excavations at Eynsham Abbey, Oxfordshire, 1989–92*, 159–92. Oxford Archaeology Thames Valley Landscape Monograph 16. Oxford, Oxford Archaeology.

Blinkhorn, P. (2004) Early and middle Saxon pottery. In G. Hey (ed.) *Yarnton. Saxon and Medieval Settlement and Landscape: results of excavations 1990–6*, 267–72. Oxford Archaeology Thames Valley Landscape Monograph 20. Oxford, Oxford Archaeology.

Blinkhorn, P. (in prep.) *The Ipswich Ware Project: ceramics, trade and society in middle Saxon England*. Medieval
    Pottery Research Group Monograph Series.
Clarke, H. and Ambrosiani, B. (1991) *Towns in the Viking Age*. Leicester, Leicester University Press.
Dallas, C. (1993) *Excavations in Thetford by B. K. Davison between 1964 and 1970*. East Anglian Archaeology
    62. Gressenhall, Norfolk Museums Service.
Denham, V. (1985) The pottery. In J. H. Williams, M. Shaw and V. Denham (eds) *Middle Saxon Palaces at
    Northampton*, 46–64. Northampton Development Corporation Monograph Series 4. Northampton,
    Northampton Development Corporation.
Dolley, M. (1976) The coins. In D. M. Wilson (ed.) *The Archaeology of Anglo-Saxon England*, 349–71.
    London, Methuen and Co.
Ford, D. A. (1995) *Medieval Pottery in Staffordshire, AD 800–1600: a review*. Staffordshire Archaeology Studies
    7. Stoke-on-Trent, City Museum and Art Gallery.
Ford, D. A. (1999) A Late Saxon pottery industry in Staffordshire: a review. *Medieval Ceramics* 22–3, 47–65.
Hadley, D. M. (2001) In search of the Vikings: the problems and the possibilities of interdisciplinary
    approaches. In J. Graham-Campbell, R. A. Hall, J. Jesch and D. N. Parsons (eds) *Vikings and the
    Danelaw: select papers from the proceedings of the thirteenth Viking Congress, 21–30 August 1997*, 13–30.
    Oxford, Oxbow.
Hebditch, M. G. (1967–8) A Saxo-Norman pottery kiln discovered in Southgate Street, Leicester, 1964.
    Transactions of the Leicestershire Archaeology and History Society 43, 4–9.
Hodges, R. (1980) *Dark Age Economics: origins of towns and trade AD 600–1000*. London, Duckworth.
Hurst, J. G. (1955) Saxo-Norman pottery in East Anglia: part I. General discussion and St Neots Ware.
    Proceedings of the Cambridge Antiquarian Society 49, 43–70.
Hurst, J. G. (1956) Saxo-Norman Pottery in East Anglia: part II. Thetford Ware. *Proceedings of the Cambridge
    Antiquarian Society* 50, 42–60.
Hurst, J. G. (1957) Saxo-Norman pottery in East Anglia: part III. Stamford Ware. *Proceedings of the Cambridge
    Antiquarian Society* 51, 37–65.
Hurst, J. G. (1976) The pottery. In D. M. Wilson (ed.) *The Archaeology of Anglo-Saxon England*, 283–348.
    London, Methuen and Co.
Kelly, S. (1992) Trading privileges from eighth-century England. *Early Medieval Europe* 1, 3–28.
Kilmurry, K. (1980) *The Pottery Industry of Stamford, Lincs. c. AD 850–1250*. British Archaeological Reports
    British Series 84. Oxford, Tempus Reparatum.
Lucy, S. (2000) *The Anglo-Saxon Way of Death*. Stroud, Sutton.
Marshall, P. (2003) Analysis and interpretation of radiocarbon determinations from All Saints Church. In
    A. Dodd (ed.) *Oxford before the University*, 421–4. Oxford Archaeology Thames Valley Landscapes
    Monograph 17. Oxford, Oxford Archaeology.
McCarthy, M. and Brooks, C. (1988) *Medieval Pottery in Britain, AD 900–1600*. Leicester, Leicester University
    Press.
Mellor, M. (1994) Oxford pottery: a synthesis of middle and late Saxon, medieval and early post-medieval
    pottery in the Oxford region. *Oxoniensia* 59, 17–217.
Mellor, M. (2003) Pottery from All Saints Church. In A. Dodd (ed.) *Oxford before the University*, 336–9.
    Oxford Archaeology Thames Valley Landscapes Monograph 17. Oxford, Oxford Archaeology.
Mepham, L. (1997) Pottery. In A. G. Vince, S. J. Lobb, J. C. Richards and L. Mepham (eds) *Excavations in
    Newbury, Berkshire, 1979–1990*, 45–67. Wessex Archaeology Report 13. Salisbury, Trust for Wessex
    Archaeology Ltd.
Myres, J. N. L. (1969) *Anglo-Saxon Pottery and the Settlement of England*. Oxford, Clarendon Press.
Myres, J. N. L. (1977) *A Corpus of Anglo-Saxon Pottery of the Pagan Period* (2 vols). Cambridge, Cambridge
    University Press.
Nailor, V. (1984) A preliminary note on a late Saxon ware from Nottingham. *Medieval Ceramics* 8, 59–63.
Richards, J. D. (1987) *The Significance of the Form and Decoration of Anglo-Saxon Cremation Urns*. British
    Archaeological Reports British Series 166. Oxford, Tempus Reparatum.

Richards, J. D. (1992) Anglo-Saxon Symbolism. In M. O. H. Carver (ed.) *The Age of Sutton Hoo*, 131–48. Woodbridge, Boydell.

Rogerson, A. and Dallas, C. (1984) *Excavations in Thetford 1948–59 and 1973–80*. East Anglian Archaeology 22. Gressenhall, Norfolk Museums Service.

Smedley, N. and Owles, E. J. (1963) Some Suffolk kilns: iv, Saxon kilns in Cox Lane, Ipswich 1961. *Proceedings of the Suffolk Institute for Archaeology* 29, 304–35.

Timby, J. (1988) The Middle Saxon pottery. In P. Andrews (ed.) *Southampton Finds Volume One: the coins and pottery from Hamwic*, 73–121. Southampton Archaeology Monograph 4. Southampton, Southampton City Museums.

Wilson, D. M. (1976) Craft and industry. In D. M. Wilson (ed.) *The Archaeology of Anglo-Saxon England*, 253–82. London, Methuen and Co.

Wade, K. (1988) Ipswich. In R. Hodges and B. Hobley (eds) *The Rebirth of Towns in the West AD 700–1050*, 93–100. Council for British Archaeology Research Report 68. London, Council for British Archaeology.

Williams, J. H. (1974) A Saxo-Norman kiln group from Northampton. *Northamptonshire Archaeology* 9, 46–56.

Young, J. and Vince, A. (2005) *A Corpus of Anglo-Saxon and Medieval Pottery from Lincoln*. Lincoln Archaeological Studies 7. Oxford, Oxbow.

OF TOWNS AND TRINKETS: METALWORKING AND METAL DRESS-ACCESSORIES IN VIKING-AGE LINCOLN

Letty ten Harkel

Any attempt to understand the dynamics of everyday life in a Viking town – indeed, in any town – must involve critical analysis of the identities and actions of its people. The collective identities of a town's inhabitants create the identity of the settlement, just as the actions of its occupants underpin the dynamics of everyday life. As evident from the range of approaches adopted in the other chapters in this book, there are many different methodologies involved in the study of past identities and actions, including thematic approaches as well as data-specific analyses. This chapter focuses on the significance of metal dress-accessories as a means to reconstruct the identities of the inhabitants of Viking-Age Lincoln.

The use of dress-accessories for studying social and ethnic identities is widespread (Crane 2000; Damhorst *et al.* 2005; Davis 1992). It has previously been addressed in the context of the Scandinavian settlement of England by scholars such as Thomas (2000; 2001), Owen (2001), Kershaw (2008; 2010) and – specific to the historic area of Lindsey – Leahy (1993; 2007; Leahy and Paterson 2001). The majority of theoretically engaged academic debate focusing on the interpretation of items of dress nevertheless pertains to the post-medieval and modern periods (see, for example, Crane 2000; Damhorst *et al.* 2005; Davis 1992; Parkins 2002; Wilson and De la Haye 1999), resulting in an often-stated assumption that early medieval dress (or 'costume') does *not* constitute 'fashion' in the same way as modern clothing does. For example, Davis (1992, 29) placed the beginnings of fashion in the 13th or 14th century:

> Fashion's rise in the West had much to do with the emergence at about this time of a town bourgeoisie to rival feudal aristocracy's secular monopoly of wealth, power, and display.

Since the publication of Davis's (1992) work, however, it has become accepted wisdom that the emergence of 'fashion' did not happen overnight. For example, Wilson and De la Haye (1999, 3) proposed that items of dress count as 'fashion' when it can be demonstrated that changes in their form and decoration were intrinsically related to social change. A question that springs to mind is whether this was already the case in the Viking Age.

This chapter investigates the relationship between the form and decoration of Viking-Age dress-accessories and social change. It addresses the following questions: is it possible to identify a relationship between the form and decoration of Viking-Age dress-accessories and broader changes in society, such as the Scandinavian settlement and the urbanisation process? Are changes in manufacturing processes and techniques related to social change? To put it more concisely, how can the production and style of 9th- to 11th-century dress-accessories from Lincoln, placed within its regional context, shed light on the study of Viking-Age urbanism?

As part of the importance of Lincoln's Viking-Age metalwork assemblage lies in the spatial distribution of the objects, this chapter first provides a brief summary of the town's late 9th- to early 11th-century archaeology (also see Stocker, this volume), incorporating discussion of the evidence for metalworking. This will be followed by a discussion of finished artefacts from Lincoln. Analysis will focus on the manufacture, style and distribution of the objects, placing them in the context of data from rural Lincolnshire, as included in the *Portable Antiquities Scheme* (*PAS*) database. Finally, this evidence will be used to analyse and reconstruct the actions and identities of Lincoln's inhabitants, providing insight into the dynamics of everyday life in a Viking-Age town in England.

Metalworking in Viking-Age Lincoln

Lincoln was situated at the junction of the rivers Witham and Till, in the southwest of the historic region of Lindsey, which, together with Kesteven and Holland, would make up the territory of *Lincolnescire* (Lincolnshire) at the time of the 1086 *Domesday* survey (fig. 11.1). The archaeological sequence of the former Roman *colonia* of Lincoln is comprehensively discussed elsewhere (Stocker 2003), but a number of observations are worth repeating here. The topography of the Viking-Age settlement consists principally of four main areas: the walled Upper and Lower Cities (formerly the 1st-century Roman fortress and walled *colonia*) and the extra-mural areas of Wigford, south of the River Witham, and Butwerk, to the east of the Lower City (Jones *et al.* forthcoming; Steane *et al.* 2001) (fig. 11.1).

The earliest evidence for post-Roman activity in Lincoln consists of a small chapel or church with associated burials, focusing on a likely saintly burial, at St Paul-in-the-Bail in the Upper City (Gilmour 2007; Steane *et al.* 2006; Vince 2003a, 144–50) (fig. 11.1). Opinions on the origins of this churchyard vary but all place it in either the early or middle Anglo-Saxon periods. The most significant collection of metal dress-accessories predating the late 9th century has been found on this site as well, consisting of a silver Trewhiddle-style buckle and strap-end and a silver Carolingian buckle. The finds came from various residual contexts, but the discovery of four 9th-century Lunette coins – likewise from various residual contexts – on the same site has led to the suggestion that these objects either represent a dispersed hoard, or dispersed grave goods (Vince 2003a, 144–50; but see Steane *et al.* 2006, 201–2).

Additional evidence for activity predating the second half of the 9th century has been found in the southeastern part of the Lower City, along Silver Street at the Saltergate site (fig. 11.1), where a handful of unfurnished burials were uncovered during routine excavations, and radiocarbon dated to the very late 7th to earlier 9th centuries (Jones *et al.* forthcoming; Vince 2003a, 154–5; 2003b, 204). It has been suggested that the evidence represents another religious foundation, associated with the postulated double foundation of St Peter-at-Pleas and St Peter-at-Arches, near the southern entrance gate where the Roman road known as Ermine Street enters the Lower City (Vince 2003a, 144–5; see also Stocker, this volume). Other evidence from this period consists of some unstratified pottery scatters near the Upper and Lower Cities and some small finds, including a middle Anglo-Saxon buckle and a handful of pins that could

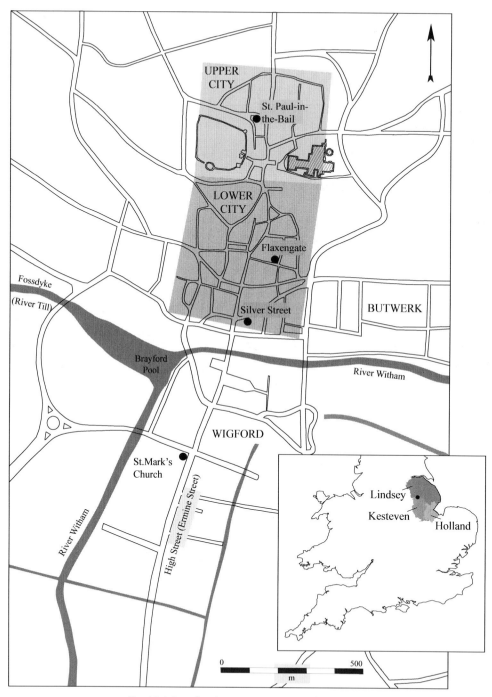

Fig. 11.1 Lincoln, showing sites mentioned in the text.

be of either middle or late Anglo-Saxon date, from the Lower City (Ten Harkel 2010, app. 11; Vince 2003a, 153–4, fig. 8.14). Recently, however, excavations conducted in 2009–10 at the bus station by Allen Archaeology revealed evidence for middle Anglo-Saxon structures. These would almost certainly have been located on what used to be Thornhill Island in the River Witham, and may indicate the presence of a middle Anglo-Saxon extra-mural *wic* or trading settlement, possibly comparable to Fishergate in York (Mick Jones *pers. comm.*).

Significant evidence for economic activity in Lincoln dates to the late 9th century, contemporary with Scandinavian settlement in England. Excavations revealed an increase of activity in the southeast corner of the Lower City, in the vicinity of the Silver Street burials. Evidence included planned house plots with associated Stamford-ware crucibles as well as moulds, scrap-metal – such as copper-alloy wire, bars, ingots and sheet metal – and (part-) finished artefacts, indicating non-ferrous metalworking (Bayley 2008a; Vince 2003b, 284). In the course of the 10th century, occupation spread to the extra-mural areas of Wigford and *Butwerk*. Various sites in Wigford, including St Mark's church, also produced evidence for non-ferrous metalworking (Foley 1981, 16; White 1992, 5–6). The manufacturing evidence from *Butwerk* was more restricted to pottery production, although this impression is possibly due at least in part to the relative lack of excavations in this part of Lincoln.

Occupation in the Upper City increased in the second half of the 10th century. Here, too, non-ferrous metalworking took place, the most significant evidence having been unearthed to the east of the church at St Paul-in-the-Bail, in a sunken-floored building overlying some earlier graves in the cemetery (Steane *et al.* 2006, 167–9). It is worth noting, however, that there is significantly less evidence for economic activity from the Upper City for this period than from the other parts of Lincoln. It is possible that here, too, the evidence is skewed because of a lack of excavations, although the elevated position of the Upper City and its relative distance from the River Witham suggest that this part of the settlement was not a practical location for manufacturing activity either, rendering it likely that occupation of the Upper City had a different character compared to elsewhere.

The evidence from St Mark's church (Wigford) and St Paul-in-the-Bail (the Upper City) reveals a spatial correlation between late Anglo-Saxon burial activity and metalworking, which corresponds to a broader pattern that witnesses an increase in metalworking activities on church lands. Hinton (2000, 115; 2003, 273) has contrasted this evidence with the middle Anglo-Saxon travelling smith's grave in Tattershall (Lincolnshire). The smith was given a furnished burial and was accompanied by his metalworking tools and a box of scrap metal, but was interred in a liminal position between two territories, suggesting that his trade invested people with a mixture of fear and respect. Hinton argues that the Church was responsible for the transformation of the Anglo-Saxon smith's status from a travelling craftsman with magical powers to a socially accepted craftsman in the service of the Church (also see Ten Harkel 2011, 25). In Lincoln's case, the Church, by attracting specialised craftsmen to the former Roman *colonia*, had a direct influence on the economic growth of the town.

The importance of the Church for stimulating economic activity and ultimately the urbanisation process raises questions about the relationship between ecclesiastical sites and the developing towns. Blair (2005, 98), arguing in favour of minsters (rather than *wics*) as proto-urban settlements, views 'the city' as a place that was 'stately, commodious, and populous, protected by physical boundaries and legal privileges, a place of righteousness and refuge, above all holy'. Despite the overwhelmingly ecclesiastical character of the surviving archaeology within the town walls and the possibility that it was, indeed, an important religious centre prior to the later 9th century (Gem 1993), it is doubtful, however, that middle Anglo-Saxon Lincoln ever fitted Blair's description. Indeed, a more populous and commodious 8th- to 9th-century settlement from Lincolnshire was the supposedly ecclesiastical centre (at least for part of its existence) at Flixborough (Loveluck 2007; Loveluck and Atkinson 2007). Nevertheless, the importance of the Church in Lincoln's early development should not be disregarded. This is of particular interest in the context of the evidence for Scandinavian influences on the metalwork (see below) and the possibility that there were Scandinavians amongst the metalworkers, as tentatively suggested by a soapstone vessel sherd of Scandinavian provenance that was reused as an ingot mould, found at the Saltergate site in the immediate vicinity of Silver Street in the Lower City (Bayley 2008a, 20; Jones *et al.* forthcoming). Evidence for the close co-operation between the – originally pagan – Scandinavian elite and the Church has previously been noted on the basis of the earliest coinages and stone sculpture from Scandinavian-controlled Yorkshire (Bailey 1980; Blackburn 2004, 332; Hadley 2006, 35–6; Lang 1976). The Church was not only instrumental in decreasing the marginal position of metalworkers in Anglo-Saxon society, but also that of the Scandinavian settlers.

It has been argued that the emergence of urban centres such as Lincoln caused the decline of non-ferrous metalwork production in rural centres, such as the abovementioned centre at Flixborough. Here, non-ferrous metalworking occurred on a scale that was larger than the immediate needs of the settlement in the 9th century, but came to an end in the 10th century (Loveluck 2007, 102–5, 117). Indeed, very limited evidence for 10th-century non-ferrous metalworking from rural Lincolnshire has been identified to date, exceptions including a die used for making foils in *Jellinge*-style that was found at Stickford (*PAS* NLM1063; Leahy 2007, 151) and a silver droplet identified as metalworking waste, dated to *c.* AD 850-1000, from the parish of Brampton in West Lindsey (*PAS* YORYM-FA6027). A number of ingots, including a copper-alloy example from Market Rasen in West Lindsey (*PAS* DENO-63EB93), a silver ingot from Roxby cum Risby (*PAS* NLM-683755) and a gold ingot from the Gainsborough region (*Treasure* 2001, 50), may represent bullion, and, thus, do not represent conclusive evidence for non-ferrous metalworking.

There is less evidence that ironworking was exclusively a characteristic of urban economies. The evidence from Viking-Age Stamford (Lincolnshire) indicates that the town became an important centre for iron production, but this may be related to the prevalence of bog ore from the fen edge – where Stamford was located – and valley bottoms in the East Midlands (Cowgill 1994, 25; Mahany *et al.* 1982). Ironworking continued at Flixborough into the 10th century as well, whilst evidence for later 10th-century ironworking has also been identified on the Barrow Road-site in Barton-upon-Humber (Bradley 2002, 5; Gardner and Bunn 2006, 5) and iron smelting may have taken place at Cherry Willingham (Everson *et al.* 1991, 89; Everson and Stocker 1999, 9) and Cumberworth (Green 1997, 6). Ironworking also took place in Lincoln on a limited scale (Vince 2003b, 282–4). This may indicate that blacksmithing was not specialised to the same extent as the production of dress-accessories, but was carried out at settlement level to provide for the immediate needs of a community.

The suggestion that the production of dress-accessories was a specialised craft in the late Anglo-Saxon period is confirmed by the evidence from Structure 20 on the Flaxengate site in the Lower City (Perring 1981). In features associated with this building were a large number of finished and unfinished hooked tags with both triangular and circular shapes but mostly with the same ratchet-style decoration (fig. 11.2). In total, the Flaxengate excavations produced at least 45 copper-alloy specimens as well as seventeen iron examples, strengthening the suggestion – based on the large number of iron dress-accessories retrieved during the Flixborough excavations (Evans and Loveluck 2009) – that dress-accessories made of ferrous metals were much more common in the Anglo-Saxon period than was previously thought.

Although decoration in ratchet-style is by no means unique to Lincoln, analysis of the distribution of hooked tags in the same decorative style from the rest of Lincolnshire, (based on a search executed in 2009) revealed that a significant percentage occur along transport routes connecting to Lincoln, along Ermine Street, which runs along the raised contour of the Lincoln Edge, and some of the more important

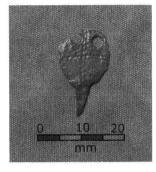
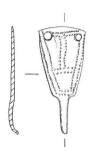
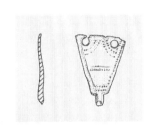
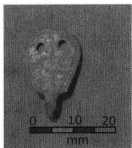

Fig. 11.2 Four examples of hooked tags of the type produced in Lincoln, all found at the Flaxengate site (photographs by the author; drawings by Dave Watt, copyright City of Lincoln Council, and reproduced with kind permission of City of Lincoln Council).

riverine routes such as the Trent and Ancholme. The fact that – to an extent – Flaxengate products may have circulated in the surrounding region (fig. 11.3) contrasts with Astill's (2006, 248) recent conclusion that the evidence for metalwork production in many of the West-Saxon *burhs* 'indicates a craftsman working to satisfy the demands of a patron rather than mass production for a wider clientele'. However, as will be evident from the discussion below, the production evidence for the hooked tags is exceptional in terms of its quantity even within Lincoln, suggesting that only certain types of dress-accessories were mass-produced and therefore suitable for circulation amongst a wider clientele. Nevertheless, the fact that mass-production occurred at all confirms a broader pattern whereby economic activity in the towns of the Scandinavian-controlled regions of England occurred much earlier than in the West-Saxon and Mercian *burhs* (Astill 2009, 265), suggesting that the growth of the Scandinavian towns was from an early stage inherently related to economic productivity, more so than in its West-Saxon and Mercian counterparts.

Dress-accessories from Viking-Age Lincoln

Moving on from the production process to the finished artefacts, it is time to turn to the 'trinkets' from the title of this paper.[1] The term 'trinkets' reflects the sentiment held by various scholars of the period (*e.g.* Hinton 2005; Leahy 2007, 166–7; Owen-Crocker 1986, 206) that the increasingly mass-produced nature of many dress-accessories and use of base metals

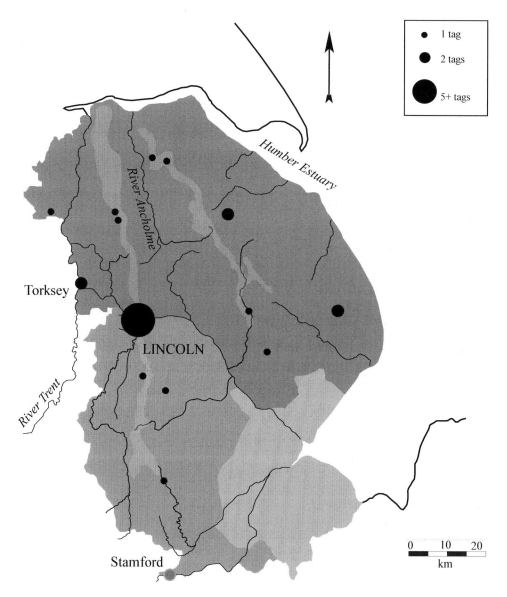

Fig. 11.3 Distribution of hooked tags with ratchet-style decoration possibly produced in Lincoln. The Lincoln Edge is indicated in a lighter shade of grey, running roughly north-south. Lincoln is situated in a 'gap' in the limestone escarpment where the River Witham turns east (drawn by the author, based on analysis of data from the PAS, collated in 2009 in the context of the author's PhD research).

indicated a decline in standards of workmanship. Whereas this may hold true to an extent, there are other ways of interpreting these developments in the production of dress-accessories. As discussed in the opening section of this chapter, the distinction between fashion and dress is that the former can be related to social change. It has already been demonstrated that changes

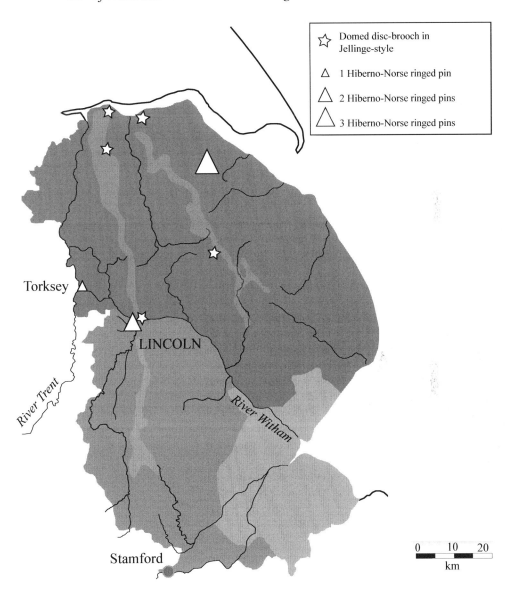

Fig. 11.4 Distribution of artefact types of 'Scandinavian' character (drawn by the author, based on analysis of data from the PAS, *collated in 2009 in the context of the author's PhD research).*

in the organisation of production – such as the increasing urbanisation of the metalworkers' trade – is an inherent aspect of broader changes in the ecclesiastical and secular structures of society. The following section looks deeper into these issues by studying finished artefacts to shed light on the emergence of Viking-Age Lincoln.

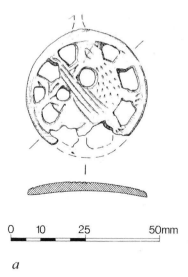

0   10   25   50mm

a

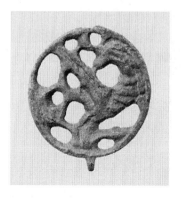

b

Fig. 11.5 Pendant from The Park (p70 <ae171>) (source: Colyer et al. 1999; reproduced by permission of C. Colyer, B. J. J. Gilmour and M. J. Jones and the Council for British Archaeology) with one of its Danish parallels (National Museum of Denmark d255-1999; copyright National Museum of Denmark).

To begin with the relationship between the form and decoration of Viking-Age dress-accessories and the Scandinavian settlement, as stated above, many of the dress-accessories from Lincoln display clear Scandinavian influences and some may even have been produced in Scandinavia. A clear example is a convex brooch in *Jellinge*-style from St Mark's Station in Wigford (zeb95 <442>), of a type identified by Kershaw (2010, 317, fig. 11) as possibly being of southern Scandinavian manufacture. Comparison with objects listed on the *PAS* website revealed that domed brooches in *Jellinge*-style are relatively rare in Lincolnshire. Three came from the area of the Trent and Humber estuaries, an important nodal point in the communications between York, the Midlands and the wider North Sea world including Scandinavia. A gilded silver example was found in Whitton (*Treasure* 2000, 30–1), with additional examples of copper alloy from South Ferriby (Leahy and Paterson 2001, 196, fig. 10.7) and Roxby-cum-Risby (*PAS* NLM-0F69C5), the –*by* suffix of the latter two place-names displaying clear Scandinavian influences as well. A fourth domed brooch in *Jellinge*-style was found in Sixhills (*PAS* NLM4529). All examples were found in Lindsey, the area to the north and east of the Rivers Trent and Witham (fig. 11.4), suggesting the area to the north of Lincoln had stronger 'Scandinavian' affinities than the region further south.

Excavations in Lincoln have also produced two openwork pendants from Grantham Place (gp81 <44>) and The Park (p70 <ae171>), both made of copper alloy and depicting a winged quadruped. In the published literature (Mann 1999, 152), they have been described as being reminiscent of *Borre*-style, a 9th- to 11th-century Scandinavian-derived art-style. In fact, the decoration of these pendants is typical of ornaments of 11th- to 12th-century date from Scandinavia, the pointed wing being a feature of Romanesque art with clear parallels in *Ringerike* and *Urnes* art styles, including an ornament from an 11th-century grave in Lund (Mårtensson 1963; Anne Pedersen *pers. comm.*). Pedersen (*pers. comm.*) has identified some particularly close parallels from Denmark, currently in the collection of the National Museum in Denmark (D179/2000 and D255-1999) (fig. 11.5). Pendants had gone out of fashion in England after the early Anglo-Saxon period (Leahy and Paterson 2001, 195). It would, therefore, seem safe to assume that these objects were also of Scandinavian manufacture, although the close similarities between the two Lincoln pendants has led to the suggestion that they may have come from the same mould, which might suggest manufacture in Lincoln itself (Mann 1999, 152). If so, they represent further evidence for a Scandinavian presence amongst the Lincoln metalworkers, in this case dating to the 11th or early 12th century. Exchange of manufacturing expertise was not uncommon in the 11th century, as the reigns of Æthelred and Cnut also witnessed the production of coin dies in Lincoln for his Danish coinages (Stafford 1978), whilst pottery was produced in 11th-century Denmark that was virtually indistinguishable from Lincoln wares (Vince 1995).

There are more dress-accessories with Scandinavian influences. A strap-end, found at 181–3 High Street in Wigford, belongs to Thomas type 4, a group of multi-headed copper-alloy strap-ends in derived *Borre*-style that betray 'Norse' influences (hg72 <ae5>) (Steane *et al.* 2001, 130; Thomas 2001, 39–45). A type of dress-accessory commonly regarded as 'Hiberno-Norse', based on their occurrence in Dublin, York and the Irish Sea region, are the so-called ringed pins, broadly dated to the 9th to 11th centuries. Two examples have been found in Lincoln, from Broadgate East (be73 <ae164>) and Flaxengate (f72 <ae290>), in or near the southeast quadrant of the Lower City. Both belong to the plain-ringed polyhedral-headed type (Fanning 1994, 70–88), the most common ringed pin type found in Dublin (Fanning 1994, 10). The only ringed pins that have been found elsewhere in Lincolnshire were again from Lindsey. One comes from Torksey, the site of a Viking winter camp in 872/3 (Brown 2006, no. 280), whilst three possible additional fragments have been found in Riby, near the Humber (*PAS* LIN–143411, LIN–134231 and LIN–145C85) (fig. 11.4).

Dress-accessories from Lincoln also shed light on the integration of the Scandinavian settlers into Anglo-Saxon society. The Flaxengate excavations produced a flat disc brooch made of copper alloy, decorated in *Borre*-style with four symmetrical strands of knotted interlace set around a central lozenge (f72 <ae302>). Brooches of this type include a mixture of Anglo-Saxon and Scandinavian styles, combining Scandinavian-style decoration with Anglo-Saxon object type; disc brooches in Scandinavia were usually convex (Kershaw 2010; Margeson 1997, 23). This type of flat disc brooch is particularly common in East Anglia, leading to the suggestion that their production centre was located in Norwich or elsewhere in East Anglia (Margeson 1997, 23, fig. 28; Hinton 1974, 20, fig. 13). The distribution of these brooches in rural Lincolnshire reveals a concentration near The Wash, as well as the Humber estuary and along the various transport routes leading to Lincoln (fig. 11.6). The importance of the North Sea coast and the Humber as a transport route has also been argued on the basis of the distribution of stone sculpture across Lincolnshire (Everson and Stocker 1999).

Stylistic details of dress-accessories from Lincoln also bear witness to much wider European influences that reached England from the late 9th century onwards. Excavations in the Lower City produced two flat disc brooches made of cast lead alloy, found at The Park (p70 <pb13>) and Grantham Street (sw82 <386>). One the basis of their similarities, it was suggested that they came from the same mould (Mann 1999, 157–8); pieces of scrap-lead suggest that lead-working did take place on this site (White 1982), although the collection of stone and clay moulds from Flaxengate do not fit any of the brooches actually found in Lincoln (Bayley 2008a, 17, fig. 10). Both brooches were decorated with identical relief decoration consisting of a central boss surrounded by two lozenge-shaped plain borders, surrounded by four crescent-shaped lines with ladder-pattern decoration arranged in the shape of a cross surrounded by a ladder-pattern border. In each space between the arms of the cross, there are two pellets (Mann 1999, 156–7)

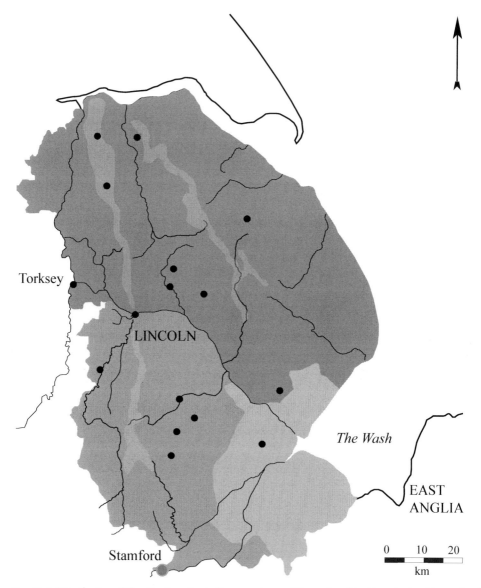

Fig. 11.6 Distribution of flat disc-brooches in Borre-*style, possibly produced in East Anglia (drawn by the author, based on analysis of data from the* PAS, *collated in 2009 in the context of the author's PhD research).*

(fig. 11.7). The laddered cross-design with curved arms that characterises these objects is found more widely across early medieval Europe, including the Frisian region, East Anglia, Yorkshire and, further south, London (Gabor Thomas *pers. comm.*; Weetch in prep.; Whitney-Lagen in prep.). The decoration also shares elements with that of some of the lead-alloy brooches found in York (Mann 1999, 157), in particular the 'ladder-pattern' decoration, which Tweddle (2004,

452) identifies as 'false filigree', reflecting southern English and Ottonian fashions. One example is known from elsewhere in Lincolnshire, found in Barrow-upon-Humber and currently on display in the North Lincolnshire Museum (cat. no. BRBC1) (Rosie Weetch *pers. comm.*).

The possibility that continental Frankish influences became more widespread in England in the wake of the Scandinavian settlement has also been suggested in the context of the ceramic evidence. From the late 9th century onwards, wheel-thrown pottery was produced in the emerging towns in the Scandinavian-controlled regions of England that bore strong similarities in form and manufacturing technique to continental pottery types from the Rhineland and northern France, leading Vince (1993) to suggest that Frankish potters migrated to England in the wake of the Scandinavian settlement (see also Kilmurry 1980). Although Blinkhorn (this volume), suggesting an earlier date for the innovations in pottery production, argues strongly against this notion, dating evidence relating to the emergence of these Frankish-

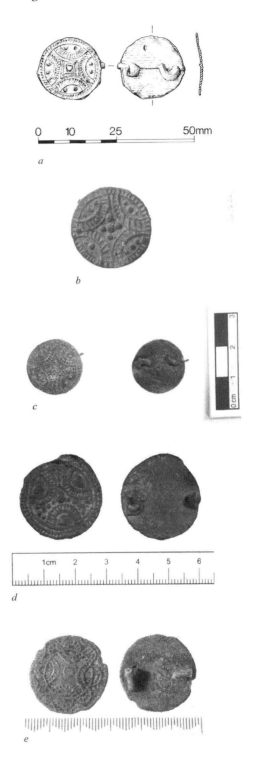

Fig. 11.7 Flat pewter disc-brooch from The Park (p70 <pb13>) (source: Colyer et al. 1999; reproduced by permission of C. Colyer, B. J. J. Gilmour and M. J. Jones and the Council for British Archaeology), with decorative parallels: b) metal-detected find from Barrow-upon-Humber (North Lincolnshire Museum BRBC1) (photograph by Rosie Weetch; reproduced with kind permission of the North Lincolnshire Museum); c) find from Vintry House excavations in London (Museum of London VRY89.V176.2399) (photograph by Christopher Witney-Lagen; reproduced with kind permission of the Museum of London); d) metal-detected find from the East Riding of Yorkshire (PAS YORYM-B664E6) (reproduced with kind permission of the PAS); e) metal-detected find from the Thetford area, Norfolk (PAS SF-4BD9B2) (reproduced with kind permission of the PAS).

styled pottery types from Lincoln, at any rate, which Blinkhorn does not include in his discussion, seems to fall inside the period of Scandinavian control in this region.

To return to non-ferrous dress-accessories, other production evidence from Lincoln consists of two unfinished finger rings made from flat tapering strips of copper alloy, found at 181–3 High Street in Wigford (hg72 <ae50> and <ae12>). A finished example, decorated with three rows of punched decoration, was found in the Lower City, at West Parade (wp71 <ae41>) (published in Colyer *et al.* 1999, 226, fig. 109, 4). No comparable artefacts were found elsewhere in Lincolnshire, but this may be an issue of recognition, as strips or small rings of copper alloy may not be immediately recognised by metal-detectorists as objects of archaeological significance.

Two very similar copper-alloy wire pins with glass heads, tentatively dated to the late Anglo-Saxon period, were also found in the Lower City, at Flaxengate (f72 <ae197>) and Motherby Hill (mh77 <ae2>). In the light of the evidence for copper-alloy wire and glass production from Flaxengate (Bayley 2008a; 2008b), it is not unlikely that they were produced there. Again, no comparable objects have been found elsewhere in Lincolnshire. Some of the copper-alloy wire found at Flaxengate may also have been related to the production of copper-alloy wire rings, found in significant numbers during excavations in the southeast quadrant of the Lower City. Some of these rings, including examples from the recent excavations at *The Collection* (Malone 2009) as well as Flaxengate, have their ends twisted together, placing them firmly within the late Anglo-Saxon period, whilst others are plainer and therefore more difficult to date on art-historic grounds alone. These artefacts are too ubiquitous, however, to allow for meaningful analysis of rural distribution patterns, not in the least because – again – they are only very rarely recognised by metal-detectorists.

Evidence for contact with other Viking towns exists as well, most notably in the shape of a small lead-alloy pendant from a late 11th- to 12th-century context at St Mark's Station in Wigford (z86 <676>), similar to silver examples from Birka, Sweden, and displaying significant similarities with an example from Coppergate in York, identified as a miscast and therefore almost certainly produced there (Bayley 1992, 780, fig. 340). On the whole, however, the most abundant evidence for contact between Viking towns consists of Stamford-ware pottery, which occurs in large numbers from the late 9th century onwards. Over the course of the 10th century, the use of domestic pottery from Stamford and also from Torksey (Lincolnshire) increases, whilst very limited quantities of Leicester, York and Nottingham ware occur in Lincoln as well (Young and Vince 2005). A few York-minted Viking coins have, furthermore, been found in late 9th- and 10th-century contexts, as well as one St Edmund's coin from Scandinavian-controlled East Anglia, whilst the 10th-century St Martin's coinage from Lincoln displayed similarities with near-contemporary York coinages (also see Stocker, this volume; Williams, this volume) (Blackburn 2006; Stewart 1983).

Religion, ethnicity and status in Viking-Age Lincoln

The previous discussion has demonstrated how the form and decoration of dress-accessories from Lincoln bears witness to broader changes in society, such as the Scandinavian settlement and the urbanisation process. It is clear that new ethnic influences arrived in Anglo-Saxon society in the wake of the Scandinavian settlement. It has also become evident that some of the artefacts produced in Lincoln – the hooked tags with ratchet-style decoration – were produced on a large scale and may have had a regional distribution, whilst other types of dress-accessories were produced on a smaller scale. There is also evidence for varying levels of contact between Lincoln and other emerging towns, although this is very slight on the basis of the metalwork alone. To understand the identities and activities of Lincoln's inhabitants, however, one should not merely look at the evidence that is there, but also at the evidence that is *not* there. Perhaps more pertinent than the objects found in Lincoln are those that have *not* been found.

A striking characteristic of Lincoln's metalwork assemblage is the absence of expressions of religious identity. In contrast to the metalwork assemblage from the Viking encampment at Torksey (Brown 2006; James Graham-Campbell *pers. comm.*), there are no Thor's hammers or cross pendants from Lincoln, nor are there any brooches with cross-shaped decoration except perhaps the rather stylized examples depicted in fig. 11.7. If overt expressions of religious identity reflect tensions between different religious groups, the absence of such objects from Lincoln fits well with the picture of integration of Christian belief into the daily lives of the Scandinavian settlers, as discussed previously. In this context it may be worth pointing out that there is no evidence for the *production* of dress-accessories with clear Scandinavian influences in Lincoln either that predate the 11th century, when Scandinavia was in the process of converting to Christianity. The earliest production evidence from Lincoln – the hooked tags, the finger rings, the lead-alloy brooches and the wire pins – all belonged to quite generic or pan-European object types, suggesting that the metalworkers who settled in Lincoln, despite some of them probably being of Scandinavian descent, were not investing in expressing their Scandinavian identities to any significant degree (see Hall 2000 for a discussion of the same phenomenon in York).

Worth noticing as well is the absence of decorated metal horse-harness accessories – basically, dress-accessories for horses – from Lincoln. The only possibly pre-Conquest metal harness fittings from Lincoln are an 11th- to 12th-century copper-alloy strap-loop with minimal incised decoration (f72 <ae234>) and some 11th-century copper-alloy decorative strapping (f72 <ae48>, both from Flaxengate (Ten Harkel 2010, ch. 5; White 1982, 39). Late Anglo-Saxon horseshoes and iron spurs have also been found, however, confirming that horses *were* used in Lincoln at the time. Examples of 10th- to 11th-century horse harness fittings from the rest of Lincolnshire are numerous, including more than 100 decorated stirrup fittings and some 50 other decorative harness fittings. These were often executed in Scandinavian-derived decorative styles, sometimes gilded, suggesting that equestrian activity was an elite activity, a suggestion that is confirmed by written sources such as *Beowulf*, *The Wanderer* and *The Husband's Message*, all of which were entrusted to parchment in the late Anglo-Saxon period. As the 10th century witnessed an increase in the amount of metal horse harness accessories from all over the country – during the middle Anglo-Saxon period, these seem to have been made of more perishable materials – it may be possible to suggest that the Scandinavian settlement caused a revival in the status of equestrian activity.

The highly decorative nature of some of the equestrian equipment from the rural parts of Lincolnshire contrasts with the crude quality of the Lincoln fitting (fig. 11.8), serving as a reminder that horses had multiple functions, not only as status symbols but also as work animals. The absence of high-status horse harness fittings from Lincoln furthermore suggests that the use of horses as status symbols – adorned with decorative metalwork – occurred mostly *outside* the town, whilst *in* towns, horses were used – if at all – for more utilitarian purposes. This could well mean that Lincoln's population did not belong to the landholding elite, who preferred to reside on the 'rural' estates that formed the bases of their power (Ten Harkel 2011).

Fig. 11.8 Horse-harness fitting (strap-loop) from Flaxengate, Lincoln (photograph by the author; reproduced with kind permission of the City of Lincoln Council) and other horse harness fittings: b) harness pendant from Hibaldstow (PAS NLM-3CD626) (drawn by Marina Elwes); c) stirrup-mount from East Kirkby (PAS NCL-76AEA7); d) strap-divider from Boston (PAS NLM168) (drawn by Marina Elwes); e) stirrup-mount from Winteringham (PAS NLM1077) (drawn by Marina Elwes) (reproduced with kind permission of the PAS).

The absence of late Anglo-Saxon weaponry from Lincoln seems to confirm that Lincoln's population did not subscribe to the kind of warrior-like masculine identity that stands central to Hadley's (this volume) chapter.[2] The distribution of stone funerary sculpture confirms this. On the basis of the fact that there is frequently only one funerary monument per parish in rural Lincolnshire, Everson and Stocker (1999) have proposed that these stones represent the funerary monuments for the 'founders' of these parishes, erected in the 10th century during an ongoing process of parish formation and fragmentation related to changes in landownership that occurred in the wake of the Scandinavian settlement. In Lincoln itself, there are no definite 10th-century pieces from the Lower City, whilst contemporary sculpture from the Upper City occurs only at the church of St Paul-in-the-Bail and the Cathedral (Everson and Stocker 1999). In Wigford, however, the cemeteries of St Mark's and St Mary-le-Wigford both produced large quantities of 10th- to 11th-century funerary sculpture, leading to their interpretation as the graveyards of the emerging mercantile elite, whose growing wealth enabled them to express their social aspirations in ways similar to the landholding elite (Stocker 2000; also see Stocker, this volume). Did these mercantile communities include metalworkers? Certainly, it is possible that some of the smiths active in Wigford were buried in the cemeteries of St Mark's and St Mary-le-Wigford. However, it is notable that there is a paucity of sculpture from the Lower City, which produced the most abundant evidence for metalworking activities. Assuming that the occupants of the Lower City would be buried in their local parish churchyard, this suggests that, on the whole, metalworkers did not engage in funerary display through sculpture. Does this mean – as Astill (2006, 248) suggests – that metalworkers operated to serve the demands of an aristocratic patron (secular *or* ecclesiastical) and were thus excluded from the expression of social aspiration on their own parts? Or does this mean that, during the period that the erection of funerary sculpture was a fashionable way to express status and/or social aspiration, non-ferrous metalworkers, whose position in society was undergoing significant change, had not (yet) reached the level of independence and wealth that allowed them to invest in conspicuous display themselves? These questions will be explored in more detail in the final part of this chapter.

Discussion: everyday life in Viking-Age Lincoln

So far, the study of fashion and its production in Viking-Age Lincoln has revealed many aspects of the identities and actions of its inhabitants. The production of dress-accessories increasingly took place in towns, although metalworking for more utilitarian purposes – such as blacksmithing – continued to take place in rural settlements. The Church was an important driving force behind the increased monopolisation of non-ferrous metalworking in the emerging towns and the increased social acceptability of the craft. Producers of dress-accessories were not part of elite society, but may have worked for a variety of patrons or clients, most clearly demonstrated by the relatively widespread regional distribution of hooked tags. Some of the metalworkers were of Scandinavian descent, although there is no evidence that those active in Lincoln invested their products with overt references to ethnic or religious identity.

What else can be learnt about the dynamics of everyday socio-economic life in Viking-Age Lincoln? With the benefit of hindsight, it is possible to suggest that the evidence from Lincoln represents a phase in the development that saw the transformation of metalworking as a peripatetic and liminal lifestyle – represented by the smith who was buried near Tattershall Thorpe – to a highly respected urban craft, represented by the metalworkers' guilds of the medieval period. The metalworkers of Viking-Age Lincoln belong somewhere in the middle phase of that change and – partially or perhaps wholly because of the influence of the Church as an important patron during the transformation of their craft – did not yet take part in the same forms of conspicuous display – such as the erection of funerary sculpture – as the landholding elite or the postulated merchants from Wigford. Despite this, their importance to Lincoln's economic growth is expressed in the central location of the workshops, in the heart of the Lower City, where they continued to be located until after the Norman Conquest. In this respect the metalworking industry differs from Lincoln's pottery industry, which was forced outside the city walls to extra-mural *Butwerk* in the course of the 10th century, contemporaneously with a decline in the quality and distribution of Lincoln-produced wares (Young and Vince 2005).

It is significant that the production of iron continued to exist on a more widespread scale, as it bears witness to the increased diversification of smiths working with different types of metal, as has been suggested by Hinton (2003, 263), with those working with non-ferrous metals enjoying higher status than those working with ferrous materials. The concentration of non-ferrous metalwork production in Lincoln, as in other Viking Age towns in England, became a characteristic aspect of the emerging 10th-century towns. The use of base metals and application of simple, repetitive decoration that could be executed quickly was not so much a decline in workmanship as a way to increase production speed and lower cost, thus adding significantly to Lincoln's viability as the economically prosperous town it became in the later 10th and 11th centuries.

Lincoln's metalworkers were clearly intent on economic success. The presence of Scandinavian metalworkers may give the impression that this was another expression of a more general interest in obtaining wealth that existed amongst the Scandinavians, but there is evidence that there was an Anglo-Saxon element amongst Lincoln's population as well. The flat disc brooch form, the variety of shapes of the hooked tags and the occurrence of copper-alloy pin types that were already common during the middle Anglo-Saxon period suggests a degree of continuity with the preceding period. The stratigraphic sequence from St Paul-in-the-Bail reveals no obvious break in the later 9th century, when the Scandinavian settlement took place. What is more, the first wheel-thrown pottery produced in Lincoln from *c.* 870, the so-called Lincoln Kiln Type (LKT), used the same clays and tempers as preceding hand-made Maxey-type wares, suggesting that at least some of the potters who were active in Lincoln were familiar with middle Anglo-Saxon pottery production processes (Vince 1993, 161). Object types like the flat disc brooch with *Borre*-style decoration reveal that integration into Anglo-Saxon society took place rapidly.

In short, it is clear that the production and style of 9th- to 11th-century dress-accessories can shed much light on Viking-Age urbanism, in particular on the activities and identities of its inhabitants. Of course, the analysis of one category of material culture never paints the complete picture. For that reason, this chapter occasionally referred to conclusions based on different data. Much work remains to be done, however, on widening the debate through comparative research with other contemporary settlements from England and abroad, and integrating metal-detected rural assemblages with finds retrieved during urban excavations. Only then will a comprehensive picture of everyday life in Viking towns emerge.

Acknowledgments

Many people have contributed in some way to this paper. First of all, my thanks must go to *The Collection* in Lincoln for providing access to the objects, records and x-rays. Jenny Mann was a bottomless source of knowledge and information regarding the Lincoln small finds. Mick Jones kindly allowed me to read the drafts for the Lower City volume ahead of publication and shared his extensive knowledge of Lincoln's archaeology with me. I am much indebted to Anne Pedersen for sharing her knowledge of southern Scandinavian Romanesque art, and to James Graham-Campbell for his much needed help in identifying a number of artefacts. Thanks must also go to Philippa Walton at the British Museum for identification of an object that turned out to be Roman, and to Gabor Thomas and Rosie Weetch for their second opinion on a number of objects and ideas. Chris Whitney-Lagen drew my attention to the London parallel to the lead-alloy flat disc brooches from Lincoln. This paper is ultimately based on my PhD research, which was supervised by Dawn Hadley. Her support and tireless editing over the years were invaluable. Dawn Hadley, Mick Jones and Jenny Mann kindly read and commented on an earlier version of this paper.

Notes

1 This paper discusses only a selection of dress-accessories from Viking-Age Lincoln. See Bayley and Ten Harkel (in prep.) for a more comprehensive discussion of the assemblage.

2 Excavations in Nottingham did, however, reveal two weapons burials that have been interpreted as belonging to Viking warriors (see chapter by Hadley, this volume).

Bibliography

Astill, G. (2006) Community, identity and the later Anglo-Saxon town: the case of southern England. In W. Davies, G. Halsall and A. Reynolds (eds) *People and Space in the Middle Ages 300–1300*, 233–54. Turnhout, Brepols.

Astill, G. G. (2009) Medieval towns and urbanization. In R. Gilchrist and A. Reynolds (eds) *Reflections: 50 Years of Medieval Archaeology, 1957–2007*, 255–70. Society for Medieval Archaeology Monograph 30. Leeds, Maney.

Bailey, R. N. (1980) *Viking Age Sculpture in Northern England*. London, Collins.

Bayley, J. (1992) *Anglo-Scandinavian Non-Ferrous Metalworking from 16–22 Coppergate*. The Archaeology of York 17 (7): The Small Finds. London, Council for British Archaeology.

Bayley, J. (2008a) *Lincoln: evidence for metalworking on Flaxengate and other sites in the city: technology report*. English Heritage Research Department Report 67. Portsmouth, English Heritage.

Bayley, J. (2008b) *Lincoln: evidence for glass-working on Flaxengate and other sites in the city: technology report*. English Heritage Research Department Report 68. Portsmouth, English Heritage.

Bayley, J. and Ten Harkel, A. (in prep.) Metalwork and metalworking in Viking-Age Lincoln.

Blackburn, M. A. S. (2004) The coinage of Scandinavian York. In R. A. Hall (ed.) *Aspects of Anglo-Scandinavian York*, 325–49. The Archaeology of York 8 (4): Anglo-Scandinavian York. York, Council for British Archaeology.

Blackburn, M. A. S. (2006) Presidential address 2005: currency under the Vikings. Part 2: the two Scandinavian kingdoms of the Danelaw, *c.* 895–954. *The British Numismatic Journal* 76, 204–26.

Blair, J. (2005) *The Church in Anglo-Saxon Society*. Oxford, Oxford University Press.

Bradley, J. (2002) *An Archaeological Evaluation on Land at Barrow Road, Barton-on-Humber, North Lincolnshire*. Unpublished Humber Archaeology Report 97.

Brown, H. (2006) *Torksey, Lincolnshire, in the Anglo-Scandinavian Period*. Unpublished MA dissertation, Centre for Medieval Studies, University of York.

Colyer, C., Gilmour, B. J. J. and Jones, M. J. (1999) *The Defences of the Lower City: excavations at The Park and West Parade 1970–2 and a discussion of other sites excavated up to 1994*. The Archaeology of Lincoln 7 (2). York, Council for British Archaeology for the City of Lincoln Archaeology Unit.

Cowgill, J. (1994) Desperately seeking slags. *Lincoln Archaeology* 1993–4, 25.

Crane, D. (2000) *Fashion and its Social Agendas: class, gender and identity in clothing*. Chicago, University of Chicago Press.

Damhorst, M. L., Miller-Spillman, K. A. and Michelman, S. O. (eds) (2005; 2nd edn) *The Meanings of Dress*. New York, Fairchild Publications.

Davis, F. (1992) *Fashion, Culture and Identity*. Chicago, University of Chicago Press.

Evans, D. and Loveluck, C. (eds.) (2009) *Life and Economy at Early Medieval Flixborough, c. A.D. 600–1000: the artefact evidence*. Excavations at Flixborough 2. Oxford, Oxbow.

Everson, P. and Stocker, D. (1999) *Corpus of Anglo-Saxon Stone Sculpture Volume 5: Lincolnshire*. Oxford, Oxford University Press.

Everson, P., Taylor, C. C. and Dunn, C. J. (1991) *Change and Continuity: rural settlement in north-west Lincolnshire*. London, HMSO.

Fanning, T. (1994) *Viking Age Ringed Pins from Dublin*. National Museum of Ireland, Medieval Dublin Excavations 1962–81, series B, vol. 4. Dublin, Royal Irish Academy.

Foley, K. (1981) *Glass- and Metalworking: industrial material from Anglo-Scandinavian Lincoln.* Unpublished MSc thesis, Institute of Archaeology, University of London.

Gardner, R. D. and Bunn, D. (2006) *Proposed New Hotel Site, Barrow Road, Barton-on-Humber, Lincolnshire: archaeological desk-based assessment and geophysical survey.* Unpublished Pre-Construct Archaeology Report.

Gem, R. 1993. The episcopal churches of Lindsey in the early 9th century. In A. Vince (ed.) *Pre-Viking Lindsey,* 123–7. Lincoln Archaeological Studies 1. Lincoln, The City of Lincoln Archaeology Unit.

Gilmour, B. (2007) Sub-Roman or Saxon, Pagan or Christian: who was buried in the early cemetery at St Paul-in-the-Bail, Lincoln? In L. Gilmour (ed.) *Pagans and Christians – From Antiquity to the Middle Ages: papers in Honour of Martin Henig, presented on the occasion of his 65th birthday,* 229–56. British Archaeological Reports International Series 1610. Oxford, Archaeopress.

Green, F. J. (1997) *St Helen's, Cumberworth: assessment report.* Unpublished Hampshire Archaeology TVAT Report 04/97.

Hadley, D. M. (2006) *The Vikings in England: settlement, society and culture.* Manchester, Manchester University Press.

Hall, R. A. (2000) Anglo-Scandinavian attitudes: archaeological ambiguities in late ninth- to mid-eleventh-century York. In D. M. Hadley and J. D. Richards (eds) *Cultures in Contact: Scandinavian settlement in England in the ninth and tenth centuries,* 311–24. Turnhout, Brepols.

Hinton, D. A. (1974) *A Catalogue of the Anglo-Saxon Ornamental Metalwork 700–1100 in the Department of Antiquities, Ashmolean Museum.* Oxford, Clarendon Press.

Hinton, D. A. (2000) *A Smith in Lindsey: the Anglo-Saxon grave at Tattershall Thorpe, Lincolnshire.* The Society for Medieval Archaeology Monograph Series 16. London, Maney.

Hinton, D. A. (2003) Anglo-Saxon smiths and myths. In D. Scragg (ed.) *Textual and Material Culture in Anglo-Saxon England: Thomas Northcote Toller and the Toller Memorial Lectures,* 261–82. Cambridge, D. S. Brewer.

Hinton, D. A. (2005) *Gold and Gilt, Pots and Pins: possessions and people in medieval Britain.* Oxford, Oxford University Press.

Jones, M. J., Steane, K., Darling, M. J., Mann, J., Vince, A. and Young, J. (forthcoming) *The Archaeology of the Lower City and Adjacent Suburbs.* Lincoln Archaeological Studies 4. Oxford, Oxbow.

Kershaw, J. (2008) The distribution of the 'Winchester' style in late Saxon England: metalwork finds from the Danelaw. *Anglo-Saxon Studies in Archaeology and History* 15, 254–69.

Kershaw, J. (2010) *Culture and Gender in the Danelaw: Scandinavian and Anglo-Scandinavian brooches, 850–1050.* Unpublished DPhil thesis, Institute of Archaeology, University of Oxford.

Kilmurry, K. (1980) *The Pottery Industry of Stamford, Lincs. c. AD 850–1250: its manufacture, trade and relationship with continental wares, with a classification and chronology.* British Archaeological Reports British Series 84. Oxford, Tempus Reparatum.

Lang, J. (1976) Sigurd and Weland in pre-Conquest carving from northern England. *Yorkshire Archaeological Journal* 48, 83–94.

Leahy, K. (1993) The Anglo-Saxon settlement of Lindsey. In A. Vince (ed.) *Pre-Viking Lindsey,* 29–44. Lincoln Archaeological Studies 1. Lincoln, Lincoln Archaeology Unit.

Leahy, K. (2007) *The Anglo-Saxon Kingdom of Lindsey.* Stroud, Tempus.

Leahy, K. and C. Paterson (2001) New light on the Viking presence in Lincolnshire: the artefactual evidence. In J. Graham-Campbell, R. A. Hall, J. Jesch and D. N. Parsons (eds) *Vikings and the Danelaw: select papers from the proceedings of the thirteenth Viking Congress, 21–30 August 1997,* 181–202. Oxford, Oxbow.

Loveluck, C. (2007) *Rural Settlement, Lifestyles and Social Change in the Later First Millennium AD: Anglo-Saxon Flixborough and its wider context.* Excavations at Flixborough 4. Oxford, Oxbow.

Loveluck, C. and Atkinson, D. (2007) *The Early Medieval Settlement Remains from Flixborough, Lincolnshire: the occupation sequence, c. AD 600–1000.* Excavations at Flixborough 1. Oxford, Oxbow.

Mahany, C., Burchard, A. and Simpson, G. (1982) *Excavations in Stamford, Lincolnshire, 1963–1969.* The Society for Medieval Archaeology Monograph 9. London, Maney.

Malone, S. (2009) *Excavations at the site of* The Collection, *Danes Terrace, Lincoln.* Unpublished Archaeological Project Services Report 20 (09).

Mann, J. (1999) Other artefacts. In C. Colyer, B. J. J. Gilmour and M. J. Jones, *The Defences of the Lower City: excavations at the Park and West Parade 1970–2 and a discussion of other sites excavated up to 1994*, 146–69 and 224–36. The Archaeology of Lincoln 7 (2). York, Council of British Archaeology for the City of Lincoln Archaeology Unit.

Margeson, S. (1997) *The Vikings in Norfolk*. Norfolk, Norfolk Museums Service.

Mårtensson, A. W. (1963) Gravar kring stavkyrkan. In R. Blomqvist and A. W. Mårtensson (eds) *Fynd fra Ultima Thule: en berättelse om vad grävningarna för Thulehuset i Lund avslöjade*, 43–66. Archaeologica Lundensia: Investigationes de Antiqvitatibus Urbis Lundae II. Lund, Almqvist & Wiksell Int.

Owen, O. (2001) The strange beast that is the English Urnes style. In J. Graham-Campbell, R. A. Hall, J. Jesch and D. N. Parsons (eds) *Vikings and the Danelaw: select papers from the proceedings of the thirteenth Viking Congress, Nottingham and York, 21–30 August 1997*, 203–22. Oxford, Oxbow.

Owen-Crocker, G. R. (1986) *Dress in Anglo-Saxon England*. Manchester, Manchester University Press.

Parkins, W. (ed.) (2002) *Fashioning the Body Politic: dress, gender, citizenship*. Oxford, Berg.

Perring, D. (1981) *Early Medieval Occupation at Flaxengate, Lincoln*. The Archaeology of Lincoln 9. London, Council for British Archaeology.

Stafford, P. (1978) Historical implications of the regional production of dies under Æthelred II. *The British Numismatic Journal* 48, 35–51.

Steane, K., Darling, M. J., Mann, J., Vince, A. and Young, J. (2001) *The Archaeology of Wigford and the Brayford Pool*. Lincoln Archaeological Studies 2. Oxford, Oxbow.

Steane, K., Darling, M. J., Jones, M. J., Mann, J., Vince, A. and Young, J. (2006) *The Archaeology of the Upper City and Adjacent Suburbs*. Lincoln Archaeological Studies 3. Oxford, Oxbow.

Stewart, I. (1983) The anonymous Anglo-Viking issue with sword and hammer types and the coinage of Sihtric I. *The British Numismatic Journal* 52, 108–16.

Stocker, D. (2000) Monuments and merchants: irregularities in the distribution of stone sculpture in Lincolnshire and Yorkshire in the tenth century. In D. M. Hadley and J. D. Richards (eds) *Cultures in Contact: Scandinavian settlement in England in the ninth and tenth centuries*, 179–212. Turnhout, Brepols.

Stocker, D. (ed.) (2003) *The City by the Pool: assessing the archaeology of the City of Lincoln*. Lincoln Archaeological Studies 10. Oxford, Oxbow.

Ten Harkel, A. T. (2010) *Lincoln in the Viking Age: a 'town' in context*. Unpublished PhD thesis, University of Sheffield.

Ten Harkel, L. (2011) Land or gold? Changing perceptions of landscape in Viking Age Lincolnshire. *Assemblage* 11, 15–33.

Thomas, G. (2000) Anglo-Scandinavian metalwork from the Danelaw: exploring social and cultural interaction. In D. M. Hadley and J. D. Richards (eds) *Cultures in Contact: Scandinavian settlement in England in the ninth and tenth centuries*, 237–55. Turnhout, Brepols.

Thomas, G. (2001) Strap-ends and the identification of regional patterns in the production and circulation of ornamental metalwork in late Anglo-Saxon and Viking-Age Britain. In M. Redknap, N. Edwards, S. Youngs, A. Lane and J. Knight (eds) *Pattern and Purpose in Insular Art*, 39–48. Oxford, Oxbow.

Tweddle, D. (2004) Art in Pre-Conquest York. In R. A. Hall (ed.) *Aspects of Anglo-Scandinavian York*, 446–58. The Archaeology of York 8 (4). London, Council for British Archaeology.

Vince, A. (1993) Forms, functions and manufacturing techniques of late ninth- and tenth-century wheelthrown pottery in England and their origins. In D. Piton (ed.) *Travaux du Groupe de Recherches et D'Etudes sur la Céramique dans le Nord – Pas-de-Calais; Actes du Collque D'Outreau (10–12 Avril 1992)*, 151–64. Numéro hors série de Nord Ouest Archéologie.

Vince, A. (1995) A Lincolnshire potter in Cnut's Denmark? *Lincoln Archaeology 1994–1995*, 44.

Vince, A. (2003a) Lincoln in the early medieval era, between the 5th and 9th centuries. In D. Stocker (ed.) *The City by the Pool: assessing the archaeology of the City of Lincoln*, 141–56. Lincoln Archaeological Studies 10. Oxford, Oxbow.

Vince, A. G. (2003b) The New Town: Lincoln in the high medieval era (*c*. 900 to *c*. 1350). In D. Stocker (ed.) *The City by the Pool: assessing the archaeology of the City of Lincoln*, 159–296. Lincoln Archaeological Studies 10. Oxford, Oxbow.

Weetch, R. (in prep.) *The Late Saxon Brooch: social identities and artistic expression in late Saxon England.* Unpublished PhD thesis, University of Reading.

White, R. (1982) *Non-Ferrous Metalworking on Flaxengate, Lincoln, from the 9th–11th centuries.* Unpublished MSc dissertation, Institute of Archaeology, University of London.

White, R. (1992) *Non-Ferrous Metalworking in Lincoln: assessment of potential for examination and outline of resource implication (1st Draft).* Unpublished document, Lincolnshire County Council.

Whitney-Lagen, C. (in prep.) *The Manufacture and Meaning of Early Medieval Pewter Dress Accessories in Britain.* Unpublished PhD thesis, Institute of Archaeology, University of London.

Wilson, E. and de la Haye, A. (1999) Introduction. In A. de la Haye and E. Wilson (eds) *Defining Dress: dress as object, meaning and identity*, 1–9. Manchester, Manchester University Press.

Young, J. and Vince, A. (2005) *A Corpus of Anglo-Saxon and Medieval Pottery from Lincoln.* Lincoln Archaeological Studies 7. Oxford, Oxbow.

MAKING A GOOD COMB: MERCANTILE IDENTITY IN 9TH- TO 11TH-CENTURY ENGLAND

Steven P. Ashby

kamb koþan; kiari: þorfastr
'A good comb Thorfastr made'
(British Museum 1923, 117–18; Barnes and Page 2006, 292–5)

Sometime around the 11th century, a combmaker known as *Thorfastr* made a comb, and marked its case with the above inscription. In 1851, the case was recovered from a site in or near to Lincoln (see Barnes and Page 2006, 292), and now sits on display in the early medieval galleries of the British Museum. Relatively speaking, the case has become well known, as it is unusual in that it provides us with the name of an artisan who may – perhaps – have been operating in Lincoln in the late Viking Age or medieval period. The inscription's potential for public engagement is thus high, and this has been exploited to good effect. However, archaeological commitment to the object has been relatively limited in scope. While much work has been undertaken on the origin and dating of the inscription, less time has been devoted to questions involving its context, meaningful content, or the reason why it was written. If the inscription was intended as a form of advertising, then that tells us something about the level of literacy amongst the comb-consuming community. More broadly, however, it raises the question of whether combs themselves can be 'read' (see Ashby 2011b). This chapter begins from the premise that such a reading is possible, and that all combs are 'inscribed' with the identity of their manufacturer, if not their name.

Approaches to artefacts and identity

The role of combs in the production and manipulation of identity has previously been discussed (Ashby 2006a; 2006b), but it remains unclear *whose* identity was being expressed, to whom it was being communicated, and on whose behalf. It is therefore germane to consider more generally how one might begin to access and understand the processes involved in the production and maintenance of identity through portable material culture. Weissner (1983) has shown how within any single artefact or artefact type (in her case the projectile points of the Kalahari San), style may exist in a diverse range of physical attributes. Moreover, artefacts may communicate both emblemic style, referring to conscious affiliation or group membership, and assertive style, which is personally-based, concerned with individual identity, and may be either conscious or

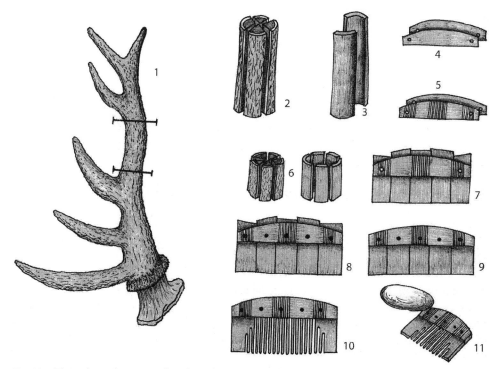

Fig. 12.1 The authorised sequence of comb production (drawn by Hayley Saul, based on originals from Ulbricht (1978) and Ambrosiani (1981); copyright Hayley Saul).

unconscious (Weissner 1983, 257–8). Weissner demonstrates that the relationship between these two aspects of stylistic expression is complex, and the ways in which they combine are unpredictable; thus, analysis of the ways in which material culture was used in communication must be context-specific.

In the commercial environment of Anglo-Scandinavian York or Lincoln, where most combs are likely to have been produced as stock for sale, rather than created to order, interpretation of assertive style is subject to certain confounds. Consumer choice was necessarily limited by the range of forms and designs that the combmaker opted to create, although once purchased combs may have been customised with inscriptions, graffitti, and other personal expressions of style. However, though combs from Scandinavia sometimes feature remarkably articulate representations of identity (see, for instance, the Christ figure inscribed on a comb from Sigtuna; Tesch 1987, fig. 8), with the exception of Thorfastr's combcase, comparable examples are surprisingly rare in British contexts. Elsewhere (Ashby 2011b), I have proposed that form and ornament might best be interpreted by means of a linguistic analogy, but this is not the only conceptual mechanism by which they may be understood. It has long been argued that social meaning is invested in all aspects of material culture, rather than simply in an arbitrarily defined repertoire of objects, traits or motifs that are sufficiently complex, ornate, or 'non-functional' to act as transmitters of style (Richards 1987; Cumberpatch and Blinkhorn 1997). Yet, in the light of Weissner's work, it is clear that even the identification of those artefact attributes that might carry stylistic information is far from straightforward. Accordingly, this chapter focuses not on style, but on technology, and on choice.

Technological choice

The approach developed here draws upon the work of social anthropologists (particularly Ingold 2000; Lemmonier 1993b). The study of form and ornament in traditional, typological terms remains fundamental, as does comprehension of the production and communication of meaning through style (see Weissner 1983; Ashby 2011b), but we should also consider the subtle mechanisms by which meaning, identity and belonging may have been communicated through morphological variation. Important in this respect is Lemonnier's (1993a) work on the social embeddedness of technological choice, the plurality of approaches to manufacturing, and the subtle reproduction of shared *habitus* through technological traditions (see also Ingold 1993; Van der Leeuw 1993). For Lemonnier (1993b, 2, 16), techniques (whether of living, making, or using) are learned behaviours that are culturally and spatially variable, yet made temporally persistent and robust through the power of tradition and conservatism. He perceives a need to study these techniques as 'social productions', and argues that the 'set of constraints' within which material culture is produced includes not only material considerations – such as the physical properties of bone or antler – but also an important suite of cultural and symbolic constraints, and mental rules regarding the ways in which tasks should be undertaken. Lemonnier (1993b, 16–21) sees politics, identity, status and social distinction as key agents in the formulation of technological choice. We may thus postulate that in the Viking Age – a time characterised by significant culture contact and social change – the existence of any variation in manufacturing practice was potentially socially significant. Furthermore, in a wide-ranging study of pottery manufacture, Van der Leeuw (1993) has demonstrated that the way in which a vessel is conceptualised has important implications for the approach taken to its manufacture, and in particular to the nature and sequence of the key stages of the production process. This consideration holds particular promise for the study of early medieval combs, given the complexity and level of investment dictated by the manufacturing sequence.

More recently, Ingold (2000) has shown that people, rather than learning techniques in the abstract, develop them through the experience of engaging with the world in which they live. This is not wholly inconsistent with the 'social' model of technology outlined above; learning of course remains key to the construction of knowledge. However, this knowledge is not imparted directly from teacher to apprentice as an abstract canon of ideas, but is developed through guided involvement with the environment. For us, the implications of the work of Ingold, Lemonnier and others are that combmaking is best understood in terms of tradition, and that this tradition reflects the negotiation of social and practical concerns through engagement with the local environment (including materials, tools, the provision and organisation of working space). To develop this approach it is thus necessary to delineate the parameters of variation: the nature of the industry; the means by which combs were made; and the choices and alternatives that were available to the manufacturer.

Technological choice in practice: combs

Organisation

We begin with the organisation of the craft. Early medieval combmaking is envisioned, almost universally, as an itinerant craft (*e.g.* Ambrosiani 1981; Callmer 2002; Hansen 2005; Nicholson 1997), a deduction based primarily on what is seen as the small size of deposits of manufacturing waste excavated at sites such as Hedeby (formerly Denmark, now Germany), Birka (Sweden) and Ribe (Denmark). Supporting arguments related to a perceived uniformity of the European comb corpus, and to geographical disparities in the availability of raw material, are relatively easily dismissed (see Ashby 2006a; in press b). Following some initial dispute, in which Ulbricht (1978) claimed that the manufacture of combs was a part-time activity, while Ambrosiani (1981) argued for an itinerant mode of production (see also Christophersen 1980a; 1980b), Ambrosiani's model has since been accepted as received wisdom. Yet, while elegant, the latter requires qualification (Ashby 2006a; in press a; in press b). Quite apart from any concerns with the interpretation of deposit size, there are a number of logical problems. For example, Ambrosiani's proposed means of raw material acquisition (receipt, on arrival at market, of antlers collected by members of the local community) seems logistically complex and vulnerable to disruption or collapse. The model also proposes an unrealistic and unnecessary level of organisational uniformity; why should combmakers work in the same way, in all areas, at all times, irrespective of political, social, economic, or tenurial circumstance?

There is also a problem of scale: over what distances should we envision these combmakers moving? There is a realistic possibility that peripatetic combmakers worked on a circuit that took in York or Lincoln and their hinterlands, and one might perhaps accept the idea of seaborne combmakers travelling between the nodal towns of the Baltic as part of a community of travelling artisans and traders (see Sindbaek 2007a; 2007b; 2008). However, it seems unlikely that the combmakers from either region were in regular contact with their counterparts from across the North Sea. The reasons for this are social, rather than economic. It seems unlikely that the manufacturers of an artefact so important in both the daily lives of people – and in the production of their identities – would live a life so detached from regional community. After all, the effectiveness of *Thorfastr*'s advertising was entirely dependent on his being known to local communities. Thus, while the 'itinerant combmaker' model offers a reasonable explanation for the nature of the Scandinavian evidence, any wider application must critically consider both context and scale. Ambrosiani made no claim for the validity of her model beyond the confines of the Viking Age, but that has not deterred others from applying it (implicitly or explicitly) to earlier or later contexts. Moreover, we should resist the temptation to shoehorn our evidence into this familiar narrative. Rather, by accepting the inevitability of variation and contingency, it becomes possible to investigate new aspects of early medieval society, including urban and mercantile identities.

Method

There is a similar received wisdom that the process of comb manufacture is well understood (see Smirnova 2005, 24 for a direct statement to this effect), and a familiar sequence of production is frequently outlined (see figs 12.1 and 12.2). This model is rarely questioned, and often thought so familiar that rehearsal is deemed unnecessary (*e.g.* Mainman and Rogers 1999, 1905; see also Smirnova 2005, 24). The identification of this *chaîne opératoire* goes at least as far back as

Stage	Description	Potential Choices
1	Antler tines cut from beam	Antler pre-softened? How?
2	Antler tines split into four	Tools
3	Removal of porous core	Tools
4	Shaping of blanks	Use of clamp, fixative, and/or end riveting.
5	Decoration	Tools, roughing-out, motifs, arrangement, overall scheme.
6	Billets cut from sections of antler beam	Use of a clamp, or vice or jig in a more settled workshop.
7	Assembly	Means of securing: clamp, vice, temporary pegs, fixative agent such as animal glue?
8	Drilling and riveting	Positioning of perforations for rivets. Use of bone pegs, iron or copper-alloy rivets, or rolled copper-alloy sheet. Heating of rivet prior to hammering out.
9	Levelling of comb back	Tools: Saw or rasp.
10	Teeth-cutting and shaping	Special-purpose saw? Secured with a jig, vice, clamp, or holder (see Galloway and Newcomer 1981, 82)? Degree of teeth-shaping and sharpening deemed necessary (see Ambrosiani 1981, 45).
11	Polishing and finishing	Burnishing, staining, inlaying, plating. Tools and materials used.

Fig. 12.2 Key tasks involved in the production of a composite comb, and some of the technological choices involved in each task.

Hilczerowna's (1961) work at Gdansk, which was followed by similar reconstructions of the sequences employed at other Polish sites, such as Wolin and Kolobrzeg (see Cnotliwy 1973, 44–59, 313–14), and the idea of an ordered programme of tasks reached a wider audience in the work of Ulbricht (1978) at Hedeby. In all of these cases, the production sequence was reconstructed from inferences made about the waste and finished products recovered from a given site, but there is often an implicit assumption that the process was widespread and immutable in detail from the late Roman period onwards.

The investigations upon which this production model is built do have a firm empirical basis (see Hilczerowna 1961; Cnotliwy 1956; Ulbricht 1978; Ambrosiani 1981, 103–18; Galloway and Newcomer 1981; summarised in MacGregor 1985). In her influential study, Ambrosiani (1981, 117) compared the waste produced via her experimental comb reconstructions with that excavated at Ribe. However, while this form of comparative analysis is fundamental to enquiry

	Probably Red Deer	Probably Reindeer	Probably Elk	Total Antler (inc indet antler)	Bone	Other Material	Indeterminate Material	Total
York (Waste)	111			166	77	1	15	259
Coppergate, York (combs)	32 (70)			52 (146)	21 (29)	1	(4)	74 (179)
Lincoln (combs)	1 (7)			1 (18)	7 (18)	1 (3)	3 (1)	12 (36)

Fig. 12.3 Raw materials in combs from sites in Lincoln (small and tiny fragments in parentheses). For detailed breakdowns by site and chronology, see Ashby 2006a: tables 7.25 to 7.27.

into the archaeology of crafts, the fact that the waste products appear to 'match' is, of course, not in itself evidence that the processes involved (or their sequencing) were identical. The root of this oversimplification lies in Ambrosiani's understanding of technology as fundamentally driven by efficiency. For instance, with reference to shaping of blanks and the removal of unwanted material, Ambrosiani (1981, 117) states that 'we found it much better to work with the rasp than the chisel, and the reason the Ribe comb-maker did not, must have been that his [*sic*] was not as efficient as ours'. This belief in efficiency as the driver of technology is also central to Galloway and Newcomer's (1981) classic account of practical investigations into comb manufacture. Yet we have seen that efficiency is not the only factor involved in the determination of technological practice, and that social and symbolic considerations (however elusive) must equally be taken into consideration.

As it stands, what we might term the 'authorised sequence' is rather one-dimensional and static. It leaves a number of important questions unanswered: how was each of these techniques undertaken in practice? Was the sequence completely immutable? Galloway and Newcomer (1981) have suggested that some of the stages in the sequence might be transposed; application of ornament might, for instance, be moved from step 5 to a position following steps 6 or 7. Even so, the rationale for the fixity or otherwise of a particular stage seems, again, to be rooted in the idea of maximising efficiency (*e.g.* Galloway and Newcomer 1981, 82–3), and alternative justifications for sequence formulation are not considered. This belief in the pre-eminence of efficiency also influences the authors' discussion of the possibility (first raised in Hilczerowna 1961) of combmakers amassing a stock of components in order to maximise output. This may well have been a key consideration in some contexts, but, alternatively, the primary consideration may have been to preserve the integrity of the process of 'making'. Indeed, the movement from raw antler to finished article may have been laden with meaning, and undertaken as a coherent quotidian ritual (see also Edmonds 1999, 15–31), rather than as a series of discrete, unconnected tasks.

To summarise: much has been learned through systematic study of combs and production waste from a range of early medieval contexts across Europe (*e.g.* Cnotliwy 1956; Ulbricht 1978; Ambrosiani 1981; MacGregor 1985; Smirnova 2005), as well as from experimental reconstruction of the manufacturing process (Galloway and Newcomer 1981), but it is dangerous to assume that we know all we can about the process of comb production. Even if we are willing to accept a certain uniformity and systematisation in the manufacture of these objects, we should still ask why things were done in the way they were. Following Lemonnier, the reasoning may not always (or ever) be generated purely out of a mechanistic drive for efficiency, but from the convergence of technical and cultural concerns with material and technique.

To apply this abstract emphasis on factors other than efficiency, we need to identify aspects of comb manufacture that might conceivably play host to technological variation. Such aspects include raw material use and treatment, production and finishing of blanks, assembly of components, application of ornament, cutting and shaping of teeth, finishing and polishing. By way of summary, fig. 12.2 enumerates some of the manufacturing sequence's possible loci of variation. In the following discussion the focus moves from the variability of the sequence of production to the individual stages in which we may be able to identify further potential technological choices. This is followed by a case study from northern and eastern England, in which analyses of several of these phenomena are undertaken, such that the expression of identity becomes visible at a range of scales.

Materials

The combmaker is presented with a number of options regarding raw material use. Combs may be fashioned from postcranial bone (typically bovid and equid ribs and metapodials, but other longbones may be used), antler (typically red deer, *Cervus elaphus*; reindeer, *Rangifer tarandus*; or elk, *Alces alces*), horn (although the scale of its use is difficult to assess given its perishability; Biddle 1990) and, rarely, ivory (Lasko 1956). A key concern for the combmaker must simply have been material availability. Investigations are ongoing, but based on macroscopic identifications of combs and waste, and initial proteomic analyses of a number of comb fragments, reindeer and elk antler do not seem to have been accessible to the combmaker working in England (Ashby 2006a; in press b; see Buckley *et al.* 2009 for the proteomic method involved).

The preference for antler over bone has a basis in their respective physical properties (MacGregor and Currey 1983), but this, in itself, does not explain its ubiquity in the Viking Age, as postcranial bone was commonly used in middle Anglo-Saxon combmaking (Riddler 1992, 149). Indeed, the development of Viking-Age towns would presumably have made postcranial bone (in the form of butchery waste) more easily accessible to the combmaker than was previously the case. The explanation may lie in the re-organisation of the craft of combmaking, and consequent changes in access to antler. However, given that postcranial bone represents a serviceable substitute, the phenomenon probably has a more complex, and possibly socially embedded, cause. In sum, it is safe to say that the combmaker's choice of raw materials, while fundamentally grounded in knowledge of their physical properties, was, nonetheless, influenced by social, economic, and logistical concerns.

Methods of raw material pre-treatment may also have been diverse (see MacGregor 1985, 63–5). It may have been considered important to work antler when fresh, when seasoned, or when soaked. Soaking may have involved a range of different chemical agents, including water, oil, sorrel, or wood ash (see Cnotliwy 1956, 152). Potential soaking pits are known from Grodzisk Mazowiecki (Poland) (Cnotliwy 1956, 153), and – perhaps – Naes (Denmark) (Hansen and Høier 2000; Christiansen 2006). Given the implications of the identification of any such features for the 'itinerancy' model (reliance on permanent soaking pits may be indicative of a sedentary mode of production), it is perhaps unsurprising that discussion has tended to focus on the 'need' (or otherwise) to soak antler prior to working it. There has been little consideration of the possibility of regional variability, or of the roles of tradition and inherited knowledge in this technological choice.

Form

Once materials have been acquired and treated as necessary, the combmaker then needs to decide which parts of an antler may be used for the various comb components. To a large degree this must have been dictated by dimensions, morphology and grain (see Smirnova 2005, 24), and the orthodoxy is that tines were used for the production of connecting plate blanks, while the beam was the source of toothplate billets (see Ambrosiani 1981, 103). In reality, however, decisions would have been governed by the combmaker's experience and knowledge of working with particular materials, as there are important differences in the gross morphology and internal macrostructure of red deer, reindeer and elk antler (see Ashby 2006a, 81–7; Ambrosiani 1981, 112), and the particular dimensions of a given beam will also have been significant. Moreover, at some point in the manufacturing process the combmaker must begin to envision the intended form of the comb. As overall aesthetics are dependent upon dimensions, profile and section, rather than the characteristics of individual components, we might argue that such a decision must have been made early in the production sequence, perhaps even at the outset. This may be so, but the form of the finished artefact is not a passive reflection of any such mental blueprint, but rather emerges through practice: a negotiation between the potentials of the material and the skills of the combmaker (see Ingold 2000, 406–19).

Ornament

The elements of ornament that are easily visible today (that is, the aesthetics of the decoration itself, rather than the process by which it was envisioned, marked out and inscribed) are best studied in stylistic terms (see Carr and Neitzel 1995 for a review). It is nonetheless appropriate to recount briefly some of the decorative choices available to a combmaker. Though in other contexts (notably in the medieval towns of Scandinavia, *e.g.* Wiberg 1987; Flodin 1989; Hansen 2005) ornament might incorporate a range of openwork designs, in Viking-Age England it was generally limited to the use of incised lines (including chevrons, lozenges, saltires, cross-hatch, and simple interlace) and ring-and-dot motifs. While the former were probably produced using saws, knives, or fine scribing implements, the latter must have been dependent on the use of either compasses, or some form of punch or drill (*e.g.* Galloway and Newcomer 1981, 83–4). It is likely that the application of incised interlace and complex, interwoven strings of ring-and-dot followed some form of initial 'marking out'. Moreover, even simpler forms of ornament are frequently arranged according to particular decorative schemes (see Ashby 2006a, 157–8) that may also have involved some form of 'roughing out', analogous to the pencil used by Galloway and Newcomer (1981, 83) in their experiments. Exactly how this was done doubtless varied in time and space, and is one element of the manufacturing process that remains lost to us.

Assembly

Beyond material concerns and the aesthetics of form and ornament, another potential area of variation is the detailed means by which a comb is produced. As we have seen, technological choices may include the sequence in which key tasks are undertaken, the choice of tools for a particular task, or the manner in which those tools are applied. These are all conditioned by the way in which the object and its production are conceived in the mind of the combmaker, which is in itself borne out of a combination of inherited knowledge and experience of working with particular tools and materials (see Van der Leeuw 1993; also Ingold 2000, 339–48).

Archaeologically visible indicators of these choices might include the presence and nature of marks created by tools, or the degree to which these traces and osteological structures are hidden by finishing and polishing. Furthermore, we might consider the ways in which the combmaker dealt with the mechanical and aesthetic issues of how best to assemble the various comb components. For example, a comb may be fixed together using rivets made of iron, copper alloy, or (less commonly) skeletal materials, and the rivets may pass through the centrepoint of each toothplate, through the edges between plates, between alternating edges, or may be positioned in a range of decorative arrangements (see Smirnova 2005, 37; Ashby 2006a) (fig. 12.4).

Variation in rivet technologies has both chronological and spatial dimensions, but when one focuses on the Viking Age, rivet arrangements

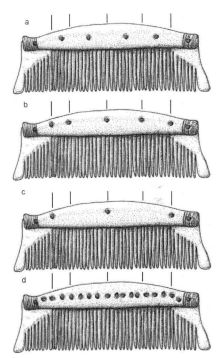

Fig. 12.4 Riveting methods (a) Central (b) Every Edge (c) Alternating Edge (d) Decorative (the author, after an original drawing by Pat Walsh, copyright Northamptonshire Archaeology).

in particular show useful patterning. On a European scale, tradition appears to have been discretely regionalised (Smirnova 2005, 29–38; Ashby 2006a, 163). For example, the 'central' and 'every edge' techniques common in Norway and Sweden are rare in England, as is the 'decorative' technique, which can be seen as a characteristic of late Viking-Age Scandinavia and areas within its cultural and economic milieu. In contrast, the 'alternating edge' technique is not well evidenced in northern Scandinavia, though it is present at Hedeby, where the range of practices evidenced is diverse (Tempel 1970).

Given this diversity, factors other than efficiency must be relevant. For individual combmakers the choice was probably unconscious; ethnographic studies of crafts have demonstrated that in such cases a given artisan might tell an outside observer that their method was the best – or only – way to accomplish the task. Thus, although it is clear that tools and materials offer a range of possible pathways down which one may proceed, to the combmaker there is in fact only one way to 'make a good comb'. The artisan learns their craft according to certain tenets, and – in the absence of external influence to do otherwise – continues to manufacture according to those tenets.

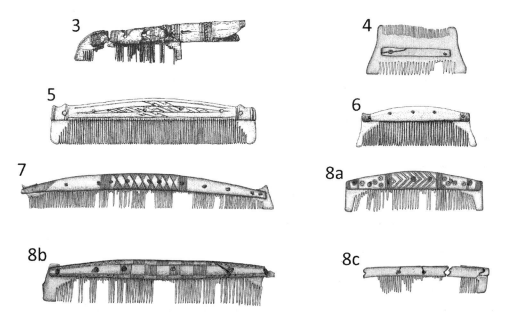

Fig. 12.5 Combs referred to in the text. Based on a typology developed in Ashby 2006a; see also Ashby 2011a (Types 4, 7, 8a, 8b and 8c drawn by Hayley Saul; Types 5 and 6 drawn by Pat Walsh, copyright Northamptonshire Archaeology; Type 3 drawn by Frances Chaloner, reproduced by permission of Julian D. Richards).

The technology of combmaking in Viking-Age England

Thus far, we have moved from the abstract to the generalised, and it remains to see how these concepts may be employed in the particular case of the Anglo-Scandinavian towns of York and Lincoln. Although their disparate sample sizes preclude detailed quantitative comparison, one may nonetheless note some general patterning in materials, morphology and manufacture. Antler largely dominates over bone among the combs of Viking-Age York and Lincoln, and in general there is no evidence of a relationship between material and morphology. All antler combs that could be identified to probable species were of red deer, hinting at a heavy local component to manufacture. Of course, there are exceptions, and Type 4 riveted mounts are generally made from postcranial bone (largely split ribs). Figure 12.3 shows the results of raw material analyses of combs from multiple sites in York and Lincoln (alongside comparative data from a sample of waste material from Coppergate, York). Notwithstanding the limitations of sample size, and the overall preference for antler, bone does seem to be more important at Lincoln than it does at York, particularly at Flaxengate, while waste deposits at the latter site are indicative of a preference for butchered over shed antler (see Mann 1982). That raw materials were less dominated by shed red deer antler than was the case at York might be indicative of a less structured supply network. Perring (1981, 42–3) has further argued that the small scale of manufacture at Flaxengate, coupled with the fact that waste was not consistently concentrated in particular buildings, is symptomatic of a cottage industry conducted from 'otherwise domestic buildings'. However, it should be noted that this antler-working is not easy to connect with

Type	Iron	Copper Alloy	Unknown N/A	Total
Type 3	15 (16)		(13)	15 (29)
Type 4	17 (10)		7 (26)	24 (36)
Type 5	2 (2)		(2)	2 (4)
Type 6	24 (18)	(1)*	1 (12)	25 (31)
Type 7	42 (22)		(7)	42 (29)
Type 8a	5 (8)		(5)	5 (13)
Type 8b	9 (8)		(3)	9 (11)
Type 8c	3 (2)	1		4 (2)
Type 9	3 (2)	1 (2)		4 (4)
Total	120 (88)	2 (3)	8 (68)	130 (159)

*Fig. 12.6 Variation in rivet materials according to type, in combs from northern England. Small and tiny fragments (i.e. those less than 50% complete) are shown in parentheses. *XRF analysis shows rivets to be composed of iron, and plated with copper alloy.*

combmaking, given that secure contexts have proven elusive (see Mann 1982, 1–2), and a number of other forms of objects were recovered unfinished (Perring 1981, 42–3). Neither in York can we show all bone and antler waste to relate to combmaking. If, however, one accepts MacGregor's (1985) argument that the Viking Age was characterised by specialisation in materials rather than products (so that it is more satisfactory to speak of an 'antler-worker' than a 'combmaker'), then it must follow that many waste deposits (particularly those with a high antler to bone ratio) relate, at least in part, to the manufacture of combs.

Turning now to the sphere of aesthetic choice, we need some form of typological framework within which to discuss morphological variation (see Ashby 2006a, 99–109; 2007). The detailed type profiles of the comb collections from York and Lincoln have been discussed elsewhere (Ashby 2006a; see also Ashby 2011a), and herein it is sufficient to provide a brief outline (fig. 12.5).

Meaningful comparison of the collections from York and Lincoln is confounded by differences in chronology, sample size, the nature of excavation, fragmentation and residuality, but it is clear that a diversity of types were in circulation at both Viking-Age York and Lincoln (see Ashby 2006a for a detailed treatment). There may be a chronological component to this variation, but once this is accounted for (see Ashby 2006a, 140–7) much may be explained in terms of particular comb forms having assigned and understood social and functional roles. Type 4 combs are certainly best understood as inexpensive alternatives to antler composite combs, while Types 5 and 6 articulate trends popular in Scandinavia and continental Europe. The associations of

Type	Alternating	Central	Decorative	Every Edge	Other	Mixed	Unknown/N/A	Total
3	7			2		1	6	16
4					22		4	26
5				1			1	2
6	10	3	1	5		3	3	25
7	37			3		2		42
8a	3			1			1	5
8b	4					2	3	9
8c	2			1		1		4
9	2		1	1				4
TOTAL	65	3	2	14	22	9	18	133

Fig. 12.7 Riveting techniques in combs from northeast England, including York and Lincoln. Only large fragments (i.e. those of which 50% or more remains) and complete combs are shown.

Type 3 are difficult to establish, but they clearly express some level of continuity from the pre-Viking period. Type 7 might similarly be seen in this light, but it also makes reference to Ireland (Dunlevy 1988) and southern Scandinavia (Tempel 1970). Though it is not clear that all of these forms were made on site, we must assume that many combs were native to the region. Thus, either there was a range of artisans each producing a discrete, limited repertoire of comb forms, or, and perhaps more probably, each combmaker produced combs according to a number of different templates, so that they were able to conduct transactions with consumers of differing aesthetic tastes. Such tastes may well have fed into cultural dialogues regarding identity, group membership and authority, but that is a discussion for elsewhere (see Ashby 2011b). Herein the key issue is that the combs were produced according to demand, and their overall form arguably tells us more about the consumer than it does the manufacturer.

The other component of aesthetic 'decision-making' relates to ornament. The York and Lincoln collections are characterised by myriad motifs, arrangements, and decorative schemes, and there is clearly a chronological component to the patterning (Ashby 2006a, 148–58). No discrete disparities between Lincoln and York were observed to overlie this temporal variation (see Ashby 2006a, tables 7.14 and 7.16). Instead, ornament seems to reflect the dominant aesthetics of the day, and the recognition of a more discrete application in the creation of identity remains elusive.

At the level of manufacturing technique, there is broad regional concordance in terms of rivet employment. Iron rivets were clearly the popular choice of fixing pin in the northern Danelaw, irrespective of time or context (fig. 12.6). The few exceptions, such as a Type 6 comb from York with copper-alloy-plated rivets (see MacGregor *et al.* 1999; Ashby 2006a, fig. 7.27, no. 1512), are best interpreted as displaced 'foreign' pieces, and do not detract from the overall regional homogeneity. Moreover, the 'alternating edge' style of rivet arrangement dominates at both York and Lincoln, and across northeast England more generally (fig. 12.6). The occasional deviant examples probably represent combs displaced by trade or travel, and it is interesting that such examples are largely restricted to combs of Types 6 and 8 (types frequently recovered outside of England; see Ambrosiani 1981; Dunlevy 1988). It is interesting to note that further south, the 'alternating edge' technique also seems to dominate at *Hamwic* (Southampton, Hampshire) and London, and it may be characteristic of England, or perhaps even the British Isles as a whole.

Discussion

I have shown elsewhere (Ashby 2006a; in press a) that there is considerable diversity of manufacturing practice across Europe, even in combs of broadly similar form and ornament. This has important implications for the nature of the trade. Although combmakers may have had contact with their counterparts in other regions, and combs themselves certainly became displaced through travel and trade, regional manufacturing traditions seem to have remained discrete. In particular, though there is little sign of local variability, York and Lincoln's combs are clearly different from those found in mainland Europe and Scandinavia (Ashby 2006a, 99–128; 2011a; *cf.* Ambrosiani 1981; Flodin 1989). Though no doubt inspired by the Norse Type 5 and 6 combs, materials and techniques of manufacture differed in important respects from those in Scandinavia.

My particular concern here has been the origin of this patterning in manufacturing tradition. If not aesthetics, what prompted the genesis of such 'invisible' differences in technique? I have argued that such technological choices may, although only implicit in the mind of the combmaker, have a sound basis in tradition, inherited knowledge, and experience, and are thus subject to regional or cultural norms. In this particular case, this similarity of practice is indicative of a shared technological tradition in northern and eastern England. Whether this extended further within the British Isles is unclear, but it is certainly consistent with the material seen by the author to date. Given the evidence for contact and familiarity with forms popular elsewhere in northern Europe, the evidence for a discrete 'school of manufacture' is of note; it is not stretching the evidence too far to speak of this as a mercantile identity. Whether explicit or implicit, technological choices were the shared inheritance of multiple generations of combmakers in the region, and these choices in many ways bound them together as a reference community. That community was characterised by – indeed defined by – commonality of practice, shared perspectives on material and method, and the promotion and perpetuation of mutually understood norms through apprenticeship and experience. The possible existence of a community of itinerant craftworkers and traders operating widely throughout the 'nodal towns' of the Baltic region (Sindbaek 2007a; 2007b) does little to diminish the significance of the English tradition with which it was counterpointed. The presence of some combs made to the 'English' format at trading settlements such as Hedeby (see Tempel 1970) may relate to trade, travel, or the presence of English combmakers in the region, but the paucity of combs of this form in towns further north suggests that their influence did not successfully permeate into the system.

The approach outlined herein has much potential to elucidate social aspects of early medieval craft and industry beyond the world of the combmaker. Whether we are concerned with ceramics or irons, textiles or sculpture, we need to question the assumption of efficiency-led production, and think more carefully about the processes by which technology is created, learned, and manipulated. Such an approach, which pays sufficient attention to the social elements of craft, is the only way by which we can hope to understand why the comb Thorfastr made was good.

Bibliography

Ambrosiani, K. (1981) *Viking Age Combs, Comb Making and Combmakers in the Light of Finds from Birka and Ribe*. Stockholm Studies in Archaeology 2. Stockholm, University of Stockholm.

Ashby, S. P. (2006a) *Time, Trade and Identity: bone and antler combs in northern Britain* c. *AD 700-1400*. Unpublished PhD thesis, University of York.

Ashby, S. P. (2006b) Trade in Viking-Age Britain: identity and the production and distribution of bone and antler combs. In J. Arneborg and B. Grønnow (eds) *Dynamics of Northern Societies: proceedings of the SILA/NABO conference on Arctic and North Atlantic archaeology, Copenhagen, May 10th–14th, 2004*, 273–9. Studies in Archaeology and History 10. Copenhagen, Publications from the National Museum.

Ashby, S. P. (2007) *Bone and Antler Combs*. Finds Research Group Datasheet 40.

Ashby, S. P. (2011a) An atlas of medieval combs from northern Europe. *Internet Archaeology* 30 (3).

Ashby, S. P. (2011b) The language of the combmaker. A study of craft and technology in early medieval England. In J. Baron and B. Kufel-Diakowska (eds) *Written in Bones: studies on technological and social contexts of past faunal skeletal remains*, 9–24. Wrocław, Institute of Archaeology, University of Wrocław.

Ashby, S. P. (in press a) Disentangling trade: combs in the North and Irish Seas in the long Viking Age. In J. H. Barrett and S.-J. Gibbon (eds) *Maritime Societies of the Viking and Medieval World*. London, Maney.

Ashby, S. P. (in press b) A study in regionality: hair combs and bone/antler craft in the Northern Danelaw. In D. Petts and S. Turner (eds) *Early Medieval Northumbria*. Turnhout, Brepols.

Barnes, M. P. and Page, R. I. (2006) *The Scandinavian Runic Inscriptions of Britain*. Runrön 19. Uppsala, Institutionen för nordiska språk.

Biddle, M. (1990) Toilet equipment: combs of horn and bone. In M. Biddle (ed.) *Object and Economy in Medieval Winchester*, 678–90. Winchester Studies 7 (2). Oxford, Clarendon Press.

Blinkhorn, P. (1997) Habitus, social identity and Anglo-Saxon pottery. In C. G. Cumberpatch and P. Blinkhorn (eds) *Not So Much A Pot, More A Way of Life: current approaches to artefact analysis in archaeology*, 113–24. Oxford, Oxbow.

British Museum (1923) *A Guide to the Anglo-Saxon and Foreign Teutonic Antiquities*. London, British Museum.

Buckley, M., Collins, M., Thomas-Oates, J. and Wilson, J. C. (2009) Species identification by analysis of bone collagen using matrix-assisted laser desorption/ionisation time-of-flight mass spectrometry. *Rapid Communications in Mass Spectrometry* 23, 3843–54.

Callmer, J. (2002) North-European trading centres and the early medieval craftsman: craftsmen at Åhus, north-eastern Scania, Sweden ca AD 750–850. In B. Hårdh and L. Larsson (eds) *Central Places in the Migration and the Merovingian Periods: papers from the 52nd Sachsensymposium, August 2001*, 125–57. Uppåkrastudier 6. Lund, Almquiest & Wiksell Intl.

Carr, C. and Neitzel, J. E. (eds) (1995) *Style, Society, and Person: archaeological and ethnological perspectives*. New York, Plenum Press.

Christiansen, D. V. (2006) Naes – a late Iron Age and Viking Age coastal settlement. In K. M. Hansen and K. B. Pedersen (eds) *Across the Western Baltic*, 257–66. Vordingborg, Sydsjællands Museum.

Christophersen, A. (1980a) *Håndverket i Forandring: studier i horn- og beinhåndverkets utvikling i Lund* ca *1000–1350*. Acta Archaeologica Lundensia 4 (13). Lund, CWP Gleerup.

Christophersen, A. (1980b) Raw material, resources and production capacity in early medieval comb manufacture in Lund. *Meddelanden Fran Lunds Universitets Historiska Museum* (NYA SE Part), 150–65.

Cnotliwy, E. (1956) Z badan nad rzemioslem zajmujacym sie obróbka rogi i kosci na Pomorzu Zachonim we wczesnym sredniowieczu. *Materialy Zachodnio-Pomorskie* 2, 151–79.

Cnotliwy, E. (1973) *Rzemiosło Rogownicze na Pomorzu Sczesno redniowiecznym.* Wroclaw, Polska Akademia Nauk Instytut Historii Kultury Materialnej.

Cumberpatch, C. G. and Blinkhorn, P. (eds) (1997) *Not So Much A Pot, More A Way of Life: current approaches to artefact analysis in archaeology.* Oxford, Oxbow.

Dunlevy, M. M. (1988) A classification of early Irish combs. *Proceedings of the Royal Irish Academy* 88 (C11), 341–422.

Edmonds, M. (1999) *Ancestral Geographies of the Neolithic. Landscapes, monuments and memory.* London, Routledge.

Flodin, L. (1989) *Kammakeriet i Trondheim ca 1000–1600.* Trondheim, Riksantikvaren.

Galloway, P. and Newcomer, M. (1981) The craft of comb-making: an experimental enquiry. *University of London Institute of Archaeology Bulletin* 18, 73–90.

Hansen, G. (2005) *Bergen c. 800–1170: the emergence of a town.* The Bryggen Papers, Main Series No. 6. Bergen, Fagbokforlaget.

Hansen, K. M. and Høier, H. (2000) Naes – en vikingetidsbebyggelses med hørproduktion. *Kuml. Årbog for Jrsk Arkaeologisk Selskab* 2000, 59–89.

Hilczerowna, Z. (1961) *Rogonictwo Gdanskie w X–XIV Wicku.* Gdansk, Gdanskie Towarzystwo Naukowe.

Ingold, T. (1993) The Reindeerman's Lasso. In P. Lemonnier (ed.) *Technological Choices: transformation in material cultures since the Neolithic,* 108–25. London, Routledge.

Ingold, T. (2000) *The Perception of the Environment.* London, Routledge.

Lasko, P. (1956) The comb of St Cuthbert. In C. F. Battiscombe (ed.) *The Relics of Saint Cuthbert,* 336–55. Oxford, Oxford University Press.

Lemonnier, P. (ed.) (1993a) *Technological Choices: transformation in material cultures since the Neolithic.* London, Routledge.

Lemonnier, P. (1993b) Introduction. In P. Lemonnier (ed.) *Technological Choices: transformation in material cultures since the Neolithic,* 1–35. London, Routledge.

MacGregor, A. (1985) *Bone, Antler, Ivory and Horn: the technology of skeletal materials since the Roman period.* London, Croom Helm.

MacGregor, A. and Currey, J. D. (1983) Mechanical properties as conditioning factors in the bone and antler industry of the 3rd to the 13th century AD. *Journal of Archaeological Science* 10, 71–7.

MacGregor, A., Mainman, A. J. and Rogers, N. S. H. (1999) *Craft, Industry and Everyday Life: bone, antler, ivory and horn from Anglo-Scandinavian and medieval York.* The Archaeology of York 17 (2). York, Council for British Archaeology.

Mainman, A. J. and Rogers, N. S. H. (1999) Craft and industry: the range of the evidence. In A. MacGregor, A. J. Mainman and N. S. H. Rogers (eds) *Craft, Industry and Everyday Life: bone, antler, ivory and horn from Anglo-Scandinavian and medieval York,* 1903–16. The Archaeology of York 17 (2). York, Council for British Archaeology.

Mann, J. E. (1982) *Early Medieval Finds from Flaxengate, 1: objects of antler, bone, stone, horn, ivory, amber, and jet.* Archaeology of Lincoln 14 (1). London, Council for British Archaeology.

Nicholson, A. (1997) The antler. In P. Hill (ed.) *Whithorn and St Ninian: the excavation of a monastic town, 1984–91,* 474–95. Stroud, Sutton.

Perring, D. (1981) *Early Medieval Occupation at Flaxengate, Lincoln.* Archaeology of Lincoln 9 (1). London, Council for British Archaeology.

Richards, J. D. (1987) *The Significance of Form and Function of Anglo-Saxon Cremation Urns.* British Archaeological Reports British Series 166. Oxford, British Archaeological Reports.

Riddler, I. (1992) Bone-working and the pre-Viking trading centres. In R. A. Hall, R. Hodges and H. Clarke (eds) *Medieval Europe 1992, Pre-printed Papers 7: art and symbolism,* 149–56. York, Medieval Europe 1992.

Sindbaek, S. M. (2007a) Networks and nodal points: the emergence of towns in early Viking Age Scandinavia. *Antiquity* 81, 119–32.

Sindbaek, S. M. (2007b) The small world of the Vikings: networks in early medieval communication and exchange. *Norwegian Archaeological Review* 40 (1), 59–74.

Sindbaek, S. M. (2008) Routes and long-distance traffic: the nodal points of Wulfstan's voyage. In A. Englert and A. Trakadas (eds) *Wulfstan's Voyage: the Baltic Sea region in the Early Viking Age as seen from shipboard*, 72–8. Roskilde, Viking Ship Museum.

Smirnova, L. (2005) *Comb-Making in Medieval Novgorod (950–1450): an industry in transition*. British Archaeological Reports International Series 1369. Oxford, Archaeopress.

Tempel, W.-D. (1970) Die Kämme aus Haithabu (Ausgrabungen 1963–64). *Berichte über die Ausgrabungen in Haithabu* 4, 34–45.

Tesch, S. (1987). *Kyrkolunden: en historisk och arkeologisk tillbakablick*. Märsta, Sigtunahem.

Ulbricht, I. (1978) *Die Geweihverarbeitung in Haithabu*. Die Ausgrabungen in Haithabu 7. Neumünster, Wachholtz Verlag.

Van der Leeuw, S. (1993) Giving the potter a choice: conceptual aspects of pottery techniques. In P. Lemonnier (ed.) *Technological Choices: transformation in material cultures since the Neolithic*, 238–88. London, Routledge.

Weissner, P. (1983) Style and information in Kalahari San projectile points. *American Antiquity* 48 (2), 253–76.

Wiberg, T. (1987) Kammer. In E. Schia (ed.) *De Arkeologiske utgravninger i Gamlebyen, Oslo*, 202–8. Bind 3. Oslo, Alvheim and Eide.

CRAFT AND HANDIWORK:
WOOD, ANTLER AND BONE AS AN
EVERYDAY MATERIAL IN VIKING-AGE
WATERFORD AND CORK

Maurice F. Hurley

This chapter discusses the role of craft working in late Viking-Age towns, drawing on evidence from a wide range of raw materials that are represented in the archaeological record. During the 10th to 12th centuries, the Viking towns were clearly the product of the Viking Age and are not conceivable without interaction with the native population. This 'marked fusion' (Simms 1990, 41) is defined by the term Hiberno-Norse and the term is used in this paper when referring to the late Viking Age (*c.* 1014–1170) in Ireland. In the Hiberno-Norse towns some crafts were important and constant, some flourished briefly only to fade into obscurity, while others were always marginal. The working of two raw materials will be taken to illustrate the various aspects of craft in the Irish towns; namely wood and bone/antler. Despite the limited archaeological evidence for interactions of towns with their hinterlands and irrespective of political allegiance and ethnicity, the towns cannot have existed in isolation. Craft knowledge, skills and information on new technologies must have easily transcended political and ethnic boundaries, and these form the focus of this chapter.

As it is only possible to compare like with like, the challenge of placing the evidence in a broad context drawing general conclusions is considerable. The variability of preservation even within one town can skew the picture and make comparative analysis pointless. Comparisons between towns, where all the variables are not considered, is even more risky and comparing the material from deep, sealed and anaerobic urban layers with finds from dry rural sites is pointless. For example, preservation conditions in Waterford varied widely depending on the underlying geology; in areas of gravel substrata, preservation of organic material was poor while in adjoining areas overlying clays preservation was excellent. Variable rates of deposition seem also to have had an effect on preservation, while other post-depositional factors, such as the insertion of stone-filled foundation trenches and drains, had the effect of aerating and dewatering the ground. In Waterford, preservation conditions are at an optimum for the late 11th to mid-13th centuries, while in Cork preservation is better for the mid-12th to late 13th centuries.

Despite methodological difficulties, the study of organic materials provides important new insights into the relationship between towns and their rural hinterlands, which has been the focus of debate over many years (Bradley 1988; 2009; Clinton 2000; Geraghty 1996; Sawyer

1970, 90; Simms and Fagan 1992; Valante 2008), in particular regarding sourcing of wood as a raw material (Hurley 1997a, 42–3; O' Sullivan 2000, 77–85; Tierney 1998). Perceptions of the distinctiveness of Hiberno-Norse towns are influenced not only by environmentally determined factors that create good conditions for the preservation of organic materials in many towns, but also by historical evidence for the political and ethnic distinctiveness of Irish urban populations. Irish towns emerged in the context of Scandinavian influences and most of today's Irish port cities and towns – namely Dublin, Waterford, Cork and Limerick – developed in a Hiberno-Norse milieu (Wallace 1992). Moreover, contemporary native Irish texts such as the *Annals of the Four Masters* (O'Donovan 1851) and *Cogadh Gaedhel re Gallaibh* (Todd 1867) referred to the residents of the towns as 'foreigners' (Lucas 1966). When the Anglo-Normans invaded Ireland in 1170, the towns, which had already emerged as regional administrative foci, served as fortified bridgeheads and ideal command centres for colonial development (Bradley and Halpin 1992; 1993). Yet, while Hiberno-Norse towns evidently fostered trade and commerce and served as conduits for foreign commodities and new ideas (Hurley 2006), they cannot be viewed in isolation from the rural hinterland from whence their raw materials were obtained (Bradley 1988). Indeed, the raw materials of rural Ireland formed the main export items of medieval Irish ports to Britain and the port towns of northwest France and the Low Countries (O'Sullivan 1937; Hurley 1999), and were essential for the sustenance of urban populations.

Craft and handiwork in Hiberno-Norse Ireland

On seeing the range of superior quality artefacts discovered in Viking-Age and Hiberno-Norse towns, it is tempting to view the towns as veritable craft and trade emporia, the implication being that all the residents were exclusively craftsmen. It is argued here that many people, while primarily merchants, warriors or food producers, possessed a range of skills and that the division of labour, as we understand it today, was not a significant feature of daily life.

The term 'craft' implies an occupation or trade requiring a special skill, with all those specialists in the trade regarded as craftsmen and collectively referred to by reference to the main product output, such as potters, coopers, smiths and weavers. Handiwork, however, is taken to mean the production of items on ad-hoc bases (for personal use) as the need arises. In high medieval urban society, crafts were undoubtedly the preserve of professionals who worked in their individual trade to the exclusion of others. By contrast, small artefacts made from wood and bone were, in many instances, one-off items produced by people for their own needs. The line between craft and handiwork is somewhat blurred, however, when production of the items in question evidently required a high level of skill and precision or the possession of specialised tools, in which case it is defined as craft. By contrast, large numbers of mundane objects, where the raw material required only limited modification, cannot in themselves be taken as evidence for craftsmanship or specialisation. For example, not all staves can be confidently attributed to professional coopers. Indeed, even in the 19th century, long after the moment when coopering became an organised craft servicing the brewing, distilling and food provisioning industries, rough (or 'white') coopering was still practised by men outside the regulated craft/industry to service the needs of farmers (Coleman 1944, 83). Thus, solely from an archaeological perspective, looking at a limited sample of artefacts, the differences between one stave and another may be merely one of degree in skill and specialisation and the full implications of the craft or non-craft means by which each was produced are not appreciated.

The identification of the level of specialisation for the production of particular artefacts rests on a number of criteria. Obviously, the complexity of the process, the possession or use of specialised tools and access to rare or highly valued raw materials are significant factors in identifying craft specialisation. Similarly, in distinguishing locally produced items from imports, we tend to assume that it does not make sense to import objects that could be made from locally available raw materials. However, this assumption pre-supposes the existence of sufficient demand for the product to sustain a craftsman as well as availability of the requisite skill and technology. Ceramics are a case in point in medieval Ireland of the fallacy of this presupposition. Although the technology and raw materials were available, glazed ceramics were not produced in Ireland until the later 12th century. Prior to this, glazed wares were imported from Britain and France for over 100 years and are common finds in all Irish port towns. Long after local ceramic centres were established in the 13th century, imported pottery continued to dominate the assemblages of Cork and Waterford (Gahan and McCutcheon 1997; Gahan *et al.* 1997; Hurley 1989, 35–45; McCutcheon 1995; 1997; 2003) but to a far lesser degree in medieval Dublin (McCutcheon 2006).

In any evaluation of the place of craft in late Hiberno-Norse towns, it is necessary to outline the current state of archaeological evidence. As stated in the introduction to this chapter, environmental conditions are of singular importance. The preservation of organic material in many Irish cities is very good. The evidence from Dublin is particularly spectacular. Anaerobic conditions occurred throughout much of the Viking Age and medieval levels and extensive excavations have taken place over many years (Simpson 2000; Wallace and Ó Floinn 1988). Anaerobic conditions also prevail throughout most of the low-lying island city of Cork and in parts of Waterford. With the exception of crannogs (lake dwellings) and bogs, these conditions rarely exist outside the cities. Consequently, it is difficult to undertake worthwhile comparative studies between the cities and their rural hinterlands. While we may assume that organic raw materials were utilised at all periods and in all environments, wood-, bone- and leather-working and textile production are generally not discussed by archaeologists when these materials are not represented in the excavated assemblages. Arising from the limitations of survival, it may appear that the craft skills of medieval rural Ireland were limited and impoverished by comparison with those of the flourishing towns, where bewilderingly rich assemblages of artefacts in every available raw material and diversity of form are represented. As the raw materials were only obtainable from rural environments and the towns must have consumed large quantities of these, a complex relationship between town and country must have prevailed. The following sections discuss the evidence of wood and bone/antler to illustrate these links.

Wood as a raw material

Wood was the most commonly used raw material in Hiberno-Norse Waterford and Cork. It was, in many forms, used extensively as a building material and the majority of household furnishings and many utensils were made of wood. Wood was also used in combination with other materials; for example, most iron implements and tools had wooden handles. The earliest wooden artefacts from Waterford date to the mid-11th century, but the majority in both Waterford (Hurley and McCutcheon 1997, 553–633) and Cork (Hurley 1997b; 2003) were found in 12th-century contexts. It is important to stress that the distribution of wooden objects is not indicative of a preference for wood by certain citizens, classes or even in certain periods, but merely reflects environmental conditions, which enabled the survival of organic material.

Some of the wooden artefacts are single surviving examples of a type of object, but where multiple examples of one category survive over a broad date range, often very little change in form or working technique is apparent. The most noteworthy example of change in form is perhaps reflected in the occurrence of carved cylindrical churns in the late 11th to mid-12th century (fig. 13.1), which was replaced by a predominance of stave built vessels in the later 12th century, a technique which continued throughout the medieval period and beyond.

Almost all of the wood used for artefacts and structural purposes in Cork and Waterford was of native origin and was likely to have been locally felled. At least sixteen native species are represented in the Waterford assemblage (Hurley and McCutcheon 1997, 554–6) and seven in Cork (Hurley 1997b, 275–8), and included yew, oak, ash, alder, hazel, birch and hawthorn. The only possible imported species represented in the archaeological record are Scots pine, boxwood and cork. The Scots pine found in 11th-century Waterford may be from the remnants of native woodland, but it may equally be derived from re-used ships timbers of Scandinavian origin. Similarly, the boxwood may be from Irish grown introduced species, but is more likely to represent a foreign import, as boxwood combs are known to have been widely sought and imported over long distances along the River Volga trade routes from the Black Sea Coast of the Caucasus (Kolchin 1989, 139). The cork represented as net floats was almost certainly imported to Cork and Waterford from Iberia (Hurley 1997b, 278). While imported wood may have been acquired for highly specialised purposes and items, the woodworkers chose native species for most objects on the basis of suitability for technique of manufacture and intended use. It is apparent from the consistent preferences for particular types of wood that the woodworkers, and perhaps the majority of the population, were familiar with the properties that characterise the native varieties of wood. Softer woods, such as ash and alder, were preferred for bowls, which were lathe turned. Alder was frequently used for dowels because it was easily carved yet tough and water resistant. Alder also seems to have been preferred for vessels of high quality, and significantly all the Waterford mazers[1] (fig. 13.2) were turned in this wood.

The harder woods, such as oak and yew, were rarely used for turning, but yew was used for the vast majority of carved utilitarian objects, which needed to be strong and durable. Yew was preferred because it has greater elasticity and strength than any other timber grown in the Irish climate. Items made from yew rarely warp or crack and because of these qualities it was evidently chosen for archers' bows (fig. 13.3) as well as other items requiring precision. Similarly, spoons, handles, tuning pegs, pins, spindles, net-braiding needles and gaming pieces, all of which were in regular use and subject to shock or pressure, were predominantly made of yew. It is possible, however, that yew is disproportionately represented in the assemblages, as it is more likely to survive in conditions where preservation qualities in the ground are marginal, resulting in the decay of softer woods. Oak was used for many of the larger wooden objects such as shovels, rakes, shingles, roof finials and furniture (Hurley 1997b; Hurley and McCutcheon 1997), and it predominated amongst the timbers used for structural purposes (Hurley 1997a) due to its unique properties of great strength and durability.

Large carved vessels, such as cylindrical churns and troughs, were made from ash and alder (fig. 13.1). These woods were easily carved and less liable than oak or yew to split when cut into thin-walled cylinders. Smaller stave-built vessels generally had yew side-staves but some were of oak, and the majority of vessel heads and bases were of oak. Most of the staves from the larger tubs and casks were made of oak. The hoops generally consisted of split yew branches with the bark pared off, yew evidently being the preferred material because of the flexibility

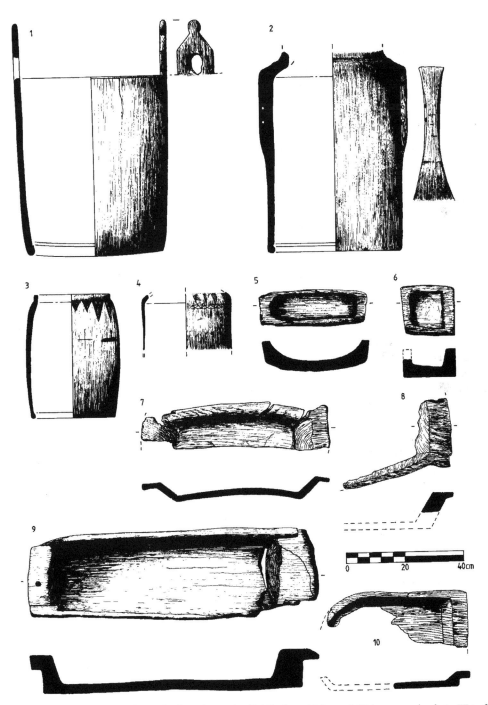

Fig. 13.1 Examples of churns (1-4) and troughs (5-10) from 11th- and 12th-century levels in Waterford (source: Hurley et al. 1997).

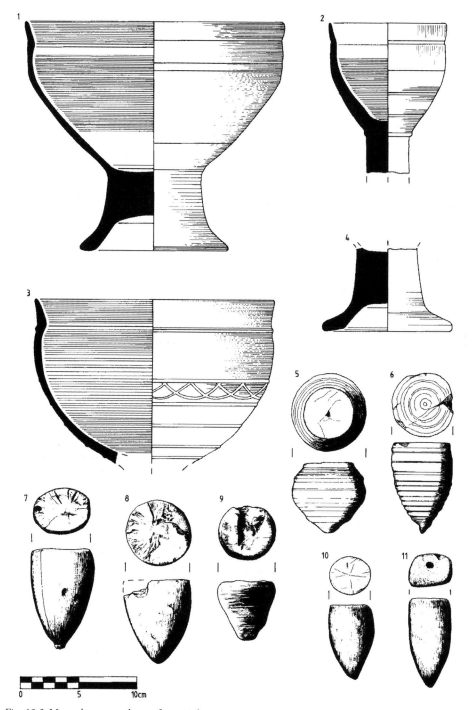

Fig. 13.2 Mazer hanaps and cores from 12th-century contexts in Waterford (source: Hurley et al. *1997).*

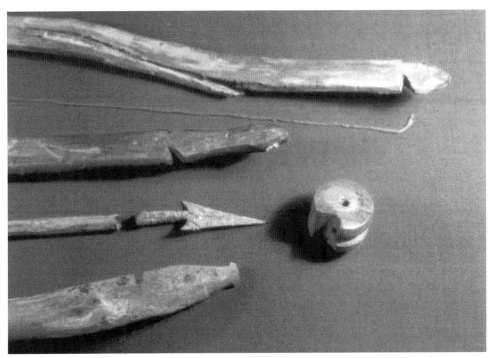

Fig. 13.3 Archery material from Waterford: ends of three wooden bow-staves (12th century), silk cord (possibly a bow-string), bone crossbow-nut (early to mid-13th century), arrowhead and shaft (mid-12th century) (photograph Waterford City Council).

and elasticity of the wood. In the late 12th century, withies of hazel, wrapped by willow twigs or bark, were used to bind the staves. Yew rods were used as hoops from the 13th century for churns and large casks, until iron bands replaced these in the post-medieval period.

Urban craft or rural handiwork?

A substantial body of research exists concerning the raw materials from which wooden artefacts were made (Kelly 1976), but it is less certain where the wooden artefacts were produced. Was the wood brought as un-worked logs into the towns, where resident specialised craftsmen manufactured artefacts, or did country people trade their craftwork with the town-folk in exchange for exotic imports? There is no definitive answer, but a combination of both processes seems likely. There is no means of quantifying the amount of rural produce traded as raw material or finished product, but we do know for certain that wood was worked in both Cork and Waterford, as a large quantity of woodworking waste, including many cores from turned bowls, was recovered. Many of the 12th- and 13th-century urban strata are largely comprised of woodchip. At Christ Church, Cork, for example, a 'reddish brown layer' of woodchips, almost one metre deep, covered much of the site (Cleary 1997, 32) and in the Arundel Square/Peter Street area of Waterford, woodchip and shavings, as well as tree bark and twigs, were the predominant components of organic layers (Hurley 1997a, 556).

Several forms of artefact were widespread throughout the medieval world of northwest Europe, especially in the port towns; notwithstanding, strong native traditions are visible in the range of artefacts in 11th- and 12th-century Irish towns. For example, there are numerous parallels between items found in Cork and Waterford and those from contemporary levels of the crannogs in Gaelic-dominated rural Ireland (Johnson 1999). Native elements are also strong in the styles of decoration on wooden artefacts from Waterford (Lang 1997, 634–6). It could, therefore, be argued that locally based craftsmen, working with native materials, were in regular contact with all areas with which Cork and Waterford had trading connections, that is, with the hinterland and other seaport towns in Ireland, Britain and the western European seaboard. It is likely that new ideas or examples were brought to Ireland from abroad and used (as prototypes, as it were) to inform Hiberno-Norse craftsmen who then undertook large scale production of the items applying native stylistic elements. There was evidently no need to continue to import items from abroad when these could be made in Ireland from locally obtained raw materials.

Woodworking techniques

A number of techniques are apparent within woodworking. These include turning, coopering, basket making and carving. Of these crafts, as we shall see, it is likely that turning and coopering were specialised, while basketry and carving may be largely domestic activities. A discussion of each of these techniques follows.

Wood turning

Wooden vessels were certainly turned within the walls of the towns, as evidenced by the discovery of 38 cores during the Waterford City Centre excavations (Hurley and McCutcheon 1997, 573–5). It seems likely that in the 12th century, each household had more wooden vessels than ceramic ones, and there must have been considerable demand for these items. Despite the ubiquity of turned wooden objects, no definitive evidence for a 'wood-turner's house' has been identified in either Waterford or Cork. Of the fourteen plots excavated at Peter Street in Waterford, containing evidence for *c.* 90 houses of 11th- and 12th-century date (Hurley *et al.* 1997, 34–165), not one house plot or area produced unequivocal proof of a long-term resident wood-turner. Some evidence for woodturning was certainly represented in every house plot where organic materials were well preserved, but the concentrations of wooden items were merely reflective of preservation conditions. A similar situation holds true for Cork (Hurley 1997b, 278–81). Wooden bowls were predominantly recovered from cesspits, while cores were neither found in significant concentrations, nor in association with more significant concentrations of wood shavings than found elsewhere on the site (Cleary 1997, 32), nor were they found in association with finished or unfinished wooden vessels. The greatest concentration of wood working waste found in Waterford was in mid-12th-century extra-mural dumps making up the backfill of the 11th-century defensive ditch at Bakehouse Lane (Hurley and McCutcheon 1997, 574–6), where several cores were found in association with waste from other crafts such as leather working, coopering and bone and antler working.

The possibility arises that some itinerant craftsmen served the needs of a few large ports and the markets in several smaller towns. By analogy with modern usage, in the early part of the 20th century, the owner of the Borrisokane (Co. Tipperary) pole-lathe 'not only supplied local needs and did business at fairs, but also did a considerable trade with wholesale firms in Dublin, Cork and Galway' (Ó Ríordáin 1940, 30). The reciprocating pole-lathe, which is very different from the modern rotary lathe, is believed to have been used from the late Iron Age (Ó Ríordáin 1940, 30; Earwood 1993, 184–95) to modern times and was a portable item. Ó Ríordáin (1940, 30) states that

> In essentials it consists merely of a wooden bench with adjustable head-stocks. The place of the pole may be taken by a living branch of a tree and this was frequently done by the Welsh turners who were thus able to work in the open, at fairs and elsewhere, and so to produce goods to the order of the costumers on the spot.

An early 19th-century account describes turners basing their activities in the wood: '[they] generally build a hut in the wood that is being cut and reside there while the timber is felling, buying and working those kind of trees most suited to their purpose and paying for them as the manufactured goods are sold' (Thompson 1802, 253). Wood turning seems to have always remained a 'folk craft' and the wood turners never formed guilds. This may be largely due to the decline in demand for wooden table vessels in urban areas in the late medieval period at a time when many other craftsmen were forming guilds. Nonetheless, the craft continued to flourish in rural Ireland (Ó Ríordáin 1940).

To summarise, wood turners were certainly working in 11th- and 12th-century Waterford and Cork, but uncertainty remains regarding the scale of the craft and its organisation. Wood turning may never have become established as a sustainable craft with permanent full time resident craftsmen and some of the production may have taken place in woods outside the towns. The scale of the craft was such, however, as to allow for its survival, but the standard of craftsmanship that produced the 12th-century Waterford mazers (Hurley and McCutcheon 1997, 564–72) 'with their carefully controlled [design] matching the high standard of workmanship' (Lang 1997, 635) is unparalleled in the wooden bowls of later date. The two mazer fragments from Cork (Hurley 1997b, 295–9; Hurley and Price in prep.) are of a lesser quality, but large numbers of finely turned bowls and platters continued to be produced in both town throughout the 13th century.

Coopering

The practice of coopering to produce vessels involved the use of multiple jointed staves bound with hoops and fitted with a base, which was either a single disc or multiple (end) staves. Coopering was well established in Ireland by the early Christian period, as evidenced by the 9th-century stave built vessels from Lissue Rath (Co. Antrim) (Bersu 1947, 154). However, in Waterford, very few staves were recovered from 11th-century contexts, although the numbers increased dramatically from the mid-12th century onwards. In Cork, the earliest staves are similarly from the mid to late 12th century (Hurley 2003), becoming more numerous in the 13th century. There appears to have been a preference for carved rather than coopered vessels in the late 11th and early 12th centuries. Several carved cylindrical churns and troughs were found in Waterford (fig. 13.1), and comparable items have recently been found in 12th-century Cork (Hurley and Price in prep.). Nonetheless, stave-built and carved vessels have been found in association elsewhere in Ireland, for example in 10th-century levels at Ballinderry Crannog No. 1 (Co. Westmeath) (Hencken 1936, 134–65), and in 7th-century contexts at Deer Park Farms (Co. Antrim) (Earwood 1993, 272).

Parts of a carved vessel were recovered from an early 12th-century context at South Main Street, Cork (Hurley and Price in prep.). Only part of the rim and shoulder survive, with three additional fragments that appear to come from the walls of the vessel. From these limited remains, it is apparent that the body of the vessel was carved from a single piece of wood and – with the exception of the insertion of the base – there would have been no composite element in the construction. The slope of the shoulder is indicative of a churn-type vessel and this form is further enhanced by the lid seating; in other words, the lid would have fitted inside the rim and rested on an internal protruding ridge. As the mouth was considerably narrower than the straight-sided body of the cylinder, the base must have been pressed into a shallow groove on the inner wall of the cylinder. The vessel is carved from alder wood, which was comparatively soft and easily carved or gauged out. The use of alder contrasts with the use of oak or yew for composite stave building. The vessel was cut from a tree trunk using a laborious technique that required a considerable expenditure of time but a lower standard of skill than cooperage (Earwood 1993, 234–45). Hencken (1936, 218) wrote of similar vessels of late 10th-century date from Ballinderry Crannog No.1, and made the following observations:

> In every case these vessels have been hollowed out of a large log, and a groove has been cut inside near the base of the resulting cylinder to hold the solid wooden disc that forms the bottom. The cylinder must then have been steamed or otherwise softened and the bottom pressed into place from underneath. In hardly any case would it have been possible to have inserted the base from the top.

The churn or keg from Cork is of a type of vessel that has not been found in urban contexts post-dating the late 12th century. It is closely paralleled by three vessels from Waterford (fig. 13.1), which were recovered from contexts dating from the late 11th to the mid-12th century. One was used as a cistern in the floor of a late 11th- to early 12th-century sunken featured structure or cellared building. It is likely that these vessels were superseded by stave-building in urban contexts, while the archaic technique persisted in some parts of rural Ireland until the 17th century, when it had become virtually obsolete in the rest of Europe (Earwood 1993, 237). The churn fragments from Cork have traces of decoration on the cylinder walls and possibly the shoulder of the vessel, while the decoration on the Waterford vessels generally occurred on the shoulder (Hurley and McCutcheon 1997, 616–18). The decoration is of type that has been described as 'rustic or even primitive ornamentation' (Lang 1997, 634). The motif consists of vertical and horizontal lightly incised lines with panels of pendant, chevrons or 'vandykes'. The motifs belong to 'the Insular repertoire of ornament ... [and] such motifs are long-lived in Ireland' (Lang 1997, 635).

A wide variety of vessels of different sizes were coopered. Coopering was a highly skilled craft, and was still widely practised until the early 20th century (Coleman 1944, 79–88), by which time coopers, unlike wood turners, had unions and guilds (Caulfield 1876, 289). The status to which coopering rose in the post-medieval/early modern period, by comparison with other wood crafts, was no doubt due to the significant use of casks for beer, spirits and salted meats, as well as for the trade and export of provisions such as butter, meat and fish; exports of all of these were particularly significant in Cork City (O'Sullivan 1937). While the coopering of casks was highly skilled, and was generally a practice based in towns, a cruder form called 'white coopering' (Coleman 1944, 82) was practised by semi-skilled men who were not regarded as craftsmen. Their products were usually straight-staved, without the barrel bulge characteristic of casks, and included wash-tubs, drip-tubs and coal-buckets. For farm use, churns, noggins, butter tubs and cream butts were also produced (Coleman 1944, 82). Presumably, similar types of stave vessels were made in towns during the Hiberno-Norse period, when urban economies were largely based on the handling of agricultural produce. In addition, stave built vessels were probably used domestically for jugs or other table vessels. It is likely, therefore, that in the 11th and 12th centuries the status of coopers was very similar to wood turners. Coopers may have done other carpentry, but they were certainly highly skilled and full-time wood workers.

Basketry
It is less certain that basketry was recognised as an established craft in Hiberno-Norse Waterford and Cork, although the relatively small number of finds makes it harder to assess the quality of the baskets that were used in these towns. A well-preserved basket of late 12th-century date was found in Waterford (Hurley and McCutcheon 1997, 618) and fragments of a basket have been found in Cork in mid-13th century levels (Hurley 1990, 77–8 and fig. 18, no. 16). Seven solid wooden discs from Waterford with perforations around the circumference were identified as the bases of baskets (Hurley and McCutcheon 1997, 618); however, one rectangular fragment (Hurley and McCutcheon 1997, fig. 16: 24.4) is now considered more likely to be the base of a birdcage. Baskets and panniers must have been used to transport most raw materials and produce, much as plastic and cardboard are used today. Fish, eggs and solid fuel have traditionally been carried in baskets (Evans 1957, 205–10). Wooden wicker beds were still in use in rural Ireland in the 19th century (Kinmonth 1993, 165) and while little is known of such items in the Viking Age, a description of the sack of Dublin in 1000 (Todd 1867, 112–13) records the taking away of beds and soft furnishing from Dublin by the men of Munster. Likewise, wicker cradles, still in use in the Aran Islands at the turn of the 20th century, were objects made by highly skilled craftsmen (Kinmonth 1993, 174) and were regarded as 'objects of great sentiment [passing] from mother to daughter for many generations' (Mason 1936, 78). Judging from the late 19th-century photographs of markets in Cork City, wicker cradles were still common and the basket was the ubiquitous container not only for carrying preserved items but also for trade and display of goods (Kinmonth 1993, 174–5, plate 280; also see Hurley 1999, fig. 6). Professional basket makers may have found sufficient demand for their wares in Hiberno-Norse towns the size of Cork and Waterford, but many types of baskets have traditionally 'been made by country people or fishermen and never by professional basket makers' (Wright 1975, 342). Women may have produced baskets as a domestic craft. Access to coppiced hazel and willow as a raw material was essential for people involved in basket weaving. Such raw materials may have been traded by country people at urban markets and fairs.

Carving
Carved objects may have been made by any or all of the woodworkers discussed here, or may in many instances have been made by the people who were engaged in one or more other occupations, such as fishermen, farmers, warriors, weavers and musicians. Wood carving was probably more often than not carried out by the users of the objects. The technical knowledge possessed by non-professionals cannot be easily imagined by those of us accustomed to today's availability of mass-produced commodities. The embellishment of carved objects with designs, or the application of owners' marks, was probably also done by the users. Some were no doubt better than others. Examples of these variations can be seen on distaffs found in 12th- and

13th-century Waterford (Hurley and McCutcheon 1997, 588). One of these was decorated in a style described as 'ubiquitous in folk art of all times and places' (Lang 1997, 636). The decoration was extensive but the execution crude. In the early Irish law texts of the 8th century (Kelly 1988), it is stated that 'masters in yew carving had a special social rank' (Mitchell 1976, 178), because the wood was difficult to work and prized for high-grade carpentry. The more sophisticated gaming boards and chess-pieces, as well as longbows (Halpin 1997, 546–52), were probably made by professionals who specialised almost exclusively in the production of such particular items. It cannot be established archaeologically whether all or any of these artefacts were made in towns or even locally produced. On the other hand, examples of smaller carved objects, especially toys, were probably made at home. Examples include a carved wooden animal head and a wooden toy knife from Cork (Hurley 1982, 302–5, fig. 16. 1. 7 and 16. 2. 5; Hurley 1997b, 182–3), a toy knife from Waterford (Hurley and McCutcheon 1997, 597–8) and a small decorative wooden boat from Cork (Hurley 2010, 161, fig. 15. 3) (also see McAlister, this volume). There is no reason to presume that these were made by craftsmen, but it is more likely that they were made at home by fathers for their sons (Hurley 2012, 22).

Woodworking tools

Each stage of woodworking from felling to fine carving required different tools. Skilled crafts, such as turning and coopering, also needed their own specific range of tools. However, few metal tools exclusively related to woodworking have been identified from Hiberno-Norse contexts. There are, however, many tools that could have been used for woodworking but were probably multi-purpose, such as knives. Most large woodworking tools, such as axes, were equally applicable to structural work as to the fashioning of artefacts.

The axe was predominantly used for felling and cutting trees. There is also evidence for the use of an adze (*i.e.* a hollowing implement for shaping and dressing wood, the use of which is indicated by shallow, scallop-shaped depressions on the wood). There is no evidence that large planks were sawn, but rather they were cleft radially, probably by wedge and mauls. Saws may have had a limited use in joinery for 12th-century timber-framed houses, but there is no diagnostic evidence. On the whole, it seems that saws were used only for the production of combs and other small items. There is little evidence for the use of the saw for felling or cutting up wood until the 16th century (O'Sullivan 1994, 21), although the saw is listed along with the axe, billhook, adze and auger in the 8th-century law tracts as essential tools for 'a prosperous farmer' (Kelly 1997, 485).

Carving on larger timbers was generally done with chisels, which were used for creating grooves, notches and mortises on timber-framed houses and thresholds. Perforations were frequently carved, but some appear to have been drilled. Carving of all small artefacts was apparently done with knives. A specialised set of hollowing chisels with either hooked or straight blades must have been used for wood turned on a lathe. Specialised coopering irons have been identified amongst metal artefacts from Waterford and Cork (Scully 1997a, 469–74; 1997b, 173–4). Drilling with spoon-bits seems not to have been introduced until the 13th century (Scully 1997b, 173–4). Twist-bits were found in 14th-century contexts in Cork (Hurley 1990, 67–8, figs 14.5 and 15.3). Some holes were burned through the wood with pointed, red-hot irons. Small hooks and chisels must have been used to carve items such as wooden spoons.

Antler and bone

Preservation

In Waterford, the largest number of bone and antler artefacts was recovered from house floors, associated backyards and pits of 12th- and early 13th-century date, while in Cork, the date range is somewhat later, falling between the mid-12th to early 14th centuries. Significant cultural differences between the Hiberno-Norse and early Anglo-Norman period (after 1170) are not apparent in the artefactual assemblage. Contexts dating to both of these periods were in most cases sealed with prevailing anaerobic conditions, leading to excellent organic preservation. In contrast, bone and antler artefacts from both earlier and later levels are infrequent and fragmentary, which largely reflects survival rates. Horn (the outer keratin layer of horns of cattle and goats) rarely survives even in the most favourable conditions. There is only one horn comb from Waterford (Hurley 1997c, 658) and two from Cork (Hurley 1997d, 243–50). The only other well-preserved horn artefact is part of a late 11th- to early 12th-century possible blast horn or drinking horn from Waterford (Hurley 1997c, 679–81).

Red deer (*Cervus elaphus* L.) was the only native species of deer present in Ireland in the late Hiberno-Norse period and it would have found the semi-wooded environment an ideal habitat. Roe (*Capreolus capreolos* L.) and fallow (*Dama dama* L.) deer were native to Great Britain, but absent from Ireland. Venison played a very minor role in the diet of the inhabitants of 12th-century Waterford (McCormick 1997, 836–7) and 12th-century Cork (McCarthy 1997, 351; 2003, 380). It must be assumed that shed antler was collected in the wider hinterland of the towns, as the high proportion of naturally ruptured burrs present in the assemblages testifies to the availability of intact shed antler to the urban craftsmen. The antler had to be collected as soon as it was cast (March to May), because shed antler is frequently devoured by rodents or by the deer themselves. This collection was most likely done by country people familiar with the habitats of the deer. The antler may then have been sold to, or bartered with, urban-based craftsmen. Alternatively, the craftsmen themselves may have spent an annual season collecting from the countryside what they needed. In view of the scale of production in Waterford and Cork and the association of horn cores and antler, it seems more likely that horn and antler working were urban-based crafts in which the raw materials were supplied in an organised fashion.

The amount of discarded antler in late 11th- and 12th-century contexts is very high, and fragments were often large. Complete antlers, large lengths of shafts adjacent to burrs (and occasionally crowns) and long tine off-cuts, all of which contained usable portions of antler, were frequently discarded. The amount of discarded antler in late 12th-century contexts is in sharp contrast with the 13th century, when use of antler was more economical, with smaller proportions of waste. This increased thrift may be a consequence of a diminished supply of the raw material.

Bone was more readily available within the towns as 'cattle were the principal source of meat' in Hiberno-Norse and medieval Waterford (McCormick 1997, 822) and Cork (McCarthy 1997, 350–6; 2003, 377). It is likely that supply exceeded demand for bone from craft workers at all times. Bone was generally used for objects where the natural shape of the material lent itself to minimum modification. The most obvious examples are the wide flat split ribs, which were used for casket mounts, proximal ends of mammal long bones, used for spindle whorls, and pig and sheep metapodials, used for toggles and 'buzz-bones'. Bird bones were ideal for whistles

Fig. 13.4 Evidence for the production of antler combs in mid-12th-century Waterford (photograph Waterford City Council).

and flutes. Tubes and needle cases could be made from long bones of small animals with little or no alteration. The natural diversity and plentiful supply of bones as a raw material led to greater diversity of form for a wider range of objects than was obtainable with antler.

Working methods

Antler, bone and, to a lesser extent, horn were used for specific types of objects where the salient characteristics of the raw material could be maximised. It is difficult to be sure to what extent antler working was a domestic handicraft or well-developed craft. The greatest amount of evidence is for the late 11th to early 13th centuries, and in that period it was certainly a highly specialised craft with comb making being the central element (also see Ashby, this volume).

Antler combs (fig. 13.4) exhibit a high standard of expertise and were certainly the work of craftsmen who possessed specialised tools and highly developed skills. Other objects, such as gaming pieces, may represent by-products of comb making, and for production of these objects specialised tools were also necessary. Furthermore, the components of stringed musical instruments, where precision was essential, were undoubtedly the work of professionals.

Bone objects may sometimes have been professionally made, but many required little skill to produce, as they are frequently 'no more than the adaptation of the natural feature of certain bones' (Adams and Sheppard 1990, 251). The use of proximal ends of mammal bone for spindle whorls and the bone and antler cylinders is a case in point. Examples of an intermediate category of objects, either the work of specialists or that of skilled handymen, include flutes and whistles, needles and pin-beaters.

The antler and horn waste in the late 11th- to early 12th-century ditch fills and mid-12th-century extra-mural dumping in Waterford is probably derived from workshops. Particularly large concentrations of antler waste (burrs, tines, various off-cuts and slices) were also found in the early 12th-century habitation debris of two adjoining properties fronting on to Peter Street in Waterford (Scully and McCutcheon 1997, 88–93, PS1 and 2, L6; Hurley and McCutcheon 1997, 653). Antler waste was also found in or adjacent to nearby houses, though in lesser quantities. In all of these cases, the antler was associated with bone and horn cores exhibiting various saw marks. The antler and horn waste in the ditch was possibly derived from specific industrial-type workshops located close to the rampart – perhaps outside of the 11th- to 12th-century defences in the unexcavated areas to the west (Hurley 1997e).

There is little indication of the type of objects produced from horn in Hiberno-Norse towns. Not until the post-medieval period is there extensive evidence for the use of horn for combs (Dunlevy 1988, 370–1), which was when many of the crafts common in the medieval towns were formalised into guilds and documented (Jeayes 1905, 11–14). By that time, the use of antler for combs had almost ceased and been replaced by horn.

Working Methods and Tools

There is no direct evidence for the tools used for antler and bone working in Hiberno-Norse Waterford and Cork. From the artefacts themselves, as well as from the waste, however, there is a considerable amount of evidence for the use of saws. Saws were used to cut bone and antler into appropriate lengths for further working. The teeth on all of the combs were sawn, as were casket mounts, discoid gaming pieces, needle cases, the modified antler tines in their various forms, and the bone and antler cylinders. Other tools were used to shape the artefacts: drills, gouges and punches to perforate; knives to carve and shape; and inscribing tools with a fixed or variable radius were used to decorate. While a variety of such tools is represented in the assemblages of Cork and Waterford (Hurley 1990, 67; Scully 1997a, 469–74; 1997b, 172–4), inference for their possible application is more 'readable' on the bone objects themselves. The use of inscribing tools, for example, is evident only on gaming pieces and occurs probably no earlier than the late 12th century. Some of the antler waste was roughly chopped with an axe, but this evidence is minimal by comparison with the number of sawn pieces.

Dot-in-circle roundel motifs rarely occur on the combs, but are frequent on the decorative casket mounts from Waterford (Hurley 1997c, 654–5). This does not necessarily imply the existence of separate craft workshops or different craftsmen for these two artefact types. The application of roundels to the flat surfaces of casket mounts was easily achieved with scribing bits of various fixed-radii, while the convex surfaces of comb connecting plates made use of this instrument impractical. Dot-in-circle roundels were also common on the flat surfaces of discoid gaming pieces, but were rarely used on hemispherical pieces. Gaming pieces made from those parts of antler – unsuitable for comb making due to the high proportion of spongy tissue – were particularly common in the assemblage from medieval Cork (Hurley 1997d, 250–3) but less common in Waterford where antler was obviously in more plentiful supply.

Most of the shaping of small bone and antler objects – such as needles/pin beaters, bone tubes/needle cases and the perforations in toggles and 'buzz-bones' – was done with a knife. Perforations, however, were more commonly drilled, probably with spoon bits and not with twist-drills until the 14th century (Hurley 1990, 67). Files may have been used, although none was identified in Cork or Waterford.

Conclusions

In the absence of evidence for 9th- and 10th-century settlement in Waterford and Cork, it is difficult to know to what extent Scandinavian influences prevailed on the 11th- and 12th-century culture of these towns. Some elements of Scandinavian influence certainly remained apparent in the material culture (Hurley 2010). The assemblages of wooden and bone artefacts are mostly of local production in readily available raw materials. The craftsmen were based in the towns using raw materials obtained from the hinterland, indicating that a strong interdependence between town and countryside must have existed. Not every artefact can be seen as the work of a specialist and many items were produced by semi-skilled people whose main occupation may have been in other activities. High standards of craftsmanship, once attained, did not necessarily remain consistent and many factors such as availability of raw material and demand were obviously influential in maintaining standards and output.

Acknowledgements

I would like to express my thanks to Vincent Price for assistance with the bibliography, text and illustrations.

Note

1   Mazers or mazer hanap: a drinking cup. They were bowls that stood on a pedestal consisting of a stem and foot. They were mostly made of lathe-turned wood but decorative precious metal rims or other applied decoration were sometimes added (*Encyclopaedia Britannia* 1911, 8.582). Hope (1987, 129) has stated that 'of all the drinking vessels in use from the 13th to the 16th century, none were so common and so much prized as those known as mazers'. The origin of the word mazer is thought to be derived from an Old High German word *másá* meaning a spot; a mazer is therefore so called from being a bowl of 'spotted wood'. The highly valued spotted or speckled maple wood was frequently used for these vessels (Hope 1887, 129). In Ireland, drinking vessels referred to as 'meader' or 'mether', frequently translated as 'meade bowl' (Evans 1957, 99; Woodmartin 1886, 103), probably represent the Gaelic rendering of the word mazer in a language that does not contain the letter z (Hurley and McCutcheon 1997, 566).

Bibliography

Adams, G. and Sheppard P. (1990) Bone, antler, ivory and horn working 1: the industry and its by-products. In M. Biddle (ed.) *Objects and Economy in Medieval Winchester*, 251–2. Oxford, Clarendon Press.

Bersu, G. (1947) The *rath* in the townland of Lissue, Co. Antrim: report on the excavations in 1946. *Ulster Journal of Archaeology* 10, 30–48.

Bradley, J. (1988) The interpretation of Scandinavian settlement in Ireland. In J. Bradley (ed.) *Settlement and Society in Medieval Ireland*, 49–78. Kilkenny, Boethius Press.

Bradley, J. (2009) Some reflections on the problem of Scandinavian settlement in the hinterland of Dublin during the 9th century. In J. Bradley, A. J. Fletcher and A. Simms (eds) *Dublin in the Medieval World: studies in honour of Howard B. Clarke*, 39–62. Dublin, Four Courts Press.

Bradley, J. and Halpin, A. (1992) The topographical development of Scandinavian and Anglo-Norman Waterford City. In W. Nolan and T. P. Power (eds) *Waterford History and Society*, 105–29. Dublin, Geography Publications.

Bradley, J. and Halpin, A. (1993) The topographical development of Scandinavian and Anglo-Norman Cork. In P. O'Flanagan and G. Buttimer (eds) *Cork History and Society*, 15–44. Dublin, Geography Publications.

Caulfield, R. (1876) *The Council Book of the Corporation of the City of Cork from 1609–1643 and 1690–1800.* Guildford, Billing and Sons.

Cleary, R. M. (1997) Christ Church site excavations. In R. M. Cleary, M. F. Hurley and E. Shee Twohig (eds) *Skiddy's Castle and Christ Church Cork: excavations 1974–77 by D. C. Twohig*, 22–100. Cork, Cork Corporation.

Clinton, M. (2000) Settlement patterns in the early historic kingdom of Leinster (seventh to mid twelfth century). In A. P. Smyth (ed.) *Seanchas: studies in early medieval Irish archaeology, history and literature in honour of Francis J. Byrne*, 275–98. Dublin, Four Courts Press.

Coleman, J. C. (1944) The craft of coopering. *Journal of the Cork Historical and Archaeological Society* 44, 79–88.

O'Donovan, J. (ed.) (1851) *Annals of the Kingdom of Ireland by the Four Masters* (7 vols). Dublin, Hogges & Smith.

Dunlevy, M. (1988) A classification of early Irish combs. *Proceedings of the Royal Irish Academy* 88 C, 341–422.

Earwood, C. (1993) *Domestic Wooden Artefacts in Britain and Ireland from Neolithic to Viking Times.* Exeter, Exeter University Press.

Encyclopaedia Britannia Vol. 8 (1911, 11th edn) Cambridge, Cambridge University Press.

Evans, E. E. (1957) *Irish Folk Ways.* London, Dover Publications Inc.

Gahan, A. and McCutcheon, C. (1997) Medieval pottery. In M. F. Hurley and O. M. B. Scully with S. W. J. McCutcheon *Late Viking Age and Medieval Waterford: excavations 1986–1992*, 285–336. Waterford, Waterford Corporation.

Gahan, A., McCutcheon, C. and Twohig, D. C. (1997) Medieval pottery. In R. M. Cleary, M. F. Hurley and E. Shee Twohig (eds) *Skiddy's Castle and Christ Church Cork: excavations 1974–1977 by D. C. Twohig*, 109–29. Cork, Cork Corporation.

Geraghty, S. (1996) *Viking Dublin: botanical evidence from Fishamble Street.* Medieval Dublin Excavations 1962–81, series C, vol. 2. Dublin, Royal Irish Academy.

Halpin, A. (1997) Archery material. In M. F. Hurley and O. M. B. Scully with S. W. J. McCutcheon *Late Viking Age and Medieval Waterford: excavations 1986–1992*, 538–53. Waterford, Waterford Corporation.

Hencken, H. O. N. (1936) Ballinderry Crannog No. I. *Proceedings of the Royal Irish Academy* 43 C, 103–239.

Hope, W. H. St John (1987) On the English medieval drinking bowls called Mazers. *Archaeologia* 50, 129–93.

Hurley, M. F. (1982) Wooden artifacts from the excavations of the medieval city of Cork. In S. McGrail (ed.) *Woodworking Techniques before AD 1500*, 301–11. British Archaeological Reports International Series 129. Oxford, British Archaeological Reports.

Hurley, M. F. (1989) Excavations at Grand Parade II (part 1). *Journal of the Cork Historical and Archaeological Society* 94, 27–45.

Hurley, M. F. (1990) Excavations at Grand Parade II (part 2). *Journal of the Cork Historical and Archaeological Society* 95, 64–87.

Hurley, M. F. (1997a) The use of wood as structural material. In M. F. Hurley and O. M. B. Scully with S. W. J. McCutcheon *Late Viking Age and Medieval Waterford: excavations 1986–1992*, 40–4. Waterford, Waterford Corporation.

Hurley, M. F. (1997b) Wooden artefacts. In R. M. Cleary, M. F. Hurley and E. Shee Twohig (eds) *Skiddy's Castle and Christ Church Cork: excavations 1974–1977 by D. C. Twohig*, 274–310. Cork, Cork Corporation.

Hurley, M. F. (1997c) Artefacts of skeletal material. In M. F. Hurley and O. M. B. Scully with S. W. J. McCutcheon *Late Viking Age and Medieval Waterford: excavations 1986–1992*, 650–98. Waterford, Waterford Corporation.

Hurley, M. F. (1997d) Artefacts of skeletal material. In R. M. Cleary, M. F. Hurley and E. Shee Twohig (eds) *Skiddy's Castle and Christ Church Cork: excavations 1974–1977 by D. C. Twohig*, 239–73. Cork, Cork Corporation.

Hurley, M. F. (1997e) The defences. In M. F. Hurley and O. M. B. Scully with S. W. J. McCutcheon *Late Viking Age and Medieval Waterford: excavations 1986–1992*, 20–34. Waterford, Waterford Corporation.

Hurley, M. F. (1999) Archaeological evidence for trade in Cork from the 12th to the 17th centuries. In M. Gläser (ed.) *Lübecker Kolloquium zur Stadtarchäologie im Hanseraum II: Der Handel*, 13–24. Lübeck, Verlag Schmidt-Römhild.

Hurley, M. F. (2003) Wooden artefacts. In R. M. Cleary and M. F. Hurley (eds) *Excavations in Cork City 1984–2000*, 349–59. Cork, Cork City Council.

Hurley, M. F. (2006) Gateways to southern Ireland: Cork and Waterford in the 12th century. In D. Ó Riain-Raedal and D. Bracken (eds) *Reform and Renewal: Ireland and Europe in the 12th century*, 36–56. Dublin, Four Court Press.

Hurley, M. F. (2010) Viking elements in Irish towns: Cork and Waterford. In J. Sheehan and D. Ó Corráin (eds) *The Viking Age: Ireland and the West. Proceedings of the Fifteenth Viking Congress*, 154–65. Dublin, Four Courts Press.

Hurley, M. F. (2012) Children and youth in medieval Cork and Waterford. In M. Glässer (ed.) *Lübecker Kolloquim zur Stadtarchäologie im Hanseraum VIII: Kindheit und Jugend, Ausbildung und Freizeit*, 13–24. Lübeck, Verlag Schmidt-Romhild.

Hurley, M. F. and McCutcheon, S. W. J. (1997) Wooden artefacts. In M. F. Hurley and O. M. B. Scully with S. W. J. McCutcheon *Late Viking Age and Medieval Waterford: excavations 1986–1992*, 553–633. Waterford, Waterford Corporation.

Hurley, M. F. and Price, V. (in prep.) The wooden artefacts. In *Excavations at South Main Street, Cork*.

Hurley, M. F. and Scully, O. M. B. with McCutcheon, S. W. J. (1997) *Late Viking Age and Medieval Waterford: excavations 1986–1992*. Waterford, Waterford Corporation.

Jeayes, I. H. (ed.) (1905) *The Academy of Armory, or a Storehouse of Arnoury and Blazon. By R. Holme (1688)*. London, Roxburghe Club.

Johnson, R. (1999) Ballinderry Crannog No. 1: a reinterpretation. *Proceedings of the Royal Irish Academy* 99, 23–71.

Kelly, F. (1976) The Old Irish tree-list. *Celtica* 11, 107–24.

Kelly, F. (1988). *A Guide to Early Irish Law*. Dublin, Dublin Institute for Advanced Studies.

Kelly, F. (1997) *Early Irish Farming: a study based mainly on the texts of the 7th and 8th centuries AD*. Dublin, Dublin Institute for Advanced Studies.

Kinmonth, C. (1993) *Irish Country Furniture 1700–1950*. New Haven, Yale University Press.

Kolchin, B. A. (1989) *Wooden Artefacts from Medieval Novgorod*. British Archaeological Reports International Series S495i and ii. Oxford, British Archaeological Reports.

Lang, J. T. (1997) Decorated wooden artefacts. In M. F. Hurley and O. M. B. Scully with S. W. J. McCutcheon *Late Viking Age and Medieval Waterford: excavations 1986–1992*, 634–50. Waterford, Waterford Corporation.

Lucas, A. T. (1966) Irish-Norse relations: time for reappraisal? *Journal of the Cork Historical and Archaeological Society* 64, 62–75.

Mason, T. (1936) *The Island of Ireland: their scenery, people, life and antiquities*. London, B. T. Batsford Ltd.

McCarthy, M. (1997) Faunal remains: Christ Church. In R. M. Cleary, M. F. Hurley and E. Shee Twohig (eds) *Skiddy's Castle & Christ Church Cork: excavations 1974–1977 by D. C. Twohig*, 349–60. Cork, Cork Corporation.

McCarthy, M. (2003) The faunal remains. In R. M. Cleary and M. F. Hurley (eds) *Excavations in Cork City 1984–2000*, 375–90. Cork, Cork City Council.

McCormick, F. (1997) The animal bones. In M. F. Hurley and O. M. B. Scully with S. W. J. McCutcheon *Late Viking Age and Medieval Waterford: excavations 1986–1992*, 819–53. Waterford, Waterford Corporation.

McCutcheon, C. (1995) The pottery. In M. F. Hurley and C. Sheehan (eds) *Excavations at the Dominican Priory, St. Mary's of the Isle, Cork*, 85–96. Cork, Cork Corporation.

McCutcheon, C. (1997) Pottery and roof tiles. In M. F. Hurley (ed.) *Excavations at the North Gate, Cork*, 75–102. Cork, Cork Corporation.

McCutcheon, C. (2003) Pottery. In R. M. Cleary and M. F. Hurley (eds) *Excavations in Cork City 1984–2000*, 197–235. Cork, Cork Corporation.

McCutcheon, C. (2006) *Medieval Pottery from Wood Quay, Dublin*. Dublin, Royal Irish Academy.

Mitchell, F. (1976) *The Irish Landscape.* London, Collins.

Ó Riordain, S. P. (1940) The pole-lathe of Borrisokane, Co. Tipperary. *Journal of the Cork Historical and Archaeological Society* 45, 28–32.

O'Sullivan, A. (1994) The craft of the carpenter in medieval Ireland; some hints from the book of illuminations. *Irish Association of Professional Archaeologists Newsletter* 19, 18–22.

O'Sullivan, A. (2000) The wooden waterfronts; a study of their construction, carpentry and use of trees and woodland. In A. Halpin (ed.) *The Port of Medieval Dublin: archaeological excavations at the civic offices, Winetavern Street, Dublin 1993*, 62–95. Dublin, Four Courts Press.

O'Sullivan, W. (1937) *The Economic History of Cork City for the Earliest Times to the Act of Union.* Cork, Cork University Press.

Sawyer, P. H. (1970) The Vikings and the Irish Sea. In D. Moore (ed.) *The Irish Sea Province in Archaeology and History*, 86–90. Cardiff, Cambrian Archaeological Association.

Scully, O. M. B. (1997a) Metal artefacts. In M. F. Hurley and O. M. B. Scully with S. W. J. McCutcheon *Late Viking Age and Medieval Waterford: excavations 1986–1992*, 428–89. Waterford, Waterford Corporation.

Scully, O. M. B. (1997b) Ferrous and non-ferrous metal artefacts. In R. M. Cleary, M. F. Hurley and E. Shee Twohig (eds) *Skiddy's Castle & Christ Church Cork: excavations 1974–1977 by D. C. Twohig*, 165–91. Cork, Cork Corporation.

Scully, O. M. B and McCutcheon, S. W. J. (1997) Catalogue of houses: Peter Street. In M. F. Hurley and O. M. B. Scully with S. W. J. McCutcheon *Late Viking Age and Medieval Waterford: excavations 1986–1992*, 53–136. Waterford, Waterford Corporation.

Simms, A. (1990) Medieval Dublin in a European context: from proto-town to a chartered town. In H. B. Clarke (ed.) *Medieval Dublin: the making of a metropolis*, 52–70. Blackrock, Irish Academic Press.

Simms, A. and Fagan, P. (1992) Villages in Co. Dublin: their origin and inheritance. In F. H. A. Aalen and K. Whelan (eds) *Dublin City and County: from prehistory to present*, 79–119. Dublin, Geography Publication.

Simpson, L. (2000) Forty years a-digging: a preliminary synthesis of archaeological investigations in medieval Dublin. In S. Duffy (ed.) *Medieval Dublin I*, 11–68. Dublin, Four Courts Press.

Thompson, R. (1802) *Meath: statistical survey of the County of Meath.* London, Graisberry and Campbell.

Tierney, J. (1998) Wood and woodlands in early medieval Munster. In M. Monk and J. Sheehan (eds) *Early Medieval Munster: archaeology, history and society*, 53–8. Cork, Cork University Press.

Todd, J. H. (1867) *Cogadh Gaedhel re Gallaibh.* London, Longman.

Valante, M. (2008) *The Vikings in Ireland: settlement, trade and urbanisation.* Dublin, Four Courts Press.

Wallace, P. F. (1992) The archaeological identity of the Hiberno-Norse town. *Journal of the Royal Society of Antiquaries of Ireland* 122, 35–66.

Wallace, P. F. and Ó Floinn, R. (1988) *Dublin 1000: discovery and excavation in Dublin 1842–1981.* Dublin, National Museum of Ireland.

Woodmartin, W. G. (1886) *The Lake Dwellings of Ireland.* Dublin, Hodges & Figges.

Wright, D. (1975) The baskets. In C. Platt and R. Coleman-Smith *Excavations in Medieval Southampton 1953–1969, ii*, 341–2. Leicester, Leicester University Press.